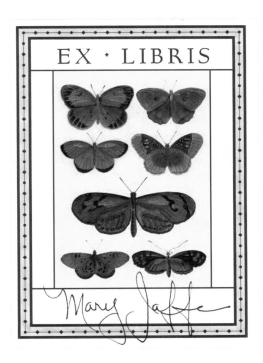

PILGRIMAGE IN MEDIEVAL ENGLAND

Chaucer's Wife of Bath from a fifteenth-century manuscript of *The Canterbury Tales*. (*Cambridge University Library*)

Pilgrimage
in Medieval England

Diana Webb

Hambledon and London
London and New York

Published by Hambledon and London, 2000
102 Gloucester Avenue, London NW1 8HX (UK)
858 Broadway, New York, NY 10003–4812 (USA)

ISBN 1 85285 250 X

A description of this book is available from
the British Library and the Library of Congress

Typeset by Carnegie Publishing,
Chatsworth Road, Lancaster,
and printed on acid-free paper and bound
in the UK by Cambridge University Press

Contents

Illustrations

Between pages 78 and 79

Text Illustrations

Illustration Acknowledgements

The author and publishers are grateful to the following for permission to reproduce illustrations: the Ashmolean Museum, pl. 13; Basil Blackwell Ltd, p. 15, from David Hill, *An Atlas of Anglo-Saxon England* (Blackwell, Oxford, 1981), p. 152; Cambridge University Library, pp. ii, 110; Helen Lubin, pp. 210, 211; the National Gallery, pl. 4; the National Monuments Record, pls 5–12.

Abbreviations

AB	*Analecta Bollandiana*
AM	*Annales Monastici*, ed. H. R. Luard (4 vols, *RS*, 36)
CCR	*Calendars of Close Rolls*
CEPR	*Calendars of Entries in the Papal Registers Relating to Great Britain and Ireland*
CIPM	*Calendars of Inquisitions Post Mortem*
CLR	*Calendars of Liberate Rolls*
CM	Matthew Paris, *Chronica Majora*, ed. H. R. Luard (8 vols, *RS*, 59)
CPR	*Calendars of Patent Rolls*
CS	Camden Society
CYS	Canterbury and York Society
Foedera	Thomas Rymer, *Foedera, Conventiones, Literae ac cujuscunque Generis Acta Publica* (3rd edn, 10 vols, The Hague, 1745)
GA	*Gesta Abbatum Monasterii Sancti Albani a Thoma Walsingham, Regnante Ricardo Secundo, ejusdem Ecclesiae Praecentore, Compilata*, ed. H. T. Riley (3 vols, *RS*, 28, pt 4)
GP	*Willelmi Malmesburiensis Monachi Gesta Pontificum Anglorum Libri Quinque*, ed. W. Hamilton (*RS*, 52)
LC	*Literae Cantuarienses: the Letter Books of the Monastery of Christ Church Canterbury*, ed. J. Brigstocke Sheppard (3 vols, *RS*, 85)
Leland	*Leland's Itinerary in England and Wales*, ed. L. Toulmin-Smith (5 vols, London, 1964)
LP	*Letters and Papers, Foreign and Domestic, of the Reign of Henry VIII*
Materials	*Materials for the History of Thomas Becket, Archbishop of Canterbury*, ed. J. C. Robertson (7 vols, *RS*, 67)
RS	Rolls Series
SS	Surtees Society
VCH	*Victoria County History of the Counties of England*
Walsingham	*Chronica Monasterii S. Albani*, ed. H. T. Riley (2 vols, *RS*, 28, pt 2).

For my children
Eleanor and Richard

Introduction

The dominant image of medieval pilgrimage entertained by many English readers is derived from Chaucer's *Canterbury Tales*. Begun probably around 1388, it was abandoned and left unfinished when the poet died in 1400. From a pilgrimage with which most of his audience would have been familiar, by experience or from hearsay, Chaucer fashioned a narrative framework for the stories he wanted to tell and the gallery of social types whom he wanted to depict telling them; just as Giovanni Boccaccio (with some of whose work Chaucer was familiar) used the flight of a group of fashionable young people from plague-stricken Florence in 1348 for the same purpose. Chaucer's satire seems to be of the social types rather than of pilgrimage as such, although the presence in the company of certain disreputable characters whose religious understanding is open to doubt, and of others who really should not have been there, may be taken as genial criticism of pilgrimage as actually practised. Into the first category come, for example, the Miller and the Pardoner (who as a professional indulgence seller was in a sense involved in the same business as the proprietors of shrines); into the second, the Monk and the Prioress, who strictly speaking should have remained within their respective cloisters.

Although not all the topographical details can be certainly established, Chaucer's pilgrims were clearly following a standard itinerary, which can be verified from other records of journeys from London to Canterbury and, continuing on the same road, to Dover.[1] Like most moderately well-to-do pilgrims, they were on horseback. Departing from Southwark, they made their first overnight stop at Dartford, fifteen miles out, and their second at Rochester, arriving at Canterbury on the third day. Chaucer did not live to see them all the way to the shrine, but the anonymous author of a later continuation, *The Tale of Beryn*, depicts their arrival and behaviour there and at the inn, and supplies further picturesque and plausible detail.[2]

The Wife of Bath must be numbered among the members of Chaucer's company who have most captured the imagination of posterity. We are informed that before taking the road to Canterbury

> thries hadde she been at Jerusalem;
> She hadde passed many a straunge strem;
> At Rome she hadde been, and at Boloigne,
> In Galice at Seint-Jame, and at Cologne.
> She koude muchel of wandrynge by the wey.

She was, therefore, an exceedingly well-travelled international pilgrim, who in addition to visiting the three major shrines (the Holy Land, Rome and St James of Compostela) had venerated the Virgin Mary at Boulogne and the Three Magi in Cologne Cathedral. Everything we are told about her suggests that she would have acquired enhanced status in local society on the strength of her experiences. Many Englishmen and women will have shared at least some of her journeys. Some (like Chaucer's Knight) were also what we now call 'crusaders', but what contemporaries, even as late as the fourteenth century, still often called pilgrims (*peregrini*). A 'crusade' was originally a *peregrinatio*, and the Holy Land crusade so remained until specialised terms with a more specifically military slant, like 'general passage' (*passagium generale*), came into use in the course of the thirteenth century.

There were words, in Latin and in Greek, for the things pilgrims did and wished to do (prayer, vow, sacrifice, thanksgiving), but no single word for the people who did them or for the whole complex of their activities. This may seem ironic in view of the fact that our word 'pilgrim', like its cognates in many modern European languages (*Pilger, pèlerin, peregrino*), is derived from the Latin word *peregrinus*; but this in fact originally meant a 'foreigner' or 'stranger', a disadvantaged being, cut off, at least temporarily, from his roots. The Greek *xenos* had similar meanings, but could also denote 'guest' and in some contexts was as close as the language came to a word for 'pilgrim'. The Latinised term *xenodochium* was frequently used in the medieval period to mean a hostel or hospital which might accommodate pilgrims among other 'strangers'. The Latin *hospes*, which could mean either 'host' or 'guest' and from which 'hospital' and 'hospitality' obviously derive, seems not to have been used to designate a pilgrim, except in so far as he or she was incidentally the inmate of an inn, hostel or hospital; *hospitium* might designate a special lodging for pilgrims but could also mean a general- purpose inn. While *peregrinus* and its derivatives were more and more frequently used in the early medieval centuries to describe pilgrims and pilgrimage (*peregrinatio*), they took a long time to shed their original connotations of foreignness and alienation. In the usage of Bede and his contemporaries, *peregrinatio* had a specialised religious meaning, but it was not exactly what we now usually understand by 'pilgrimage'.

This book is principally concerned with pilgrimages undertaken by English men and women within England. Their journeys to shrines overseas are mentioned only incidentally. I have confined myself mainly to England, with occasional mentions of the rest of the British Isles, and there is, as the reader will discover, a strong emphasis on the local and the small-scale. It is often difficult to delineate the boundary which divides 'pilgrimage' from the more or less everyday resort of people to their neighbourhood shrines, and some readers may feel that several of the pilgrimages and 'shrines' which I mention are barely worthy of the name. Our imaginative picture of the pilgrim tends to be of a long-distance traveller, if not necessarily of so determined a globetrotter at the Wife of Bath, but how long in fact did a journey have to be to qualify as a pilgrimage?

A working definition has been suggested, in a recent study of pilgrimage in ancient Greece: 'any journey undertaken for a specifically religious purpose, and which involved an overnight stay at the pilgrimage centre'.[3] The second part of this definition is perhaps less applicable to medieval pilgrimage. Miracle stories and other written sources, as well as material evidence such as finds of shrine souvenirs, help to give an impression, albeit a very patchy one, of the clientele and catchment areas of medieval shrines. One conclusion that can be drawn from this evidence is that a great deal of pilgrimage, in England as elsewhere, took place over distances which were sometimes surprisingly short. In the early fifteenth century, Margery Kempe of Lynn, who went in her time to Rome, Jerusalem and Compostela, Assisi, Wilsnack and Aachen, was one day invited to go two miles from where she lived on pilgrimage to a church of St Michael the Archangel. It is unlikely that this little expedition involved an overnight stay, but Margery explicitly called it a pilgrimage.[4] The long-haul pilgrimage to an overseas shrine was the exception rather than the norm, and was regarded as a correspondingly momentous and prestigious undertaking. The author of a study of Hindu pilgrimage sites in India has suggested that the long journey to the high-status shrine tends to be undertaken in the hope of spiritual benefit or enlightenment, the lesser journey to the lowlier shrine for more mundane, problem-solving purposes.[5] Certainly a late medieval housekeeper would not have gone to Jerusalem in the hope of finding her keys, but she might (as an anonymous Lollard preacher complained) spend more than the keys were worth on a little journey to an English shrine of the 'servant saint' Zita of Lucca.[6]

The pilgrim's journey might be short not only in distance but in duration, as long as the essential elements of self-abnegation and abandonment of familiar ties were present at least in miniature:

> Whoever goeth on pilgrimage to John Thorne [*recte* Shorne], to our Lady of Walsingham, to St Anne in the wood [at Brislington near Bristol], left his father

and mother and brethren for the time that he was from home; therefore Our Lord's promise applied to him; therefore, let him put in the box at the shrine of the saint whatever he would he should receive a hundred times as much in the present world and in the world to come everlasting life. [7]

These were the views of Dr Edward Powell, dean of Salisbury, who was replying to Hugh Latimer's preaching against pilgrimage and other traditional practices at Bristol in Lent 1533. The belief defended by Powell underlay much medieval popular pilgrimage, although people continued to make lengthy pilgrimages, and there continued to be pilgrims (sometimes scarcely distinguishable from vagabonds) for whom pilgrimage, or the appearance of it, was a way of life.

For much of the medieval period, the radical dissimilarity of *peregrinatio* from all that normal people considered most comfortable and desirable gave it power not merely as a form of asceticism, a means to a greater spiritual perfection, but as a form of penance, a way of purging the soul of the dross of sin, either of particular sins or sin in general. In part because of the hardship involved in all travel, pilgrimage came to be regarded as a form of self-denial available to persons who had not embraced the permanent ascetic and penitential regime of the monk. Further conditions might be attached to it, or voluntarily embraced by the pilgrim: that it should be performed barefoot, in fetters or under certain dietary restrictions, all of which enhanced its penitential character. The association opened up possibilities, which ecclesiastical authorities were able to exploit, of using pilgrimage as penance and punishment for offences against the moral and spiritual code, whether committed by monks, clerics or laymen. The original impulse seems to have come from Irish Christianity, and the practice was disseminated, as penitential discipline was imposed on the laity as well as the clergy, through the use of the handbooks known as penitentials.

The use of pilgrimage as penance (which in early times often bore the very strong marks of its resemblance to exile) did not meet with universal approval. There were obvious hazards in sending disaffected monks or persons guilty of crimes of violence off on long journeys where they were effectively liberated from the supervision of anyone who knew them. As practised in much later centuries, for example by the Inquisition in southern France or by thirteenth- and fourteenth-century bishops, the culprit was directed to a specified destination, told when to set out, and often required to bring back a certificate of performance. There was obviously room in such a scheme of things for a short local pilgrimage to be imposed as penance for a relatively trivial offence. English bishops sometimes required the penitent merely to come to the cathedral bearing a candle and stand before the high altar while mass was said: it was the public humiliation as much as the journey (which might or might not be called a 'pilgrimage') which was penitential.[8]

Similarly, journeys both long and short could earn the pilgrim an indulgence. The award of indulgences in respect of pilgrimage, which became common in the twelfth century, formalised the pilgrim's hope of acquiring merit, and even quantified it. The meaning of indulgences, often misunderstood today, was not infrequently misunderstood in the medieval period. Indulgences were the product of two intertwined developments: the extension of penitential discipline to all Christians and the growing belief in Purgatory as a place, or state, in which penance which for any reason the penitent had failed to perform in his or her lifetime could be completed. Purgatory was believed to exist in time (by contrast with Heaven and Hell, both eternal), and therefore indulgences came to be commonly described in terms of so many days, weeks, months or years. Indulgences properly understood did not earn God's forgiveness of the sin itself; that could only be achieved by adequate repentance, and was signalled by the priest's absolution of the penitent. In the very early medieval period this was conferred after the penance had been performed; later it came, more encouragingly, to precede it. A pilgrimage in quest of an indulgence could only properly be undertaken when the penitent was contrite and had been shriven by his or her priest: the same applied to going on crusade. After the launching of the First Crusade in 1095, it rapidly came to be believed that the pope had awarded what came to be called a 'plenary' indulgence, one which wiped out all penance incurred by the individual, at least to those who died on the expedition. This spiritual privilege, which did not always require the death of the beneficiary, was granted subsequently to those who took the cross in order to fight the enemies of the church both in the Holy Land and elsewhere. Non-military pilgrims did not receive equal privileges until Boniface VIII awarded a plenary indulgence to pilgrims who went to Rome in the first Jubilee year in 1300 and fulfilled certain specified requirements. By the end of the fourteenth century, numerous shrines, such as that of St Thomas Becket at Canterbury, were seeking the grant of plenary indulgences on certain special occasions.[9]

The same shrine could therefore be the destination of both voluntary and involuntary pilgrims. The voluntary category might include people coming out of pure devotion, seeking of their own free will to expiate a sin, hoping for the cure of sickness or help with some other difficulty, wishing to give thanks for benefits already received or seeking an indulgence. A journey, however short, had to be involved, but it was perhaps just as important to the definition of a pilgrimage that it was for the participants an *occasion* in their lives, whether it was triggered by the need to seek a cure or by some other personal crisis, or whether it marked a seasonal feast or merely a day out, not something to be undervalued in the medieval period given the monotony and drudgery of most people's daily round.

To think that the generality of pilgrims visited shrines in the hope or expectation of either experiencing or witnessing a miracle may be a misleading inference from the miracle stories which are inevitably a major source of information about pilgrimage. That people who lived, on average, short lives, with little in the way of effective medicine or pain relief to ease their passage, sought help, hope and strength from pilgrimages is of course not to be denied; but then as now miracles were not the experience of the majority, even if it is acknowledged that medieval observers were more likely than we are to regard gradual or partial cures as miraculous. In life and in death, individuals believed they might acquire spiritual merit from pilgrimage; there were also clearly elements of fellowship and festivity involved when parties of neighbours banded together to make long or short journeys to a shrine. All these motives might be involved when an indulgence was known to be available on a principal feast-day, not least in the high days of summer when travelling was in some ways at least a little less wearisome. Major feast-days were not infrequently accompanied by fairs and markets, which constituted an additional attraction. Almost any church was potentially a place of pilgrimage, even if it was extremely local. English bishops frequently offered indulgences for the benefit of small churches and chapels, whose visitors are most unlikely to have come from outside the locality, or at most would be passers-by on their way elsewhere. These indulgences were often in effect money-making devices, intended to assist rebuilding or refurbishment, much like church roof repair funds at the present day. It is clear also that there was a great deal of pilgrimage which never received any kind of official sanction, except that of the blind eye, and undoubtedly there was much that has left no record at all.

Pilgrimage over longer distances, and to the more famous shrines within England, was undertaken by a wide range of people. Some, like Margery Kempe, also went during their lives to the major shrines of Christendom; for others Walsingham or Canterbury represented the journey of a lifetime, a radical departure from the normal round. This relationship between the local and the less local is sometimes reflected in the provisions of wills. In 1531 John Benett of Raunds in Northamptonshire made elaborate provision for a pilgrim to go on his behalf to Walsingham, at a total cost of 12s. 4d. He then allocated a number of smaller amounts for pilgrimages to shrines within his native county, none of which was going to cost more than sixteen pence.[10] In 1349, a group of Wiltshiremen were in the church at Box, near the Somerset border, 'as pilgrims' at the Feast of the Assumption (15 August), as they recalled at an inquest held twenty-four years later.[11] Were these 'pilgrims' *en route* elsewhere, perhaps to Glastonbury, when they happened upon the parochial celebrations of the Assumption; or had the parish church of Box become the goal of a local pilgrimage which gained in volume from its position near a major road to Bath and Bristol?

In trying to evoke something of the breadth and variety of all this devout activity, I have drawn on a wide and miscellaneous range of sources. These of course include miracle-collections, without which we would know much less about pilgrim behaviour and practices than we do, but bishops' registers, wills, chronicles and the records of royal government also contain valuable information. It need hardly be said that not every English saint, cult or shrine is mentioned here, nor has every possible source been scrutinised. Much that is published I have not been able to examine, and much that is unpublished remains to be discovered. It should also be emphasised that the subject is pilgrimage, a physical action undertaken with a religious purpose, rather than the cult of the saints as such: the cult of the saints encompassed practices other than pilgrimage, but pilgrimage also expressed impulses in which the veneration of a saint (or the Virgin, or Christ Himself) mingled with others equally human, but less specifically 'religious'.

A great deal of previous writing on English pilgrimage has centred, for understandable reasons, on Thomas Becket and Canterbury, but two more broadly-based studies are particularly worthy of remark. Ronald Finucane's justly celebrated *Miracles and Pilgrims*, first published in 1977, arose from an interest in medical history and grew into an investigation of what could be discovered from miracle stories, not only about disease and cure, but about many other aspects of social life. Finucane's attention to the (usually rather restricted) catchment-areas of shrines has been a particularly valuable contribution. Much more recently, the emphasis of Ben Nilson's *The Cathedral Shrines of Medieval England* (1998) is as the title promises: on the greater shrines, their architecture and setting, on the practices which revolved around them and the offerings made at them. It is to be hoped that the focus of the present book is sufficiently different to be of interest, and that I have been able to give a picture which (apart from being enjoyable) will arouse the reader's interest in finding out more.

My thanks are due to Tony Morris for enthusiastically embracing the idea for this book, Martin Sheppard for his indefatigable labours in bringing it into the light of day and to my husband, as always, for all imaginable support and encouragement on the home front.

1

Beginnings

There were pilgrims in what is now England not only before there were Englishmen, but before there were Christians.[1] The idea of journeying to a sacred place in search of enlightenment or cure was familiar to the Romans and to the peoples they incorporated into their empire, including the Egyptians, the Greeks and of course the Jews. The monumental structures of Roman Bath overlaid (and all but obliterated) an Iron Age healing shrine. The previously presiding deity, Sulis, was assimilated to the Roman Minerva and such assimilations took place elsewhere. Elsewhere too archaeologists have unearthed structures which may have been shops selling votive offerings, or hostels for the accommodation of overnight visitors, for some of whom sleeping at the shrine was a necessary part of the healing process, as it would be for many of their medieval successors. Some things change little over time. Our own behaviour when confronted with pools or springs, wells or fountains, even in surroundings as unpropitious as those of a hotel lobby, links us to our pagan pilgrim ancestors. At Bath seventeen pre-Roman coins have been discovered in the forerunner of the King's Bath, and coins as votive offerings have been found in many of the other pre-Christian shrines which have been excavated in England.

To surmise that there was continuity of 'pilgrim' behaviour in England as elsewhere is one thing, but to demonstrate continuity of use at particular sites, from pagan through Roman to Anglo-Saxon times, is quite another. We have little evidence from which to construct a picture of Christian pilgrimage in Roman Britain. The Anglo-Saxon incursions of the fifth century may well have both disrupted religious practice and obliterated evidence, although their precise effect on Romano-British Christianity, and indeed the precise extent of the Christianisation of Roman Britain, are still matters of debate and investigation. The patient work of archaeologists continues to amplify our knowledge as opportunity affords; but the verbal testimony is scanty and unlikely to be added to.

The best-known word-picture of early Christianity in England is given by the Northumbrian monk Bede in his *Ecclesiastical History of the English People*, completed in 731, by far the most familiar to modern readers of the many works of scholarship to which he devoted his unobtrusive life.[2] For his knowledge of a period that was almost as remote from him as the Reformation is from us he was naturally dependent on such earlier sources as he possessed, notably the gloomy diatribe of the northern monk Gildas, *The Ruin of Britain*, written in Wales perhaps about 540, but possibly earlier.[3] Bede's own information was much better about some parts of England than others, and his vision of the past was shaped by his wholehearted commitment to the up-to-date Romanised principles of the English church which had been established in a series of phases since the mission of St Augustine in 597, under the aegis of Pope Gregory the Great. Bede knew pretty much what there was to be known by someone in his position, but neither his viewpoint nor his sources of information equipped him to answer all the questions that we might like to ask. Nevertheless, he offers some evidence for the possibility of Christian continuity between his England and its past, which may imply continuity of pilgrimage practices.

Roman Britain had not been entirely without the martyrs who all over the Christian Roman world were the first individuals to be venerated as saints, to do miracles and to attract pilgrims to their graves. Drawing on Gildas and other early sources, Bede tells the story of England's protomartyr, St Alban. Having refused to sacrifice to the pagan gods, the saint was led to execution. At the appointed place he caused a spring to bubble up at his feet and was then beheaded. These two details, the spring and the beheading, take on added meaning when seen in the context of pagan reverence for both water-sources and the human head. Bede identifies the place of the martyrdom as a hill outside the Roman Verulamium, and continues:

> Here when peaceful Christian times returned, a church of wonderful workmanship was built, a worthy memorial of his martyrdom. To this day, sick people are healed in this place and the working of frequent miracles continues to bring it renown. [4]

It seems from this that Bede believed that Alban had been continuously venerated at Verulamium ever since the 'wonderful church' was first built (whenever that was). He also described how another saint, Germanus of Auxerre, visited Alban's tomb on his visit to Britain in 429, to give thanks for the success of his mission against the Pelagian heretics, and enriched it with further relics. It is thought likely that St Albans Abbey is built on or very near the site of the martyrdom, where it is known that there was a cemetery, located outside the walls of the Roman settlement in accordance with the usual custom.[5]

This may not have been the only instance of continuity of relic veneration beyond the fifth century, but it is the only one to which Bede himself bears direct witness. In more general terms he refers to the continued existence of churches, most notably the ancient foundation of St Martin on the east side of Canterbury, where, he believed, Bertha, the Frankish Christian wife of Ethelbert of Kent, worshipped before the conversion of her husband and his kingdom at the end of the sixth century.[6] This marked the first successful stage in what proved to be the long drawn out and far from smooth re-establishment of the Roman church in England. Ethelbert eventually gave Augustine and his missionaries the liberty 'to build *or restore* churches', although these may have been architectural shells without a living congregation. We have no evidence that any of them were or had been places of pilgrimage. The site chosen for what became St Augustine's Abbey, important because it was intended as a royal and episcopal mausoleum, overlay a Roman inhumation cemetery, which may in the course of time have become a Christian burial place; but it is not known that it was distinguished by the possession of any particularly holy remains.

There is one faint clue to the existence of a surviving cult in St Augustine's *obsecratio*, a request addressed to Pope Gregory for relics of the martyr Sixtus. Augustine had discovered that a saint of this name, presumably a Romano-British martyr, was being venerated, or at least remembered, at Canterbury itself or somewhere in its neighbourhood. Augustine was uncertain about this personage, because he was performing no miracles and there was no reliable account of him. The pope in response sent him relics of the martyr Pope Sixtus II to replace those of this questionable local saint.[7] If an apparently Christian cult could create difficulty because there was no certain information about it, the customs and observances of the pagan Anglo-Saxons created considerably more. Pope Gregory outlined a policy for Augustine in a famous letter which was actually addressed to his fellow-missionary Abbot Mellitus and is reported by Bede. The central passage, though so often quoted, is worth quoting again. Mellitus was to tell Augustine

> what I have decided after long deliberation about the English people, namely that the idol temples of that race should by no means be destroyed, but only the idols in them. Take holy water and sprinkle it in these shrines, build altars and place relics in them. For if the shrines are well-built, it is essential that they should be changed from the worship of devils to the service of the true God. When this people see that their shrines are not destroyed they will be able to banish error from their hearts and be more ready to come to the places they are familiar with, but now recognising and worshipping the true God. And because they are in the habit of slaughtering much cattle as sacrifice to devils, some solemnity ought to be given to them in exchange for this. So on the day of the dedication or the festivals of the holy martyrs, whose relics are deposited there, let them make themselves huts from the branches of trees around the churches which have been converted out of shrines, and let them celebrate the solemnity with religious feasts.[8]

If this policy was carried out (and as the pope hinted, it was a way of economising on building materials), continuity not of cult but of cult-site would have been achieved at least in some places. A popular local shrine might be created on the site of a once-pagan temple. Pope Gregory's recommendation that the people be encouraged to erect do-it-yourself accommodation around churches on the occasion of religious festivals may indicate that he had been given good information about English pagan customs. The pagan Anglo-Saxon temple excavated at Yeavering in Northumberland contained a pit full of animal bones, almost all the skulls of oxen. The heads, it has been suggested, were reserved for the god, while the carcases were consumed by the revellers. Outside the temple were 'the marks of successive stake- or bough-built huts'. [9]

Bede was familiar with various kinds of pilgrimage, but he only consistently applied the term *peregrinatio* to one of them and probably never thought of classifying them as a single phenomenon. True *peregrinatio* was self-exile for the love of God, which did not necessarily involve a known or defined destination. Secondly, it was possible to undertake a journey to a particular holy place, most frequently Rome, and sometimes practitioners of 'true' pilgrimage did this as well. Thirdly, the afflicted had recourse to shrines where they experienced miraculous cures: these were necessarily shorter journeys in terms of both distance and duration, and were undertaken by humble people. Bede refers to this practice, but never calls it *peregrinatio* or indeed gives it a generic name at all. To this list we can add the attendance of the people at religious festivals which Pope Gregory hoped to encourage, for this too became a characteristic form of medieval short-distance pilgrimage.

In several places Bede refers to men (and women) who had detached themselves from their roots and their kin so as to increase their heavenly deserts. For some of them, the destination was Ireland, fittingly in view of the fact that this concept of self-exile for the sake of repentance and spiritual improvement was characteristically Irish. Many Irish monks crossed the seas, to England, to Scotland and to continental Europe, on the same quest.[10] This was *peregrinatio* in the strict sense, making oneself a stranger or alien for the Lord's sake, but Bede perceived that it could bear different nuances. The many who had left England in the days of bishops Finnan and Colman, he wrote, did so 'either for the sake of religious studies or to live a more ascetic life'. [11] A related purpose was to learn the religious life in continental houses which were better grounded in monastic discipline than the fledgling English communities could yet be. Bede named Brie (that is the convent of Faremoutier), Chelles and Les Andelys as the most popular destinations of high-born and virtuous Englishwomen such as Ercengota, the daughter of Edbald of Kent and the future saint Sexburga.[12] A little later, Hilda, destined in fact to become abbess of Whitby, wished 'to cross over to Gaul, leaving her home and all that she had to live as a stranger for the Lord's sake in the monastery of Chelles'.[13] Chad, the future bishop of Lichfield, returned to England after a period of spiritual exile in Ireland, but his companion Egbert remained there until he too felt new urges which, like Hilda's, were not destined to be fulfilled in the form in which he conceived them. He wanted either to preach to the Frisians and other pagan peoples of northern Europe, or, failing that, to go to Rome. In the end it was revealed to him that he must instead go and reform the monasteries founded by St Columba. He therefore sent Willibrord to undertake the Frisian mission in his place. Two other English priests, both called Hewald, who had been in 'exile' in Ireland, also went to Frisia and there found martyrdom.[14]

Like their Irish counterparts and models, these Englishmen and women were directing their steps not so much to foreign shrines as to schools of spiritual instruction: celebrated religious houses, celebrated teachers, the mission field or the ascetic proving-ground of eremitical solitude. Glastonbury in St Dunstan's early days as a monk in the early tenth century was much frequented by Irish *peregrini*, as well as by 'other crowds of the faithful', because it was believed that St Patrick was buried there. The Irish brought with them books which nourished Dunstan's spirituality. Dunstan's first post-conquest hagiogapher, the monk Osbern, remarked that a practice which in other people 'good will' made into a custom, custom had made natural to the Irish.[15]

Egbert however had reached a point where he wanted to go to Rome, and Bede recorded an increasing traffic in that direction in the later seventh century. Several English kings either expressed a desire to give up their thrones and retire to Rome or actually did so: Oswiu of Northumberland (who was prevented by death, in 670), and then successively Caedwalla and Ine of Wessex. 'At this time', Bede observes, 'many Englishmen, nobles and commons, layfolk and clergy, men and women, were eager to do the same thing.' [16] Later Coenred of Mercia and Offa, son of Sighere of the East Saxons, both went to Rome and ended their days serving at the tomb of St Peter. [17] Self-exile, for these 'kings who opted out',[18] necessarily took a special form: they hoped to associate themselves in death with the prince of the apostles. For churchmen also Rome had special meaning both as a source of authority and also of relics and other religious impedimenta with which they enriched their English churches. The abbot Benedict Biscop of Monkwearmouth (d. 689) was a prime example, and St Wilfrid (d. 709) another. In a homily in Benedict's memory, Bede stressed that, unlike some others, he had derived great spiritual benefit from his travels, which he loved to recall in old age.[19] Wilfrid, successively abbot of Ripon and bishop of York, was a vigorous proponent of Roman orthodoxy, but for that and other reasons he frequently managed to antagonise both the kings of Northumbria and his fellow churchmen. He went to Rome more than once to lay his grievances before the pope, and like Benedict he was an indefatigable collector of relics while he was there.[20] Of another churchman, Oftfor, who went to Rome some time before he became bishop of the Hwicce around 691, Bede remarks that this journey 'in those days was considered to be an act of great merit', as if the greater frequency of the practice in his own time was diminishing its value.[21]

The journey to Rome could for some be an act of abnegation and exile, but others, such as Wilfred and Benedict, went with a more or less clear-cut purpose in view and with every intention of coming back. This particular journey conveyed merit and put the pilgrim in touch with the sources of the Catholic faith. So, in a different sense, did the altogether exceptional enterprise of going to the Holy Land, which Bede mentions only once, albeit at some length, when he gives edited extracts from the book on the Holy Places by Adomnan of Iona, the biographer of St Columba, which he thought an admirable piece of work for people who had no prospect of seeing Jerusalem with their own eyes.[22] In the 720s another Englishman, Willibald, was visiting the Holy Land. His travels, which he related in old age to his kinswoman the nun Hugeberc, well illustrate the rich interaction of motives and destinations in the practice of these high-born and high-minded Anglo-Saxons. Setting out in the spirit of self-exile, he went first to Rome with his brother Winnebald and their father (who died on the way at Lucca), and there spent some time before leaving Winnebald and setting out for Jerusalem, in quest of a greater perfection. Returning to Rome after many adventures, he was directed by the pope to the German mission field, which had already absorbed Winnebald, and there he ended his days as bishop of Eichstätt in Bavaria.[23]

These overlapping forms of Christian 'pilgrimage', with their variously penitential, ascetic and missionary characteristics, do not much resemble the pilgrimage practices of earlier pagan civilisations, or for that matter pilgrimage as most later medieval Europeans (and Englishmen) would have understood it. There were, however, other practices flourishing in Bede's England which would have been much more recognisable to a pagan Celt or Roman on the one hand, or to a thirteenth-century Englishman on the other. Of several holy personages Bede records not only that they did miracles in their lives but that cures were sought and found at their tombs. The horse-litter in which Erkenwald, bishop of London, was carried when he was ill was preserved and continues to cure many people afflicted with fevers and other complaints. Not only are people cured who are placed in or near the litter, but splinters cut from it and taken to the sick bring speedy relief.[24]

There were also healing miracles at Barking Abbey, which Erkenwald founded, and at the tomb of the virgin Etheldreda at Ely, and of Cuthbert and his successor Edbert at Lindisfarne.[25] In one place Bede offers a little detail about the mode of access to such a shrine. Chad was buried at Lichfield

> in a wooden coffin in the shape of a little house, having an aperture in its side, through which those who visit it out of devotion can insert their hands and take out a little of the dust. This dust, if mixed in water, was most effective in diseases of both man and beast.[26]

A similar medium was employed to effect cures at St Cuthbert's tomb at Lindisfarne. The monk and bishop Cuthbert (d. 687), who combined northern Celtic traditions with Romanised loyalties, ranks as one of the greatest of English saints, and his relics were treated by his community in a manner which, it has been suggested, owes more to Gaulish saints' cults than to any of the native traditions of the British Isles.[27] Cuthbert's body was given a magnificent interment; found to be incorrupt eleven years later, it was translated to a new burial place. One day an exorcist from the monastery was sent for to attend a boy who dwelled in the locality and who was possessed by an evil spirit. The priest advised that the boy's father should actually bring him to the holy place, 'to be prayed for at the relics of the martyrs'. At first, he derived no benefit from his visit and continued to rave and shout horribly. One of the monks was then divinely inspired to take some dirt from the place where the water in which Cuthbert's body had recently been washed had been thrown out, and to make it into a potion which he poured into the sufferer's open mouth, bringing about the desired cure. The boy then went with his father on a tour of the *loca sancta* at the monastery, offering up prayer and thanksgiving 'before the relics of the martyrs'. Here we get a glimpse of a sort of itinerary followed by worshippers around a sacred site.[28] It is clear that this particular miracle was credited to Cuthbert, and stones and dirt from the same place effected other cures afterwards, but the monastery was already hallowed by the various relics which it enshrined.

Cuthbert effected several posthumous miracles either at his burial-place or at longer range by means of relics such as the shoes he had worn in the tomb. When his disciple Edbert joined him in the same grave, he also joined him in working miracles at the site 'if the faith of those who seek them admits of it'. It is very striking however that by far the greater number of the wonders related by Bede were performed by Cuthbert in his lifetime. The saint's concern for the members of his community and others who were subject to his pastoral care was conspicuously demonstrated by his power to do miracles for them while he still lived. That this power should be seen to extend beyond death was obviously important, not least because it established the saint's likeness to the apostles and martyrs, but perhaps it was not as yet more important. The decisive shift of emphasis to *post mortem* miracles, which were the principal stuff of later medieval collections and the indispensable proof of sanctity, took place over a period of centuries.

Of all Bede's wonder-workers the most conspicuous was in some respects the oddest. King Oswald of Northumbria was killed at the battle of 'Maserfelth' (perhaps Oswestry) against the pagan Mercians in 642.[29] It is not clear that he was in any genuine sense a martyr for the faith, and Bede does not give him that title, but he displayed the power to sanctify not only the eventual burial sites of the various portions of his dismembered body but other places associated with his life and death. Bede remarked that many miracles took place both at the spot where he planted the standard of the cross before the battle at 'Heavenfield' (near Hadrian's Wall) where he secured his throne, and through the agency of splinters of wood taken from the cross. The monks of nearby Hexham inaugurated the custom of going to Heavenfield on the eve of the anniversary of Oswald's death, keeping vigil there and in the morning celebrating mass. Bede noted that 'a church has lately been built [there], so that the place has become still more sacred and worthy of honour in the eyes of all'.[30] The place of Oswald's death was similarly sanctified: 'Many miracles are related which took place either at that site or through the soil taken from it.' A traveller who experienced the miraculous cure of his horse there spread the news and the paralysed daughter of an innkeeper was taken there and cured.[31] There is no apparent evidence of clerical sponsorship in the miracles first reported from the place of Oswald's death. The horse, which was apparently the first living being to feel the benefit of the saint's power, may have been performing a role in the story consistent with its own place in a warrior culture: it was, after all, a warrior king whose holy blood had been shed at the scene.

Here again motifs with an ancient pedigree are visible. Oswald's head and hands were severed from his body by Penda, king of the Mercians, and hung on stakes: it is not clear where, but perhaps at a pagan cult site. A year later Oswald's brother, Oswiu (himself to be venerated as a saint), mounted a raid and rescued them. Oswald's pagan enemies clearly regarded the king's head as a notable trophy. When recovered, it was quietly interred at Lindisfarne as if it was not thought right to accord too much prominence to a 'relic' which had significance for pagans. The other portions of the

body, however, became focal points of Oswald's cult: the arms were enshrined at the dynastic centre of Bamburgh and the rest of the body, after
some initial reluctance on the part of the monks, at Bardney in Lincolnshire.
Relics and cult-centres subsequently multiplied. Numerous holy wells or
springs, at Heavenfield and elsewhere, came to be associated with Oswald's
cult. One at Winwick supposedly marked the place where the king died,
and one at Oswestry commemorated the spot where a raven dropped his
right arm. Such examples are at least suggestive of continuities with ancient
religious practices.[32] Oswald was by no means the only saint to be associated
with holy wells, and we have already seen that St Alban, before being
beheaded, caused a spring to gush from the ground at his feet.

That there may well have been in all these instances local continuities
with 'Celtic' belief should not of course lead us into the obviously absurd
contention that the Iron Age peoples of Britain had been alone, or unusual,
in venerating springs or according supernatural potency to heads. The cult
of Sulis at Bath would have looked familiar to a visitor who was acquainted
with healing water cults in Italy, while the veneration of the head as a source
of power and energy was widespread. We are inclined to see Roman busts
as mere portraiture, but in their origin they possessed a deeper significance.[33]
The head-reliquaries of medieval Europe belong to the same genealogy.
There is of course very good reason behind a sentiment which still animates
head-hunting peoples at the present day. It was doubtless observed that
beheading was a remarkably effective way of disposing of even the most
resistant martyr, as the later legend of St Katherine of Alexandria testifies:
what her famous wheel could not achieve, a sword did. The miraculous
reunion of head and body became a leitmotif of certain saints' legends,
including that of Edmund of Bury.

The 'Celts' therefore exemplified widespread and basic beliefs which both
their pagan and their Christian Saxon successors in England found it equally
easy to accept. Bede had no apparent difficulty in believing that, when the
two Hewalds were martyred by the Frisians, a spring burst forth from the
ground at the place of their death. Pilgrimage as a 'popular' phenomenon
in Anglo-Saxon and later England can be seen, in part at least, as resting
on a substratum of such common beliefs. In advocating the discreet Christianisation of pagan shrines, Gregory the Great was wise not only in his
own generation but for many generations to come. This of course is not
at all the same thing as saying that every Celtic or pagan Saxon cult-site
had a Christian successor or, conversely, that every Christian pilgrimage
centre of the later middle ages rested on pagan foundations. Cults of all
kinds waxed and waned, and relics migrated, as Oswald's head did when
it accompanied St Cuthbert's remains on their later wanderings before

coming to rest at Durham. Changing settlement patterns and the growth of towns, as well as the human need for novelty, created, and went on creating, new cult-centres.

Bede lays the foundations for our knowledge of early English pilgrimage, even if he would not have applied the word *peregrinatio* to most of it. He might well have found it difficult to understand the modern usage which subsumes short or long 'pilgrimages' to shrines in search of cures or to pay a quick debt of worship under the same denomination as the long-distance *peregrinatio* which took an Irish or English monk the Lord knew whither for the love of Christ. The former meaning has all but obliterated the latter, at least in the western world. The essential element of 'wandering' far from one's familiar roots was lacking in what might be a very short journey from which the traveller hoped and expected to return, but this modification of the concept can be seen as both cause and consequence of the growing practice of pilgrimage by men and women who were in no sense living a religious life.

Bede could not, of course, foresee the future political shape of the English kingdoms and their gradual merging into one, nor the depredations of the Vikings which so disrupted the ecclesiastical life which was his prime concern. It is of little importance for present purposes to decide whether the Viking destruction of shrines and religious houses was motivated by deliberate pagan hostility to Christianity or whether it was a common-sense strategy of attacking soft targets where movable wealth in the form of precious metals was concentrated.[34] The destruction of St Etheldreda's shrine at Ely in 860 and the uprooting of St Cuthbert's community from Lindisfarne in 875 are only the most celebrated examples. In 869 the Danes also created a martyr who would become the focus of one of the major pilgrimage cults of medieval England when they murdered Edmund, king of East Anglia. In the tenth century there was an interlude of reconstruction of church and kingdom under the kings of the house of Wessex. Ely was restored in 970 as a community of monks, and after a century which included a prolonged stay at Chester-le-Street, St Cuthbert's relics were established at Durham in 995. The Danish menace was however briefly renewed in the early eleventh century. Canterbury was sacked in the autumn of 1011 and Archbishop Alfege was captured and martyred at Greenwich. The Dane Cnut, on becoming king in 1016, made it his business to conciliate opinion by patronising prominent shrines, and this remained a normal preoccupation of the kings of England.

Elsewhere in western Europe there was a marked increase in the volume of writing about the saints in and after the eleventh century, but the contrast between the amount produced then and the amount surviving from earlier epochs was unusually marked in England. The Viking destruction not only of shrines but of writings, although impossible to quantify with any degree of exactness, may well have been considerable. So at least some Anglo-Norman writers certainly believed when they failed to find sources for the lives of the old English saints. The difficulties that they encountered handicap us, too, when we try to obtain a picture of pilgrimage in England before the Norman Conquest.

2

Saints and Conquerors

In the 1120s the chronicler William, a monk of Malmesbury in Wiltshire, wrote a history of the English church, entitled *Gesta Pontificum* (*The History of the Bishops*). He confessed that he had found the task more difficult than the writing of his earlier *Gesta Regum* (*History of the Kings*). The reason was the relative paucity of source material, a problem he mentioned several times by way of apology or explanation. St Rumonus, for example, was allegedly buried in a beautiful shrine at Tavistock, but there was no written evidence: 'You will find this in many parts of England, all historical record eliminated, I believe, by enemy action (*violentia hostilitatis*), just the bare names of saints and the knowledge that they claim miracles.' [1]

Similar disclaimers are made by other post-conquest hagiographers. It is tempting sometimes to dismiss them as mere commonplaces: 'Naturally, the saint I am celebrating did innumerable miracles; the fact that there is no information about them can be blamed on the negligence of our ancestors.' In 1110 the monks of St Albans, who had acquired control of the priory of Tynemouth, translated the Northumbrian royal saint Oswiu (d. 651) to a new shrine, and one of the monks wrote an account of the saint and his miracles. [2] In the opening words of his prologue, he stated that 'the carelessness of the ancients dictates that modern diligence will fail in many of its attempts'. In this particular instance, the 'ancient fathers' were much to be censured for leaving Oswiu's life enveloped in silence; even Bede had not treated either his life or his death adequately. He had been buried obscurely, albeit in a stone sarcophagus, on the banks of the Tyne, among a 'rude' people who did not invest burial places with much splendour; although he was venerated by those who had known him, his memory was gradually extinguished in the upheavals which afflicted northern Christianity. Oswiu's revival began with the *inventio* (discovery) of his relics in 1065 under Earl Tostig, and culminated in their translation to a new shrine in 1110. [3] This took place on 20 August, which was also the supposed anniversary of the saint's death and was now established, or re-established, as Oswiu's major festivity. The miracles recorded by the monk of St Albans belonged to this new epoch; we know nothing about any earlier pilgrimage.

A similar pattern appears elsewhere in a number of local variations. A saint not much more recent than Oswiu, the royal abbess Milburga (d. 715), was buried at Wenlock in Shropshire, but William of Malmesbury noted that the site was unknown, again thanks to the destruction of ancient records 'by the violence of enemies and time'. She was 'rediscovered' in 1102 as work proceeded on a new church for the Cluniac monks who had taken the site over around 1080. It may be that the event, and the account that was written of it, which gives vivid details of cures of leprosy and other afflictions among the local people, was contrived to help establish the French monks in their possession of Wenlock in difficult times early in the reign of Henry I.[4] Here, as with Oswiu, we are in effect being told that there was no pre-conquest cult or, more precisely, none that post-conquest authors knew about.

There had been one distinctive, but non-discursive, Anglo-Saxon form of written commemoration of the saints: the list of 'resting places'. Only one pre-conquest example survives, the *Secgan*, which can be dated to after c. 1030, but there is evidence, again from post-conquest sources, that there may have been several more. They had potential as guides for pilgrims, but the manner of their arrangement does not suggest that this was the primary use for which they were intended.[5] It was a chronicler writing almost a century after the Conquest, Hugh Candidus of Peterborough, who, in giving a version of one of these lists, said that he had done so 'for the convenience of the readers, so that he who wishes to visit any saint will know where he can find him'.[6] Whether or not this was a consideration in the minds of the original compilers, it readily occurred to the Anglo-Norman monk a century or more later.

Much has been written about the attitude of the Norman conquerors to the saints of old England.[7] Whether or not it was the Conqueror's original intention, the Conquest resulted in the imposition of a new, non-English ruling class on the kingdom, and the transformation embraced the church and its lands. By 1100 no native Englishman was a bishop or ruled an abbey of major importance. The custodians of the English saints were now men of French speech and a Latin culture which they often deemed superior to that of the conquered. They had to decide on their policy towards saints who were unknown to them and who sometimes possessed uncouth names and obscure histories. A few rabidly xenophobic Normans may have genuinely believed that there had been no saints in England, or that no Englishman could be a saint, and in some miracle stories real or alleged slights of this kind prompted an affronted saint to confound the sceptics and command their devotion henceforth. In the event, the men who became bishops, abbots and non-native inmates of religious communities, secular

The resting-places of the saints as described in the late Anglo-Saxon period.
Many of these remained places of pilgrimage until the Reformation.

and monastic, in the post-conquest kingdom, discovered powerful incentives to conciliate and glorify the saints under whose patronage they now found themselves living.

The sense that the resident saint was, in England as everywhere in Christendom, the entrenched *genius loci* emerges strongly. Many of the saints the newcomers had venerated in their several homelands (for not all were Normans) remained there; their patronage could hardly be imported wholesale into England, although new church dedications (such as the many to St Nicholas) reflected cults popular with the conquerors. The communities which now had to be ruled, and the men and women who served them in town and country, remained for the most part English, and they knew who their 'undying landlords' were. Conversely, where the natives had apparently permitted their saint to slide into obscurity, it might seem appropriate to the new landlords, as at Wenlock or Tynemouth, to identify themselves with the neglected saint and to enshrine him or her in a visible and befitting manner. Here it was not the saint that was open to doubt or criticism but rather the treatment which, it was claimed, he or she had latterly received.

The frequent absence of written sources for these saints was, however, a real difficulty for serious and respectable men who were imbued with the idea that an authentic cult must be supported by written evidence. William of Malmesbury said that he did not want to hold the relics St Ethelwold had collected at Thorney up to ridicule, but asked how it was possible to talk of miracles when you had no record of them.[8] The striking efflorescence of Anglo-Norman hagiography in the century after the Conquest owed much to the urgent need to repair a defective record, in so far as it was possible to do so. The impulse doubtless often came from religious communities who wanted the credentials of themselves and their saints firmly established in the eyes of the new rulers of the kingdom.

Often the interests of these writers extended only to one community and one, or at least one principal, saint. The archdeacon Herman at the end of the eleventh century wrote of the miracles of St Edmund.[9] Simeon of Durham around 1100 was principally concerned with his own church and with St Cuthbert,[10] while the history, property rights and saints of Ely, above all Etheldreda, were documented in the third quarter of the twelfth century by the compiler of the *Liber Eliensis*.[11] Other individuals cast their net wider. Perhaps the most influential was Goscelin of St-Bertin, who came to England, perhaps in 1058, as secretary to the bishop of Sherborne, and eventually became a monk of St Augustine's Abbey at Canterbury. His chief loyalty in later life was to St Augustine's, but in between times he was virtually a freelance writer of saints' lives.[12] His work was well known to twelfth-century writers such as William of Malmesbury and the compiler of the *Liber Eliensis*, and also probably to Eadmer, an English-born monk of Christ Church, the cathedral monastery of Canterbury and a local rival to St Augustine's. Eadmer, who was born about 1060 and died about 1130, is best known as an historian and as the biographer of his archbishop, St Anselm, but he also wrote lives of several Anglo-Saxon saints, including St Wilfrid (whose relics Christ Church claimed), St Oswald of Worcester and York, and a previous archbishop of Canterbury, St Dunstan.[13] William of Malmesbury had both a deep attachment to the west country and his own St Aldhelm of Malmesbury, and a much broader awareness. Another leading hagiographer of the period, Osbert of Clare, a native of Suffolk, was first and foremost a Westminster man; he rose to be prior of the monastery, but failed in his ambition to be elected abbot when Gilbert Crispin died in 1117, and spent much of the rest of his career in exile from Westminster. Although he is perhaps best known as the devotee and hagiographer of Edward the Confessor, his periods of enforced absence from Westminster enabled him to deepen his knowledge of other English saints.[14]

It remained true that the best efforts of piety and scholarship could not entirely make good what did not exist. The 'many miracles' with which a saint was routinely credited were essential to his or her *curriculum vitae*, but the details were rarely available and not, in fact, indispensable, since it was not the principal purpose of this literature to describe popular pilgrimage. The first biographer of St Oswald of Worcester (d. 992) digressed from his main subject to record the murder of Edward, brother and briefly successor of King Edgar, in 979; in the following years 'so many miracles were performed at his tomb, that no one could write them down as fast as they were performed'. So indeed we must suppose, for no record of them survives.[15] Oswald refounded Winchcombe Abbey during the 960s, but the monks were temporarily expelled some years later, and it seems unlikely that the cult of the ninth-century Mercian child-prince Kenelm was as yet firmly established there. Goscelin of St-Bertin wrote a life of the saint some time between 1045 and 1075, claiming that Kenelm had from the beginning performed innumerable miracles, but significantly only a few 'of the many of modern times and our own' were described, and we are bound to suspect that these 'many', if they ever happened, were not actually on record.[16] When Goscelin described the life of Werburga of Chester, he mentioned her miracles in broad generic terms but gave no particulars, probably because he was unable to do so. William of Malmesbury is only a little more informative: 'The merits of this virgin are proclaimed at Chester and her miracles extolled. Although she is promptly favourable to the petitions of all, she is especially quick to give heed to the prayers of women and children.' He refers elsewhere to the practice of oral exposition of miracles by *custodes*. [17] Sometimes, perhaps, these *custodes* possessed written records of miracles which no longer exist; perhaps, however, they simply conserved oral traditions, and we have no way of knowing how old these may have been. Edward, Kenelm and Werburga alike attracted pilgrims to their shrines in later centuries, but we know little or nothing about their early activities.

This virtual absence of miracle-collections makes it effectively impossible to write the history of pilgrimage in England before the year 1000, and the eleventh-century record is patchy by later standards. The blame may lie with the destructive activities of the Danes or the literary negligence of Anglo-Saxon shrine custodians or a combination of the two. Both were invoked by post-conquest writers. Even in the more settled conditions of the tenth century the guardians of the saints may not have been as interested in promoting them to a popular audience as their twelfth-century successors came to be. William of Malmesbury wrote admiringly of the achievements of St Dunstan, who had been one of the leaders of the tenth-century reform of the English church, and implied that the improved veneration of the saints was an important part of his programme:

> Monasteries arose throughout the island, the altars of the saints were heaped with a mass of precious metal, and the conduct of the builders was not inferior to the beauty of the buildings.[18]

Dunstan began his career in high ecclesiastical office as abbot of Glastonbury, an ancient monastery with a wealth of relics and saintly associations. Yet he himself may not have been the most forward of the reformers in encouraging popular access to the saints.[19] It was not invariably the case in pre-conquest England (or elsewhere in Europe) that this was encouraged as it was to be later. Relics were not always conspicuously elevated or tombs located for maximum accessibility to the populace. The miracles performed by the saints for pilgrims to their shrines constituted only a proportion of their activity. The ceremonial parade of them in processions, and the export of secondary relics (dust from the tomb, snippets of cloth) over long or short distances, from early times provided other means by which they could make their power felt.[20] In repose they might prefer to share the seclusion of their guardians. Monks undoubtedly had incentives, including economic incentives, to attract offerings, but their own liturgical and devotional routines had to be safeguarded and access to the saints might be preferentially granted to persons of high status with whom they had property and political dealings.

The cult of Dunstan's associate, St Oswald of Worcester, illustrates the point.[21] At his funeral, orphans and widows, *peregrini* and the poor, monks and clerks, all flocked to the scene; later, 'the blind were illuminated through Oswald's prayers, and on his feast day demons were expelled and the sick healed'. [22] Eleven or twelve years later, Oswald's miracles (not particularised) prompted a translation of his relics. It was thought inappropriate that one through whose merits God daily performed so many great works should be left lying in the earth, not only because this position was inherently undignified, but because 'there was easy access to all and sundry, and he was perhaps more exposed than was proper to those who were less worthy'. It was decided therefore to remove him to a place which was 'not frequented by secular persons, and removed from irreverent access'. This may mean that Oswald was relocated behind the high altar. On a certain feast day a dumb man of Worcester was able 'somehow' (*quadam vice*) to approach the tomb; here the saint appeared to him in a vision, brandishing his staff as if to drive him from the vicinity, but he cured him nonetheless. There was clearly a tension between two equally pressing needs: to advertise the saint's powers, yet to preserve the mystery and dignity of a great lord in the court of heaven. If the people could approach him only with difficulty, Oswald could however be brought to them; the reliquary was portable and was carried around the city of Worcester to quell fires or epidemics.[23]

At Canterbury, Dunstan was instantly recognised by the Christ Church community as a saint, but it is not at all clear that he was presented as such to a wider public: his tomb seems to have been somewhat inaccessible. In contrast, to take active steps to encourage the interest of the general public in a saint and to see that the results were recorded in detail was to make a very deliberate decision. The most impressive of late Anglo-Saxon miracle collections resulted from such a decision, taken by Ethelwold of Winchester, a reforming associate of Oswald and Dunstan.[24] On 15 July 971 Ethelwold carried out the translation of one of his predecessors, Swithun. The deliberation of this action is the more notable because Swithun had lapsed into almost total obscurity after his death in 862, as William of Malmesbury noted. The background to the translation was provided by the expulsion of secular clergy from the cathedral in 964 and the substitution of monks.[25] Swithun now wished to be brought from the unobtrusive burial place outside the cathedral which he had himself chosen to a more becoming place inside it; by implication this was because the church itself was now being fittingly ruled and magnificently rebuilt.

An account of the miracles Swithun performed to mark the occasion survives from the hand of Lantfredus, a monk of Winchester, and is datable to 971–73.[26] Lantfredus significantly observed that 'The life and conduct of this marvellous bishop are unknown to us, because there are no writings

[about them].' ²⁷ One of the most striking features of his account is that
he not only describes the miracles but estimates their number:

> After the body of the most holy bishop was placed within the church, as I have
> said, four or five sick persons received cures at his tomb in the space of three
> days. After the three days, and for about five months, there was rarely a day on
> which sick people were not cured in the church where the relics of the holy man
> were deposited: sometimes more, sixteen or eighteen, sometimes fewer, five or
> three, or more often seven, eight, ten, twelve, fifteen. We have seen more than
> two hundred in ten days cured by the merits of the saint, and in the course of
> a year, who knows how many? We have seen the open spaces around the said
> monastery so filled with crowds of invalids that a traveller could hardly find a
> way of getting to it. After some days, so many of them were cured, by God's
> grace, by the merits of the saint that even inside the church there were scarcely
> five sick people to be found.²⁸

Lantfredus gives some details about individuals and their places of origin.
There were sixteen blind persons from London, two men and two women
from Essex, three blind women from the Isle of Wight, a blind noblewoman
from Bedfordshire, the blind *praepositus* of Abingdon Abbey. One lame
suppliant who, one feels, was lucky to escape without the saint counter-
manding his cure, got up and left the church at high speed as soon as he
realised that he was mobile, either out of sheer excitement or in order to
avoid making an offering, but he left his crutches behind. They, and the
testimony of the bystanders, proved what had happened. Bishop Ethelwold
gave directions that the monks of Winchester must enter the church every
time a cure was announced and offer praise and thanksgiving to God. They
murmured at this when they found themselves being woken three and four
times in the night, and it was necessary for the saint himself to convey a
stiff warning that, if they ceased from their praises, the miracles would
cease; if they persevered, wonders as yet undreamt of would result.

Winchester boasted a notable concentration of population by tenth-
century standards, and the close physical proximity of reformed religious
houses there may have created an exceptionally competitive environment.²⁹
Swithun was the saint of the Old Minster, which was being rebuilt on a
magnificent scale uncomfortably close to the New Minster, which only
moved to Hyde in the suburbs of the city early in the twelfth century. The
relics of the Breton St Judocus, or Josse, had been brought to the New
Minster in 903. A man who fell prey to two mysterious harpy-like creatures
was first advised by friends to have recourse to St Josse, but it was Swithun
who effected his deliverance. The city contained yet a third major focus
of saintly activity at Nunnaminster, where the royal saint Edburga lived.
After Edburga's death in 960 it was again Ethelwold who was responsible

for translating her relics to a new shrine, and she too was supposed to perform cures. [30]

Lantfredus's account of the miracles of St Swithun is of inestimable value, for it shows that, as we might indeed expect, the practice of pilgrimage and the conventions of miracle stories were familiar to the English in the late tenth century. He was obviously well-acquainted with the *topos* of the suppliant who went with only partial success, or no success at all, to other saints. There was the blind nobleman who went to Rome, only to be told about Swithun's powers by English pilgrims there and to return 'to the region whence he had come'. A repentant parricide from foreign parts came to England to seek the aid of the saints and the tight iron band girding him burst at Swithun's shrine: it was hung up in the monastery in proof of the miracle. (This was a stock story which was told of many other saints.) Some of these competitive miracles provide evidence for contemporary pilgrimage to shrines elsewhere in England. A lame Londoner got the use of one foot back from St Augustine at Canterbury but on hearing of Swithun's merits came to Winchester to complete the cure. More interesting still is the story of the young man from Collingbourn in Wiltshire who had been blinded in an accident and who was diverted to Winchester after setting out with the intention of keeping vigil at Shaftesbury, 'where reposes the body of the most holy and venerable Elgiva, mother of the most glorious and pious Edgar, king of the English, at whose tomb many sick persons receive bodily healing through the omnipotence of God'. [31]

Like Winchester, Canterbury offered a populous environment rich in ecclesiastical communities and associations. Although on Lantfredus' evidence Augustine's shrine was operative around 970, activity here seems to have gathered momentum in the mid eleventh century. The city suffered severely, with much of Kent, from the renewed Danish incursions of the early eleventh century. In 1011 these culminated in the capture and martyrdom of Archbishop Alfege. In 1023, with Cnut' s blessing, Alfege's relics were brought back from London to Canterbury and installed in the cathedral, and in the latter half of the century Osbern, monk and precentor of Canterbury, wrote of his life and translation.[32] In 1035 Cnut also authorised the translation of the Kentish royal saint Mildred to St Augustine's Abbey from her original burial place at Minster on the Isle of Thanet. Towards the end of the century Goscelin wrote an account of this translation and the subsequent miracles which gives some picturesque detail of local pilgrimage practices and constitutes a rare source for a cult continuing through the period of the Norman Conquest. The abbots of St Augustine's were careful to maintain the church at Minster (which was their property) as a secondary shrine, solemnly processing there every year to celebrate the saint's July feast day and to entertain local notables.[33]

Between Mildred's coming and the end of the century, St Augustine's was progressively transformed by massive rebuilding, first by Abbot Wulfric and then by the Norman conquerors.[34] Meanwhile the monks of Christ Church were not inactive. The *Life* of St Dunstan which was written at the end of the century by the monk Osbern (who had written about Alfege), and another a little later by Eadmer, provide at least some retrospective evidence for his growing popularity in the mid eleventh century. A prayer composed *c.* 1020 called upon him as 'the healer of various sick people who visit your tomb'.[35] Osbern refers to 'books of Dunstan's miracles which now scarcely survive', which he had excerpted, but admitted that most of the miracles he recounted had been performed 'in our own times'. This seems most likely to mean before the Conquest and the fire of 1067.[36] This disaster, which enforced the relocation of shrines and extensive rebuilding, combined with Archbishop Lanfranc's hesitations over the cults of his predecessors to plunge Dunstan's cult and others into a temporary obscurity; but by 1100, with St Anselm's support, his stock was once again high.[37]

The picture given by Osbern and Eadmer is of a local pilgrimage with the standard attributes. A blind man of Lenham was directed in a dream to go to Dunstan, significantly described as *pater patriae*, and lament his sins; at Canterbury he begged permission, on the strength of the saint's instructions, to spend the night in prayer in the church. In the middle of the night he began to smell 'all kinds of odours' emanating from the tomb and was cured. The popular character of the pilgrimage is best illustrated by the cautionary tale of a rich and noble priest of Folkestone who, although paralysed, at first disdained to seek Dunstan's help because it meant mixing with 'a company of the poor, who flocked thither from all parts in hope of recovering their health'. Eventually he was persuaded to go, borne on the shoulders of his *clientes* and accompanied by 'no small multitude of kinsfolk', who seem to have been quite as active as the sufferer himself in calling tearfully upon the saint's assistance. Duly cured, he returned to Folkestone and gave a great feast, at which, unfortunately, the guests began tactlessly to praise God for his mercy in not rejecting a man of power, but granting him the chance of repentance along with 'his poor'. This was more than the priest's social prejudices could endure and he burst forth, 'Are you reckoning me as one of those paupers, when you say that I was cured among them? It's not so, for if Dunstan had never existed, the outcome would have been the same.' He then had a paralytic stroke from which he did not recover.[38]

This noteworthy incident led to greater veneration of the saint and more miracles. There are other touches of local colour, such as the story of the old blind woman who was cured only on her way home, when she was left without a guide on a bridge over the Stour. Pilgrimages had to be carefully timed: a lame man who went to Canterbury, but failed to obtain a cure, was on his way home when Dunstan appeared to him with apologies that he had been busy when he called; if he returned to the shrine now, he would be attended to.[39] Like many other saints, Dunstan implicitly encouraged recourse to other Canterbury relics and festivities. 'A virgin devoted to God', blind from birth, went to Christ Church when the community celebrated its general relic feast, on 23 August, the vigil of St Bartholomew and St Ouen (of whom the cathedral possessed relics). She received permission to keep watch overnight in the church, and stood in prayer by the tomb (*juxta requiem*) of St Dunstan, duly receiving her sight. The bell of St Dunstan was rung and 'the whole city' came running to bear witness, and weep, at the miracle; there were 'many thousands' of them.[40]

Dunstan's posthumous fortunes were complicated by the fact that he was associated with two major cult-centres, Glastonbury where he had been born and became monk and abbot, and Canterbury where he died as archbishop. This gave rise, by around 1100, to a contest between the two for the right to claim possession of his relics, which entered its final round as late as 1508.[41] The Glastonbury claim was that the sack of Canterbury by the Danes in 1011 had led (in somewhat mysterious circumstances) to the 'rescue' of the relics by monks of Glastonbury.[42] Osbern and Eadmer preserve evidence that there was in fact a two-way flow in the eleventh century between Canterbury and Glastonbury to do honour to Dunstan. This illustrates what might be termed the professional involvement of monks and clergy, not merely in the liturgical celebration of saints but in physical pilgrimage to them. Osbern had himself been to Glastonbury and gives an account of his own ecstatic reactions to the sight of Dunstan's tiny cell. He wept when he remembered how often the saint had come to his aid in his afflictions, and reflected:

> This was the young man's home, this was his bed, this a sight for the whole world. But the huge and spacious walls of cities cannot be compared to these narow confines, since today, through them, the fever-stricken receive their health, the frenzies of demons are quietened, and much sickness is healed.[43]

This enthusiasm resembled the sentiments pilgrims were expected to feel at Rome or in the Holy Land. Osbern seems not have heard of the claim that Dunstan was bodily present at Glastonbury. Among the arguments with which Eadmer sought to refute this impertinence, in a letter written *c.* 1120, was the fact that, as old Glastonbury monks would be able to testify, before the coming of the Normans their abbot used to visit Canterbury every year, with four or more of his monks, and stayed there for several days to do honour to Dunstan on his feast-day. This would not have made sense if Glastonbury had possessed the relics.[44]

Some writers record or imply at least a temporary decline in the fortunes of their saints around 1066. William of Malmesbury observed of St Albans that 'it never entirely succumbed to ruin'.[45] The materials at the disposal of Matthew Paris when he compiled the early history of the abbey in the mid thirteenth century included a great deal of information about the building work of successive abbots in the early medieval period, which seem to imply the continuous veneration of the saint, at least within the community itself. The relics were supposedly carried off by the Danes to Odense but later recovered; on their return they performed many cures both in the convent and among the people.[46] As to a wider public for the cult, however, we get little clue until the reign of Edward the Confessor. By then, at least, the road between London and St Albans was sustaining a flourishing traffic of both pilgrims and other travellers, and the safety and passability of that road was of more than charitable interest to the convent. The twelfth abbot, Leofstan,

> taking pity on all those who were in peril, such as travellers and merchants and also pilgrims who came to the church of St Alban for the expiation of their sins and the well-being of their bodies, made the roads safer, and had the dense woods from the slopes of the Chilterns as far as London cut back, especially along the royal road which is called Watling Street, smoothed out bits of difficult going, built bridges and had steep tracts of road reduced to a safer level.[47]

The monastery lost some of its lands to William I, however, and also had to face the claim of the monks of Ely that they possessed the saint's relics:

> Therefore reverence for the holy martyr Alban was impaired, and the display of the customary veneration, as was the case with the other saints of the kingdom, such as the blessed Edmund and the blessed Cuthbert and many others; as a result there were fewer miracles in their churches.[48]

The cult of Edmund, the king of East Anglia martyred by the Danes in 869, displays yet another variant on what is becoming a familiar pattern. At the end of the eleventh century, the archdeacon Herman described the humble covering that was first provided for the relics and commented that if Edmund had done any miracles during the period immediately after his death they went unrecorded.[49] The translation of the saint's remains to Bury around 915 and the establishment of a community to watch over them provided a setting for the development of the cult, but once again we have to wait for the eleventh century for any record of Edmund as thaumaturge. With the accession of Cnut and the institution of monks at Bury in 1020 the conditions were at last established for Edmund's development not merely as the protector of East Anglia but as a national English saint. A succession of kings – Cnut himself, the Confessor, Harold – paid homage to him, and it is from this period that Herman dated what might be termed 'mass' pilgrimage:

> From various parts of greater Britain (*Britanniae majoris*) many people visit the saint for their health. Some receive what they need straight away, some after an appointed interval, but no one goes away ungrateful because the saint, with the aid of faith, has not had pity on them.[50]

Subsequently the miracles became less frequent, but this was not for want of power, rather because there were, for some reason, fewer worshippers. Those who came received their cures as always. With the Norman abbot Baldwin and then the Norman Conquest the story entered a new phase; the saint who had established himself as the patron of all Englishmen (and Anglo-Danes) now added the Normans to his constituency.

There can be little doubt that the years around and after 1000 saw religious communities busily engaged in the acquisition and translation of relics, even if we are often dependent on post-conquest accounts of them. In about 1001 the monks of Ramsey discovered the relics of Ivo, supposedly a Persian bishop who had lived and died as a hermit at Slepe, on the Ouse near Huntingdon, with three of his companions, and translated them to Ramsey.[51] To judge from the account that was written by Goscelin for the monks between 1087 and 1090, it was an important part of the monks' strategy to promote Ivo as a popular, wonder-working saint whose power was displayed not just at his new burial place at Ramsey, but even more at the place of his life, death and discovery at Slepe, and especially at the spring which flowed there.[52] Abbot Ednoth, who carried out the translation, was clearly not blind to the importance that healing waters had, and would continue to have, in popular religion. He built a church at the spot which was so designed that half the spring was inside it and half outside, 'so that whether the door was open or locked, the boon of the water was available to visitors'.

The miracles collected by Goscelin are not precisely dated; it is not easy, therefore, to know how many of them belong to the early eleventh century, and how many were recent when he described them. Abbot Ednoth was cured of gout in Ethelred's reign; Goscelin himself was cured of gout and toothache. Ivo was a European specialist in delivering penitent killers from their chains, drawing clients from Venice, Saxony and Cologne. Two of a little group of Saxon penitents were delivered from their bonds by Etheldreda at Ely, but the other two had to come to Ramsey. A boy from Hampshire, congenitally weak in his hands and feet, was partially cured by St Edward the Martyr at Shaftesbury before coming to Ramsey, where he was completely cured and remained 'to serve the saint'. One of Ivo's miracles was specifically designed to refute any suspicion that drinking at the saint's spring was a superstitious paganising practice. A monk in the entourage of an unnamed foreign abbot who paused to drink the water objected that

> it did not become a prudent and religious man to lend himself to the folly and superstition of rustics; they are often known to frequent springs, being deceived by pagan error, and, seduced by the illusory marvels of demons, to venerate the bones of all sorts of dead people, as if they were the relics of saints. [53]

Having uttered this ill-advised criticism the monk promptly fell ill. To William of Malmesbury, St Ivo was the 'most efficacious saint in all England' and the easiest to invoke when he was writing in the 1120s, but by this time the cult had entered upon a new phase with the decision to develop Slepe as a new town and market centre.[54]

In 1014 a monk of Ramsey, Elfward, was made abbot of Evesham, and proved himself an indefatigable collector and promoter of relics.[55] At his request, Cnut bestowed the relics of the Mercian royal saint Wistan on Evesham, moving them from Repton, while the same abbot paid London merchants the 'fit price' of one hundred marks for St Odulf, a saint of Frisian origin whose relics had allegedly been stolen by Viking raiders from Stavoren.[56] It can reasonably be supposed that a prime motive of all this acquisitive activity was to enhance Evesham's heavenly security and earthly prestige, not to mention those of its abbot, and that the encouragement of pilgrimage and the offerings that facilitated building and the decoration of the church were probably an integral part of the strategy. Evesham already possessed its own ancient saints, Ecgwin (d. 717) and Credan (d. 796). On an embassy to Harthacnut in Flanders in 1039, Abbot Elfward was in danger of shipwreck and, as both the Evesham and the Ramsey chroniclers reported, he vowed to augment the public celebrations of Ecgwin's translation. The Ramsey chronicler said that he promised the saint that he would not only make a silver shrine for his relics but see to it that the cult was more widely celebrated by the faithful. He duly completed the new shrine for the saint, the original having been despoiled by the Danes, and by pontifical authority (in his capacity as bishop of London) commanded 'all the people' to flock to the festivities, which took place on 10 September.[57]

Elfward's successor at Evesham, Mannius, was a great builder and continued his work by making shrines (*feretra*) for both Odulf and Wistan.

The next abbot, Agelwin, appointed in 1059 when Mannius was stricken with paralysis, survived well into the Norman epoch. As he enjoyed the favour of the Conqueror, Evesham's saints were spared hostile scrutiny until Walter, a chaplain of Lanfranc, became the first Norman abbot in 1077. Walter supposedly permitted himself to wonder how it was that the English people, sprung from a stock adorned by so many saints, could have been subjugated by the French: perhaps the saints were not so holy after all. He decided therefore to apply Lanfranc's advice and test the relics by fire. He was impressed by the result: the bones did not even change colour. Indeed, he was so impressed that he took some of the relics on a fund-raising tour to raise money for the rebuilding of the church. They were exhibited at Oxford (where they performed at least one healing miracle), London, Winchester and elsewhere.[58]

Ecgwin in particular was a miracle-worker.[59] Prior Dominic's *Life* of him leaves the reader in no doubt that the saint had done miracles on a regular basis ever since his death, ministering to both physical and spiritual problems. His fame had grown to the point that 'crowds of people came to that place to seek remedies for both body and soul'.[60] Once again, however, the detailed miracle stories date from no earlier than the reign of the Confessor. They are followed by a description of the scenes to be witnessed in the church both regularly and on the saint's major feast-day. This is all highly conventional, but for that very reason it will serve to illustrate the experience of pilgrimage as it was visualised by the custodians of shrines. It is framed in a not unfamiliar historical perspective :

> Making many enquiries into the miracles of St Ecgwin, and often talking about them with trustworthy and venerable persons adorned with goodness, we have tried to put on record what we have gathered from many people, that in the olden time, before the coming of the Normans into England, the monastery was through the workings of God's mercy so often lit up by the miracles of this holy man that it was rare for the sun go down on a Saturday without some sick person, in the grips of some infirmity or trouble, having obtained relief through St Ecgwin. If you had been there, you would have seen now one, now two, often more, invalids coming for the sake of their health, approaching the altar or being brought by others, flinging themselves on the ground, pouring forth prayers, groaning, all alike hoping for their health. You would have seen some blind, others lame, some deaf, others mute, many lepers or paralytics or people painfully bound with irons, or besieged by some other infirmity. There were demoniacs too in this pitiful assembly. But often the divine grace, through the merits of St Ecgwin, was present, illuminating the blind, raising up the lame, restoring hearing to the deaf and speech to the mute, cleansing the leprous, healing the paralysed and not failing to cure the other sick. Through the merits of St Ecgwin

many who were painfully fettered with iron in expiation of their crimes were miraculously liberated. For when a certain person who was suffering thus devoutly sought the protection of St Ecgwin and begged for the mercy of God and his saint by spending the night frequently at the tomb of the saints (*circa sanctorum memoriam frequentius incubans*), one day the Almighty gloriously displayed his pity, and cut the iron from the sufferer with such force that it sprang a long way from its original place and filled the church with its clatter, while all present marvelled and praised God with one harmonious voice. At that time the feast of St Ecgwin was celebrated most honourably, with the utmost reverence, and a multitude of the people flocked to it; the immense pomp, the crowds, the abundant joy were equally remarkable. [61]

Two principal contexts for pilgrimage and the performance of miracles are thus indicated at Evesham: what might be termed the regular round, in which Saturday, the vigil of the weekly feast-day, was a favoured time for miracles; and the saint's major festivity, on 30 December, which attracted important visitors. Prior Dominic seems to locate Evesham's golden age in the pre-conquest past, which may be nothing more than conventional nostalgia, but is consistent with the picture he gives of the promotion of the abbey's saints by the abbots in the first half of the eleventh century.

A number of typical patterns emerge from these patchy records. There was clearly a great deal of activity, in church-building and the promotion of cults, in the middle years of the eleventh century, and there is convincing evidence of popular pilgrimage even if we are usually dependent on later accounts of it. This activity was continued and augmented by the Norman conquerors. Waltham Abbey, not far to the north of London, provides an illustrative example. Rebuilt on a large scale under the patronage of Duke Harold to house perhaps the most celebrated of the monumental crucifixes which were venerated in late Anglo-Saxon England, it was consecrated in 1060, ahead of Edward the Confessor's Westminster. Harold supposedly came to venerate the Cross before departing for the battle at Hastings, and the crucified Christ bowed His head in foreboding sorrow as he left. The Conqueror subsequently gave permission for Harold's body to be taken to Waltham for burial. The estates of the church suffered some spoliation in the next half-century, but Henry I assigned it to the queen's dower, and he and Matilda were benefactors. Waltham had links with Durham which were reflected in the rebuilding which took place early in the twelfth century, and which took into account the needs of pilgrims in so far as it was 'designed to provide a setting for the Holy Cross as well as serving the needs of the canons'.[62]

For some of the kingdom's most ancient saints, including several who had been known to Bede, revival seems to have gathered momentum after the Conquest. The monks of Lindisfarne, driven from their home by the Viking raids in 875, carried St Cuthbert's relics (and also St Oswald's head) with them and settled temporarily at a number of places, including Chester-le-Street, until they came to rest at Durham in 995.[63] The settlement at Durham created the conditions for a stable development of the cult, which after the Norman Conquest was crowned by the establishment of monks as the saint's custodians and the rebuilding of the church on a massive scale. The installation of monks altered the conditions in which pilgrims were permitted to approach the shrine, not least in so far as women were prohibited from doing so and the myth fostered that this was at the saint's own command. A detailed record of Cuthbert's miracles was not produced, however, until much later in the twelfth century.[64] Similarly, the miracles of St Etheldreda recorded in the *Liber Eliensis* are virtually all of twelfth-century date. [65]

Other saints whom Bede had known experienced similar fortunes. There is very little evidence for the cult of Erkenwald of London in the pre-conquest period, but by the time William of Malmesbury was writing in the 1120s, renewed interest was stirring. The church of St Paul's was being rebuilt after the disastrous fire of London in 1087, and the episcopate of Bishop Maurice (1087–1107) seems to have witnessed a revival of miraculous activity. Maurice was a patron of Goscelin of St-Bertin, who is supposed to have dedicated a lost account of Erkenwald's miracles to him. This may well have been the source of William's knowledge that the miracles were of 'recent' as well as ancient fame: Erkenwald, he said, was held in the greatest reverence at London. The canon Arcoid, who compiled a collection of the miracles some time after 1140, explained that the beneficiaries of the saint's many early miracles had unfortunately entrusted them to memory rather than to writing; he was able only to report a very few of quite uncertain date, which are presumably meant to have occurred before the episcopate of Bishop Maurice. [66] Ithamar of Rochester seems to have plunged into a more complete pre-conquest obscurity. William of Malmesbury knew nothing more than what Bede had said of him, which was very little. Like Erkenwald, however, he benefited from the Norman rebuilding of his church, and began to do miracles which were written up in the 1140s.[67] The pattern is exemplified yet again in John of Beverley (d. 721), who had ordained Bede himself priest. John's life was written for Archbishop Aldred of York (1061–70) by a clerk called Folcard; he says nothing about his sources, and the miracles he recounts had all been performed in the saint's lifetime, although Folcard claimed that cures of all kinds were being performed at his tomb.[68] Once again, the surviving miracle stories are of twelfth-century date or later.[69]

Another saint who had been known to Bede was particularly close to
William of Malmesbury's heart. William effectively dedicated the fifth book
of the Gesta Pontificum to Aldhelm of Malmesbury (d. 709), whose posthumous fortunes exemplify the familiar pattern.[70] William was confident that
the saint had done many miracles after his death. In the ninth century a
shrine was made for him in metalwork, on the back of which his miracles
were depicted in relief. This led one to suppose, William observes, that a
book of miracles existed at that time, but was lost during the Danish
invasions.[71] A period of revival began with Dunstan, who bestowed many
gifts on the abbey but also, foreseeing the depredations of the Danes, removed
the relics from their precious metal shrine to a stone tomb.[72] The miracles
which William relates belong mostly to another period of revival, the later
eleventh century. Now Aldhelm had to establish his credit with the new
Norman rulers. He took a step towards this objective when he restored the
sight of a fisherman from the Isle of Wight who had spent three frustrating
years at Christchurch in Hampshire in the hopes of a cure before coming
to Malmesbury. This emboldened the Norman abbot Warin, who had to
learn reverence for the saint, to replace the relics in Dunstan's shrine and
prepare for a ceremonial translation at which Osmund of Salisbury, himself
a canonised saint of the future, officiated in 1078, taking away an arm of
the saint which he bestowed upon his own cathedral.[73] This was a striking
demonstration of reverence for an ancient English saint on the part of a
new, non-English bishop. Lanfranc was at the royal court when he received
the report of one of Aldhelm's next miracles and he ordered his annual
celebration throughout England. A fair was instituted at Malmesbury to
accompany the celebrations. William describes how popular recourse to the
saint was managed. The custodians, after carrying the shrine in procession,
so positioned it across the doors that it could only be approached by people
who prostrated themselves, and there they strove, emboldened by faith, to
obtain 'a sum of many vows' from the saint for the outlay of a penny or
halfpenny. This was Aldhelm's 'everyday work' and he sent no one away
empty-handed.[74]

In reporting Aldhelm's miracles from this period, William may have had
at his disposal the records that he lacked for other saints and earlier times,
and he was also able to include cures he had witnessed himself. A picture
familiar from other miracle collections emerges: suppliants most often came
from near Malmesbury and elsewhere in Wiltshire, but also from Gloucestershire and as far afield in England as Lincolnshire. More exotic, and
perhaps less believable if only because it so much resembles stories told
about several other saints, was the deliverance of the penitent homicide
from Cologne who, having been to Rome and Jerusalem, shed at Aldhelm's

shrine the last of the iron bands with which he was girded. The pious Ernulf of Hesdin received a cure from the saint which a famous physician of Malmesbury was unable to achieve, and departed for Jerusalem, hoping not to return. 'Jealous oblivion' may have swallowed up Aldhelm's many earlier marvels, but he had survived into a society characterised by a lively concern for the written record, which would not now be revisited by the Danish menace.

Pilgrimage in pre-conquest England largely eludes our scrutiny. The landscape was undoubtedly honeycombed with local cults but we rarely catch a glimpse of them. Goscelin of St-Bertin gives one such glimpse. A rich merchant of Canterbury lost all his worldly wealth and was overcome by sorrow and ignominy. His wife tried to get him to put his trust in God, and with her approval he promised to make a pilgrimage to St Margaret, whose feast-day (20 July) fell on the octave of St Mildred's (that is the eighth day after). 'To obtain the favour of the martyr', he vowed that he would 'go barefoot to her church, twelve miles from the city, to which innumerable healing miracles had attracted crowds of people'. During the night he dreamt that he was on his way and had reached the 'hill which is called Berhamdun'. Here he experienced a vision of St Margaret and St Mildred and was directed to undertake a pilgrimage to Rome.[75] St Margaret was popular everywhere; in Kent there were twenty-two church dedications to her. [76]

There are other tantalising glimpses which archaeology may help to amplify. The crypt of the largely Anglo-Saxon church at Wing, Buckinghamshire, contained an ambulatory which was reached by stairs from the nave and seems to have housed relics in a screened-off central area. It is as yet unknown what gave Wing its obvious importance; but the recent examination of the skeleton of a young girl, found in the unusually extensive pre-conquest cemetery adjacent to the church, suggested to the excavators the possibility that she had been brought to the church in the hope of a cure, for her remains bore distinct marks of long-term pain and disease.[77] There were probably numerous such pilgrimages which left no trace in written records.

Meanwhile pilgrimage of another kind persisted, not as clearly distinguished from proper Christian practice as churchmen both English and Norman thought it should be. The Laws of Cnut pronounced a comprehensive condemnation of paganism:

It is heathen practice if one worships idols, namely if one worships heathen gods and the sun or the moon, fire or flood, wells or stones or any kind of forest trees, or if one practises witchcraft or encompasses death by any means, either by sacrifice or divination, or takes any part in such delusions.[78]

Stones, trees, and especially wells, would continue to plague the champions of orthodoxy for centuries to come, but very often their veneration was disguised and assimilated. At Steyning in Sussex a stone on which, it was said, a shepherd-saint called Cuthman used to sit while watching his flock was held in great veneration by the inhabitants in later times, because 'God had conferred many benefits through it'. The saint, still venerated in the sixteenth century at Chidham, twenty-five miles distant, lived in the ninth or perhaps the eighth century, but the place-name Steyning, first documented in the mid ninth century, may mean 'dwellers at a stone'; if so, the suspicion arises that veneration of the stone may have been prior to that of the saint.[79] In around 1200 there was a flourishing holy well at Wye at Kent. The place-name 'Wye' signifies 'idol' or 'heathen temple', and the first references to it, in the eighth and ninth centuries, suggest that the people of the area were identified as 'the dwellers by the heathen temple'. Whether this temple was associated with the spring is of course another question, but Wye was an important early centre, a *villa regalis*, situated on a major ancient trackway.[80] These instances and others like them raise once again questions about continuity, or at least recurrence, in the use of sacred sites over long periods.

In 1102 a council held at Westminster under the direction of Archbishop Anselm singled out the veneration of springs for disapprobation, but added a further prohibition: 'that no one should, with audacious innovation, treat springs or dead bodies or other things as holy, which we have known to happen, without episcopal authorisation'.[81] It has often been assumed that the reference to unauthorised veneration of dead individuals was a hit at the cult of Earl Waltheof, put to death by the Conqueror in 1076 for complicity in rebellion. Interred at Crowland in the fens, he was translated into the church in 1092, and did miracles which were known to William of Malmesbury. The prior of Crowland told William not only that the body was incorrupt, but that Waltheof's severed head had been reconnected to his body, with only a thin red line indicating the join; this detail clearly likened him to St Edmund of Bury. The Norman Conquest had created a situation in which the native English were not only keen to uphold the veneration due to their traditional saints, but also potentially inclined to honour those who died in defence of the English and their rights. For a time, at least, King Harold's status was highly equivocal: his tomb at Waltham was moved in the 1120s, as if to avoid attracting the attention of pilgrims coming to venerate the Holy Cross.[82] Although religious virtues

were claimed for Waltheof, there was little question but that this was a
political 'martyrdom'; in the eyes of the English he was a guiltless victim
of the invaders. William of Malmesbury piously hoped that this was true.
He noted that the site of Crowland, although inaccessible, was in fact
continuously frequented, ostensibly on St Guthlac's account.[83]

The 1102 decree may have been directed, however, at more than one
target. Archbishop Anselm rebuked the abbess of Romsey for permitting
the veneration of a dead man whom 'certain people want to treat as a saint'.
The abbess had sought Anselm's advice but, he said, had then disregarded
it. It seems that the dead man's son was keeping a perpetual vigil at his
father's grave, and the abbess was told to expel him from the town and
not to allow him any further opportunity for remaining by the tomb. The
archdeacon of Winchester was to enforce this sentence. It is hard to see
how this letter can refer, as some have thought, to the cult of Earl Waltheof. [84]
Both political martyrdoms and the unlicensed cults of more inconspicuous
individuals would continue, like the veneration of holy waters, to concern
the rulers of England throughout the medieval period.

3

From Wulfstan to Becket

It is hardly controversial to assert that England by 1100 was rapidly becoming more and more unlike the England Bede had known, and not only because of foreign conquest. This was a period of rapid demographic growth and the acceleration of economic activity in country and town. The Domesday Survey for Suffolk records the expansion that had overtaken the community that clustered around one major pilgrimage site, the abbey of St Edmund, in a single generation after 1066. The numbers of tenants and tradespeople who served the needs of the saint and his community had grown, and there were 342 houses now on land which had been under the plough in the reign of the Confessor.[1] It should not be too fanciful to suppose that, like other human activities, pilgrimage experienced an increase in tempo and volume in this more populous and slightly more developed society. The very ardour of the post-Conquest refurbishment of the old saints of England prompts the question of whether the Anglo-Normans were not only trying to repair the deficiencies of past record, but also fostering and responding to a new surge of devotional activity.

The writers who tried to reconstruct the record of the pre-conquest saints were living through changes which had both religious and economic implications for the custodians of shrines and for the church in general. A bigger population created both pastoral challenges and opportunities for profit. How were the saints to be presented to this numerically growing public in a way which inculcated the proper spirit of both reverence and generosity? Another influence on twelfth-century hagiographers was the development of official concepts of sanctity, of which one was particularly important and relevant to the relationship between the saints, their custodians and a wider public. This was the increasing emphasis on miracles done *post mortem* rather than on the *in vita* miracles performed by the living saint. It became a requirement of the formal canonisation procedure which was taking shape in the twelfth century that an authenticated record of miracles *post mortem* should accompany petitions for canonisation.[2] The evidence of miracles *in vita* (usually included in the written life of the candidate which formed part of the dossier) would be considered, but those which God had consented to perform in response to the saint's intercession after his or her death occupied a privileged position, as being beyond the scope of the mere illusionism or sleight of hand which the magicians of the pharaohs had been able to perform.

Saints had of course always performed wonders after their deaths. These were not by any means exclusively curative in nature. Two particularly important types of miracle *post mortem* might be described as visions and vengeance. Just as it was one of the attributes of the holy man or woman in life to see visions and exercise prophetic powers, so, after death, he or she might reappear to favoured (or sometimes disfavoured) individuals conveying insights from eternity or pronouncing doom. Saints were also active *post mortem* in defending the interests and members of the community to which they had belonged when alive and indeed still belonged in death. Frequently this meant taking revenge, whether drastic or merely corrective, on those who infringed the community's property rights or other privileges. Miracles of this kind were especially relevant to the possessing community and its neighbours, or to those further afield with whom it had property relations. The saint's visions in life and apparitions after death, and his or her healing miracles in life or death, also tended first and foremost to benefit or relate to members of his community, its servants, dependants, neighbours and patrons. Scrutiny of the miracles reported by Bede and those attributed to Cuthbert, Wilfrid or other Anglo-Saxon saints reveals a high proportion of this type, as well as of miracles performed *in vita*.

The saints always exercised powers of both attraction and repulsion. They protected and ministered to their own, which might mean fending off the assaults of outsiders; but they also impressed and overawed these outsiders by the selective demonstration of a power not merely to control and punish people beyond the inner circle of their dependants but to forgive and cure them. The wider relationships thus created sometimes amounted to a form of clientage, which could take several forms. Occasionally the beneficiary might decide to become a member of the inner circle, spending the rest of his or her days in the service of the shrine. Some pilgrims returned to their everyday lives but vowed regular future gifts, offerings or pilgrimages. For the generality of pilgrims the relationship was less binding and more transient.

The shift towards an emphasis on miracles *post mortem* and on miracles done for outsiders was accompanied by another, which accelerated in the later medieval centuries. Miracles of healing (and other kinds of assistance) performed in response to prayers and vows offered not at the shrine itself but at long range became more numerous. These prayers would normally be accompanied by a vow to visit the shrine when the desired benefit had been received, bringing an offering either once and for all or annually, perhaps on the saint's major feast-day. This can be seen as reflecting an ever greater emphasis on the miracle as a transaction between the saint and his client, the latter remunerating the former (or his custodians) for benefits received.[3] Geoffrey Chaucer bore witness to this long-term transition when he remarked at the beginning of the General Prologue to the *Canterbury Tales* that pilgrims went to the holy blissful martyr 'that hem *hath holpen* when that they were seke'. The shift clearly depended on effective publicity: miracle-seekers had to know about a saint before they could offer their prayers and vows from afar. This knowledge could be obtained by word of mouth, for example preaching or the testimony of friends and neighbours who had already been pilgrims to the shrine; by the dissemination of secondary relics; or, at a later period, by the multiplication of images, culminating in the prints and woodcuts of the fifteenth and sixteenth centuries.

The gradual transition to an emphasis on posthumous and long-range miracles was naturally reflected in hagiography. William of Malmesbury's *Life* of Wulfstan, bishop of Worcester (d. 1095), the last of the Anglo-Saxon saints, represents a type that was becoming less common. William's *Life* is a version of the now lost Anglo-Saxon life by the monk Colman (d. 1113) which, it is thought, may have been sent to Rome late in the twelfth century in support of Wulfstan's canonisation.[4] Its chief emphasis is on the saint's holy life and pastoral solicitude; only a few posthumous miracles are described, which show him acting in defence of the community, notably by obtaining the return of stolen books. Wulfstan also did favours for individual monks:

> It came to be a custom among the Worcester monks that if they ailed at all in body or were troubled in mind they whispered it to the bishop just as though he were still alive. He received the prayers of all in the large lap of his charity, and granted so many of their petitions that I believe that if any went away unsatisfied, it was not that the saint could not, but that the man who asked was unworthy, or the thing asked was unnecessary.[5]

The constituency to which Wulfstan ministered certainly extended beyond the walls of the cathedral monastery. Whenever he was commemorated with psalms and masses, 'the citizens were lavish in almsgiving', and 'he himself freely granted the petitions of them that entreated him – and there was none who sought him in faith but gained the boon of his intercession'. While the phrasing does not exclude the possibility that the saint drew suppliants from far afield, the emphasis is on the church and city which had been his responsibility in life. In the *Gesta Pontificum*, William of Malmesbury added more up-to-date information about miracles that he knew were being done in his time. His phrasing tends to emphasise the breadth and celebrity of Wulfstan's operations. 'Waves of people' attended his exequies, making offerings and 'adoring' his corpse. The deliverance of the saint's tomb from damage by fire a few years after his death was a public event, and therefore more celebrated than his 'everyday' miracles of assistance to people in their 'domestic necessities', which surpassed the power of speech or writing to enumerate. Not the least significant aspect of the tomb's escape was the fact that the reed-mat (*natta*) on which suppliants lay overnight awaiting their cures was also untouched by the blaze. No one went away empty-handed from the shrine.[6] Of these twelfth-century miracles and their beneficiaries, we have only a few details supplied by the author of an abbreviation of William's *Life*. Wulfstan was canonised in 1203, and his miracles as we have them were mostly collected over the following twenty years or so.[7]

Saints had usually originated as the possessions of religious communities, and so they remained, but the needs and aspirations of those communities now increasingly suggested the desirability of making their treasures select-ively available to a wider audience. So intense was the promotional activity generated by shrines in the twelfth century, whether in response to rising levels of demand or to the perception of possible profit or both, that there is the occasional hint of impropriety. William of Malmesbury noted that the monks of Peterborough claimed the arm of St Oswald and that, even as he wrote, a 'great exhibition' was being made of a shrine containing it, but he had his doubts about this relic. Hugh Candidus of Peterborough was, unsurprisingly, less sceptical, reporting that the arm not only performed numerous cures but had had other solidly practical effects: an exhibition of it to King Stephen elicited the gift of his ring, the payment of forty marks out of what he owed the abbey, and also (on another occasion) charters of liberties.[8]

The development of the relationship between a saint and the wider com-munity is evoked in an account of the 'liberties' of the church of St John of Beverley written by the sacrist Alured in the middle of the twelfth century. He attributed these liberties to King Athelstan, who was grateful for the assistance the saint had given him against the Scots. He described the physical boundaries of the area covered by the church's peace, the nature (and limitations) of the sanctuary it offered to criminals and fugitives, and its prerogatives and exemptions in general. The 'nobles' of the area sought burial at Beverley, and the saint's relics were carried in solemn procession outside the town during the three days before Ascension Day, followed barefoot by 'the wiser and more noble'. On Ascension Day itself, an enor-mous crowd performed a procession around the church and the shrine was then placed by its bearers across the door of the church so that the whole people could enter the building beneath the body of the saint to hear mass. The bearers, eight in number, held their office by hereditary right; they would also carry the relics in procession if the town was threatened by an epidemic. The Ascension Day celebrations were attended by all the most notable people, not only of the three Ridings and of the city of York but of Northumbria, and they were completed by exemptions from toll and arrest for debt conferred on all merchants who brought goods to the town.[9]

There may, then, have been a shift in the actual relationships between the saints, their custodians (who were still predominantly monks) and the outside world; certainly there was in the way that relationship was described. These shifts suggest a somewhat more settled society which was experiencing at least a small increase in mobility and speed and security of communication. The saints were increasingly shown acting on behalf of rank outsiders whose only connection with the shrine was occasional and opportunistic and who were not its tenants, dependants or subjects. Their value to the saint and his or her guardians was twofold. Pilgrimage meant what can best be described as prestige, the dissemination to a wider public of news of the saint's power, the splendour of the shrine and its surroundings, and the hospitality and political and social influence of the monks. It also meant offerings. Their value must have varied, but to judge by surviving later medieval evidence could sometimes be considerable. It has already been pointed out that in and after the eleventh century massive church building and rebuilding programmes were afoot in England. Reconstructions intended, in part at least, to accommodate pilgrims also looked to pilgrims for help with the finance. The saints in the twelfth century can be seen more clearly than before to be catering for a broader public than just the communities which conserved their relics, but this was not a sudden, overnight transformation and the extent of it is hard to measure, thanks to the shortcomings of earlier records. The quality and quantity of recording certainly improved. Sometimes, with the development of the formal canonisation process, it was intended to serve new purposes, but old saints, who were not candidates for canonisation, still required celebration and commemoration. St Mildred provides an excellent example of an ancient saint for whom a long silence was broken in the eleventh century; the slightly more ancient Etheldreda of Ely was promoted to a remarkable degree in the twelfth.

The three books of the *Liber Eliensis* were compiled at different dates between 1131 and 1174, perhaps by the Richard who was successively sub-prior and, from 1177 to about 1189, prior of the cathedral monastery.[10] He drew extensively on older materials, but the miracles were recent, and they suggest a keen awareness that the cult had been assiduously promoted before a wider public since 1100. In 1106, shortly before Ely became an episcopal see, Etheldreda was translated to a new shrine, and the bishop of Norwich preached 'about the life and death and miracles of the blessed virgin and the marvellous incorruption of her holy body'. These ancient attributes, well-known as they would have been to the learned who had read Bede, were now being brought to the attention of a larger audience; as with St Cuthbert, bodily incorruption strongly implied miraculous powers. The message was underlined by heavenly signs: 'Then there were renewed the ancient miracles which we read happened at the discovery of the body of the blessed martyr Stephen.'[11] These seem to have been meteorological rather than curative in nature – thunder, lightning, fire from heaven – but no less impressive for all that. The cures followed, and the author repeatedly insists on the effectiveness of well-publicised miracles. When a certain Withgar was cured of a crippling condition,

> The news travelled far. Flocks of invalids were attracted, and marvels of healing were performed which for the most part, thanks to their number and the shortage or negligence of writers escape our memory, except for a few which we will truthfully recount.[12]

The value of publicity is repeatedly stressed. The local man who disregarded his priest's injunction to observe Etheldreda's feast (an infraction of discipline which the saints regularly punished) suffered a punitive accident which left a splinter of wood embedded in his flesh, causing him great suffering. He was cured when after a year he came penitently to the shrine. When he returned 'to his province' he took the piece of wood with him as evidence, thereby effectively spreading news of the saint's powers. Miracles performed by portable secondary relics (such as Etheldreda's vestments, the old dalmatic in which her body was wrapped and the tunic she had worn while still an earthly queen) had the same effect, proving that she did not do wonders at her burial place alone: 'These and similar [miracles] spread the fame of the saint far and wide.' There are a number of informative references to standard pilgrimage practices. For example, Etheldreda herself on one occasion gave detailed instructions for the measuring of a sufferer's body so that a candle could be made of the same length to offer at her altar:

> Go and make a length of wick and run it around the sickbed on whch he lies, that is from the head along the right-hand side to the feet, then from the feet up the left-hand side to the head, and then putting wax on the wick make a candle. If he gets well enough, let him bring this candle to the Isle of Ely to the church of the virgin Etheldreda, or send it by some faithful messenger, so that he may through her prayers recover from this illness.[13]

Miracle stories often suggest competition between shrines by narrating cures which suppliants had proved unable to obtain elsewhere, but the promotion of Etheldreda, as of any saint, could also be assisted by the cultivation of friendly relations with neighbouring shrines: at least those pilgrims who had the time and the money could be encouraged to perform regional circuits. If Etheldreda occasionally did miracles for natives of Bury, she was also courteous enough to direct a young monk of Ely to St Edmund,[14] while St Edmund appeared in a vision to a peasant of Exning, telling him to go to the bishop of Ely with instructions to build a causeway across the marshes from Soham to Ely 'so that I may visit my most blessed Lady Etheldreda'. One of the monks undertook the work, which was achieved to the wonder of all. [15] It would hardly have brought Edmund all the way from Bury, but its building does symbolise the growing concern of the age with improved access and communications, which did not solely benefit pilgrims.

Water, of which there was no shortage in the vicinity of Ely, played its part in Etheldreda's cult as it did in the cults of many saints. The monks dug out a cistern on the site of her original burial place in the cemetery, from which her sister Sexburga had translated her into the church in 695. Crowds of pilgrims could approach this source of healing while the monks were in choir. One of the most elaborate miracle stories in the *Liber Eliensis* concerns the poor man from Northampton who, suffering from a severe dropsy, arrived at the church just as the monks were about to take their meal and the *custos* came to shut the doors. The latter was unsympathetic to the poor man's pleas to be admitted, if only to the saint's well, but eventually reflected that he himself was likely to be punished if it was learned that he had 'offended a pilgrim'. He therefore let him into the cemetery, remarking unhelpfully that the well was deep and the bucket wasn't there. When the pilgrim had located the well a jet of water rose out of it and spread over the courtyard, so that he could drink even without a bucket. He invoked the saint and promptly expelled all the noxious matter which was inflating him. The graceless *custos* now tried to get rid of him, sarcastically asking whether he had drunk his fill, and took a little convincing that in fact he had. [16]

The fairs of 'St Audrey' at Ely date from Henry I's reign (that is, from the same period as the establishment of the bishopric and the renewed promotion of the saint) and are only one example of the association of shrines and fairs to be found all over England, as indeed all over Christendom. In the mid twelfth century it was claimed that Archbishop Aldred of York had obtained from Edward the Confessor the right to hold a fair at Beverley on the Feast of St John the Baptist (24 June); anyone attending, whether they came 'by reason of prayer or of the fair' enjoyed safe-conduct by land and water.[17] William of Malmesbury sardonically remarked that a fair was established at St Aldhelm's feast late in the eleventh century 'so that those who were not lured by the sanctity of the confessor might be attracted by the desire for goods'.[18] 'Holy days' were, for many, holidays indeed, a good day out in a world of restricted mobility and few personal possessions. Limited purchasing power doubtless helped to account for the production of 'tawdry', originally St Audrey's lace 'chains', which had been touched to the shrine, and which were still available at Ely on the eve of the Reformation.[19] Another fair, granted by Henry I in 1115, was held at Salisbury around the Feast of the Nativity of the Virgin (6 September). Around 1150, Bishop Jocelin moved Salisbury's Feast of Relics from an unnamed date to 17 September; the church thus built up a concentrated period of activity and celebration in this propitious month.[20]

A fair of national importance grew up under the control of the monks of Ramsey in association with the shrine of St Ivo at Slepe in Huntingdonshire. The continued popularity of the healing spring at Slepe after the discovery of the relics of the saint and his companions in about 1001, and without doubt the economic expansion of the age, suggested new opportunities to the monks. About a century after the original translation of the relics to Ramsey, inhabitants of Slepe were reported to have seen a brilliant ray of light extending from the village as far as Ramsey, seven miles distant. It was therefore resolved that the relics of Ivo's three companions should be restored to the church at Slepe,

> so that that church too should be more honourably regarded and better known, and better and more devoutly frequented by the people, by the intercession of their patrons [who were] now present. [21]

The monks thus upheld the honour due to Ramsey as the resting-place of Ivo himself, while reaping the benefits of the development of a subsidiary shrine on one of their estates. As both pilgrimage and commercial centre the place had its advantages, being only three miles from Huntingdon, where a royal castle commanded the crossing of the Ouse by the old Roman road, Ermine Street. In effect the abbot and convent created a new town at Slepe, building a mile of road on a huge causeway across the floodplain of the Ouse and a new bridge (already in existence in 1107) to link the settlement more effectively into the communications network.[22] An Easter fair was granted, significantly, in 1110, and the new town gradually came to be known as St Ives. The association not only of pilgrimage and fair, but of pilgrimage, fair and spring can be paralleled elsewhere.

Bury had its fair around Edmund's principal feast on 20 November. By the time the redoubtable Samson became abbot in 1182 the opportunities for profit this afforded to both London merchants and to the citizens of Bury were giving rise to acrid disputes with the monks. The latter were certainly aware of the growth of towns and markets in England generally, and believed that the townsfolk of Bury, the descendants of the enlarged community described in Domesday Book, were growing richer to the detriment of the rights of the abbey: for example, they claimed the right to set up shops and booths in the marketplace, haggling over the payment of an annual sum to the monks in compensation. When Samson refused to recognise the claim of the London merchants that their royal privileges conferred exemption from toll at the fairs of St Edmund, they boycotted the fairs for two years, 'from which', Jocelin of Brakelond significantly observed, 'our market suffered great loss, and the oblations received by the sacrist were greatly diminished'.[23]

When Samson updated the miracles of St Edmund, he added a story, supposedly dating from the late eleventh century, to illustrate how the saint might be publicised to a popular audience and how hazardous this could be unless done with great discretion.[24] The monk Herman, a popular preacher, once exhibited the clothes in which the saint had suffered martyrdom to a large crowd at the feast of Pentecost. This crowd evidently consisted of common folk, for three weeks later a group of persons of rank arrived, devoutly requesting the boon which had already been bestowed on their social inferiors. Herman complied, with the consent of the other brethren, and the pilgrims kissed the relics and departed; but rumour was now busily at work, and a huge crowd of both sexes assembled who 'demanded the fruits of their journey'. It was judged unthinkable to send them away unsatisfied, so a wooden platform like an altar was erected in the middle of the apse, and the reliquary was placed upon it; the previous exhibition had been in the presumably more confined setting of the crypt. Herman arrived and showed the crowd the saint's shirt, pierced by spear-points and stained with blood. Previously he had permitted his audience just a glimpse of the relic, but now he took it right out of the casket and invited all present to kiss it. The result, as Samson succinctly put it, was that 'There was an unseemly rush and the altar was heaped with gifts'.

The spectacle was witnessed by a pious elderly virgin, Seietha, who, being worthy, experienced a fragrance of unearthly beauty when she kissed the shirt. She remembered, however, how her friend Tolsinus, sacrist under Abbot Baldwin, had paid for his presumption in handling Edmund's bodily remains with a prolonged spell in Purgatory. That very night Herman fell seriously ill, and Tolsinus appeared to Edwin, another monk who had been involved in the exhibition, and sternly denounced the sacrilege that had been committed 'to capture the favour of the common people (*vulgus*)': some of the holy blood with which the garment was soaked had fallen to the ground and was lost. On the third day Herman died. Samson does not speculate as to his eternal destiny, but points the obvious moral about the necessity for reverent treatment of the saints. Living and writing when he did, Samson, who is said to have preached to the people in the East Anglian vernacular, should have known all about the techniques and temptations of appealing to 'the common people'. [25]

Samson was also keenly aware how the saint's relics could be manipulated in support of his own authority as abbot. In 1198 he was absent from the monastery when fire broke out and dramaged the shrine. There was good reason to be concerned about the carelessness which had led to the fire, for the fact that it had taken place could not be hidden from the wider public; pilgrims who came to the church early the following morning to make their oblations had already heard about it, and the 'hideous appearance presented by the burning' prompted rumours that the relics themselves had been damaged. On his return Samson tried to get the monks to divert some of their own living allowances to the repair of the shrine, but this scheme foundered on the opposition of the sacrist, who observed that St Edmund could perfectly well repair his own shrine if he so desired. Samson then announced his intention of translating the saint and carrying out a ceremonial inspection of the relics. A three-day fast by way of preparation was announced to the people, and the monks were misled into believing that the ceremony was going to take place publicly, which would indeed have made sense if Samson's sole purpose had been to reassure the pilgrim public. In fact he carried it out in private, and only a few brethren were privileged to see the relics. The event, although publicised beyond the monastery, was thus used as a gambit in the abbot's battle with a party among his own monks. Samson had handled the relics with his own hands and, with his authority thus enhanced, dismissed the shrine guardians and imposed new regulations on their successors. [26]

Accounts of miracles are an indispensable source for the story of pilgrimage, in the twelfth century as earlier and later, but it must be repeated that not all pilgrims either sought or experienced miracles. Many probably came in obedience to custom and to enjoy a day out, particularly as fairs and games often accompanied the celebration of a saint's annual festivity. There was also a more generalised expectation of spiritual benefit. Thomas Becket's pilgrims are repeatedly described simply as coming 'to pray'; wonderful and unexpected things sometimes then happened to them. Certainly more pilgrims will have heard about miracles, narrated by shrine custodians, than ever had first-hand experience of them. From the twelfth century on, the pilgrim might also hope by a decent display of piety and contrition to earn an indulgence. A pilgrimage made to secure an indulgence would, like any other, be accompanied by an offering. It may well have been that in the minds of many pilgrims shrines were places where spiritual goods were obtained against the proper payment, not unlike the fairs and markets which so often went on outside.

The final entry in the *Liber Eliensis* records the death of Thomas Becket. With the murder in Canterbury Cathedral on 29 December 1170 by four knights of King Henry II,[27] who either thought they were doing his bidding or hoped to earn his favour, we reach an epoch in the history of English pilgrimage. It was not just a fortuitous alliance with Geoffrey Chaucer across a gap of two hundred years that secured for Becket the position he still enjoys as the dominant figure in that history.[28] The more populous, expansive society of late twelfth-century England provided a fitting backdrop to the development of the new cult, but the saint's career, the manner of his death, and the city in which he died and was enshrined all presented special features which help to account for its extraordinary success.

Most saints began by being saints in the eyes of those who had known them in life, and of the communities which remembered them and preserved their relics. In the early twelfth century, Wulfstan of Worcester provides a good example of a recently living saint, known and venerated as such on the strength of a reputation earned during his career as the last surviving Anglo-Saxon bishop. By contrast, although Becket achieved veneration, and indeed canonisation, so rapidly that he could be treated as a saint by many people who had seen and known him and indeed outlived him for many years, he was made a saint by the manner of his death, as his usual appellation, 'the martyr', makes plain.[29] This did not prevent conventional saintly characteristics being read back into his life, a process which was greatly assisted by the discovery that he had worn a louse-ridden hairshirt, regarded by some as almost automatic proof of sanctity.[30] The complexity of his life and reputation, however, was such that, at least until his standing as a saint was firmly and officially established, he presented different faces to different people.

From being the friend, servant and chancellor of Henry II, Becket had in 1162 become archbishop of Canterbury (at the king's instigation). There is no real reason to doubt the sincerity of the transformation, if transformation in fact it was, which made him the dedicated archbishop and defender of the rights and immunities of the English church against the same king. He had, after all, once been a household clerk of Archbishop Theobald of Canterbury. Nor is this view necessarily compromised by the suspicion that he was a man who would have played with total commitment whatever role in life he was called upon to play. It was all but inevitable, however, that some at least of those who remembered him in his earlier roles had doubts about him in his last one, and some of his posthumous miracles had the function (or so those who recorded them believed) of confounding such sceptics. In another camp were friends and well-wishers who shared Becket's principles but had sometimes had their doubts about his tactics. Such people had less difficulty in accepting his sanctity and indeed hailed him as a martyr, even chiding Pope Alexander III for his tardiness in proclaiming the canonisation, although a three year interval, in normal circumstances, would hardly have seemed excessive.

It is naturally more difficult to assess how Becket's sanctity was perceived by the ordinary inhabitants first of Canterbury and Kent, and then of England and beyond, who came to the tomb or invoked the martyr from afar, including the many who had no direct knowledge or recollection of the late archbishop. The circumstances of the murder were clearly of capital and immediate importance. Several eye witnesses of the event survived to report what they had seen. John of Salisbury, the archbishop's friend, and the greatest of contemporary English 'men of letters', was one. Benedict of Peterborough, who may have been another eyewitness, reported that after the initial acrimonious interview between Becket and the four knights, John characteristically remonstrated with Thomas about his inability to take advice and his tendency to make matters worse.[31] John remained to witness the murder when the knights came rampaging back and pursued Becket into the cathedral. Another clerk, Edward Grim, also stayed by the archbishop's side and was wounded in the arm. He bore witness to Thomas's desire for martyrdom: ironically, Becket was unwilling to be persuaded to take refuge in the cathedral for fear that the knights would in fact respect sanctuary and deprive him of his crown. It was consistent with his hopes that he forbade the monks to bar the doors of the cathedral against their onslaught.[32] The monk William fitz Stephen, who stayed with Becket until the danger overwhelmed his courage, later had the duty of receiving pilgrims at the shrine and composed both a *Life* of the saint and one of the two major miracle collections, in which he included an account of the murder. There was no lack of testimony, therefore, to the intrepidity and determination of the saint and the gratuitous savagery of his murderers. The action of Hugh Mauclerc in slicing off the top of the dead man's skull with his sword and spreading the brains over the pavement, mingled with blood and bone, was widely reported. John said that in this the murderers were more cruel than Christ's executioners who, seeing that He was already dead, forbore to break his legs.[33]

All martyrs were to a degree Christlike, but few of the many saints who were venerated as martyrs had the benefit of such detailed first-hand reportage. An archbishop, one of God's anointed, had been brutally done to death in his own cathedral. Here was sacrilege, as well as martyrdom: and here too was blood. The mere fact of violent death seems to have been sufficient to secure the reputation of martyrdom for some quite unlikely candidates, and the case was strengthened if the element of sacrilege was also present.[34] Was Becket universally perceived as a martyr for the rights of the church, or was the immediate response, at least, more visceral? The archbishop's blood, spilled in his own cathedral church, was an immediate focus of attention. Benedict describes the appearance of the body: there was blood like a diadem all around the head, but the face was free of it except for a trickle which ran down from the right of the forehead leftwards across the nose. Immediately, some anointed their eyes with the blood which lay on the pavement, others brought vessels in which to carry away drops of it, and others cut pieces off their clothes to dip into it. Whether it was just members of the community and the archbishop's household who were doing this, or whether there had been a concourse of outsiders, is not made entirely clear. There was, understandably, a period of total confusion in which people could do what they wished.[35]

It is difficult not to acknowledge the exceedingly primitive aspect of this kind of devotional reaction. In the course of time, Becket's blood, diluted to homeopathic levels of efficacy in vials of water, became an important agent of miraculous cures and of the dissemination of his cult to distant parts of Europe. Ampullae containing Becket 'water' were made at Canterbury and distributed to pilgrims from the early days of the cult, rapidly becoming the badge of the Canterbury pilgrim.[36] Gerald of Wales described how, when he and some companions waited upon the bishop of Winchester at Southwark, the bishop knew instantly that they had been at Canterbury by the *signacula* around their necks.[37] Such ampullae functioned as much more than souvenirs. If Becket performed a large number of miracles at long range, it was sometimes by means of visions, but it was certainly often by means of his 'water'. This water was special in that it was supposedly a tincture of the martyr's blood, but water otherwise associated with saints and their tombs had long been credited with miraculous powers. Earlier in the century Eadmer had told how a vessel of water in which St Dunstan's walking-stick had been washed was kept in the cathedral at Canterbury and effected cures.[38]

Many of the early pilgrims to Becket's shrine may well have known something about his career as archbishop and the ostensible reasons for his death. Inhabitants of Canterbury and of the estates of the archbishop and the cathedral priory, in Kent and elsewhere, would have had very good reason to be informed about events which had had an impact on their own lives, when royal officials moved in to confiscate and expropriate the property of the king's enemies. News, however garbled, must have spread. What we cannot know precisely is the relative importance in any one pilgrim's mind of murder, sacrilege and blood, the archbishop's status as a martyr for the rights of the church or simply as an opponent of the king, and whatever personal qualities of holiness, such as charity to the poor or bodily austerities, which he was known or rumoured to have exemplified.

It was largely because of the extraordinary circumstances of Becket's death that the cult went through a preliminary period of suspense while the cathedral, polluted by the murder, remained bereft of divine service and the world awaited the resolution of the political consequences. The church was not reconsecrated until almost a year later, on 21 December 1171, but since the previous Easter it had been open to those who desired to venerate the place of the martyr's death; before that, people had been admitted only secretly. As Gervase of Canterbury described it,

> The first miracles took place around his tomb, then throughout the crypt, then throughout the church, then throughout Canterbury, then throughout England, and France, Normandy, Germany, and, in short, throughout the whole church of Christ throughout the world. [39]

The rapid dissemination of relics was a vital part of this process.

A story told by Benedict (and later somewhat altered by William fitz Stephen) vividly evokes some of the tensions of this early phase.[40] There was not only scepticism in some quarters about Becket's sanctity, but an uncertain political climate. A monk of Reading Abbey called Elias was afflicted by severe leprosy and wished to betake himself to St Thomas, but feared that he would not obtain the necessary permission from his abbot. He pretended therefore that he wanted to go to the hot springs of Bath, for which he obtained permission. He set off westwards and then turned back eastwards. It was the time of the very first miracles, before the martyr's credentials were established beyond cavil and before large numbers of people were making the pilgrimage. On his way to Canterbury Elias met a knight who was well known to him and who dissuaded him from his intention, lest, if it became known among the great men of the kingdom that he had performed the pilgrimage, harm should come to his monastery. The knight had a positive alternative to offer, for he produced a phial of the martyr's water and urged the monk to taste it. Elias venerated the relic, tasted the water and washed his face with it. He then switched course again to Bury St Edmunds, where he obtained from a friend a piece of cloth tinged with

Thomas's blood. He wrang it out in water and washed himself, washing the leprosy away. On his return to Reading, the abbot suspected from the completeness of his cure that he had been to Canterbury and not to Bath, and got the true story out of him.

Henry II was far too intelligent a ruler not to sense the need to come to terms with the burgeoning cult. To do so would smoothe his path with the pope, but that was only one consideration. Any lingering reluctance he may have felt was dispelled by the crisis he encountered in 1173–74 in the form of a rebellion by his sons, who mustered an impressive coalition of allies against him. By this time most of the miracles recorded by Benedict of Peterborough and William fitz Stephen in two massive collections had already taken place. These two men, as monks of Canterbury, seem successively to have had the responsibility of recording evidence of miracles at the shrine, and William fitz Stephen's collection was presented to Henry at the royal request.[41] William was able to include (doubtless much to the king's gratification) an account of the well-publicised penance which Henry performed at Canterbury in July 1174. This was reported by the chroniclers, for the most part, in glowing terms and a variety of intriguing detail.

According to William, Henry dismounted at the leper hospital of St Nicholas at Harbledown on the outskirts of Canterbury and continued on foot, going barefoot from the church of St Dunstan to the shrine.[42] Roger of Hoveden tells us that his 'tender feet', unaccustomed to this rough usage, bled copiously.[43] Gervase of Canterbury says that when Henry had performed his penance and received 'discipline' from the monks, he remained at the shrine all night, not only not eating but not even going out to answer the calls of nature. After this vigil he toured the altars of the upper church and then returned to the tomb in the crypt. At dawn he heard mass and then, having drunk the holy water of the martyr, joyfully went on his way 'signed with an ampulla', that is to say wearing, probably on a cord about his neck, the lead ampulla of the martyr's 'water'.[44]

Few chroniclers of this episode failed to note another event which they saw as no accident. William the Lion of Scotland, one of the hostile coalition which had formed against Henry in 1173, was captured at the precise moment of the king's Canterbury journey. Wiliam of Newburgh is emphatic: this came about 'so that the reward of his pious act should be seen not to follow, but rather to accompany it, and that there should be no doubt about the matter'.[45] Henry thus initiated not only his personal rapprochement with the saint and his shrine, but what proved to be a long tradition in which Canterbury figured prominently in the itineraries of English monarchs and also of their distinguished foreign visitors. The ease and speed of this development of course owed a great deal to Canterbury's location on the ancient high road from London to Dover. Already rich in saints, it would never have been a backwater, but the consequences of Becket's death reveal it as, so to speak, a major shrine waiting to happen. The presence of kings, or their distinguished guests, at Canterbury cannot always be taken to mean that pilgrimage was their reason for being there; on the other hand, if they were passing through Canterbury to or from Dover or Sandwich they could now scarcely avoid doing reverence to the martyr.

On 25 May 1175 Henry visited Canterbury again with his eldest son, Henry the Young King, who according to Ralph Diceto followed his example in all things save that the father continued his devotions, vigils, prayers and fasting for three days.[46] Canterbury soon attracted other high-profile visitors. On 20 April 1177, the Wednesday before Easter, Philip, count of Flanders (another of Henry's enemies in 1173–74), arrived at Dover and proceeded straight to Canterbury, where Henry met him on the following day and then escorted him back to Dover, giving him fifty silver marks 'in aid of his pilgrimage'.[47] The flow continued with the archbishop of Rheims, whom Henry met there in July 1178.[48] In the following year came the most eminent of foreign visitors to date. Louis VII of France came to Canterbury in late August 1179 in thanksgiving for the recovery of his only son and heir, the future Philip Augustus, from a serious illness. He endowed the shrine with the great ruby, the Regale, which remained there until Henry VIII's covetousness became too much for him, and he also made the monks an annual gift of decent French wine, which they received for many years to come.

This pilgrimage illustrates the point that the proximity of Canterbury to Dover made possible state visits which, unless they were to be combined with diplomatic business at London or elsewhere in the kingdom, could be quickly accomplished and easily monitored by the king or his representatives. Louis was met by Henry himself at Dover on 22 August and re-embarked, having performed his pilgrimage, on the 26th.[49] When the archbishop of Rheims came to Canterbury again in 1181, Henry sent word that he wished to speak with him, and the archbishop came to Winchester to do so.[50] Theobald, count of Blois, was a visitor in 1184 and stayed with the king for fifteen days. Later that year the count of Flanders came again, this time accompanying the archbishop of Cologne. Henry met the pair at Dover, but on this occasion the pilgrimage, which was duly performed en route to London, was incidental to diplomatic business Henry had with the archbishop concerning the king's son-in-law Henry the Lion, the deposed duke of Saxony.[51]

Becket's murder was a cause célèbre, and it occurred in a social and temporal context which was propitious for the development of a major pilgrimage. There would be no backwardness now in recording and publicising the new saint's miracles, at least once it was plain that there was going to be no royal threat to the cult. In the collections of Benedict of Peterborough and Willliam fitz Stephen we find the full range of saintly activity both on behalf of suppliants and in chastisement of detractors and defaulters. Most of the miracles were not novel in character: that was hardly to be expected. The newest of saints still had to do the things which suppliants wanted done, and people's needs and problems came in a limited number of forms.

The potency of the cult was revealed in, and enhanced by, the proliferation of secondary shrines where Becket could be venerated and the benefits of his intercession tapped. Perhaps the most considerable of these secondary shrines was the hospital of St Thomas of Acon, founded in about 1190 by the husband of the saint's sister, Agnes, on what was believed to have been the site of his birthplace in London. It enjoyed privileged status and received numerous indulgences down to the Reformation.[52] Almost any association with Becket could suffice to create such a site. Benedict of Peterborough reported that very soon after his death a cross was erected at Newington in Kent to mark the spot where he had paused to confirm local children, on his last journey from Canterbury to London, and numerous miracles were performed there in the early years of the cult.[53] William fitz Stephen records the cure a Herefordshire woman received by 'putting herself through a window where the blessed Thomas at stood at a writing-desk when he was performing the office of scribe for the king'.[54] In such instances the place – the cross, the window – amounted to a relic of the saint, comparable to the more conventional relics, such as vestments or phials of the martyr's 'water', which conveyed Becket's power far afield.

Churches and chapels were being dedicated to Thomas within a very few years of his death, and often obtained grants of indulgence which may have encouraged dwellers in the locality to seek the martyr there. Waltham Abbey was a rather special case, as Henry II contributed generously to the fabric as part of his reparations for his involvement in Becket's death. In 1188 the infirmary chapel was consecrated to Becket, and received a commemorative indulgence from the bishop of Hereford, a former canon of Waltham.[55] There were many others with less exalted patronage and more remote locations. William fitz Stephen tells how Becket appeared at Devizes, together with his namesake the apostle, first to a deaf man and then to a blind man, with instructions to build a chapel to the martyr there. This itself became a place of pilgrimage where cures were effected.[56] The possession of relics could establish a local pilgrimage, accessible to people who could not or would not make the journey to Canterbury. A man of Chester obtained some relics of the martyr (part of his hairshirt and bloodstained vestments) as protection against the marauding Welsh and installed them in the monastery of Whitchurch in Shropshire, very near the present Welsh border. Here they promptly began to do miracles, not least for Welsh clients. One, called Griffin, was directed by a vision of the saint to go to Canterbury to complete his cure, while a woman who had been for seven weeks unable to retain food drew lots, 'as is the custom in those parts', to discover which of two nearby churches, one dedicated to the Virgin, the other to the Archangel Michael, she should visit to seek help. She was directed by means of a vision to go to Whitchurch, and there offer 'a penny, obtained by honest toil'.[57] Another shrine remote from Canterbury was Carlisle Cathedral, which by the end of the thirteenth century had obtained the sword with which Becket had been martyred, a considerable attraction.[58]

It was not just at Canterbury, then, that Becket made his presence felt. This helped to ensure his virtually immediate impact on the cults of other saints. It is scarcely an exaggeration to say that no saint in England (or more precisely the custodians of no saint in England) could henceforth afford to ignore the example of the martyr of Canterbury. This was not just a matter of crude competition for offerings but of maintaining the honour of other and older saints in the face of this challenge, particularly in the early years when Becket's miracles were at their most numerous and the dissemination of his cult most explosive. If all saints were one in the source and the nature of their power, could the others now demonstrate their equality?

It is therefore understandable that there should be a great deal of evidence in the closing decades of the twelfth century that the guardians of other shrines were coming to terms with the dominating presence of the new martyr and taking what steps seemed necessary to strengthen and revivify the appeal of their saints. When William of Malmesbury mentioned Frideswide (d. 727), the virgin martyr of Oxford, he said nothing about any recent miracles. Members of her Oxford community were among the early beneficiaries of Becket's powers. First the canon and chamberlain Robert, who was severely afflicted by diarrhoea, was cured by the martyr's water, and then the prior himself, Robert of Cricklade, who observed this miracle and rebuked two brethren who had previously been disbelieving, was driven to Canterbury by infirmity. He was Benedict of Peterborough's first-hand informant, and is probably represented in one of the Miracle Windows being helped to approach the shrine.[59]

On 12 February 1180, with royal approval, and in the presence of Richard, archbishop of Canterbury, and others, Frideswide's relics were translated to a new shrine, and an updated collection of miracles was produced by Prior Philip.[60] The influence of Becket's cult on this collection can be discerned in the employment of the *topos* of the miracle performed by one saint which another (perhaps greater and more celebrated) has either proved unable or unwilling to perform or has specifically delegated. There are several examples of this simple generic story among Frideswide's miracles. A number of her clients had supposedly gone to the shrines of other unspecified saints before coming to her, and she also performed cures for women from the territory of St Edmund and St Alban. Becket, however, is specifically mentioned four times.[61] The knight Hamo from Brittany, disappointed at Canterbury, came to Oxford not to seek a cure but to visit a kinsman, and got a pleasant surprise. The other beneficiaries were local people who obtained either a partial cure or no cure at all from St Thomas, who is however always referred to in the most reverential terms. It is not explained why Thomas proved unable or unwilling to oblige them, but the probable implication is that that the people of the locality should have had faith in Frideswide as their *genius loci*.

This implication is spelled out in the hagiographical writings of Reginald of Durham, which represent one of the most interesting responses to Thomas's new and imposing presence. Reginald's accounts of the miracles of St Cuthbert and of Godric of Finchale, the merchant and pilgrim turned hermit who died in May 1170, only seven months before Thomas himself, depict the relationship not only between two local cults, one old and one new, but the still more complex interplay between these two saints of the north and the canonised saint of the south. Reginald's collection of the miracles of St Cuthbert includes a number of examples of the 'competitive' *topos*, as the table below will indicate.[62]

The beneficiary	Other saints/shrines approached
A man from East Anglia	Edmund, Etheldreda (the pilgrim draws lots) [63]
A foreign pilgrim	The Holy Sepulchre, St Leonard of Noblat (partial cures) [64]
A pilgrim of uncertain origin	Unspecified other English saints [65]
A youth of Bergen	Becket, Edmund (the pilgrim draws lots) [66]
Unnamed	Godric of Finchale [67]
The son of a knight of Cumberland	Becket (recommends Cuthbert) [68]
A noble lady	Edmund, Thomas (the pilgrim draws lots) [69]

The beneficiary	Other saints/shrines approached
A clerk who once served Becket, now the archbishop of York	Becket (recommends Cuthbert) [70]
A woman from near Northallerton	Godric (pilgrim diverted to Cuthbert) [71]
A boy of Berwick	Becket (diverted to Cuthbert) [72]
A man of Cleveland	Becket (partial cure) [73]

Only a few of these are in fact stories of outright failure to obtain a cure at the other shrines mentioned. The foreign pilgrim, for example, who had iron fetters bound around his body and both arms, received two-thirds of his relief at the Holy Sepulchre and from St Leonard. In other instances, the suppliant never went to the rival shrine, but was advised in a vision to have recourse to Cuthbert; Becket himself told two would-be clients to do so, thus diplomatically supporting the northern saint in his patronage of his own regional sphere. In one of three stories in which the suppliant drew lots to decide which of three shrines he should try, a man from East Anglia was, however, directed away from his own regional patrons Edmund and Etheldreda.

Reginald's treatment of Godric of Finchale involved him in some still more complex plotting, in which a major theme is the cooperative relationship not only between Godric and Cuthbert but also between both of them and Becket. Appearing in a vision to a master of letters at Durham, who had been debating with his fellows why God had done so many miracles so quickly for Becket and none for Godric, Godric himself explained that in his lifetime he had taken care only of his own soul, while Thomas had been the pastor of many others. It was enough for Godric now that his soul dwelt with God,

> but soon Thomas, my brother, crowned with me in heaven, and the blessed father Cuthbert, my sole advocate, will be coming to Finchale; so that we can there bring aid to the petitions of the sick, and thus will proclaim to the world that we live together with Christ. [74]

Sometimes the faithful received visions in which two or more of the saints appeared together, sometimes also with John the Baptist, the patron of Finchale. Reginald's strategy depended on the old and respectable belief that all the saints were essentially one in the origin and mechanisms of their power. Godric's miracles were to be understood, it seems, as the work of a celestial syndicate, but as a list of cures effected at Finchale after failure or partial failure elsewhere indicates, there was more to it than that.

Beneficiary	Other saints approached
A girl of Durham	St James (twice) [75]
A woman of Hertfordshire	Becket (partial cure); Andrew [76]
Provost of 'Straintune'	Cuthbert (partial cure) [77]
Woman of Hamsterley	Cuthbert (directs her to Godric) [78]
Woman of Musselburgh	Holy places in Scotland [79]
Woman of Durham	Becket (partial cure) [80]
Woman of Sedbergh	Becket [81]
Woman of Bothale	Becket [82]
Woman of Carleton	Becket (diverted to Godric) [83]
Blind son of Uchtred de Ulchel	Becket (vow) [84]
A young knight of Normandy	Becket (vow; diverted to Godric) [85]
Girl of Northumbria	Becket [86]
Her father	Becket [87]
A youth of Durham	Becket [88]
Clerk of Cravecroft	Andrew (having once been cured by Godric) [89]
Woman of Cleveland	The Virgin at Guisborough; St Leonard (at York?) [90]
A man of Northumbria	Becket (advises recourse to Cuthbert and Godric) [91]

Godric catered for the women who could not obtain access to Cuthbert, thanks to the legend of the saint's prohibition. In one instance, a woman possessed by demons went to Durham to seek Cuthbert's help and was guided by the saint himself to Finchale; in another, Godric restored the sanity of a young girl who had thoughtlessly wandered into the precinct of St Cuthbert, a case which to Reginald demonstrated the sweetness of the alliance between the saints. On the one occasion that Cuthbert left the cure of a man incomplete, it was specifically in order to establish Godric as his colleague and assistant (*coadjutor et cooperator*) in the performance of miracles.

That suppliants should fail to obtain cures at Compostela or from St Andrew or other Scottish saints required no apology, but when Godric performed or completed a cure which Becket proved unable or unwilling to perform an explanation is usually (although not always) given. A man of Appleby actually asked Godric to cure him 'for the love of St Thomas the Martyr', and Agnes of Carleton, who had a huge ulcerated swelling on her stomach and wanted to go to Canterbury, was crisply advised by her mistress to try someone nearer at hand, as she could only move with assistance. Becket himself made the point to the man from the borders of Northumbria who had dragged himself to Canterbury:

> Why have you come here to me from Northumbria, when you have St Cuthbert, much more precious than me, and St Godric my companion, in your neighbourhood? You do not receive what you ask from them because you do not have the faith in them that you should, nor pay them the honour and reverence that you should have done. Return therefore as fast as possible, because St Cuthbert and I will come there with St Godric, and will do more curing miracles there than here.

Reginald saw that the old shrine of the great saint of the north, and the newer shrine of the lesser saint, had to be as it were re-established in relation to the cult that had now arisen in southern England with its unprecedented pulling power.

William fitz Stephen produced an ingenious face-saving formula to explain why Thomas was more effective than Edmund, and other older saints, in certain cases: the old saints had done their stint, and it was unreasonable to ask them to go on labouring in the modern age.[92] It is not surprising that Bury sources should prefer to depict the old and the new martyrs cooperating in wonder-working, just as Reginald showed Becket cooperating with Cuthbert.[93] In an elaborate story which was the last added by Thomas of Monmouth to his collection of the miracles of the supposed boy martyr, William of Norwich, Becket advised Godfrey, a citizen of Canterbury, who had incautiously gorged himself on goose, peas and ale after having three teeth extracted, not to expect a cure from him but to have recourse to Little St William. Resting at Ospringe on his way north, Godfrey prayed for good companionship on the road, and Becket promptly appeared to him, accompanied by St Edmund (although Godfrey did not recognise either of them). They escorted him at miraculous speed across the Thames, by what means he could not subsequently remember, and deposited him three miles from Bury by sunset. Here they identified themselves and left him. Godfrey was tactful enough to realise that he must do reverence to St Edmund, and then went to the inn. On the following day he went on to Norwich, in good fettle although feeling some effects from the rather dramatic haste of the previous day's journey. In this story, both Thomas and Edmund were conceding their natural rights to the boy martyr: Thomas his patronage over a Canterbury man, and Edmund his suzerainty within the East Anglian sphere. Thomas of Monmouth claimed to have seen Godfrey subsequently at Canterbury, fit and well, and to have verified the particulars of his incredible journey.[94]

The cooperative miracle involving Becket as one partner is to be found in other collections. An undated miracle of St Ivo tells how a woman blind from birth toured the shrines of England. Having been to Canterbury, she was on her way to address her prayers to Ivo when she sat down to rest not far from the shrine and fell asleep. As she slept, two men in episcopal garb appeared to her, one in the direction from which she had come, the other in the direction she was going. They placed two bright eyes in her head, and the woman joyfully realised she could see. There was no doubt that the miracle should be ascribed to Thomas and to Ivo jointly.[95] A variant tale is told by Benedict of Peterborough: a blind man of Gloucester came to Canterbury in hopes of a cure from the martyr's blood and received, it seemed, only an increase in his pain. Entering Rochester Cathedral on his homeward journey, he was in such pain as to fear imminent death; but the monks placed him before the shrine of St Ithamar and there during mass he was cured. Benedict was gracious enough not to argue with those who attributed the miracle to Ithamar, while pointing out that if the cure had taken place on the public highway it would undoubtedly have been credited to Becket.[96]

The theme of competition with Becket was usually handled more tactfully than it was in the Reading collection of the miracles of the Hand of St James.[97] This includes some striking examples of the familiar *topos*: the relic proved able to compete not only with Salisbury and other unnamed shrines, but with Canterbury, where Becket failed miserably to cure a crippled girl who then got relief at Reading. Perhaps St James was presuming on his apostolic status when he bluntly told the girl 'You will certainly not receive a cure there'.[98] However, Benedict and William fitz Stephen between them tell of three monks of Reading, including the leper Elias, who received cures from St Thomas. Moreover, there had been a connection between Reading and Becket: the archbishop had dedicated the abbey church and granted an indulgence for the pilgrimage.[99]

Less emphatic was the story included among the new miracles of St William of York which were written down in 1177. A woman of Gisburn who was 'vexed with the stone' received a vision of St Thomas in which she was instructed to come to Canterbury with a cross; she went, but without the cross, and was not cured and had to return home because of her poverty. Hearing of the cures achieved by St William, she went to York and after confession of her sins was successful. It is perhaps being hinted here that her failure to carry out Becket's instructions fully, a symptom of her sinful state, accounted for her disappointment at Canterbury. Like virtually all of William's clients, she came from the north and found solace from a northern saint. When she had been cured she joined with others in ministering to the sick at the shrine for several days.[100]

Sometimes there is the merest hint of a connection between Becket's cult and developments elsewhere. The monks of St Albans, like others, were naturally engaged throughout the twelfth century in the defence and promotion of their ancient saint. More perhaps than any other community in England, they were professionally conscious of the Roman past. Theirs, as Bede reminded all educated Englishmen, was the only English relic cult to boast such antique origins. In 1178, during the rule of Abbot Simon (1167–83), the community claimed to have discovered the relics of Amphibalus, as Geoffrey of Monmouth had for the first time named the clerk to whom Alban gave shelter, thus provoking his own martyrdom. According to the story transmitted by Roger of Wendover and after him Matthew Paris, the burial place of Amphibalus and nine companions at Redburn near St Albans were pointed out to Robert Mercer, a citizen of the town, by a vision of St Alban himself; the saint chatted amiably to Robert about local topography and answered all his questions.[101] The whole transaction is depicted as a community event involving the people of the town; both the discovery of the relics and their translation to the abbey church were marked by miracles.

Matthew Paris underlined the significance of this discovery in his *History of the Abbots*: the martyrdom of St Thomas and the *inventio* of St Amphibalus took place, he calculated, within the same seven-year period; it seemed like a renewal of the world.[102] Perhaps the need to respond to the challenge of St Thomas, as well as to vindicate the possession of St Alban himself, which was periodically claimed by the monks of Ely, was one of the stimuli which led to the *inventio* of Amphibalus. Were the monks aware that inhabitants of their town were having recourse to the new saint? A youth called William was cured of insanity by Alban, who is significantly called 'his own patron, the martyr', but had to go to Canterbury for relief from the epilepsy which subsequently afflicted him for nine years.[103]

Clients who had failed to obtain relief from Becket were cured at certain French shrines. While this is interesting testimony to his fame and his influence, it is hardly to be supposed that the custodians of every shrine in western Europe had Becket constantly at the forefront of their minds.[104] The urge to ascribe late twelfth-century development in the cults of other English saints to the influence or challenge of Thomas has sometimes to be tempered similarly in the light of the available evidence. The Winchester annalist related that in 1182 St Barnabas announced his presence by miracles at Hyde Abbey 'and the church then began to be renovated and improved'. This may tell us no more than that one of the great churches of Winchester was participating in the contemporary boom in fund-raising and church building.[105] Similarly, Adam of La Charité, abbot of Evesham for thirty years from 1160, was a great builder and benefactor of his church and completed a new shrine for St Ecgwin, to which the saint was translated in 1183.[106] If we had the records of any miracles performed by Ecgwin in honour of the occasion, we might find that we had evidence to support the suspicion that Adam and the rest of the community had Becket in mind, but we do not.

There is, however, some suggestive, although by no means conclusive, indirect evidence for such a connection. The discovery in Lancashire of an early thirteenth-century ampulla embossed with images of St Ecgwin and 'Edwin, saint and king' raises the possibility that the monks of Evesham were aware of the Canterbury model. There can be no certainty about this, as there is no known cult of Edwin of Northumbria at Evesham or anywhere outside of York and Whitby, and no evidence that Ecgwin had migrated northwards. All that can be said is that it is hard to know where the ampulla was produced if it was not at Evesham; someone, somewhere, who was interested in Ecgwin was imitating what was being done at Canterbury.[107] Another ampulla of similar date bearing the images of the Virgin and St Modwenna has been discovered in Leicestershire. In this case there can be little doubt that it came from Burton Abbey in Staffordshire where Modwenna was enshrined. The Burton Annalist recorded that both she and Wulfstan of Worcester were doing miracles in 1201.[108]

Was the renewed and successful drive to achieve Wulfstan's canonisation, after a failed attempt in the pontificate of Eugenius III (1145–53), among the side-effects of Becket's fame? Again, this cannot simply be assumed to be the case. Wulfstan's recorded miracles, which mostly date from the first quarter of the thirteenth century, reveal a strongly regional, western power base.[109] Clients came from Worcestershire itself, from Shropshire, Herefordshire, Wiltshire and Somerset, and also from Wales. Beneficiaries from elsewhere were not of course excluded: there were a few from Warwickshire just to the east, and one each from Essex, Hertfordshire and London. A pilgrimage by the bishop of Rochester is also recorded, but when the justiciar Hubert Walter visited Worcester one Lent and witnessed many miracles, he had come on royal business and to strengthen the 'fluid fidelity' of the Welsh.[110] Similar concerns would later induce Edward I to seek Wulfstan's patronage.

Wulfstan's claims to supremacy in his particular geographical sphere are underlined by the two 'competitive' miracles included in the collection. A girl of Gloucester who for eighteen years had been without the sight of one eye was told by the Virgin in a dream to go to Wulfstan, but her parents derided the idea, asking rhetorically whether it was to be supposed that the power of St Peter at Gloucester Abbey was less than that of Wulfstan at Worcester.[111] They might have reflected that the latter's presence at Worcester was indeed relatively more concentrated than that of a universal saint like Peter could be at any one English shrine, and they should also have known better than to disregard the Virgin's specific instructions. Fortunately the girl acted on her own initiative. On another occasion, seafarers from Bristol to Ireland were imperilled by storm, and each called on the saint of his choice, one on St Nicholas (an established specialist in deliverance from shipwreck) and another on Becket. It was the invocation of Wulfstan that was effective, as if the Irish Sea fell within the area of his special concern; Colman and William of Malmesbury had earlier related how the saint had intervened to put an end to the slave trade between Bristol and Ireland.[112] John Comyn, archbishop of Dublin, was among the commissioners appointed in 1202 to investigate the miracles. It is significant that a few years later Wulfstan did a couple of well-publicised miracles for Irish clients, and that one of his ampullae has been discovered in excavations in Dublin.[113]

Another major church in the west of England, Glastonbury Abbey, fell on hard times after a disastrous fire in 1184. That by itself may have been sufficient incentive for the carefully stage-managed *inventio* which uncovered the relics of King Arthur and Guinevere in 1191. Glastonbury's later medieval history was inextricably bound up with the exploitation of the Celtic and Grail legends which Geoffrey of Monmouth and innumerable romancers after him made the favourite reading of laity and many clergy alike. If further context for the *inventio* of 1191 is needed, it may be found in the claims of the English to political and ecclesiastical dominion over the Welsh and the associated desire to prove that Arthur was not the Welsh Messiah in waiting but was truly dead. Henry II himself had supposedly authorised the search for Arthur's remains, and Edward I later showed a keen interest in them. Is it then necessary to postulate, as has been suggested, that the monks of Glastonbury had an eye on Canterbury? It is interesting that they now renewed their old claim to the relics of their former abbot St Dunstan, possibly reasoning that he was now totally eclipsed at Christ Church Priory. It was a fact that Glastonbury had no single saint of pre-eminent stature. Its claims to David and Patrick, as to Dunstan, were very far from universally convincing, and many of the relics it did possess were of limited interest. Later, Joseph of Arimathea, remarkably identified as the leader of twelve missionaries dispatched to Glastonbury by St Philip, would go far to plug the gap. Late in the twelfth century the news of Becket's burgeoning cult may at least have underlined the need to take action.[114]

Thomas Becket's cult was the product of specific events, but also a reflection of twelfth-century circumstances and an influence upon later developments. With hindsight Becket can be seen as standing at the head of a number of subsequent developments in English pilgrimage. He was one of the first English representatives of the relatively new breed of papally canonised saints. Specifically, he was a canonised bishop, a type characteristic of the official English sanctity of the next century and a half. He was also a political martyr who would have later and lesser successors both lay and ecclesiastical. He was from the beginning, and remained, a dominating presence in the landscape of English pilgrimage. Analyses of the places of origin of pilgrims as revealed in miracle collections have repeatedly shown what reflection and common sense might suggest, especially given medieval conditions of travel, that the catchment-areas of virtually all shrines were predominantly local or at most regional. Becket was no exception to this rule: a statistical majority of his known pilgrims came from the more southerly parts of England.[115] Nor did he violate the other rule that miracles occurred (or were recorded) in bursts, most often shortly after a saint's death or a well-publicised translation to a new shrine, and diminished over time. When, for example, Thomas Cantilupe of Hereford was doing miracles, between 1287 and 1307, Becket was doing few or none that we know about. Chaucer could still say in the late fourteenth century, however, that pilgrims came to Canterbury to give thanks for deliverance from sickness.

Cures and miracles were anyway not the whole story. Even if the levels of excitement of the early 1170s were not permanently maintained, which was scarcely to be expected, a wealth of incidental evidence, for example from wills, chronicles and court records, suggests that Becket retained greater pulling power over medium to long distances, and also attracted more visitors from overseas, than any other saint in England, even if the absolute numbers were not great. The best competition for this wider audience was to come, between about 1300 and the Reformation, from Our Lady of Walsingham. Becket's fame (and the riches of his shrine) endured until the Reformation and earned him what may have been a uniquely savage retribution from a new King Henry who had identified him as a capital enemy of the crown.

4

Saints, Bishops and Shrine Promotion

In the second half of the twelfth century the English church acquired two canonised saints, Edward the Confessor in 1161 and Thomas Becket in 1173. Of the five canonisations performed by Innocent III in the early years of his pontificate, two were of Englishmen, Gilbert, abbot of Sempringham, in 1202 and Wulfstan of Worcester in 1203.[1] There were more to come in the next 120 years, all bishops. Hugh of Lincoln died in 1200 and was canonised in 1220 by Honorius III, who in 1226 also elevated William, archbishop of York (d. 1154). Edmund Rich, archbishop of Canterbury, who died at Soissy in France in 1240 and was buried at the Cistercian abbey of Pontigny, was canonised seven years later; his tomb became a magnet for English pilgrims well into the next century. Edmund's pupil and sometime chancellor Richard Wych, bishop of Chichester, followed him to the grave in 1253 and to sanctification in 1262. Next in the sequence came Thomas Cantilupe of Hereford, whose remains were brought back to England five years after his death in Italy in 1282. He was canonised after a longer interval, in 1320, but was clearly regarded and in many respects treated as a saint long before. With him the line of sainted English medieval bishops ended, except for Osmund of Salisbury (d. 1099), who was canonised by Calixtus III in 1457; a process had first been initiated on his behalf in 1228. There had in the meantime been one more English canonisation, of the Augustinian canon John Thweng of Bridlington, in 1401.

Already in the twelfth century the popes had indicated that canonisation would not be awarded easily and that promoters should think twice about pressing the claims of too many candidates. Papal canonisation was therefore always going to be a rarity. For at least a century and a half from the middle of the thirteenth century circumstances conspired to make it a greater rarity than had perhaps been intended. Between 1267 and 1378 only seven saints were canonised, most of them owing their promotion at least in part to French or Angevin backing; the exception was Thomas Cantilupe of Hereford in 1320. In the closing decades of the thirteenth century there was a succession of short pontificates which made it abnormally difficult to see a process through to a successful conclusion. The long Avignon residence of the popes between 1309 and 1378 witnessed greater stability, but also the continuance of the Franco-Angevin influence which had originated largely in the recurrent and ingrained papal fear of imperial designs in Italy. Then came the Great Schism, unresolved until 1417, during which canonisation came to an almost complete halt, although some hearings were conducted. The Yorkshireman John of Bridlington was among the very few saints to be proclaimed during this period. In the two centuries from 1260 to 1460, therefore, only four Englishmen were canonised.

During this long fallow period, the English authorities occasionally put forward names for consideration. Robert Grosseteste of Lincoln was repeatedly a candidate (in 1254, 1285–59 and 1307). Edward III in the early years of his reign tried to promote both Thomas, earl of Lancaster, and Robert Winchelsey, archbishop of Canterbury, the latter having already been the subject of petition in 1318–20. In 1386 and again between 1392 and 1398 Richard II pressed the claims of his murdered ancestor Edward II. All these cults, to a greater or lesser degree, had political implications. All the men involved were extremely high-profile figures in the public life of the nation. It would be rash to conclude that none of them had a popular following, but a popular following was not sufficient to guarantee candidature, let alone success, and none of these 'saints' in fact achieved even the initiation of a process. Perhaps significantly the only English candidate who did, albeit without result, was the much lowlier Thomas de la Hale, a monk of St Martin's Dover who was killed in a French raid on the town in 1295 and enjoyed a modest cult which, with royal backing, led to the initiation of an enquiry into his sanctity in 1380.[2]

The canonised saint was distinguished from others not by the intrinsic nature of his or her sanctity but by the procedure by which that sanctity had been publicly authenticated. While all canonised saints were legitimate objects of pilgrimage, pilgrimage, in England or anywhere else in Christendom, might have experienced long periods of famine as old cults lost their lustre, if it had depended on a constant supply of such officially approved saints. Canonised sainthood, in fact, accounted for only a proportion of new or renewed pilgrimage activity, which was generated from a number of sources of varied character.

There was and is a certain ambiguity about the canonised saint. The pope does not confer sanctity upon a saint; he recognises, in the name of the church, that he or she in fact possesses it. To achieve that recognition the saint has to do miracles, or rather, through his or her intercession to move God to do miracles; and for that to happen the intercession of the saint has (normally) to be sought by prayer. In other words, some kind of cult has to exist for the prospective saint to become a candidate for sanctification. The enquiries into existing cults undertaken by the Counter-Reformation church from the late sixteenth century on, which often led to approval of their continuance short of formal beatification or canonisation, turned to a very large extent on verification of the historic actuality of the cult, as well as on the scrutiny of evidence of holy life and miracles. All saints owed their promotion to influential backers and the *pietas* of interest groups such as the religious orders which possessed their relics, but they also depended to some degree on evidence that they had attracted suppliants who experienced miracles in response to their prayers and offerings. From the standpoint of the faithful, the 'official' saint had to meet their needs whether before or after canonisation, and as such he or she was largely indistinguishable from a host of others who were never canonised or even considered for canonisation.

Pre-eminent among uncanonised saints were the many, great and small, who had lived too soon to be the subjects of a papal commission of enquiry. In formal terms, their title to veneration rested on their inclusion in martyrologies and calendars. They ranged from the very greatest of them all – the Baptist, the Apostles, the Fathers of the Church – and legendary martyrs such as St Katherine and St Margaret, to figures from every period of the church's history, many of essentially local fame, whose credentials were not in question. In England, Alban from the Roman period, Cuthbert from the heyday of the Christianisation of the north, Edmund the martyr of the Danes, came into this category. All had become the possession of entrenched communities with extensive properties and privileges, whose *raison d'être* in an important sense remained the saint and his shrine, even if pilgrimage was not the major source of their income.

It was not just for economic reasons that the continuance of pilgrimage at a healthy level was welcome, if not vital, to these churches. The ancient image of the saint as the protector and if necessary avenger of his or her community's interests may have lost much of its force by the thirteenth century as more developed governmental and legal institutions came into being, but the belief that the saints could render assistance and comfort both in the trials of life and in the face of death furnished an implicit justification for the continued existence and privileges of the institutions which served their shrines. Old uncanonised saints therefore marched on, some of course more resplendent than others, into the age of the canonised saint, but this did not mean that old cults remained popular, let alone materially profitable, without the expenditure of some effort. Translation, and the award of new indulgences, were techniques applicable to old saints as to new, obvious means by which a cult could be refreshed.

New saints were usually translated to a new and more sumptuous tomb, after some lapse of time: Becket in 1220, Hugh of Lincoln in 1280, Thomas

Cantilupe of Hereford in 1349. Thus new feasts were created; Becket's translation, on 7 July, was better placed in the year to attract crowds than the anniversary of his death on 29 December, and it was to the Feast of the Translation that the Jubilee indulgences which the Canterbury authorities sought from the pope every fifty years were usually attached.[3] The grant of indulgences to mark occasions such as the translation of a saint or the dedication of a new or rebuilt church became common in the twelfth century. In his *History of the Abbots*, Matthew Paris first mentions an indulgence for St Albans in connection with the the consecration of the new church, late in 1116, which was attended by Henry I.[4] The indulgence granted by Walter Gray of York on Christmas Day 1224, on the occasion of the translation of Wilfrid of Ripon to a new shrine, contained a number of interesting provisions. The archbishop had checked that the skeleton was complete in every particular, but decided that the head should be separately located 'so that by seeing it the faith of the faithful may be strengthened and [their] devotion increased'. This implied its enclosure in a special, perhaps head-shaped, reliquary which would be located in a prominent and visible place on an altar, but might also be readily portable. It was possible for the faithful to obtain the indulgences granted by the archbishop not only in person but through their proxies if they were unable to attend. The indulgence, of thirty days, was to last from the day of the translation itself to Epiphany (6 January); on the feasts of Wilfrid's deposition or death (12 October) and of his first translation, by St Oswald in the tenth century (24 April), it would be available only for eight days.[5]

In 1215 the sixty-second canon of the Fourth Lateran Council limited the quantity of indulgence that might be granted by a mere bishop to one hundred days on the occasion of the dedication of a church and forty days for the anniversary. The pope himself, it was declared, normally observed these limits, even though he possessed the 'fullness of power' over the church; Walter Gray was well within them in 1224.[6] The popes by the end of the thirteenth century had long abandoned any such restraint on their own awards, but in its time the Lateran decree demonstrated an awareness that the granting of indulgences had proved sufficiently popular with bishops to lead to excess. In addition, the decree prohibited the veneration of relics that had not been authenticated by the Roman Church. The church had thus by the early thirteenth century developed a range of methods by which it could, in principle, control and encourage the devotions of the faithful.

The results were not quite what it might superficially appear that they should have been, that is, that new cults and new shrines were henceforth closely and centrally regulated by the official church. The boundary between what may loosely be called 'official' and 'unofficial' pilgrimage was often hazy. Canonised saints were proper focuses of pilgrimage, and would undoubtedly be assiduously promoted as such by their custodians, although this did not guarantee that they would become big attractions, but certain pilgrimages which seem to have had an essentially unofficial character were never officially condemned. It was also possible for the object of veneration to be perfectly respectable while the mode of veneration provoked concern. Some cults which did attract official condemnation, or at least anxiety, are considered later. Our present concern is with English cults which, even if they proved to be short-lived, received different types and degrees of official approval.

The St Albans chronicler Roger of Wendover noted a number of events between about 1150 and 1230 which would have been of interest to English pilgrims. Becket apart, there had been the deaths of the hermits Wulfric of Hazelbury and Godric of Finchale and of the monk-bishop Hugh of Lincoln, each of whom, Roger said, had continued to do miracles down to the present day. He also noted the discovery of the remains of King Arthur at Glastonbury in 1191. Hugh of Lincoln was canonised and St Thomas translated, both in 1220; and Roger also gave one version of the story of the Holy Rood of Bromholm, in Norfolk, whose miracles began around 1223.[7] Roger's successor as historiographer at St Albans, Matthew Paris, added that St Wulfstan was translated to his new shrine at Worcester in 1218 and that one of his ribs was sent as a gift to St Albans, 'so that he might be more greatly venerated', and also that oil seeped from the tomb of William of York in 1223.[8] Matthew characterised the first half of the thirteenth century as an age of saints, and not only in England:

> [There have been] many saints in England, above all St Edmund, archbishop and confessor, [who has been] solemnly canonised and radiates miracles at Pontigny. The hermit St Robert at Knaresborough is renowned for manifest wonders. Roger, bishop of London, too, and several others in England, and the widow St Elizabeth in Germany, the daughter of the king of Hungary, and also St Hildegard the prophetess, are distinguished by notable signs.[9]

Here saints of very varied types rub shoulders, a hermit who never attained canonisation with a bishop who did and another whose supporters believed that he should do. Of the impact of Edmund of Abingdon's canonisation, as of Becket's earlier, there can be no doubt. Like Becket, Edmund provides some excellent examples of the rapid development of secondary shrines in response to the demand for wider access to his spiritual powers. His burial place at Pontigny was much frequented by English pilgrims, some of whom seem to have regarded it as a corner of a foreign field that was forever England, an association clearly strengthened by the fact that Becket himself had spent part of his exile there. Englishwomen were accorded privileged access to this Cistercian abbey in order to pay their respects to Edmund, [10] while Archbishop Wickwane of York (1279–85) told two clerks of his diocese who wanted to make the journey there: 'Although [all] those who want go on pilgrimage to the relics of the saints deserve favourable consideration, we think we should treat with greater generosity those who want to expend pious labour on distant pilgrimages to our own saints (*sanctos nostrates*).' [11]

Edmund's miracles were not confined to Pontigny. His sisters, Margaret and Alice, were nuns at Catesby in Northamptonshire and he had left with them a *pallium* and also some painted panels which he used to carry about with him. These soon began to effect miracles which added to the pressure for his canonisation. [12] In 1260 the Waverley chronicler said that 'many and frequent miracles' were occurring at the altar of St Edmund in the church of Aston (Tirrold), between Oxford and Banbury, and in 1289 the Worcester annalist reported that 'God displayed many miracles in the chapel at Abingdon, which Edmund earl of Cornwall, warned by a dream in the previous year, built in the place where the blessed confessor Edmund was born'. [13] The earl had been named for the new saint when he was born in 1249.

Kinship or friendship with Edmund fostered other saintly reputations. Richard of Chichester was the most conspicuous example. Matthew Paris (who wrote a life of St Edmund) reported the miracles that occurred at Chichester when it was discovered that Richard had worn a hairshirt and girded himself with iron bands. The two saints were commemorated together at Dover in a chapel, still to be seen, which was dedicated by Richard to Edmund and where his own entrails were buried; but it is not clear whether this was a place of pilgrimage. Richard too was honoured at his birthplace, Droitwich in Cheshire, at a salt spring which according to legend had failed in his time but became profitable once more through his intercession. In the sixteenth century John Leland wrote of this 'In token whereof, or for the honour that the Wichemen and saulters bare unto this Richard their cuntre-man, they used of late tyme on his daye to hang about this sault spring or well one a yeare with tapestry and to have drinking games and revels at it.' At the end of the fifteenth century there was an image of St Richard, together with one of Henry VI, in the parish church of Droitwich; they had been newly repaired, 'by which there is the more resort of pilgrims and offerings to the said saints'. [14]

Matthew Paris also related that miracles were attributed to St Edmund's brother Master Robert, and to another of his disciples, Thomas of Hertford, archdeacon of Northumberland, who like Richard died in 1253. Thomas's curative miracles were reported to Matthew by a knight called John of

Lexington and prompted him to observe that, although neither Thomas nor Richard of Chichester was canonised at Rome (for Matthew did not live to see Richard's canonisation), it was not to be doubted that they were of St Edmund's fellowship in death as they had been in life. Matthew also reported that miracles were attributed to Edmund's sister Margaret when she died as prioress of Catesby in 1257. He regarded Sewal, archbishop of York (d. 1258), as another of his saintly disciples.[15]

Both the status and the celebrity of some of these figures is uncertain: did Margaret Rich do her miracles for the 'general public' or just for the members of her own community? A degree of popular confusion about some individuals may conceivably have resulted from the publicity given to indulgences such as the one the bishop of Exeter granted in January 1253 to those 'who go devoutly to pray at the tomb of the venerable father, Roger of good memory, late bishop of London, who lies in the church of St Paul's'. Indulgences were not infrequently awarded for prayers said for the souls of the deceased, but it is possible, especially when it was specified that the prayers should be offered at the graveside, that this enhanced, or even helped to create, saintly reputations such as Matthew Paris attributed to Roger of London.[16]

Roger was only one of many. If all the bishops who enjoyed a passing or local cult had in fact achieved canonisation, the list of sainted English bishops would have been much longer than it is. Robert Grosseteste of Lincoln was a strong contender and had powerful spiritual backing, as Matthew Paris reported:

> At the same time [1255] many and varied miracles occurred at the church of Lincoln and were carefully examined. As if rejoicing together, those resplendent confessors St Remigius and Bishop Hugh seemed to compete to lend their support to St Robert, who had recently gone to the Lord, so that already twenty miracles out of many, which it would be a lengthy business to recount, let alone write down, have been made public and attested before serious and trustworthy men in the chapter of Lincoln and carefully examined, for we know that deliberate lies are displeasing to God.[17]

So widespread was the conviction of Grosseteste's sanctity that the Tewkesbury annalist actually reported, under the year 1257, that he had been canonised at Rome.[18] Among his successors at Lincoln, Oliver Sutton had no compunction about calling him *beatus*, as he did the canonised St Hugh. John Dalderby in 1314 awarded forty days' indulgence for visits to his tomb,[19] as other bishops did, in England as elsewhere in Christendom, in respect of other uncanonised saints. Thomas Cantilupe of Hereford in particular attracted them long before his canonisation in 1320.

As, in Matthew's thinking, Grosseteste was welcomed by Remigius and Hugh into their fellowship at Lincoln, so another minor episcopal cult existed alongside those of Wulfstan and Oswald at Worcester. John of Coutances was bishop of Worcester from 1196 to 1198. He was remembered unfavourably for having once irreverently and furtively elevated the relics of St Wulfstan by night, but the incorruption of his body suggested that he had been of holy life.[20] In 1302 Robert Winchelsey as archbishop of Canterbury carried out a visitation of the church of Worcester and discovered that the bishop, Godfrey Giffard,

> has constructed a certain monument for his own burial near the high altar of the church, above the place where stands the shrine of the blessed Oswald ... and that the venerable body of a man who is commonly reputed holy, John of Coutances by name, still after a hundred years and more from the time of his death not yet turned to ashes but appearing undecayed to the beholder, has on this pretext been improperly removed from the place where it was accustomed to rest and to receive the veneration of the people, with the casket in which it is enclosed, and now, with the monument, occupies the place where according to the custom of other churches sedilia should be provided for the priest and other ministers of the altar at the celebration of the mass.

The altar was also receiving insufficent light as a result of Giffard's rearrangements, and the archbishop directed that his monument should be relocated lower down 'where it will be more clearly visible to those passing by' while 'the body of the aforesaid saint is to be restored to its original place and the sedilia be provided'.[21] Clearly, Winchelsey was not solely or even primarily concerned with the location of John's tomb as such, but his application of the word *sanctus* to him and the implicit acceptance of the veneration he received from 'the people' are worthy of note.

In 1257 Matthew Paris mentioned the death of Walter Suffield, bishop of Norwich, 'at whose tomb miracles were said to shine forth'.[22] Walter in fact enjoyed a modest cult at his cathedral for some while after his death. In 1305 the account rolls record offerings of £3 3s. 3d. 'at the tomb of Saint Walter', but there was an inexorable decline through the fourteenth century until only a penny was collected in 1404. In the meantime another bishop of Norwich, John Salmon (d. 1325), briefly surpassed Walter, attracting offerings of £2 7s. 8d. to his tomb in 1328. By 1342 they had declined to a tenth of that level and only 3d. was received in 1363, after which no further record was kept.[23] Here we seem to see the differential workings of 'living memory'. Both bishops left behind them a reputation for charity. Walter Suffield founded the hospital of St Giles at Norwich, which flourished until the Reformation. He had connections with men holier than himself: he served Edmund of Canterbury as an administrator, contributed to the making of the shrine at Pontigny and himself went on pilgrimage there at least once. He was also well known to Richard of Chichester. Although he himself had something of the character of the hunting parson, Suffield belonged to a generation of English bishops who had before their eyes lofty exemplars of pastoral responsibility and charitable activity.[24] He clearly did better than John Salmon in stimulating some kind of local legend, but after a century and a half its potency was exhausted.

Exeter, like Norwich, was among the greater churches of England that did not have a major saint to its credit, and here two late medieval bishops enjoyed cults: the short-lived James Berkeley (1326–27) and the very much more enduring Edmund Lacy (1419–55). The financial returns on Berkeley's cult have been charted, revealing that they fell off after the mid 1340s and had ceased altogether by the end of the century. Edmund Lacy's cult, on the other hand, may have been denied its natural life-span by the coming of the Reformation. It was locally remembered in the sixteenth century that 'many Miracles were said, and devised, to be done at his Tomb; whereupon great Pilgrimages were made by the Common People to the same'. A few sixteenth-century wills from neighbouring Somerset suggest at least some remembrance of the holy bishop, an impression substantiated by the arrangements that were in force in 1528 for remunerating the *custos* of the tomb, who was paid 'for bringing in the Pilgrims and getting their offerings'. He received 6s. 8d. if the offerings amounted to £7 13s. 4d., but only 3s. 4d. if they came to less. Lacy had suffered from an affliction of the leg bones which seems to have enhanced his appeal: evidence for this was discovered in 1943 in the form of fragments of wax votive images which had been hung up over his tomb.[25] The canonisation of Osmund of Salisbury in 1457, not long after Edmund's death, may well have acted as a powerful incentive to the canons of Exeter to try to make something of him. William Worcester saw the tomb in 1477–78 and was able to transcribe prayers, in verse and prose, that were addressed to Edmund; by the time Leland saw it, some time before 1543, it had been defaced.[26]

Further examples could be multiplied. Very early in his reign Edward III tried to get the pope to initiate canonisation processes not only for Thomas, earl of Lancaster, but for Robert Winchelsey of Canterbury, John Dalderby of Lincoln and William March of Bath and Wells.[27] Thomas of Lancaster had himself been an eager supporter of Winchelsey's sanctity. Although the cult of a prelate who had been identified with resistance to both Edward I and Edward II could not but have its political aspect, we also have some evidence of a popular cult in the form of the miracles which were attested before a Lincoln clerk appointed for the purpose in 1319.[28] Edward III wrote twice to the pope on John Dalderby's behalf, on 11 February 1327 and

20 February 1328, laying great stress on his purity of life and claiming that even in death he was displaying his charity by healing the sick, but these efforts were without result. Wells was another major church without a major cult. The short-lived drive to canonise William March (d. 1302) may have been little more than a fund-raising exercise at a time when a great deal was being spent on rebuilding. The splendour of his tomb indicates some investment in the project, and during the episcopate of Bishop John Drokensford (d. 1329) taxes were being levied on benefices in the diocese to defray the expenses of the canonisation bid and also of the 'new work' being done at the cathedral.[29] For the new king there may have been another reason for pressing the claims of former bishops of these two sees. Henry Burghersh of Lincoln (1320–40) and Drokensford of Wells had both been regarded by Edward II as enemies. On 10 March 1327, the day before he first petitioned the pope on Dalderby's behalf, Edward III directed the treasurer and barons of the Exchequer to 'exonerate' Burghersh from the amercements the previous king had imposed upon him.[30] Such consider-ations were unlikely to weigh with the pope, nor would they necessarily secure a popular following for the two late bishops.

All such cults must have relied on the discreet encouragement of a collecting-box positioned near the tombs, and also presumably on preaching in the cathedral and the locality. The presence of collecting-boxes, which were certainly placed on or near many tombs other than those of canonised saints, may conceivably have contributed to confusion about the status of the deceased. At Exeter there was a collecting-box attached to the tomb of Bishop John the Chanter (d. 1191) and much later there were pyxes for oblations on the tombs of both Bishop Lacey and Bishop Berkeley, and also on those of Bishop Grandisson (d. 1369), and of the second earl of Devon; the proceeds were divided up every quarter between the treasurer and the canons.[31] The offerings deposited in the box near the tomb of Ralph of Shrewsbury, bishop of Bath and Wells (d. 1363), were used to pay for a frontal for the high altar and other things at the discretion of the chapter.[32] There could well be a fine line between pious alms given for the benefit of a dead man's soul, especially perhaps a dead bishop's, and offerings made in quest of or thanksgiving for his intercession, just as there was a fine line between indulgences granted for prayers for his eternal wellbeing and indulgences granted for venerating him. Some ordinary pilgrims may have traversed these lines, consciously or unconsciously, when visiting a church.

When Thomas Cantilupe of Hereford was canonised, in 1320, his cult was arguably already past its best, although pilgrimage to the shrine may have continued at a respectable level almost to the end of its existence at the Reformation.[33] The bishop's chief promoter, his successor Richard Swin-field, did not live to see the happy day when his efforts were rewarded. On the face of it, Thomas got off to an inauspicious start; at the moment of his death in central Italy in October 1282 he was on his way to Rome, under sentence of excommunication laid upon him by John Pecham of Canterbury. Five years later Swinfield brought his predecessor's relics back to Hereford and began his long struggle. We know about the experiences of Cantilupe's pilgrims, as distinct from the bare and fragmentary record of their offerings, only in the period when Bishop Swinfield was working hard to generate miraculous activity. Papal commissioners came to London and to Hereford in 1307 to examine both the written records and living witnesses. The miracle collection which was compiled in support of Cantilupe's case was perhaps the most impressive since Becket's own, but it was different in form and composition in large part because of the development of the official procedure in the intervening century.[34]

Of nearly five hundred miracles recorded between 1287 and 1312, over seventy occurred at the very beginning, during the one month of April 1287. On 3 April (Maundy Thursday), Swinfield moved Cantilupe's remains from the chapel of St Mary at the east end of the cathedral to a new tomb in the north transept. Advance publicity had had its effect and miracles began before the move was effected. One of the most conspicuous was the cure of the mad Edith Oldecriste, the wife of a Hereford ironmonger. Her husband had her 'measured' to the cross in Hereford Cathedral and also to the Holy Cross of Wistanstow in Shropshire. She was brought, bound, to lie before the cross in the cathedral, but, on the advice of 'a certain clerk', was moved from the roodloft to the chapel of St Mary, where Thomas still lay. Here she received her cure, which was announced by the ringing of the bells, heard by her husband as he returned from Wistanstow.[35] Edith's cure had a sequel which reflected the peculiar circumstances in which Cantilupe's cult began. His adversary John Pecham of Canterbury was still alive (he died in 1292) and his official, Thomas of St-Omer, endeavoured to get this crucial miracle publicly attributed not to Cantilupe but to a twelfth-century bishop of Hereford, Robert of Béthune.[36]

That the first miraculés should be from Hereford itself and its immediate vicinity is unsurprising. Inhabitants of the episcopal estates in the surrounding countryside, who sometimes had personal recollections of the dead bishop or were especially open to the persuasions of the living one, also feature prominently. Word of mouth reporting attracted sufferers to the shrine and helped to create an interplay between miracles there and miracles performed at long range. John of Herlaurton, resident in the parish of Holme Lacy, who had a tumour on his neck, heard of the cure of the mad

Edith and betook himself to the cathedral, where he was seen inserting his head into one of the apertures in the side of the tomb for as long as it took him to say the Lord's Prayer three times with the Ave Maria. About a hundred people were present when he was cured. After he had been examined by the canons he was brought back into the cathedral in procession and shown to the people, and the miracle was solemnly 'published'. The procession then came to the tomb where *Benedictus Dominus Deus Israel* was sung. [37]

By such means further publicity was generated. The idea of calling upon the saint might be prompted by a previous visit to the shrine. A woman of Kilpeck had two sons who were blind or partially blind. Her sister came back from a pilgrimage to Hereford and told of Thomas's miracles. She measured the boys for the making of five candles, sending a servant to the shrine with the elder child and the candles, with instructions that he should remain there for three days and nights, placing one of the candles in the middle of the altar and one at each corner. The elder boy was cured at the shrine; his younger brother, at the very same moment, at home. [38] A woman of Ipswich, apparently dead, was revived by recourse to Thomas, on the advice of a Hereford man who happened to be passing; she subsequently came to the tomb with her husband.[39]

The practices employed to enlist the saint's aid at long range commonly included 'measuring' the sufferer with a thread or whatever lay to hand, 'according to the custom of the country', so that a candle or wax image of the proper length could be made to present at the shrine, or 'bending' a coin over the body, thus marking it for future offering. Ship-models in silver, wax or even wood, and the occasional model anchor, testified to the saint's activity on behalf of seafarers; occasionally cows or oxen were offered. A Welshman who had received an arrow wound in his head during the recent wars offered a wax head with the original arrow sticking in it, together with his best cow, which he had vowed in order to obtain the cure.[40] Persons cured at the shrine itself left behind them sticks, crutches, the litters in which they had been carried to the shrine, and even, on one notable occasion, a vehicle 'which the English call a wheelbarrow'. [41]

The story of one of the many drowned children who were resuscitated by St Thomas vividly illustrates the interplay between the shrine at the centre of the saint's power and the outside world. [42] The five-year-old Joanna, daughter of Adam Sheriff of Marden, north of Hereford, followed her parents to the tavern one Sunday evening, 'before St George' (23 April) in 1287. As there were many other children about, the parents thought nothing of it but, while playing in the garden of the house where the tavern was, she fell into a ditch or pond (*stagnum*). There was some delay in raising the clamour, for fear of involvement in legal proceedings, but when Joanna was finally extracted her father measured her to St Thomas with his belt, while all the bystanders prayed. The parents took her home and put her by the fire. Some movement was detected and the child began to expel 'humours and superfluities' and spoke. Around sunrise, her mother took her to the parish church and laid her on the altar of St Ethelbert (the established patron of Hereford Cathedral). Against the will of the neighbours, because the child was weak, her father lifted her up and rode with her to Hereford, accompanied by thirty or so neighbours as witnesses. Here the bells were rung, a procession held and the miracle 'published'. The wax image made in her likeness remained for many years hung up near the tomb, but then fell to bits with age. Every year thereafter the father, with his household, came at least once barefoot with offerings to the tomb, especially on the feast of St Ethelbert (20 May). The girl came to be known locally as 'Joanna the daughter of Adam the Sheriff, whom St Thomas revived', and many nobles from remote parts still came to see her 'in witness of this miracle'.

Adam was sixty-odd in 1307, his wife Cecilia in her fifties, and Joanna herself, who was also a witness, about twenty. Asked by the investigating commission whether he and his wife had had any devotion to Thomas before the drowning, he replied that they had been pilgrims to his tomb with other neighbours, and that they had invoked him at once. The story therefore depicts a family whose members had been among the earliest of Cantilupe's pilgrims, in April 1287, and had been coming to the cathedral at least once a year ever since. People of higher station exerted a special influence. Lord Milo, whose participation in tournaments had left him paralysed for six years, attended the translation ceremony, brought to the cathedral in a cart. Hearing of the miracles which took place on Holy Thursday and Good Friday, he made his confession and came to the tomb at Vespers on Saturday, appealing to Thomas as one noble to another. He was completely cured by morning. Because he was 'a very well-known knight' the miracle was 'well publicised' (*valde vulgatum*).[43] Cantilupe's willingness to cure sick hunting birds and war horses doubtless endeared him to upper-class clients. For Robert de Keynis of Buckinghamshire he cured not only a horse, and a hawk which had been injured by a dog, but also a pet dormouse.[44] Other pilgrims were very differently situated. The crippled John de Hanneleye of Cradley, who was cured on his return from the tomb, related that 'he had not been permitted to enter the cathedral and stay near the tomb'; one witness said of him that 'he sometimes lay on the public highway, not having anywhere else to lie'.[45]

In the upper rank of Thomas's devotees must be numbered Gilbert

of Clare, earl of Gloucester, once an opponent of the bishop, who visited
his tomb many times. Better still, Edward I and his second wife Margaret
came on foot to Hereford in 1301 with a glittering retinue which included
the king's brother Edmund and his wife, the queen of Navarre.[46] The king's
cousin Edmund, earl of Cornwall, had earlier connections with the saint
and with the shrine: he was a witness to a rather Franciscan miracle which
occurred in Thomas's lifetime, when birds flocked around the windows of
a chapel in which the bishop was preaching at Wallingford, and he was
present one day on September 1287, with the bishop of Ely, when a falcon
belonging to Ralph of Abbetost, over which a penny had been bent, was
brought to the tomb 'alive and well' .[47] As lord of the manor of Hambleden
in Buckinghamshire, Cantilupe's birthplace, Edmund dedicated an oratory
in his manor house there to the honour of God and Thomas of Hereford,
where miracles occurred.[48] Gradually the ripples of Cantilupe's celebrity
spread outwards, and in time, like Becket, he catered for individuals from
all over the British Isles, but his clientele retained a strong colouring of the
Marches, Wales and Ireland, rather like St Wulfstan's earlier in the century.
Like Wulfstan, he delivered mariners endangered in the seas between England, Wales and Ireland and also some who were engaged in the wine trade
with Gascony. Modernity demanded that he should also give attention to
those who served the king in Gascony and to both sides in the Welsh wars.
Earl Edmund was on his way to Wales when he bore witness to the miracle
of Ralph of Abbetost's falcon.

Important though the patronage of the mighty undoubtedly was, the
miracles cumulatively drew strength from their representation of a consensus
which embraced all classes of society and all parts of England. The English
bishops could therefore urge the pope, in 1294, to acknowledge what the
divine will and popular devotion, expressed in the miracles, were together
telling him.[49] For most practical purposes, Cantilupe was a saint long before
1320. In 1289, and again in 1293 and 1295, Swinfield had to intervene to
establish the allocation of the offerings at the tomb between the cathedral
treasurer and the rest of the chapter.[50] When the canonisation was at last
accomplished in 1320, certain things did however become possible. At last,
as Swinfield must have dreamed, Thomas Cantilupe's name joined those
of the Virgin and St Ethelbert as one of the patrons of the church of
Hereford.[51] It was now also officially permissible for him to be venerated
elsewhere in England. In 1334 Simon de Montacute of Worcester granted
forty days' remission to those who went 'for the purpose of devotion' to
the altars of St Thomas of Canterbury and St Thomas of Hereford in the
church of St Mary the Virgin at Oxford; two canonised saints, already linked
by name, were thus neatly linked for the purposes of devotion in one

subsidiary location.[52] This association of the two Thomases was irresistible. When Bishop Trillek was trying to raise money for his Thomas's translation 'from the humble place in which he has shone with wondrous miracles' to a new shrine, he urged his audience to hope that when it had been achieved men would say what they had said after the translation of Becket in 1220: that all things went well.[53]

Although Cantilupe's cult and canonisation bear witness to strenuous promotional efforts, it is apparent that neither canonised saints nor major cults and big pilgrimage attractions could simply be manufactured on demand. Canterbury was excellently positioned to be a major pilgrimage centre, and both the cathedral and St Augustine's Abbey possessed a sufficiency of respectable saints, but it took extraordinary and unpredictable events in 1170 to create the greatest of all medieval English pilgrimages. Norwich, Wells and Exeter never acquired a canonised saint on which pilgrim devotions could be principally focussed, while Chichester had to wait for St Richard in 1262, and Salisbury (which, however, had an important cult of the Virgin Mary) for the belated canonisation of St Osmund in 1457.

For such churches, their annual relic feast was of particular importance. Late in the twelfth century, Becket's successor Richard of Canterbury awarded an indulgence of forty days to Chichester Cathedral, which he prefaced with an eloquent exposition of the devotional function of relics, which were dispersed throughout the world so that every congregation had some memorial of the saints to ignite the divine love within them. Chichester, he said, was distinguished for its collection, and the canons proposed to 'publish' their relics on the feast of St Denis (9 October), so that it should thereby come to the notice of the general public what great patronage Chichester enjoyed, and a greater veneration for the place be instilled both in those who served the church and in the rest of the faithful.[54] At Tewkesbury Abbey, where again there was no single pre-eminent cult, the feast of relics was celebrated on 2 July, and frequent miracles were recorded there in the mid thirteenth century. In 1232 a paralytic crawled to the shrine on the feast day itself, was placed 'by the relics' (*coram sanctis reliquiis*) and arose totally cured. The Tewkesbury annalist claims more than forty miracles in different years, not always on the feast itself, but during the same high summer season when the church was clearly much frequented: the dates 3, 9, 11 and 15 July are mentioned, and later miracles took place on the feast-day itself in in 1250 and 1252. New relics were always welcome, and in 1235 the monks received a generous gift from Henry Tankerton of a varied collection which had belonged to his father.[55]

Relic feasts could be moved by episcopal authority to a more convenient or attractive time. The Salisbury relic feast was shifted at least twice in order to attract a better attendance. Bishop Jocelin, in around 1150, moved it from an unnamed date to 17 September. Confirming his action, Theobald of Canterbury spoke of the 'difficulty of the season', because of which 'the people have not been able to assemble nor have the relics been properly venerated', and awarded an indulgence of forty days for the celebration. By the early fourteenth century, however, this timing was evidently deemed to be too close to the harvest. In 1320 Bishop Roger Martival mandated the subdean of the cathedral to move the feast of relics from September to the Sunday after 7 July, candidly admitting that 'both because of other feasts at the same time and involvement in agricultural tasks, which often distracts people from divine matters, and for certain other reasons, this feast cannot conveniently be celebrated in our church'. [56]

Whether or not a church possessed a single pre-eminent cult, it was normal to welcome new acquisitions and to take every opportunity to stimulate new interest in old saints. The monks of St Albans, in the century after Becket's death, actively worked to maintain the spiritual magnetism of their church. The *inventio* of St Amphibalus in 1178 has already been mentioned. In addition, St Albans managed to acquire two new saints of modest standing, the hermits Roger (disciple and associate of the recluse Christina of Markyate) and Sigar of Northawe, who were both buried in the abbey church. Matthew Paris proudly declared that 'not only the common people but the kings of England themselves frequented their sepulchres, offering there precious hangings with which they wished the tombs to be covered'.[57] All of these improvements were eclipsed by the apparently unexpected discovery of what was believed, and may just possibly in fact have been, the original mausoleum of St Alban, during building work at the east end of the abbey church in the winter of 1256/7. The bishop of Bangor granted an indulgence of thirty days to all 'who personally venerated this *inventio*' , as did the archbishop of York, who came there on pilgrimage (*causa orationis*). Such an event could not fail to attract the notice of so self-consciously pious a king as Henry III, who came in the early spring of 1257 bearing gifts to mark the occasion.[58]

Given that even the greatest of cults waxed and waned in popular appeal, it was both natural and prudent for the administrators of churches to maintain as many pilgrim attractions as possible. St Alban apart, altars of the Virgin, St Wulfstan, St Oswiu and St Amphibalus among others could be venerated at St Albans itself, and chapels, altars and images could be multiplied to meet new needs. All major churches drew their pilgrimage income from a variety of shrines and altars. Becket's pilgrims, after 1220, did not just visit the saint's new shrine, but followed a prescribed itinerary which included the place of his murder, his original tomb, his shrine and

1. The Pilgrims' Way in Kent: a scene in King's Wood. (*Diana Webb*)

2. Boughton Aluph church seen from the Pilgrims' Way. (*Diana Webb*)

3. Boughton Aluph church: a possible sheltering-place for pilgrims. (*Diana Webb*)

4. The Wilton Diptych: Richard II presented to the Virgin by St John the Baptist and two royal saints, Edmund the Martyr and Edward the Confessor. (*National Gallery*)

5. The George Inn at Glastonbury (top) and the New Inn at Gloucester: fifteenth-century investment in accommodation for pilgrims. (*NMR*)

6. The chapel on the bridge at Wakefield. (*NMR*)

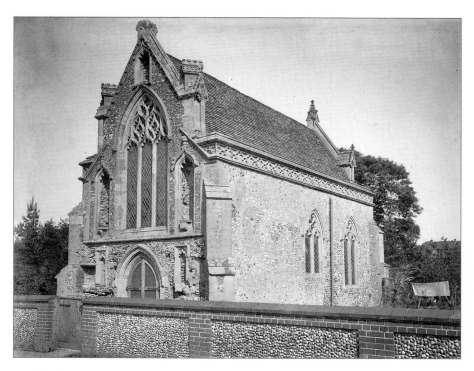

7. The Slipper Chapel at Houghton St Giles: a stopping-place for pilgrims to Walsingham. (*NMR*)

8. Four miracle windows in the Trinity Chapel, Canterbury Cathedral: pilgrims of different ages and both sexes received at Becket's shrine. (*NMR*)

9. The stairway to Becket's shrine from the south aisle of Canterbury Cathedral. (*NMR*)

10. St Thomas Cantilupe's shrine in Hereford Cathedral. (*NMR*)

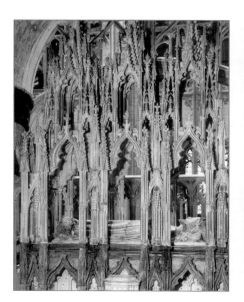

11. The tomb of Edward II in Gloucester Cathedral. (*NMR*)

12. The shrine of St Alban in St Albans Abbey (now Cathedral). The watching-loft can be clearly seen in the background. (*NMR*)

13. A selection of pilgrim souvenirs. These took the form both of badges and of ampullae which might contain holy water. (*Ashmolean Museum*)

the separate shrine of his severed scalp, every halt requiring its offering. By the fourteenth century, in obedience to the general rule that every great church had to cater for devotion to Mary, the altar and image of the Virgin in the crypt at Canterbury were an increasingly important focus for offerings and bequests, including those of royalty.[59] The pilgrim's simple linear journey to the shrine thus culminated in a tour of 'holy places' such as pilgrims to Lindisfarne had undertaken many centuries before.[60] Not only were there several shrines within major churches, in more substantial towns there was a variety of churches to be visited. At Canterbury as elsewhere, the cathedral was not the sole focus of pilgrimage; at Exeter, for example, the suburban church of St Sidwell, the priory of St Nicholas and Cowick Priory all attracted some, essentially local, custom.[61]

The patchy survival of accounts from the church of St Wilfrid at Ripon between the mid fourteenth century and the Reformation makes it possible to picture the diversity, and diversification, of sites to which it was hoped to attract offerings. Offerings were recorded on major feast days at several places in the church: St Wilfrid's head (which as we saw earlier was separately enshrined by Archbishop Gray in 1223); his original tomb; an altar of St William of York; and in the still surviving pre-conquest crypt, popularly called 'the Cruddes', where an aperture known as 'St William's needle' is to be found. The principal collections were taken during the three days of the summer fair; on Ascension Day; at the celebration of St Wilfrid's Nativity in early August; and during the winter fair, which was held around the feast of the saint's deposition (12 October). In addition there were collecting-boxes permanently sited around the church. In 1354–55 the compiler of the fabric roll recorded that these had yielded a total of £8 0s. 8d., apologetically noting that it was 'so much', because they had not been opened for two years. Normally, they were opened twice a year, at the feast of St Mark (25 April) and at Michaelmas (29 September), and they seem to have multiplied during the fifteenth century. There were some at the east end and some in the body of the church. In 1410–11 the chamberlain's accounts recorded amounts from boxes by the head-shrine, by the tomb, by the altar of St William, and in the crypt; in the body of the church there were *pixides* by images of the Virgin, of the crucifixion and of St Wilfrid himself. By 1472, in addition to those already mentioned, there were boxes on both the north and south sides of the saint's tomb, one by the image of the Holy Trinity and St Leo in the nave, another by the image of St Sitha, also in the nave, a *pix* of St Wilfrid at the west door, and several on the town bridges, most notably one which bore the name of St Sitha on Northbridge. By this time St William was yielding nothing. The monies collected in two further boxes, respectively red and white in colour, which stood 'at the feet of St Wilfrid '(presumably where his body was enshrined) and in front of the oratory of the Holy Trinity, had been generously assigned by the residentiary canons to the fabric of the church. By 1502–3 there were yet more images, of St Ninian, St Brigid, St Roche and King Henry VI. This account is by no means exhaustive.[62]

In addition to the development of a variety of focusses of devotion within a given church, the clergy often stimulated (or responded to) the public appetite for contact with the holy, and their own need to keep up with new trends in piety, by developing secondary or subsidiary shrines else-where. These might be dependencies which either provided additional centres for one or more of the cults domiciled in the mother church or nurtured an original local cult. For the community of St Albans, the church which marked the supposed place of martyrdom of St Amphibalus and his companions at Redburn represented one type and the distant priory of Tynemouth with its cult of St Oswiu another. There was nothing inherently new about this tactic. In the eleventh century the abbots of St Augustine's Abbey at Canterbury kept St Mildred's original burial-place on Thanet alive as a secondary shrine, and the abbots of Ramsey developed St Ives to take advantage of the reputation of the healing spring there. St Cuthbert did miracles on Farne Island as well as at Durham itself in the twelfth century and his tenth-century sojourn at Chester-le-Street was not forgotten: it was recalled in the wording of a papal indulgence to the church of St Mary the Virgin there in 1372.[63]

Multiple cult centres could thus arise from a variety of causes, including the dispersal of relics or the exploitation of different associations with a saint. They were not invariably under the control of the saint's major shrine, if he or she had one. At a very early period St Oswald of Northumbria was venerated at a number of places associated with his life, his death and the parts of his dismembered body, although Durham's possession of his head, which had previously been interred at Lindisfarne, gave it a major claim on him. The principal shrine of the Mercian hermit St Guthlac (d. 714) was at his burial place at Crowland Abbey in the fens, but he was also remem-bered at Repton, where he had originally been a monk; according to Thomas Cromwell's commissioners in 1536, suppliants went to Repton and placed the saint's 'bell' on their heads for the relief of headache.[64] In 1513, a Somerset testator wanted a pilgrimage performed on his behalf to 'Seynt Gollax'. As his other bequests were for west country shrines, Walsingham apart, he probably meant the shrine that had developed under the name of St Guthlac at Glastonbury Abbey, largely thanks to the coincidence that an early abbot of Glastonbury had also been called Guthlac.[65] A dedication, an altar, an image, the possession of any relic, could provide the pretext for a pilgrimage.

The *Historia Aurea* of Bury St Edmunds, compiled late in the fourteenth century, includes interesting evidence of the development of local centres of devotion to St Edmund in other parts of eastern England. Not only did Bury itself continue to attract devotees from the East Anglian region, in the 1370s the saint was doing miracles at chapels at Wainfleet near the Lincolnshire coast, which belonged to the monks of Bury and where there was a image of him, and at Lyng, a few miles from East Dereham in Norfolk, which belonged to the nuns of Thetford. The actors in these stories believed Edmund to be fully present at Wainfleet or at Lyng, as the case might be, and they directed their pilgrimages there, whether in supplication or thanksgiving, not to Bury. The Wainfleet miracles have a distinctly nautical flavour, and show Edmund at work on behalf of a constituency which included Skegness and Boston, where he rescued an unfortunate child who was precipitated into the harbour by a pig. Some fishermen of Winterton who had lost their nets called upon him jointly with Our Lady of Walsingham; sailors who had been rescued from peril near Skegness visited the chapel, presenting a ship made of wax and providing 'for a very long time' a candle to burn daily at the mass. A man of Dereham was cured of a lengthy illness when friends vowed to go to Lyng on his behalf; he set out with them but was suddenly struck dumb *en route*. His friends thought it obvious that he was not fulfilling the vow in the proper spirit and told him to take his shoes off to render himself more pleasing, which he did. Lyng supposedly drew at least one pilgrim from as far away as Kent.[66]

There were other categories of what have here been called secondary shrines. Henry I's gift of the Hand of St James to Reading Abbey effectively established it as the chief centre of Jacobean devotion in England, a point underlined when the relic cured the son of a man who had twice been to Santiago itself.[67] There were of course numerous English churches dedicated to St James, but other less illustrious saints whose major cult-centres were continental may also have developed English 'branches'. Pilgrim badges of St Hubert and St Josse, or Judocus, have been discovered at Salisbury.[68] These saints were chiefly venerated at shrines in the Ardennes and in Picardy respectively, but the provenance of the badges is uncertain and may possibly derive from English centres of their cults. If so, the badge of St Josse may have come from Winchester, where the New Minster had possessed relics of the saint since 903, while it is possible that the badge of St Hubert came from Idsworth, near the borders of Hampshire and Sussex, where the parish church is now (although not originally) dedicated to this saint and where wall-paintings of *c.* 1330, probably depicting his legend, are still to be seen.[69] If so, and if these badges were in fact acquired by inhabitants of Salisbury, they would not have made long journeys to get them.

The custodians of shrines were well aware of one another and of their promotional efforts. That awareness lies behind the commonplace miracle-story, of which several examples have already been cited, in which a certain saint succeeds in performing a miracle that another, for whatever reason, has failed to perform. Relationships between shrines were not however always competitive. Matthew Paris records that in 1242:

> on the morrow of St Michael [i.e. 30 September] the conventual church of the canons of Waltham was solemnly dedicated by William bishop of Norwich in the presence of many other venerable bishops, prelates and magnates, immediately after the [feast of[] the dedication of the church of St Paul's in London, so that pilgrims could go from the one to the other without delay. [70]

The testimony of Nicholas Wich, a monk of Worcester, at the enquiry into Thomas Cantilupe's sanctity in 1307 suggests that the relationships between the shrines of Worcester and Hereford were as much symbiotic as competitive. He knew that people all over England regarded Thomas as a saint and came to his tomb,

> because so many of these pilgrims, on their way to the tomb of the said lord Thomas, pass through the city of Worcester, that the church of Worcester annually receives ten pounds sterling in offerings as a result. Asked what these pilgrims offered in the church of Worcester that the offering could rise to this amount, he said that some gave a farthing, some a halfpenny and others a penny. [71]

Co-operation of a different kind is suggested by the discovery of a fragmentary pilgrim badge depicting St John of Beverley and St John of Bridlington together; there is other evidence that the two Yorkshire saints were venerated by the same pilgrims, but the badge is striking evidence of joint investment in the promotion of their shrines, which were only eleven miles apart. [72]

Once the pilgrim had successfully made his or her way to a shrine, there could be problems of access both physical and ideological. [73] The desirability of encouraging pilgrimage had sometimes to be balanced against other considerations. Numerous cults were based in monastic churches and in principle monastic seclusion had to be safeguarded, especially against women. St Cuthbert was supposed to have forbidden females, even young girls, to approach his shrine, and special provision might have to be made for women who wished to venerate relics or images in Carthusian or Cistercian houses. Such permissions, we may suppose, were more easily obtained by women of rank. The annalist of Cistercian Waverley recorded that Eleanor, countess of Leicester, 'a most devout lover of our house', visited the abbey in 1244 'by an indulgence of the supreme pontiff' with her husband, Simon de Montfort, and their sons, making rich offerings. [74] The custodians of Thomas Becket were old-style 'black' monks, but from the beginning they were less fussy than their counterparts at Durham. Men and women alike approached Becket's shrine exceedingly closely. The slim wife of a Flemish citizen of Canterbury found that she was unable to get her head into one of the 'windows' on the side of the shrine in order to kiss the sarcophagus; returning home with another *matrona*, her mistress, she complained that the latter, a lady of somewhat greater girth, had been able to achieve what she had not. It was not any difficulty put in her way by the monks that had obstructed her but her own sinfulness, as her mistress tactfully suggested. The madman Edward of Selling, who was amply built, had a completely different experience. He thought he saw a ghost near the shrine, and promptly 'flew to the martyr', inserting himself through one of the holes in the side of the tomb and lying with his feet by the saint's head, his head by his feet. Observing this remarkable performance, the monks pondered how they were going to get him out. They thought they would have to demolish the entire structure, but Edward suddenly emerged unaided from one of the holes. He could not subsequently manage even to get his bare shoulders into the aperture, and experiments with a slender youth proved equally fruitless. [75] The gender difference between these stories has more to do with the degree of athleticism that could be attributed to a man than with the respective moral status of males and females.

Ease of access to shrines, for pilgrims of both sexes, varied. At Winchester, since the tenth century a house of Benedictine monks, the monks' choir became more and more completely enclosed in the course of the thirteenth and fourteenth centuries. Until the fifteenth century, the shrine of St Swithun probably stood on a feretory platform behind the high altar, with a 'Holy Hole' beneath it, which permitted pilgrims to crawl from the retrochoir underneath the reliquary and thus establish closer contact with the saint. In the fourteenth century the 'Holy Hole' was remodelled and a screen built across the back of the feretory platform, which would have made the shrines on it completely invisible to anyone outside the choir. A decision to make St Swithun more accessible to pilgrims seems to have been taken in the fifteenth century, when his shrine was moved into the centre of the retrochoir, where its modern replacement now stands. [76] It was not unknown for visitations to reveal that access to shrines had been impaired by some ill-conceived alteration. Archbishop Greenfield of York complained in 1314 that on a visitation to Beverley he had been impeded in his approach to the tomb of St John by a stone altar which had been erected at its head. This was to be removed and no such obstruction to be permitted in future which might prevent 'the faithful of Christ, flocking to that church, to be able to approach the tomb freely, as they used to do'. [77] The proprietors of shrines were obliged to have all these considerations, access, the beauty of holiness and monastic decorum, constantly in mind.

The activities of the priors and abbots of St Albans are particularly well recorded in this respect.[78] Structural alterations to the fabric of the church, as well as occasional disasters, sometimes necessitated the shifting of shrines, and it might also be necessary to balance the desire for new objects of devotion against the claims of old ones which had an established place in the affections of the faithful. Under Abbot William Trumpington (1214–35), the prior, Walter of Colchester, obtained both a new crucifix and a new image of Our Lady for the church, but their predecessors were moved to the north side of the church 'for the edification of the laity and all those who came there' and to avoid any suggestion that the 'good things' which the image of the Virgin had done were being slighted.[79] Improvements were also carried out at the dependent priory of Tynemouth. Thomas de la Mare, as prior of Tynemouth before he became abbot of St Albans in 1349, spent a great deal on a new arrangement which had the effect of removing pilgrims from excessive proximity to the monks:

> he moved the shrine of the holy king and martyr Oswiu [which had been] joined to the high altar, from that place, and had it magnificently set up in the place where it now is, so that visitors (*adveniantes*) could more peacefully, freely and easily continue their devotions around the martyr.[80]

When he became abbot of St Albans, Thomas decorated the shrine of St Alban and moved the shrine of St Amphibalus from the excessively lowly position behind the altar of St Hugh into which it had had to be moved when part of the roof fell on it in 1323. This shrine had been several times relocated since the relics had first been brought into the abbey church in 1178. The altar of St Hugh housed the abbey's subsidiary relic collection and stood to the north of the shrine of St Alban, behind the high altar, in the space now known as the feretory; the altar of St Wulfstan, later known as that of the Salutation, corresponded to it on the south. Early in the fifteenth century, the 'watching loft' was built on the north side of the feretory. This was a two-storey wooden structure, from the upper chamber of which the *feretarius* could keep an eye on the shrine and the accompanying altars. The watching lofts at St Albans and in what is now Christ Church cathedral at Oxford, once the priory of St Frideswide, are the only two examples surviving in England, although watching chambers as part of the architectural fabric are also known. Later still Abbot William Wallingford (1476–84) built a high stone screen between the high altar and the feretory at St Albans, thus completely shutting off pilgrim activity from the presbytery.

At Durham, according to an engaging account composed at the end of the sixteenth century, the master of the feretory himself was not in personal attendance on the shrine, but was summoned by his clerk 'when any man of honor or worshippe weere disposed to make there praiers to god and to Saincte Cuthberte' and desired to see the shrine. The master or keeper then brought the keys and supervised the drawing of the curtains around the shrine and the unlocking of it to display the relics:

> And when they had maid there praiers & dyd offer any thing to it, if yt weare either gould sylver or Jewels streighte way it was hounge on ye shrine. And if yt weyre any other thing, as unicorne horne, Eliphant tooth or such like thinge then yt was howng within the fereture at ye end of ye shrine, and when they had maid there praiers, the clarke did let down ye cover thereof & did locke yt at every corner. [81]

Humbler pilgrims left humbler ex votos. Pilgrimage was not an activity which could totally obliterate class or economic distinctions.

The brief of the *feretarius* presumably covered all kinds of possible malpractice – including damage to the shrine itself. The practice of chipping (or even biting) pieces off shrines seems to be best documented in the earlier middle ages. Such fragments might be added to relic collections, used as portable talismans, or steeped in water to produce home remedies. The provision of purpose-made souvenirs may have diminished the need or the temptation to commit this sort of outrage, but it provided opportunities for others. Benedict of Peterborough relates an instance of theft of St Thomas's water in the days before the lead or tin ampullae were manufactured, when pilgrims took the water home in wooden vessels (*pyxides*).[82] Later, an Irish boy who came to Canterbury was given alms by the keepers of the shrine so that he could buy one of the ampullae. By chance he found one on the ground near the workshop (*ergasterium*), dropped by the seller, and picked it up, retaining the farthing he had been given. He filled the ampulla with the holy water, and, having hung it round his neck, returned to his companions who were awaiting him in the cemetery; but a great swelling promptly appeared on his neck and he was only cured when he reasoned that 'the martyr is acting for the merchant', and returned to the shrine, where he offered up the stolen phial.[83] Wax was also on sale at the shrine, which like the ampullae could prove to have miraculous qualities. This could be made either into candles or into the models of body parts (or of ships and anchors) which were frequently offered as ex votos.

Pilgrims were not usually left to their own devices but guided around the shrines in a prescribed course, certainly in a major church, while what they saw was expounded to them orally. Erasmus memorably satirised the guidance visitors received at Walsingham and Canterbury early in the sixteenth century.[84] At Walsingham, his attention was specially directed to inscriptions which, as he ironically conceded, incontrovertibly proved the authenticity of the relics they described. He was, of course, considerably more literate than most shrine personnel: he himself had set up a Greek epitaph at Walsingham which caused considerable consternation among the inmates, who had no idea what language it was written in and therefore called it Hebrew.[85] Pilgrims of course at all times included clergy and other literate persons, and specific provision was sometimes made for them, such as the *tabulae*, of which there is a surviving example from Glastonbury, now in the Bodleian Library. This was a large manuscript of six leaves, written in the late fourteenth century and mounted on a wooden frame, which recounted the history of the abbey from the time of Joseph of Arimathea. It is supposed that this was a hung from a pillar for the edification of visitors. [86] Also set up on a pillar, and dating from the late fourteenth or fifteenth century, was a brass plate inscribed with a rather shorter summary of the same history.[87] Not all the *tabulae* were so late in date: there seems to have been a record of St Edmund's translation similarly set up at Bury late in the eleventh century.[88] The ballad in praise of Our Lady of Walsingham which was printed by Richard Pynson, probably in the 1490s, must have fulfilled a similar function. The reader is instructed to 'beholde and se', which suggests that the ballad was intended for reading or recitation at the shrine itself. It summarises the history of Walsingham, and affirms that many sick have been cured there by 'Our Ladyes might' , the dead raised, and all sorts of other afflictions remedied. 'Every pylgryme' is urged to 'gyve your attendaunce, Our Lady here to serve with humble affecyon' , and the 'lettered' are invited to seek further information about the history of the site. The ballad ends with a rhapsody on the happy lot of England where 'newe Nazareth' has been built.[89]

Much of the publicity given to feast-days and pilgrimages was necessarily oral, although a foundation document such as an indulgence might be at the root of it. William Worcester noted in 1477–78 that a (bogus) indulgence of Pope Gregory VII was posted up at St Michael's Mount, with an exhortation to visiting clergy to publicise it:

> that your charges and subjects may be the more keenly enlivened to the greater encouragement of devotion and by the making of pilgrimages to obtain the aforesaid gracious gifts and indulgences may with the greater glory resort to this place. [90]

In the later fifteenth century the printed indulgence, like the woodcut image of a saint, became a possible means of publicity.[91] Badges worn by returning

A brass plate which summarised the history of Glastonbury Abbey for the benefit of visitors and pilgrims.

pilgrims may themselves have acted as advertisements and clearly quickly became recognisable. These could easily be broken or melted down, but the devotional cards which were also produced for sale were yet more ephemeral: one example survives from Bromholm Priory in Norfolk, the home of a famous Holy Rood.[92]

The control systems in operation at shrines had multiple purposes: on the one hand, to inform and to enhance the pilgrim's sense of wonder; on the other, to maintain security and ensure that the proper offerings were made. They were not, perhaps, completely watertight. In the prologue to the continuation of *The Canterbury Tales* known as *The Tale of Beryn*, the Miller and his cronies need both watching and instruction, for among their other misdemeanours they wander around the cathedral freely misinterpreting the stained glass windows according to their liking. They are called back to order by the Knight, and kneel with the others to kiss the relics exhibited to them and to pray as best they can, but their mischief-making is not finished yet. Having seen all the holy places and heard divine service, the members of the company go forth to dinner and buy themselves souvenirs (it is not made clear where) so that people back home may know where they have been. Somehow the Miller manages to secrete a large quantity of Canterbury tokens in his shirt, and then divides them with the Pardoner, but the Summoner sees them and demands a half-share. We are bound to suppose that they had a market in mind.[93] Real-life pilgrims who resembled the Miller were fit objects of criticism, which as we shall see they duly received.

There was an 'upper crust' of devotions which received particular attention from the authorities, lay and ecclesiastical. Popes and bishops alike granted indulgences to reward pilgrims to Thomas of Canterbury, Edward the Confessor at Westminster or Thomas Cantilupe at Hereford. Pilgrimage to the shrine of Osmund at Salisbury in 1457 could indirectly help to pay for the canonisation itself: in granting an indulgence to mark the translation of the relics, the pope stipulated that all the alms rendered at the tomb were to be converted to the adornment of the place and the relics. When that had been fittingly done, the surplus could go to pay the creditors who had lent money for the canonisation.[94] In granting indulgences to churches great and small, popes and bishops rarely acted on their own unsolicited initiative, but responded to petition. Everywhere, a variety of interests were involved, those of patrons as well as of others who stood to profit from a pilgrimage in a particular locality, and some relatively small churches and local cults in fact had backing from distinguished people. Many petitions came to the pope from bishops and kings and other powerful patrons. Between them, these men (and a few women) exercised a range of powers which could enhance, and perhaps sometimes damage, the prospects of English shrines.

An important part was naturally played by the kings of England, who might be influenced by personal piety, an awareness of their public duty to the major churches of the kingdom or a desire to promote particular cults associated with the monarchy itself. The mixture varied somewhat with the individual monarch, but a certain minimum involvement with the public cult of the saints was unavoidable. Royal attendance at the translations of saints old and new and at the consecrations of rebuilt or restored cathedrals enhanced the character of these events as state occasions. Some earlier medieval accounts of the translations of saints convey the impression that, for all the splendour and the impressive guest-list which might accompany them, they remained fraught with a degree of peril, an explosive miraculous potentiality which might turn to the good or the ill of the participants depending on the saint's will. It would be rash to say that this element was entirely lacking by the thirteenth century, but some chronicle descriptions of the translation of Becket in 1220 or of Henry III's second translation of the Confessor in 1269 suggest greater awe in face of the pomp and circumstance than of the relics. Of Becket's translation the Waverley annalist declared that 'such a great assembly of persons of both sexes from different parts of the earth came together that, so it is said, never in any previous time had there been so large a number of people gathered together in one place in England'. The archbishop of Canterbury, Stephen Langton, gave notice of the translation two years in advance and demonstrated the will to provide for all the needs of those who attended, even if he was not able actually to do so.[95] The Dunstable Annals, briefly describing the ceremonial, added that

> such was the banquet in food and drink, and vessels of gold and silver, and precious garments, that we read of nothing like it since the time of King Ahasuerus. It is furthermore not to be omitted that the archbishop constructed a befitting palace for this banquet, such as we think has not been seen since the time of Solomon. [96]

Bartholomew Cotton of Norwich succinctly reported: 'Never was so well-attended or glorious a translation celebrated on this earth, where so many venerable persons were present from so many different nations.'[97]

The saints did not merely receive honour themselves, they did honour to the nation. Our Lady of Walsingham did so; so did relic acquisitions such as that of the Holy Blood, which Henry III received as a gift and in 1247 installed with tremendous solemnity in Westminster Abbey. In Matthew Paris's words, it 'made England illustrous'. The occasion gave Henry III 'the opportunity to create his own festival of relics'. He bore the relic personally, on foot and in humble dress, and the bishop of Norwich, Walter Suffield, underlined the significance of the event in his sermon: Louis IX of France had the Cross of Christ, now 'the king of England,who was known to be the most Christian of all Christian princes', had received this gift 'in order that it might be reverenced more in England than in Syria, which was now nearly desolate; for in England, as the world knew, faith and holiness flourished more than in any other country throughout the world ...' The occurrence of a miracle further improved the occasion, and the king commissioned Matthew to write an account.[98]

At Westminster the king, however humble a guise he assumed, was the patron of the shrine, and he took vigorous measures to promote it. The timing of Becket's translation in early July had helped to establish it as one the major pilgrimage occasions of the English year. The timing of the feast of Edward the Confessor's translation in late October was less propitious, but that did not stop Henry III from using arbitrary powers to try to enforce attendance. In October 1248 the king not only instituted a fifteen-day fair at Westminster to mark the feast of the translation, he also banned all other fairs which customarily took place anywhere in England at the same time, including those of Ely, and all other markets in London, indoor or out. As Matthew Paris reported, the result was as intended:

> innumerable people flocked there, as to the busiest of fairs, and there the translation of the blessed Edward and of the Blood of Christ was venerated to an amazing extent (*inopinabiliter*) by the people who had been attracted and assembled there.

However, the traders were subjected to considerable inconvenience as a consequence, given the uncertainties of the October weather: they had no roof over them and not only their feet but their goods were soiled by mud and rain. Matthew also reported the remonstrances of the bishop of Ely. In 1252 the Londoners were again compelled to attend the Westminster fairs; there were such crowds as had never been seen, but the weather was appalling.[99] Despite Matthew's hyperbole, it seems unlikely that the Confessor's shrine, while it certainly attracted pilgrims, was ever among the most popular in England.

Two hundred years later, Henry VI was also eager to encourage visits to his own foundation at Eton College. In 1442 he obtained a plenary indulgence, valid for his lifetime only, for visitors to the chapel at the Feast of the Assumption. This was however very much a joint undertaking with the pope, for devotees were to be encouraged to give alms for the defence of Christendom against the Turk, and three-quarters of the proceeds, deposited in a locked collecting-box in the chapel, were to be remitted to the papal collector. Pilgrims to Our Lady of Eton were able to obtain distinctive souvenir badges.[100] A few years later Henry was displaying a more general concern for popular devotion. In the first year of his pontificate (1448–49) Nicholas V licensed the king to authorise fit persons to carry out the translation of relics within his kingdom whenever and wherever he deemed it expedient. Henry had recently

> caused it to be signified to the pope that there are kept in divers churches, monasteries and places relics of saints which alike on account of the distance of the places and the negligence of their keepers are unknown to the faithful and that, if they were shown to the people and placed in apt and honest places, the devotion of the faithful would increase and the king would thereby be greatly rejoiced. [101]

What specific results this pious initiative had is unclear.

Only a few years before the destruction of the shrines of England, Sir Thomas More remarked that pilgrimages were 'for the most parte in the handes of suche relygyous persones or suche pore paryshys as bere no greate rule in the convocacyons.' The bishops were not, in his view, the ones who were making the profit out of shrines: he argued therefore that, had they perceived criticisms of profiteering and imposture in the management of them to be justified, they would have had no great incentive to refrain from action. Not only did they not do so, they were themselves pilgrims and made 'large offrynges'.[102] They also, as he might have remarked, granted indulgences. There can in fact be little doubt that many shrines, including cathedral shrines, were monastic and many belonged to parish churches. Even where cathedrals were served by secular canons, the proceeds of shrines usually went to those who had the management of the fabric. Worcester, where the bishop claimed half the offerings, was an exception.[103]

More was, however, tacitly ignoring another vital aspect of the bishops' collective role. The clergy taken as a whole had a professional interest, both spiritual and material, in miracles and the cult of saints. Pilgrimage might occasionally present its vexatious aspects, whether these took the form of idolatry, vagrancy, crowd trouble or crime, but in its normal operations it formed an important bond between the Christian people, great and small, and the church. In common with the king, the pope and other great men, the bishops had the responsibility of upholding the order, social and divine, of which the church and its accumulated array of devotional practices was an integral part. When Henry VII died in 1509 it would have been hard to foresee that within a generation the monarchy would defect from this holy alliance.

5

Images and Indulgences

Especially after 1300, images proved an effective way of attracting devotion to both primary and secondary shrines. In March 1405 Bishop Mascall of Hereford awarded an indulgence to those who devoutly visited the church of Llanwarne, between Hereford and Monmouth, or otherwise sent or assigned a free-will offering from the goods God had given them 'out of devotion to the glorious confessor John of Bridlington in whose honour an image of the saint is erected ...'[1] This was a long way from the East Riding, and prompt work, as John had only been canonised in 1401. Bequests for lights to burn before favourite images were very common in wills. A Bedfordshire man who made his will in November 1505 left two bushels of barley for 'the sustentation of St Thos of Canterbury the whych fygure stondyth in the chancell' of the church of Marston Moretaine.[2] The setting-up of such images was of course a by-product of the wider cult, and may sometimes have commemorated a pilgrimage to the principal shrine by priest or parishioners.

The late medieval propensity to venerate images found favour and encouragement from popes and bishops alike, who granted indulgences to their devotees. Even more frequented than images of the saints were those of the crucified Christ and of the Virgin. The resultant proliferation in turn sparked a reaction. Fears, which sprang from an ancient and respectable tradition, that such devotion might lead to idolatry were in fact voiced by a few bishops early in the fourteenth century when the proliferation was becoming marked, but later tended to become a hallmark of heretical belief. Meanwhile papal indulgences, for the veneration of images as well as for other purposes, became increasingly numerous, reaching a high point, during the Great Schism, under Boniface IX (1389–1404), whose notorious generosity was one symptom of his quest for the support of Christendom. His willingness to grant plenary indulgences helped to enhance the watchfulness with which churches checked on one another: in 1402, the chronicler Thomas Walsingham reported that the monks of Ely, desiring to be equal to those of Norwich and Bury, who had obtained the grant of full remission at certain festivals, took steps to obtain a similar concession.[3]

Those who granted indulgences hoped to encourage pilgrimage and offerings for the benefit both of the pilgrim's soul and the shrine's prosperity both spiritual and material. Indulgences have an indispensable value for the student of pilgrimage but they also have many shortcomings. For one thing, it is clear that popes and bishops alike granted many indulgences of which we have no record; for another, no indulgence can tell us, in the absence of other evidence, how many people it actually attracted.[4] The mere grant is pilgrimage seen from the supply side. Even if it was a response to perceived demand, the demand may have been coming from the proprietors of shrines rather than from the 'general public'.

Other cautions are necessary. Indulgences were granted for many purposes other than pilgrimage. English bishops granted them, for example, for the saying of prayers for the departed or for the peace of the kingdom (not least in the later years of Edward II's reign), and for benefactions to roads, bridges, poor persons and other good causes. They also commonly awarded indulgences on the occasion of their consecration of a new or rebuilt church or of altars within a church. The register of John le Romeyn of York (1286–96) groups *pro forma* indulgences under headings such as 'indulgences for those who give charitable assistance from their goods to the shrine of a certain saint'.[5] Many indulgences which ostensibly encouraged resort to a church added the stipulation that the beneficiary should make some contribution to a current building or restoration programme. This was, after all, only to specify the purpose of the offering the pilgrim was anyway expected to make. The indulgence was often available also to people who sent their contribution instead of going to the church in person. There was nothing very extraordinary about this either: crusading indulgences had long been available to mere contributors. For present purposes, however, it has to be remembered that the more obviously an indulgence was a fund-raising device available on such terms, the more limited is its usefulness as evidence for actual pilgrimage.

Two indulgences granted by fourteenth-century bishops of Hereford, in themselves in no way remarkable or untypical, may be quoted here in illustration of the way that bodily pilgrimage was seen as embedded in a setting of other pious works. In 1326 Adam Orleton awarded the modest quantity of ten days' remission to those who should go *causa devotionis* to the chapel of Aldersworth in the neighbouring diocese of Worcester

> and there devoutly salute the aforesaid glorious Virgin and render assistance to her illumination at the high altar newly added to that chapel, and also piously recite the Lord's Prayer and the Angelic Salutation for the peace of Holy Church and the tranquillity of the kingdom of England.[6]

The significance of the year needs little underlining: 1326 saw the last great crisis of Edward II's reign.

On 21 November 1348 John Trillek granted an indulgence on the occasion of his consecration of altars at Vowchurch:

God who is glorious in his saints has appointed them to be fitly venerated on earth to his own glory, so that those whom he magnificently glorifies in heaven the world should cultivate to its profit and benefit. We therefore believe we are performing a duty pleasing to God and salvific to men in seeking to have places dedicated to the names of saints visited and frequented for the purpose of their appropriate veneration, and we take pious care to ecourage the devotion of the faithful to this end with alluring gifts (*allectiva munera*) of indulgences. Since therefore on 21 November in the year of Our Lord's incarnation 1348 we dedicated the high altar of the parish church of Vowchurch in the name of God, the glorious Virgin God's mother Mary, and the saints and martyrs John the Baptist, Bartholomew the Apostle, Laurence and King Ethelbert; and on the north side of the nave of the church an altar in the name of the same glorious Virgin Mary and of saints Blaise, martyr and bishop, and Martin, Gregory and Thomas, confessors and bishops, and also an altar in the southern part of the church, in the names of Mary Magdalen, Agnes, Cecilia, Catherine and Margaret, virgins and martyrs, and Milburga, virgin, trusting in the mercy of God and the merits and mercy of the aforesaid, we hereby concede to all those subject to our diocese and others whose diocesans shall ratify this our indulgence who, truly sorry for their sins, penitent and confessed, shall on each of the feast days of the said saints visit this church in honour of God and them or shall give some charitable assistance from the goods God has conferred upon them towards the lighting, vestments or other ornaments of the church, or shall assist at the establishment or painting of images in memory of them; for each of the festivals, visits or gifts for these causes, forty days of indulgence in perpetuity.[7]

This indulgence commemorated the bishop's own act of consecration. The wording of other types tended to recapitulate what the grantor had been told, and there can be little doubt that petitioners often made stereotyped claims that the church, chapel or altar for which the indulgence was being sought was resorted to by 'a great multitude' and that 'many miracles' had occurred there. What value, if any, can be attached to these declarations? Modern historians usually assume that medieval estimates of the numbers involved in battles or of the dead in epidemics arise from a non-statistical mentality. It is not so much a matter of misrepresentation as of rhetorical convention: numbers convey a sense of magnitude rather than precise information. In the present case, there were obvious advantages in vagueness. A saint was routinely 'radiant with many miracles' (*multis miraculis coruscat*); rarely if ever was there any more detail, let alone statistical exactitude. It is doubtful whether we can or should take such statements literally when they are all we have. However we choose to interpret the experiences recorded in the miracle stories of Becket or Frideswide, Wulfstan or

Cantilupe, they at least give names, ages and places of origin and describe physical and mental conditions and other problems which real individuals unquestionably suffered. Matthew Paris's reference to the twenty selected and attested miracles that were examined at Lincoln in the aftermath of Grosseteste's death edges into an adjacent territory.[8] The formulaic statements made both by chroniclers and by petitioners for the grant of indulgences, to the effect that a shrine attracted large numbers of people and witnessed many miracles, may or may not conceal a comparable reality.

With all the provisos that have just been made, indulgences have their value as a very rough guide to the landscape of shrine promotion. They certainly serve as a reminder of the multiplicity of small-scale cults and would-be cults which clamoured for the attention, and served the needs, of local populations. Among these were a host of local centres of the two cults, or more precisely the two cult-categories, which expanded rapidly in England as in Europe in the later middle ages: that of the Virgin, and those centred on the Passion and the person of Christ. Both categories demonstrated not only the power of multiplication but the power of images.

Almost all Christ-centred cults were focussed on the Passion, some on the Cross and some on the blood of Christ. Relics of Christ's blood originally tended to mean the blood actually shed at the Passion, but a sacramental version came into being, thanks largely to the greater centrality of the eucharist in the religious life of all Christians which resulted from the requirement of the Fourth Lateran Council that every adult Christian should take communion at least once annually. The English royal family acquired two notable Holy Blood relics of the older type in the thirteenth century. The first was the gift to Henry III which, as already noted, he enshrined in Westminster Abbey in 1247. The king's brother, Richard, earl of Cornwall, then acquired a relic of the Blood which had been personally authenticated by Pope Urban IV and which his son Edmund conveyed to Richard's foundation, Hailes Abbey in Gloucestershire, in 1270.[9] Although there is very little direct evidence for early pilgrimage to Hailes, its popularity mounted in the fifteenth century, with the aid of several papal grants of indulgence, and is well attested by wills and other evidence. John XXIII's grant in 1413, of ten years and ten quarantines at Whitsun and seven years and seven quarantines at Corpus Christi, was intended as a remedy for the state of dilapidation and indebtedness in which the house allegedly found itself as a result of the mismanagement of the late abbot. The pope conferred upon the abbot a privilege which was being granted with increasing frequency at this period, of hearing, or appointing confessors to hear, the confessions of pilgrims and granting absolution except in cases reserved to the apostolic see.[10] In 1487 Innocent VIII reaffirmed and amplified

John XXIII's grant of powers of confession and absolution, adding that the abbot or his appointees might

> administer the eucharist to all pilgrims to the church, as often as shall be expedient and even at Easter, without prejudice to anyone and saving always the right of the parish church and of any other, and may bless the beads of such pilgrims as touch them against the place where the blood is preserved. [11]

The papacy thus endorsed the abbey's strategy of offering to the pilgrim a complete eucharistic devotion.

Of Holy Blood shrines of the newer, sacramental, type, perhaps the best-known, at least to dwellers on the eastern side of the British Isles, was Wilsnack in north Germany. The pilgrimage which developed at Wilsnack late in the fourteenth century was focussed on three hosts which had miraculously escaped destruction in a fire. They reputedly exuded drops of blood, and English pilgrims tended to refer to the Holy Blood of Wilsnack. Margery Kempe (who also went to Hailes) went there late in life, and in 1451 two Scottish pilgrims proposed to visit both Hailes and Wilsnack, as well as Canterbury and Walsingham. Another Scottish pilgrim went on to Wilsnack after receiving a cure at Canterbury and in 1520 a mariner of Hull left money to the shrine. Pilgrim-badge finds (one of the most notable at Kings Lynn) amplify the picture.[12] No English shrine of the same type seems to have achieved like prominence, but devotion to the crucifix was omnipresent.

Relics of the True Cross were of course innumerable and familiar, and not new in the later middle ages, although in the wake of the crusades, and after the sack of Constantinople in 1204, fresh relics of the Passion flowed into western Europe from the east, and associated pilgrimage devotions accordingly rose and fell. Some were centred on miraculous crucifixes (often crucifixes which contained portions of the True Cross or other relics). The Rood of Bromholm in Norfolk was a pre-eminent example, which, as many chroniclers reported, began to do miracles in 1223 and received the enthusiastic patronage of Henry III at least down to the 1250s. It still had a public around 1400, although it no longer attracted royal interest. A papal indulgence in 1401, which permitted the prior to arrange for the hearing of pilgrims' confessions, credited the Rood with remarkable powers: sometimes certain people, their sins, it was presumed, being the cause, were 'unable perfectly to look upon the said piece, thereby sometimes incurring infirmities of divers sorts'. In 1415–16 the cellarer received a total of £32 4s. 5d. in oblations to the Rood.[13] Already before this date other crucifixes had overtaken Bromholm in fame. The cross at the north door of St Paul's in London was attracting the opprobrium of the Lollards in the late fourteenth century, as the chronicler Thomas Walsingham reported. Miracles which Walsingham interpreted as a riposte to these heretics occurred at a cross erected on the public highway at Wymondham.[14] Just to the east of London, not far off the road to Canterbury and Dover, the Rood at Bermondsey was another major attraction which was also denounced by Lollards.[15]

Occasionally there is reference not only to the miraculous powers of crucifixes but to their aesthetic and affective properties. During the rule of Abbot Michael of St Albans (1335–49), the monks discovered that there was a pilgrimage going on in their own backyard, to a crucifix newly erected in the cemetery of the parish church of St Michael. The crucifix was of marvellous beauty, carved by Master Roger Stoke, *horologiarius*, for his own intended burial place. The monks were far from querying the authenticity of the miracles that it provoked but, as the offerings grew, so contention arose between the abbey infirmarer, to whom the church was appropriated, and the vicar of St Michael's, William Puff. The case was heard in the abbey consistory and, unsurprisingly, William Puff was found guilty of withholding offerings to the amount of 40 shillings, which he had to restore to the infirmarer. The court also ordered him to pay costs.[16]

Another beautiful new crucifix, acquired by the monks of Meaux Abbey in Yorkshire under Hugh, the fifteenth abbot (1339–49), caused problems of a different kind. Like the St Albans example it was carved in great devotion of spirit, and, more remarkably, the artist worked from the nude model. The Almighty deigned to work miracles 'ceaselessly' through this crucifix, and the monks thought that 'the general devotion would be augmented' to the profit of the monastery if women had access to it. They therefore obtained permission from the abbot of Cîteaux to allow women to enter the church to venerate it. They soon regretted it. As true devotion cooled, the women whose offerings they had been so keen to encourage, taking advantage of their unwonted licence to enter the monastery, indulged their proverbial feminine curiosity, poking around the place and imposing burdens of hospitality which negated any hopes of making a profit out of them.[17] It is especially notable here that neither at St Albans nor at Meaux did the monks have qualms about the propriety of the devotion as such.

Papal indulgences afford additional evidence for local cults of Christ and the Cross. In December 1397 the Benedictines of St Mary at Monmouth obtained an indulgence for the veneration of a collection of relics of the Cross, the Holy Sepulchre, and the winding-sheet (*sindone*) and other garments of Our Lord.[18] In 1398 Boxley Abbey in Kent received an indulgence for the two principal feasts of the Cross, the 'Invention' in May and the 'Exaltation' in September, but there is as yet no mention of the miracles which in the early sixteenth century would make the Boxley Rood famous, not to say infamous. There may have been some local rivalry here from the church of Holy Cross at Bearsted near Maidstone, which was little more than three miles from Boxley and in 1425 claimed to possess an *ymago* of the Crucifixion and to attract 'great multitudes' on those same two feasts. [19] The church of SS. Peter and Paul at Drypool, now part of Hull, was in 1428 in need of repair and decoration, but it had in its favour that 'a great multitude' resorted to it on the feast of the Exaltation in September, 'out of devotion to a certain crucifix'.[20] The parish church of Stanton Harcourt in Oxfordshire similarly claimed in 1442 to attract a great multitude 'out of veneration and honour for Holy Cross'. [21] The chapel of St Laurence in the Augustinian priory of Markby in Lincolnshire contained a cross made of the 'true wood' of Our Lord's own cross which, it was said in 1475, attracted 'huge devotion' from the people of the locality; God had worked many miracles there in time past and still did, 'wherefore no small number of people flocks to that place'.[22] Other churches sought indulgences on the Feasts of the Cross without apparently claiming any special popularity or the possession of a wonder-working image, and there have been numerous finds, in London and elsewhere, of pilgrim badges of uncertain provenance which probably commemorate churchyard crosses or roods in parish churches, devotion to which has left no name and no other trace. [23]

Marian sites were innumerable and most of them were focussed on an image. Walsingham grew from its twelfth-century beginnings, slowly at first, to become the most important national shrine of England after or alongside Canterbury, as an abundance of late medieval testamentary bequests, among other evidence, reveals. Here the chief image of the Virgin, together with radiating shrines such as that of Our Lady's Milk, constituted an itinerary, described by Erasmus with gentle satire towards the end of its existence, comparable to that which the pilgrim to Canterbury followed within the cathedral. [24] Other Marian centres ministered to a more localised clientele. The church of Woolpit in Suffolk, which belonged to the monks of Bury St Edmunds, became a subsidiary centre of Marian devotion in East Anglia. A vicarage was established in the church early in the thirteenth century by the bishop of Norwich, who directed his official to value its revenues and assign the altarage and free land to the vicar. His income was to be made up to 10 marks *per annum* by the monks of Bury, who were to receive the tithes on crops and 'the offerings of pilgrims'. This was a standard division, although different solutions were found in different places to what could be a contentious issue when offerings became especially profitable, as they must have done at Woolpit.[25] The church was rebuilt handsomely in the middle of the fifteenth century, when it received many benefactions, and it became sufficiently famous to be made the butt of a satirical Lollard who referred to 'Our Lady of Foulpit'. [26] The proximity of Walsingham may have been a spur to its development. Henry VI is known to have visited it in both 1448 and 1449 from Bury, and in 1474 Lady Elizabeth Andrews left one diamond ring to Walsingham and another to Woolpit.[27]

Another local Marian shrine of some fame was the chapel of St Mary at Cleeve Abbey, near the Somerset coast. In 1320 Bishop Drokensford of Bath and Wells confirmed that the monks were to receive the oblations from the chapel as they had from its foundation. Here too there was fifteenth-century rebuilding, but the circumstances were dramatic and miraculous. When the chapel was virtually destroyed by a landslip, the image of the Virgin was found to be undamaged. The chapel was rebuilt further inland and consecrated in 1452, and in 1466 the abbey received the grant of a weekly market and two fairs to raise money for rebuilding and repair. The chapel 'soon became for the people of West Somerset a place for public ceremony, probate business and solemn oath-taking, but principally a place of pilgrimage'. [28]

Grants of indulgence and a great deal of other evidence testify to the existence of innumerable other local Marian shrines. These were, most often, focussed on an image, which might be miraculous. One of the earliest such indulgences was directed in 1327 to the bishop of Norwich for penitents who contributed to the completion of the chapel at Ipswich where a representation of the Virgin had been found underground 'and where divers great miracles have been wrought'. [29] This became a regional centre of Marian devotion which much later was well known to the Pastons. Edward III, a notable devotee of the Virgin, sent oblations to Ipswich in 1342, as he did to her chapel in the Cistercian monastery of Kingswood in Gloucestershire and several other English Marian shrines. In 1353 he visited in person the image of the Virgin at Leintwardine in Herefordshire; that this was, or had been, a local object of pilgrimage is shown by the story of one of Thomas Cantilupe's clients. She was wheeled there by her sister, but was not allowed to stay in the church and went on to Hereford instead. [30] The bishop of Worcester in 1319 conceded to the abbot of Kingswood the power to hear the confessions of any of the bishop's subjects who came to the abbey *causa peregrinationis* and wished to confess, and in March 1364 the pope referred to

> the chapel of St Mary the Virgin built between the two gates of the Cistercian monastery of Kingeswode in which chapel, as it is asserted, miracles are done by her intercession and to which many blind and lame come from England. Wales, France, Ireland and Scotland. [31]

It transpires from the abbey's petition that it was badly in need of repair, and that the monks were seeking confirmation of their sixty-year-old right to the oblations at the chapel, which suggests that this cult was another product of the early fourteenth-century surge.[32]

The siting of the chapel at Kingswood was significant. That it was external to the abbey church made it accessible to female penitents, without need for the special permissions which Englishwomen who wanted to venerate Edmund of Abingdon at Pontigny, or those who wished to inspect the beautiful new crucifix at Meaux, required. Another west country Cistercian monastery evidently adopted a similar expedient. The indulgence of seven years and seven quarantines that was granted to Tintern Abbey in March 1414 was for the benefit of those who 'visit the chapel without the west door of the church'. Here

> an *ymago* of St Mary the Virgin has been fairly and honestly and decently placed, and although the attempt has been made, has been unable to be placed elsewhere, on account of which miracle, and because mass is said daily by the monks at the altar of the said chapel, a very great multitude resorts to the chapel.[33]

To judge by Tintern's geographical position, it would have been able to call upon much the same regional public as responded to the attractions of Kingswood (which had originated as a daughter of Tintern). A more obscure shrine was said to be attracting pilgrims to the same region at very much the same time. In 1405 the chapel of St Tiriotus on the Severn near Chepstow received a indulgence of five years and five quarantines, valid for ten years: the pope had been told that 'a multitude both of English and Welsh' resorted to it.[34]

The need to make special provision for female pilgrims who desired to venerate the Virgin at the churches of strictly enclosed monastic orders was also addressed for the benefit of the Carthusians of London, when in 1399 Boniface IX awarded them a plenary indulgence, available on the major feasts of the Virgin, which, by a special dispensation, women were to be admitted to obtain. Both the indulgence and the concession to women were more restrained in 1482, when, with the encouragement of Edward IV's mother, the pious Cecily, duchess of York, who had a 'singular devotion' to this house, the pope in 1482 granted indulgence of one year and forty days to all men who visited the church every Saturday for a whole year and all women who visited the cemetery or chapel or oratory in the monastic precinct.[35]

Another metropolitan shrine of the Virgin was closely associated with the monarchy. In 1476 a papal indulgence of fifteen years and fifteen quarantines was granted to those who visited the chapel of the Virgin that was vulgarly called 'de la Pewe' at St Stephen's Westminster, at stated feasts including All Souls. In addition it was conceded that the souls for whom mass was celebrated in the chapel would receive the indulgence of St Mary 'of Scala Dei' at Sant' Anastasio outside the walls of Rome. The Roman site was well-known to English pilgrims, on the evidence of late medieval guidebooks; it commemorated a vision, supposedly experienced by St Bernard in the twelfth century, of the release of a soul from Purgatory, and the cult was especially valued for that purpose. The chapel at Westminster, the pope stated, enjoyed the devotion of Anthony Woodville, Edward IV's brother-in-law.[36] The history of the chapel, and of the richly adorned image of the Virgin which it contained, goes back at least a century before Woodville, to the reign of Edward III when the first references to it occur. Froissart referred to 'a little chapel' at Westminster, 'with an image of our Lady that worked great miracles, wherein the kings of England have always had great trust', and where Richard II prayed before going forth to confront Wat Tyler at Smithfield in 1381; this is probably identifiable as 'the Pew'. In 1480, a few years after the Scala Dei indulgence was granted, Richard Grene, Master of Arts, endowed a daily mass to be said in the chapel, referring to the many miracles which were manifested there, and in 1498 Lady Ann Scrope of Harling in Norfolk ranked 'oure Lady of Pewe' with Our Lady of Walsingham, St Thomas and St Edmund as a fit recipient of her 'grete beedes of goold'.[37]

Just outside London, the Virgin was also doing miracles at Muswell chapel in the parish of Hornsey, 'wherefore many persons have been and are wont to resort thither every year', especially at the Feast of the Assumption and in its octave, as the nuns of St Mary Clerkenwell told the pope in 1476 when they sought and obtained confirmation of their right to the oblations. The place-name, meaning 'mossy well', commemorates (like Clerkenwell itself) a 'holy well', with which the nascent cult of the Virgin may have been connected. Two years later, the nuns were building a church there, and received a grant of twenty years' indulgence at specified feasts, together with the power to appoint four priests as confessors.[38] Muswell was sufficiently well known c. 1520 to be listed among popular Marian sites in the vicinity of London. Another was Our Lady of Willesden, which yet again had no good reputation with Lollards and reformers.[39]

Numerous Marian shrines in the north of England claimed miracles. In 1428 the church of Jesmond (since 1835 part of Newcastle-upon-Tyne) and a chapel on the bridge at Corbridge both received papal grants which alleged, in identical words, that to both 'resorts a multitude on account of the divers miracles wrought therein through the merits of St Mary the Virgin'. Such stereotyped wording may seem suspect, but it is at least possible to supply some background to both claims. Corbridge, best known today for its Roman remains, stood both on the River Tyne and at an important road junction. Its midsummer fair went back to the beginning of the thirteenth century, and another at Whitsun is known to have been in existence by 1480. The Tyne was bridged at Corbridge at some point in the thirteenth century, but, as was so often the case, the bridge was frequently in need of repair. Boniface IX granted an indulgence to the chapel, in aid of the ruinous structure, in 1401. The fact that it was to be available not only during the midsummer period (it covered the feasts of St John the Baptist on 24 June and SS. Peter and Paul on the 29th) but in Whit week strongly suggests that it was aimed at the crowds attending the fairs, and that the Whitsun fair may already have been in existence. The pope did not mention miracles in 1401; perhaps the reputation of Jesmond, some fifteen miles away down the Tyne, inspired loftier ambitions at Corbridge by 1428.[40]

Newcastle antiquarians from the seventeenth century onwards were familiar with the tradition that there had been a flourishing pilgrimage at Jesmond. The chapel is first mentioned in 1351, but architectural evidence shows that it existed in the twelfth century. It was later extended with the addition of a chantry chapel on the north which had its own west door, and it has been suggested that pilgrims entered by this door, made their way to the high altar, and then left by a door in the north wall of the chapel. It seems plausible to attribute the origins of the pilgrimage to the holy well which lay in the dene to the south of the chapel. This was a warm spring which, it was reported in the early twentieth century, had once borne the inscription 'Ave Maria plena gratia'.[41] There is plentiful evidence of disputes over the ownership of the chapel. The text of the papal indulgence states that the building was 'ruinous'; this was a commonplace assertion, but perhaps the pilgrimage had fallen on hard times. Jesmond was well enough known, at least regionally, for the rector of Heslerton in the East Riding to leave money in 1472 for a pilgrimage to be done there on his account. As a Marian shrine, it thus ranked in his estimation alongside Walsingham, Lincoln, Scarborough, Guisborough, and Carlisle.[42]

Local emulation or imitation can be suspected elsewhere. In January 1393 the monks of Selby Abbey, south of York, obtained indulgences both for their own chapel of the Holy Cross and for the feast of the Assumption at the chapel of the Virgin which had been erected a century earlier on their nearby manor of Stainar. No miracles were mentioned, but a generation later, in 1442, the pope was informed that in the chapel of Stainar, 'not more than an Italian mile distant' from Selby, a certain image of the Blessed Virgin 'is frequented by all the neighbouring faithful by reason of the great and innumerable miracles which God has worked and daily works there by

the merits of the said Virgin.'[43] Little more than two miles away from
Stainar and Selby was the church of St Mary at Hemingbrough. In May
1393, only a few months after the original grant for Stainar, the pope had
granted an indulgence of four years and four quarantines on the feast of
the Assumption to the church of Hemingbrough, 'where divers miracles
are wrought'. In 1410, an inhabitant of Hemingbrough desired in his will
to be buried before the image of St Mary of Pity in the church. This may
well have been the focus of the miracles.[44]

The presence of an image of St Mary of Pity at Hemingbrough was, at
all events, a sign of the times. The repertoire of forms and styles developed
by artists ensured that the spectator, given good will and imagination, could
readily discover emotional stimulus in a crucifix which suggested Christ's
agonies, a Madonna and Child which portrayed the intimacy between
mother and son, or a *Pietà* which evoked the sufferings of the bereaved
Madonna and the slumped human reality of the dead Christ. 'Our Lady of
Pity' was one of the principal attractions at Walsingham. Margery Kempe,
admittedly an excitable subject, was moved to ecstasies of devotion by a
Pietà she saw at Norwich.[45] She does not tell us in which church it was
located, but on the evidence of papal indulgences neither the image, nor,
perhaps, her reaction to it was all that exceptional. In about 1398 an
indulgence was granted to the chapel of St Mary at Tredington in the
diocese of Worcester, 'where there is great devotion to a picture called
St Mary of Pity who holds a figure of Christ Crucified', and in 1464 a grant
to the church of St Mary de Pietate at Kersey in Suffolk remarked that
'there is a great resort of the faithful on account of the infinite miracles
which by the merits and intercession of the same virgin had been and were
being wrought daily by Almighty God at a certain image of her in the said
church'.[46] It is not unequivocally stated that this image was a *Pietà*, although
the name by which the church is known is suggestive. In 1484 the church
of Amesbury in Wiltshire was described as containing 'a chapel of St Mary
the Virgin with an image of the Saviour Crucified, to which image Thomas
de la Mare, knight, lord of Aldermaston in the said diocese, and other
faithful of those parts have a great devotion and to which they resort in great
numbers'. The indulgence was available on the feasts of the Annunciation
and Holy Cross, and it may be that the devotion was to a crucifix located
in a chapel of the Virgin.[47]

Images doubtless achieved their effects by a variety of means, ranging
from sheer emotional intensity to sheer outward splendour. In 1451 the
prior and chapter of Carlisle wished to purchase costly adornments for
their image of the Virgin. Naturally, their existing resources did not suffice
for this purpose, and forty days' indulgence was accordingly awarded to

contributors by the archbishop of York and the bishop of Carlisle, who vividly evoked the visual appeal that such images were intended to have. The prior and chapter, they declared,

> inflamed by the zeal of pious devotion, have resolved and wish, with the aid of God's grace, to cover and adorn the image or statue of the glorious Virgin with silver plates, decorated with gold, jewels, rings and many other precious ornaments, to the praise of God and the increase of the veneration, glory and honour of the aforesaid glorious Virgin, and also to ignite the devotion of the Christian faithful, by some ingenious and costly work.[48]

There is no mention of miracles, but the radiance of the Virgin thus arrayed would of itself create an aura of wonder.

Miracles effected through the merits of the Virgin were claimed at many places. Lesnes Abbey, at Erith in Kent, founded by Richard de Lucy in 1178 in the name of Thomas Becket, was in financial difficulties two centuries later, and in 1371 the brethren sought indulgences for the repair and decoration of their chapel of the Virgin 'in which our Lord has deigned of old to work many miracles'.[49] In Devon, miracles of the Virgin were claimed at Ilfracombe in 1443 and at Plym Bridge in 1450. At Plym Bridge, the pope was once again informed, 'there resorts a great multitude of faithful from divers parts of the world' and authorisation was granted to hear their confessions.[50] At Ilfracombe, the alms and oblations attracted by the wonders the Virgin had wrought in a cemetery chapel built by the parishioners gave rise to a dispute between them and the rector, not an uncommon event.[51]

Not the least interesting of these many claims was made on behalf of the chapel of St Mary de Key in the cemetery of the chapel (not a parish until the late seventeenth century) of St Nicholas at Liverpool. In 1455 the pope confirmed indulgences earlier granted by the archbishops of Canterbury and York and other English bishops, 'having regard to the devotion of the people who flock' to the chapel 'and to the miracles which God was working therein by the merits of the same Virgin'.[52] The chapel existed by 1360, and, although nothing remains of any fourteenth-century building where the parish church of St Nicholas and St Mary now stands, its medieval name and its position, albeit now further removed from the waterfront by the building of Pierhead out over the mud-flats of the Mersey, are sufficient to challenge the imagination. The Birkenhead ferry, then as now, debouched not far away, and Liverpool was a flourishing market and a port for Ireland. The clientele for the chapel was surely drawn from the clientele for the port and the market.

Among the by-products of devotion to the Virgin can be reckoned the cult of her mother, St Anne. Papal indulgences for English shrines of St Anne are concentrated in the second half of the fifteenth century, but a relatively early example was awarded in 1354 to the newly constructed chapel of St Anne and the Virgin, still to be seen over the eastern gate of the canons' close at Salisbury.[53] Was this intended as a 'station' where pilgrims entering the precinct *en route* for the cathedral (a centre of Marian devotion) might be induced to pause? A century later, in 1453, the chapel of St Anne by the seashore at Whitstable in Kent was attracting the customary 'multitude' on her feast day.[54] Seafarers were among the major beneficiaries of Anne's protection, which helps to account for the popularity of her chapel in the woods at Brislington just outside Bristol. It was said in 1463 that the popes had in the past awarded the chapel indulgences which had now lapsed. Visits had fallen off as a consequence and the chapel had become ruinous. New indulgences were now granted, and a few years later William Worcester was able to describe the chapel, with its lights paid for by the guilds of weavers and cordwainers and its thirty-two model ships and boats, which were intended for the reception of offerings and sometimes for the burning of incense. In the next century Leland recalled the pilgrimage and remarked that there was a ferry crossing at this point on the Severn.[55]

Woods and water alike provided a frequent setting for the veneration of St Anne. She was much associated with healing springs, at Buxton in Derbyshire and elsewhere.[56] In 1491 Richard Barnard, perpetual vicar of the church of Luton, had built a chapel of the saint in a certain wood nearby, where 'through the merit of St Anne many miracles are continually worked and which the faithful frequent out of continual devotion'.[57] On abundant surviving evidence from elsewhere in northern Europe, we may suppose that her cult in England drew nourishment from images as her daughter's and her grandson's did. A papal indulgence of 1482 referred to an altar of the Saviour and St Anne at Lichfield, 'on which images of Christ and St Anne have been placed'. The wording of the act by which the dean of Lichfield had founded the chantry of Jesus and St Anne in 1468 seems to imply that these were separate images, but St Anne was more commonly represented either with the Virgin, for example teaching her to read, or with both Virgin and Child in a grouping enormously popular, on the evidence of many surviving examples, all over northern Europe.[58]

These were among the fashionable devotions of the period, but old sites and old saints continued to press their claims. At a chapel dedicated to St Andrew within the bounds of the parish church of Stalham in Norfolk, the customary multitude flocked 'out of reverence for the said saint, by whose merits divers of those who visit it have been delivered from diseases', or so the pope was told in 1443.[59] Relics of various established saints continued to beckon pilgrims, none perhaps more so than the finger of St John the

Baptist 'with which he pointed to the saviour of the human race', at Mottisfont Priory in Hampshire, where, through the merits of this and other relics, it was said in 1457, God had often worked miracles and 'a multitude of people resorts at times for the sake of pilgrimage and devotion'.[60] The promoters of new local cults centred on old saints did not fail to enlist papal assistance. In 1464 the pope was told that the chapel of St Michael the Archangel at the parish church of St Mary at Hornsey, which was then 'in a solitary place', was customarily tended by persons leading a solitary life, who devoted themelves to bridge and road repair and the burial of unfortunates who were slain by robbers. Mass and the offices were celebrated there daily and by the intercession of the archangel, as it was believed, 'the most high manifests divers miracles, so that there is great devotion and resort thereto'. The indulgences which were now granted in perpetuity for the feasts of the Assumption and of St Michael himself were effectively intended to supply the place of the rents which the chapel did not possess and to make possible the completion of the buildings.[61]

The proprietors of the Anglo-Saxon saints also continued to seek the pope's aid in keeping them before the public eye. The nuns of Thetford in 1403 wished it to be remembered that St Etheldreda's shift (camisia) was most fairly and devoutly preserved there and that 'through the merits of the same God shows many notable and wonderful signs'.[62] In 1434 Pershore Abbey too claimed that God worked many miracles there; but it was also, sadly, in a parlous financial state, and so the pope granted it an indulgence on its principal feasts, including that of St Edburga.[63] Smaller churches and less illustrious saints also sought indulgences: the one awarded in 1411 to the church of St Odulphus at Pillaton in Cornwall, where on his feast-day the familiar 'multitude' resorted, is in fact the first evidence for the church's dedication and for the diffusion of the saint's cult, presumably from Evesham Abbey.[64]

A Celtic saint in a remote location also attracted the pope's beneficence, in rather special circumstances. Pius II, who lived in a very different world, was distressed to learn in 1461 that pirates around the Isles of Scilly had been despoiling not only clergy, fishermen and shipwrecked persons, but 'the faithful who go in great numbers to the chapel of St Elidius'. The saint in question was Elid or Lyde, venerated on the island which was known in the twelfth century by his name, later corrupted into St Helen's, as it is now called, and the chapel belonged to Tavistock Abbey. Apart from ordering the bishops of Exeter and St-Malo to take a strong line with the pirates, the pope now granted an indulgence of seven years and seven quarantines to benefit 'the great multitude' which resorted to it, in order to make possible its refurbishment. In the next century, apparently mistaking the saint' gender, Leland noted 'Seynt Lides isle', 'wher yn times past at her sepulchre was gret superstition'. [65]

The proprietors of ancient saints seem sometimes to have annexed more fashionable devotions to their cause. The nuns of Barking Abbey, founded by Erkenwald of London in 666, in 1400 obtained an indulgence for those visiting the cross in the oratory 'called Roodloft' on the wall of their cemetery, on a list of principal feasts which included not only those of the Cross itself but their principal saint, Erkenwald's sister Ethelburga. The Rood was not a new image, if it is to be identified as the now badly worn crucifixion group, perhaps of the twelfth century, which survives in the upper chapel of the Fire Bell Gate which is all that is left of the once venerable abbey. The nuns may have hoped to attract pilgrims, and offerings to assist with badly needed repairs, by exploiting devotion to the Cross without compromising their enclosure. Only a few years later the pope was told that the house had been damaged by floods.[66] In 1462 the church of St Chad at Wybynbury in Cheshire similarly obtained an indulgence, available on the feasts of St Chad and the Exaltation and on Easter Monday, for visitors to the chapel of Holy Cross. Power to hear confessions was also granted.[67] An image of Christ was placed near the shrine of St Cuthbert at Durham, and in 1477 the northern bishops granted indulgences of forty days for visitors to it.[68]

The more or less constant trickle of pilgrims to Becket's shrine must have provided added incentive for other Canterbury churches to seek to secure their share of the traffic. St Martin and St Augustine could offer pilgrims additional benefits from a visit to Canterbury, even if they were unlikely to be their main reason for coming. It was claimed in 1405 that the church of St Martin was visited annually by 'a multitude' on the saint's feast-day,[69] and in 1459 the abbot of St Augustine's told the pope that because of the presence of Augustine and other saints, and the past grant of papal indulgences, 'the faithful resort in great numbers with a devout heart, even from distant parts, to earn by confession and absolution the said indulgences'. He was accordingly awarded powers to hear the confessions of pilgrims of both sexes.[70] Locality nurtured pilgrimages in different ways: a shrine might be isolated but strategically sited on a road or waterway, like the chapel at Hornsey, or it might form one of a cluster which fed off one another.

A remarkable number of churches which can only have hoped to attract a local public sought the benefits of papal indulgences. Many nonetheless rested content with the forty days a mere bishop could offer, if only because seeking a papal indulgence itself meant a considerable investment of time and effort. The register of Edmund Lacy as bishop of Exeter betwen 1420 and 1455 contains numerous grants of indulgence to churches and chapels all over Devon and Cornwall and occasional related interventions in favour of local pilgrimages. In 1421 his vicar in spirituals licensed the inhabitants of the village of Mitchell in Cornwall to provide at their own expense fit priests to celebrate mass 'for themselves, and pilgrims and other travellers' in the chapel of St Francis there, on condition that the offerings 'and other emoluments' were reserved to the curate of the place. The main road linking Bodmin and Penzance still runs through Mitchell, and it seems a reasonable speculation that pilgrims who happened to pass through the village were on their way to or from St Michael's Mount in one direction, Bodmin in the other. Similar considerations may have been involved when the bishop awarded forty days to St Lugvan, not far from St Michael's Mount.[71] The monks of Canterbury who sought plenary indulgences for Becket's Jubilees, and the parish churches and churchyard chapels which attracted the modest generosity of the bishop of Exeter, must have expected to reap different rates of return.

The papacy sometimes helped to promote pilgrimage to English shrines in another, somewhat oblique, manner. While the Roman Jubilee indulgences were intended to attract pilgrims to Rome itself, the various necessities which weighed upon the popes in the fifteenth century, from the refurbishment of Rome to the threat of the Turk, disposed them to grant the benefits of these indulgences to those who were able and willing to make the appropriate offering but (for whatever reason) not the journey. This policy had in fact been inaugurated by Clement VI for the benefit of persons who had been unable to go to Rome for the Jubilee of 1350, and it was predictably much employed by Boniface IX, who made the Jubilee indulgence of 1390 available to a wide variety of people on conditions which sometimes included paying substitutory visits to local churches. In 1451 Henry VI petitioned the pope on behalf of his esquire Richard Tunstall, who had vowed to go to Rome for the Jubilee indulgence of the previous year. The demands of the service he owed to the king had made this impossible. The pope therefore granted him the indulgence on condition that he visited 'on three successive days the churches of St Paul, London and St Peter's Westminster, saying on each day seven times the Lord's Prayer and Hail Mary, and giving on the said days 10*d*. sterling to the poor'.[72] Similar replacement pilgrimages were from time to time enjoined not only on persons who wished to earn the Jubilee indulgences, but on others who had promised to perform one or all of the major pilgrimages to Rome, Jerusalem or Compostela and now wished to be absolved from their vows. This is a reminder that, if many pilgrims to English shrines had in their time also visited the major holy places of western Christendom, many more had dreamed of doing so.

Pilgrims at the shrine of St Edward the confessor at Westminster. The Confessor was in fact primarily a royal rather than a popular saint. (*Cambridge University Library*)

6

Royal Pilgrimage

The exploitation of the cult of saints was an integral part of the practice of medieval kingship. Kings enlisted the patronage of the saints by a variety of means. They obtained possession of relics by gift, purchase and sometimes *force majeure*, and they paid homage at the strongholds of the saints. This homage might take the form of pilgrimages undertaken by the monarch in person, which were normally accompanied by lavish offerings; offerings which were not lavish (as on one notable occasion when John visited Bury St Edmund's) might attract unfavourable comment. Alternatively, indeed more frequently, gifts and offerings were conveyed to shrines on the king's behalf, either on a regular annual basis, on some special occasion of festivity or thanksgiving, or to mark the great festivals of the year.

It is the evidence for actual royal journeys to shrines that most interests us here, but although such journeys did indeed possess a distinct value as part of the practice of kingship, they were only one constituent in a complex of public and quasi-public almsgiving and other devotions from which they cannot be neatly or completely distinguished. Although the king in many respects of course stood alone, the pilgrimages of the queen, queen mothers, other members of the royal family and of great nobles also seemed significant to contemporary observers. The Tewkesbury annalist, for example, carefully noted not only the visits of Richard of Clare, earl of Gloucester, to the monastery itself, but his pilgrimages to Pontigny in 1249 and to Compostela the following year; the monks helped him secure his travelling money.[1] For much of the reign of Henry III a peculiar eminence was occupied by his brother Richard of Cornwall, not only because of his royal birth but because his efforts to secure election as Holy Roman Emperor marked him out as at least an aspirant prince of European importance in his own right. Matthew Paris duly recorded his pilgrimages to St-Gilles in 1240 and to Pontigny in 1250, and his visit to Lincoln in 1255 to do reverence to Robert Grosseteste was noted by the Burton annalist.[2] His foundation of Hailes Abbey in Gloucestershire and the installation there of a relic of the Holy Blood was a gesture appropriate to his rank.

The king was the supreme patron of the churches in his realm. In laying his offerings on the altar of St Alban or St Edmund, St Thomas or St Wulfstan, he was not merely doing what was expected of him and enlisting the goodwill of the saints, but also setting a good example to his subjects great and small. When Edward I summoned a parliament to St Albans or Bury St Edmunds, his notables in effect found themselves performing an involuntary pilgrimage. Westminster, with Henry III's tireless promotion of Edward the Confessor, fell into a category all its own. Henry's gift to the abbey of the relic of Christ's blood which he obtained in 1247 was just one signal that by now Westminster was not merely a royal foundation but a shrine which derived much of its meaning from its association with the kings and their most notable palace. In one sense, the kings did not visit Westminster in the same sense that they visited other shrines; rather the world, in coming to Westminster, came to them. Henry made it his custom to celebrate the feast of the translation of the Confessor (14 October) there, and early in his reign Edward I tried to do likewise and also to spend the month of May at Westminster, celebrating there both the Ascension and Pentecost.[3] As the years went by, however, the demands of Wales, Gascony and Scotland played havoc with this tranquil design. Both Edward and his warlike grandson made ceremonial visits to Westminster to convey special messages of thanksgiving or supplication. One chronicler remarked that whenever Edward I travelled far from the kingdom he commended himself first to the saints of England, especially to Edward the Confessor.[4] In early July 1358 Edward III completed a pilgrimage tour of the country with devout supplications at Westminster before leaving for France, endowing the abbey with the head of St Benedict and announcing that he wished to be buried there and not, as he had previously intended, with the Three Kings at Cologne.[5]

The movements of relics as well as of people were significant. Relics might be described as the currency of devotion and, once acquired, did not always remain the private possession of the monarch. Some circulated as tokens of amity or diplomatic rapprochement, others remained in the royal collection. Certain really notable acquisitions were however likely to enter what may be termed the public domain, as gifts to a favoured religious foundation, where they would periodically be visited with due ceremony by the king and his entourage. The relics appropriated by Edward I in Wales had a particular significance; chief among them was a fragment of the True Cross which he brought to Westminster and which was later bestowed by Edward III on his own foundation, St George's Windsor.[6] The distribution of relics as presents, whether to other high-ranking individuals or to religious houses, fitted into the wider picture of a king's gift-giving, that vital component of his diplomatic relationships both within his kingdom and beyond, while royal pilgrimages can be seen as a part of the practice of what remained both a personal and an itinerant style of government. Pilgrimages to the major shrines of the kingdom, frequently undertaken in conjunction with other business, including military campaigns, were among the occasions on which the king displayed himself to his subjects and, in a very meaningful sense, made his presence felt.

Kings had felt obliged to forge these relationships with saints and shrines virtually from the beginning of the history of Christian, or Christianised, kingdoms. The interest which Alfonso III, king of the Asturias, took in Galicia and the shrine of St James of Compostela in a remote corner of north-western Spain has been likened to the interest taken by the ninth- and tenth-century kings of Wessex in Northumbria, and therefore in its shrines, as they looked to expand their power throughout England.[7] Writing early in the twelfth century, Simeon of Durham related that King Athelstan, while marching his army north to Scotland in 934, had visited St Cuthbert (at Chester-le-Street) 'requesting his assistance and soliciting his prayers', and offering 'many royal gifts of various kinds as an ornament to his church'. His brother and successor in the kingdom of Wessex, Edmund, visited the shrine in 945, also on his way north with an army. According to Simeon, Edmund laid upon the body two 'Greek cloths' (*pallia Graeca*), and on both occasions the members of the accompanying host rendered compulsory offerings to the saint under the king's watchful eye.[8] In Simeon's view, this homage from the kings of Wessex was owed as thanksgiving for the assistance Cuthbert had given them in overcoming the Danes and extending their hegemony over the north.

The church of Beverley in the twelfth century likewise remembered Athelstan as the author of its privileges, because of the help St John had given him in the same cause. In one version of this tradition Athelstan was on his way north to deal with the Scots when he encountered 'a sizeable crowd of poor and middling persons' in the province of Lindsey and discovered that they were on their way to Beverley for their health. He therepon decided to join them in petitioning the saint and with many tears left his knife upon the altar, promising to redeem it with rich gifts if he was victorious. Of course he was, and he returned to redeem his knife from the celestial pawnbroker. In another more elaborate version, Athelstan also bore St John's banner into battle, at the suggestion of the *custodes* of the church, saw several visions of the saint and offered his arms at the shrine on his return.[9] When later English kings needed not only help but assurance of their rights in their conflicts with the Scots, they were happy to be reminded of such traditions.

Among later Anglo-Saxon kings, Edgar (943–75), despite certain character flaws, achieved a great name as the patron of church reform and was himself remembered as a saint, at least at Glastonbury where he was buried. His son Edward achieved what was regarded as martyrdom in 979 and, when eventually buried with his mother Elgiva at Shaftesbury, enjoyed a much more general cult. Then the Danish menace reappeared. When Cnut established his dominance over the entire kingdom, he made it an integral part of his policy to conciliate its major saints. To Simeon of Durham, Cnut was 'the pious and religious king of the Angles' who displayed his veneration for St Cuthbert by walking 'barefoot to that most holy body from as far as the place which is called Garmundsway, that is, for five miles', naturally accompanying this demonstration with generous gifts.[10] Further south, Herman laid heavy emphasis on Cnut's beneficence to St Edmund and his church as a symptom of his transformation from 'wild beast' into exemplary king: it was in his time that monks were installed at Bury to watch over the saint.[11] Not to be outdone, the *Liber Eliensis* later related that Cnut liked to spend the Feast of the Purification at Ely. On one such occasion the king was approaching the church by boat and was inspired by the distant sound of the monks' psalmody to lift his voice in English song in praise of St Etheldreda. In another year, the marshes were frozen solid all around and he desired to be drawn over the ice to Ely on some sort of sledge.[12] In 1027 Cnut made a well-publicised pilgrimage to Rome which was designed to win benefits for both himself and his kingdom, and he was also associated with a number of notable translations, including those of St Wistan to Evesham and St Alfege and St Mildred to Canterbury. He established an impressive record of pilgrimages and other pious gestures undertaken with a clear understanding of their public relations value.

Kings, then, were likely to feel obliged to take note of the major shrines within their area of authority, not least perhaps in peripheral regions. For the first Norman kings, however, there were complicating factors and many competing priorities. The Conqueror's attitudes to the English were soured by rebellion, principally in the north and east, and his French bishops and abbots, as they gradually replaced their English counterparts, had to decide what their attitude to the native saints of the kingdom was to be. Simeon relates that William I sent precious jewels to Durham for the adornment of Cuthbert's image, but later, in 1072, he visited Durham in person to ascertain whether the saint's relics were really there. Accounts of what Cuthbert did to deter him from this impertinence vary. According to Simeon, he was suddenly seized with an unbearable heat which drove him from the church and in effect put him to flight.[13] The signs of accommodation and acclimatisation became more plentiful with Henry I, after half a century of Norman rule. Henry was to be found in attendance at important festivities, as when late in 1116 he and his queen attended the consecration of the new church of St Albans, where, one chronicler noted, he wore his crown. The queen was present at Winchester in 1111 for the translation of St Ethelwold to a new shrine.[14] Henry's own foundation of Reading Abbey, endowed with the Hand of St James, became a pilgrimage centre of some importance. Reading was Henry's own burial-place but not that of his successors, and although it was remembered that it was a royal foundation, it was only one shrine among many that kings might visit or benefit, and may have progressively lost its allure; Edward III is only known to have given special alms to Reading once in his reign, in 1336.[15]

With Henry II, or perhaps more precisely with Henry II and Becket, we can mark an epoch in the history of English royal pilgrimage. Henry was not without some independent pedigree as a pilgrim. In 1166 he was the earliest known visitor to the newly emergent Marian shrine of Rocamadour in southern France, and he went there again in 1170.[16] The account of his movements that is given by an anonymous chronicler who wrote with close knowledge of the royal court suggests that 1177 was the *annus mirabilis* of his pilgrimage activity. His plans were even more far-reaching than his performance, for early in the year he announced that he intended to go to Compostela and sent to Ferdinand of Leon to ask for safe-conduct, although nothing came of this. Just before Easter, Henry accompanied Philip, count of Flanders, to Canterbury and afterwards went on pilgrimage to Bury St Edmund's, arriving on the Sunday after Easter and proceeding on a further pilgrimage to St Etheldreda at Ely. Fortified thus, he went on to Geddington to receive the homage of the Welsh. As if this exposure to saints was not sufficient for one year, he also venerated the relics of St Petroc, which the prior of Bodmin brought to him at Winchester in an ivory casket. A canon of Bodmin had stolen the relics and taken them to Brittany, and Henry had intervened to obtain their restitution.[17]

Henry died in 1189 a prospective crusader, in theory at least. His successor Richard the Lionheart differed from other English kings, except Edward I and (it is easy to forget) Henry IV, in that by going in person to the Holy Land he had qualified as the highest form of pilgrim. In the relatively short time he devoted to England he was not unmindful of his obligations, although sometimes ruthless in appropriating the riches of shrines to help raise money for the crusade. After his coronation he took homage of the magnates and embarked on a perambulation of his kingdom which included pilgrimages to St Edmund and to Canterbury. Landing at Sandwich in 1194 after his unfortunately delayed return from the Holy Land, he reached London, doubtless via Canterbury, four days later and was received in solemn proession at St Paul's; then he went once again as a pilgrim to Bury and there offered 'a precious standard which had belonged to the emperor of Cyprus'.[18]

Alongside the now inescapable martyr of Canterbury the old royal martyr of East Anglia retained his claim on the attention of the kings of England. What however of the British protomartyr? John went both to Bury and to St Albans immediately after his coronation.[19] At Bury, at least, his visit disappointed the convent's expectations in that, according to Jocelin of Brakelond, instead of bringing a rich offering he took a *pallium* from the sacrist's stock to offer to the martyr without even paying for it. He made later visits to both Bury and St Albans, and showed favour to Reading and St James, but he is perhaps most notable for his patronage of the shrine of a more recent saint who was not yet canonised when he became king, Wulfstan of Worcester.

John visited Worcester as king first in 1200, again in 1204 and thereafter once in almost every year of his reign, commending himself to the saint on his deathbed.[20] He was buried at Worcester despite the claims of his own foundation, Beaulieu Abbey. Various reasons have been advanced for this apparent attachment to the last of the Anglo-Saxon bishops. It is thought possible that John, locked in conflict with the pope over the right to appoint to the see of Canterbury, sought support for his right to appoint bishops in the legend (which is not to be found in William of Malmesbury's *Life*) that Wulfstan, threatened with deposition by Lanfranc, had succesfully defended his right to keep his bishopric by appealing to the fact that the sainted Confessor had appointed him. More generally, John's predilection may reflect the growing willingness of the kings of England, a century and a half after the Conquest, to identify themselves with native English traditions. With the wisdom of hindsight we can see his reign as a turning-point in the long erosion of the position of the English kings as French princes and their increasing confinement to their island kingdom. He and his son both failed to reverse the trend. Henry III, while not notably devoted to St Wulfstan, demonstrated his attachment to the English past in other ways.

The two long reigns of Henry III and Edward I, even if we reckon only from Henry's majority, covered more than three-quarters of a century between them. They will receive particular attention here because a variety of sources enable us to document with peculiar vividness the ways in which both kings integrated their homage to the saints into their practice of kingship. Not only do they furnish ample evidence for the devotion to pre-conquest English saints which has just been mentioned, but they patronised new cults.

Henry III's reign coincided with the beginnings of pilgrimage to the Holy

Cross of Bromholm, in which he participated personally, and he was also the first king, but not by any means the last, to take an interest in the shrine of the Virgin at Walsingham. He visited both Bromholm and Walsingham for the first time in early April 1226.[21] In the following year he gave instructions for the conveyance to Bromholm of a silver model of his 'great ship', presumably the one that had recently been built at Portsmouth. This was not in fact his own gift but had been paid for by contributions collected by the *custos* of the ship, Thomas Templar. In 1234, however, Henry commissioned a silver-gilt image of himself to be sent to Bromholm. He seems to have visited the shrine every year between 1232 and 1239, between 1242 and 1248, and then in 1251 and 1256. His interest thereafter apparently ebbed, while his gifts to Walsingham became more numerous and more generous.

Not unnaturally, Henry usually combined Bromholm with visits not only to Walsingham but to Bury, often to Norwich or Ely, and sometimes also St Albans, although St Albans, lying somewhat to the west, was often incorporated into a quite different itinerary.[22] In 1235, for example, he was at Bromholm on 13 March, Walsingham on 15 March and Bury on 19–20 March; he visited St Albans in August. The king visited Bury in June 1244 and moved on to Ely, where he offered a 'garland' at the shrine of St Etheldreda, who from time to time shared in his patronage of saints both royal and Anglo-Saxon.[23] After visiting Bury in March 1245 he went on towards Bromholm and Walsingham, instructing his personal fisherman to go to Soham and send his catch after the king daily.[24] In 1248 letters patent were dated from both Bromholm and Walsingham on the same day, 18 March; on this occasion Henry had already been at Bury, between the 7th and the 11th. For much of the reign in fact, at least until the king's political and financial misjudgements began to catch up with him, it is possible to observe him engaged on an East Anglian pilgrimage tour, often undertaken in Lent.

His relationship with the old cult of St Edmund is worthy of closer attention. We have already seen that Henry's father, uncle and grandfather were all mindful of St Edmund; he was, after all, a royal saint, a martyred king, perhaps even a counterpoise to the martyred archbishop of Canterbury. Much later, Richard II had both St Edmund and Edward the Confessor depicted on the Wilton Diptych. They act as witnesses and supporters while John the Baptist presents the king to the Virgin. Richard may have felt an attraction to Edmund as to another young king; Edmund, according to legend, had become king at the age of fifteen.[25] Precisely the same considerations might have applied to Henry III, and there can be no doubt that, even if he devoted his utmost efforts to the cult of the Confessor, he also earnestly promoted the association between

Edmund and Bury on the one hand and the monarchy and Westminster on the other.

There was perhaps the more reason for him to do so as his adversaries also tended to repose public confidence in St Edmund. In 1232 the countess of Kent, wife of the disgraced Hubert de Burgh, sought refuge at Bury and her husband also came there 'to seek the help of the glorious king and martyr'. In the following year, Henry 'made peace' with the countess at Bury; her daughter, who had presumably been there with her, then went to Bromholm *causa orationis*.[26] This might be interpreted as a diplomatic as well as a pious gesture, if the king's favour to Bromholm was well known. Much later, the Bury chronicler claimed that 'the liberty of St Edmund was very precious in the sight of the barons', which made it a good place for the unpopular Peter d'Aigueblanche, bishop of Hereford, to seek asylum in 1263.[27]

Henry's eldest son was named for St Edward, and his second for St Edmund. As the king informed the abbot and convent of Bury on the child's birth in January 1245, the saint had responded to his supplications and the queen's.[28] Bury was included in the East Anglian tour Henry undertook in the immediately following Lent, and on 30 May he instructed the sheriff of Buckingham to have a window in the royal bedchamber at Brill neatly blocked up and an image of 'St Edmund standing' painted in the space.[29] Already there was an image of the saint at Westminster, for in April 1243 Henry sent orders from Bordeaux for the gilding of the diadems of the statues of both Edmund and Edward. 'An image of St Edmund the King with a crown and two large sapphires and a ruby in the crown and two emeralds and other small jewels', worth £86, was included in an inventory of furnishings at Westminster which might have to be pawned or sold to meet the king's necessities during the crisis of 1267.[30] Henry was at Bury for the saint's feast-day (20 November) in both 1235 and 1248, and in several other years he issued instructions for the rapid conveyance of offerings in wax, cloth or coin, to arrive at the shrine by that date (the saint's anniversary) and 29 April (the translation). When he visited Bury in early September 1252 he had already (while at St Albans) commissioned a crown with four floral finials, which was to cost £10, and in November he gave instructions that it was to be sent, with a quantity of gold coin and some cloth, to arrive at Bury if possible on the feast of St Edmund.[31] On 23 April 1253 he ordered gold coins and wax to be sent there, prompted by the illness of both himself and the young Edmund to remember the feast of the translation.[32]

The arrangements which had to be made for the royal household when the king conducted a full-blown regional tour can sometimes be followed in detail. Wine was frequently ordered in January and June for distribution to important stopping places, not only St Albans and St Edmunds, but Canterbury and the major stops along the way, Rochester and Faversham. Such orders were given, for example, on 7 January 1246, and on the same day the king sent twenty marks to the prior of Walsingham for the making of a gold crown for the head of the image of the Virgin, perhaps with the approaching Feast of the Purification in mind.[33] On 6 March 1255, six tuns of wine were to be sent to the king at St Albans 'by Thursday for his breakfast', as well as all the fish which came from Winchelsea to London, 'without delay'.[34] On 15 February 1256, the king was at Woodstock, and ordered that two tuns of wine should be sent to St Albans with all speed 'to place in the king's cellars there against his arrival, which will be shortly'. On the 23rd, order was given for twelve bucks to be delivered to St Albans, where he stayed between the 25th and the 28th. Henry moved on to Royston on 29 February, where, with Lent imminent, instructions were sent to the sheriffs of London to obtain twenty-five gallons of nut oil for delivery to the king at St Edmund's on the Saturday after Ash Wednesday, together with 2000 chestnuts. Henry was at Bury by 5 March, when he ordered a daily supply of mackerel, some of it salted and some packed in bread, to be sent to him while he was in Suffolk and Norfolk during Lent. On the same day he made a gift of twenty marks to the abbot and prior of Bury to help them to finish a picture in front of the high altar, and on the 8th he rewarded Mabel of St Edmund's, 'who had long served the king and queen in the making of ecclesiastical ornaments'. She was to have six ells of cloth of her choice and rabbit skins for a robe.[35]

Mabel is a reminder of the artisans and merchants on whom the king depended for the supply of the costly offerings he gave or sent to prominent shrines and of course to other lords. Mabel was certainly working for the king fifteen years earlier, for in the Michaelmas term of 1241 she was being paid substantial arrears owing to her for an embroidered cope; for whom this was intended is not stated. There is also a tribute to her expertise in a letter written from Bordeaux in July 1243, in which Henry ordered 'a standard of a good red samite, well embroidered in gold, as Mabel of St Edmund's shall best be able to manage'.[36] The king did not however always support home industries. It was possibly during his stay at Bury in 1256 that he presented the convent with an embroidered cope for which the Lucchese merchant Buono Roncino was paid eighteen marks on 29 May, but this gift may have been sent to the abbey subsequently.[37] The king moved on from Bury to Walsingham, where he is recorded between 15 and 17 March, and to Bromholm on 20 March. This seems to have been his last visit to Bromholm, and probably his last to Walsingham before he stopped there late in September 1272, less than two months before his death.

While he was abroad, Henry kept his obligations to three English shrines particularly in mind: the Confessor's at Westminster of course, but also those of St Thomas and St Edmund. In September 1254 he wrote from Gascony to his officials at Westminster with instructions that they should without fail make the offerings due from himself, his queen and Prince Edward at the shrine of the Confessor and also send 'a fine brooch, orna- mented with jewels, price ten marks', to be attached to the shrine of St Edmund. In addition they were to provide him with a hundred pounds of jewels to offer to the Confessor on his return, 'and they should have some other befitting jewels which he could offer on his arrival at Canterbury in reverence of the blessed martyr Thomas and the other saints who rest in that town'.[38] Henry of course could not ignore his responsibilities to St Thomas's shrine, and he also ensured that others did their public duty to the martyr. In May 1255 he gave orders that offerings should be provided for Eleanor of Castile, the bride of the young Edward, to present at Canterbury and at Westminster on her arrival in England. In November Buono Roncino was remunerated for cloths of gold and silk which were supplied to the princess on this occasion.[39]

The king continued to favour St Edmund in the later years of his reign. In 1262 he was again in France a month before the saint's feast and on 27 October gave instructions from Meaux that coins and gold should be sent to the shrine on his behalf.[40] He was at Bury in February 1267, but this was no tranquil pilgrimage; he was campaigning against the Disinherited, the followers of Simon de Montfort who were holding out in the Isle of Ely.[41] In the last months of the king's life he visited the town again, on his way to Norwich to punish the sacrilegious damage done by the townsfolk to the cathedral and the property of the bishop and clergy.[42] From Norwich he made his last journey to Walsingham. On this occasion, fittingly, he settled a lot of bills with Walsingham townsfolk, including purveyors of meat and bread.[43] Henry's death cemented his alliance with the martyr-king. He survived the feast of the translation of the Confessor by over a month, and died at Westminster on the feast of St Edmund in 1272.

It is unfortunate that, although we have a wealth of information about Henry's visits and benefactions to Bury, Bromholm and Walsingham, we do not have chronicle descriptions comparable to those which Matthew Paris provides for St Albans between 1244 and 1258. Matthew spoke with the king, at St Albans and at London, on several occasions, and it is he who gives us the best insight into the spirit in which Henry undertook his pilgrimages. A few days before Christmas 1244 his offerings at St Albans included a piece of precious cloth and three gold rings which were attached to the shrine, 'in remembrance of himself and to honour the martyr'.[44] In August 1252 he was accompanied by his son Edward, who offered at the shrine of St Amphibalus a piece of cloth and two rings, which the king ordered the following day should be sold and the money devoted to 'covering' the shrine. After a stay of five days, Henry proceeded to the siege of Bedford.[45] In March 1255 he came to St Albans and with great reverence prayed to the saint 'as the protomartyr of his kingdom, for himself and for his son Edward and for his other friends'.[46] Henry's visit in February 1256 came as a surprise to the convent, according to Matthew, but they benefited to the extent of four cloth hangings, one each for the altars of St Alban, St Amphibalus, St Wulfstan and St Mary.[47]

Matthew's descriptions hint that, as the reign progressed, Henry's conduct and conversation as a pilgrim to St Alban more and more reflected his specifically royal purposes. He must have been aware of the special linkage between the abbey and the Anglo-Saxon monarchy. In 1256 the monks adopted new regulations for the commemoration of their founder, or re-founder, Offa of Mercia. Matthew had already commented that no English king, not even Offa, had bestowed so many precious *pallia* on St Albans as Henry had done.[48] In March 1257 the king visited the abbey after the discovery of the supposed original tomb of St Alban, bearing lavish gifts, including a silver chalice, in which the dust discovered in the tomb was to be kept, and six silk *pannos*, one of which was to cover the newly-discovered mausoleum. It was on this occasion that Henry recited the names of the sainted kings of England, who included, besides Edmund and Edward the Confessor, Oswald, Edward the Martyr and also Oswiu, who was venerated at St Albans and its dependent priory of Tynemouth.[49]

Henry, it may be surmised, was haunted by the images of holy kings and perhaps even, with a sidelong glance at his cousin of France, whose formidable reputation anticipated his death, aspired to be reckoned among them. Henry was not above indulging in a little spiritual one-upmanship when he saw the opportunity. On one occasion Louis urged him to hear more sermons and fewer masses; Henry replied with a smile that if one had a beloved friend, one would surely prefer to see him rather than just to hear him talked about.[50] The two kings were basically of one mind, however, about the dignity of kingship. In 1264 Louis was called upon to arbitrate between Henry and the English barons and predictably annulled the Provisions of Oxford which had placed the royal power under restraint. Oxford itself soon afterwards received a royal visit which, as several chroniclers described it, demonstrated Henry's conviction of his own majesty and rectitude. According to the Annals of Oseney, he 'entered the church of

St Frideswide with great devotion, which no king had tried to do since the time of king Algar [*recte* Ethelbald of Mercia]. He conferred many goods on the church and promised more if God would give him victory over his enemies.' On 14 October the sheriff of Oxford was duly ordered to pay 100s. without delay to the prior and convent of St Frideswide; this was to be an annual grant to maintain two chaplains and also four tapers, which were to burn night and day before the shrine for the souls of the king, his predecessors and successors.[51] Henry thus sought to neutralise a tradition which, recalling the evil Ethelbald's attempt to ravish the virgin Frideswide, debarred the king himself from direct access to one of the notable shrines of his kingdom. In 1275, however, Edward I allegedly did not take the same risk; although the clergy and nobility of the city were prepared to come forth to meet him in solemn array, the king retired promptly to the castle.[52]

Henry's pilgrimages could be said to mingle purposes which were more and less obviously political. At Oxford in 1264 he was making a dramatic demonstration of royal power and piety. At St Albans and at Bury he publicly associated himself, throughout his reign, with cults of special significance in the history of the kingdom. At Walsingham and Bromholm, he was either responding to fashion or creating it: these were shrines which represented the most powerful strains of later medieval piety, devotion to the Virgin and to the person of Christ Himself. Walsingham however retained its popularity with royalty right down to the Reformation, while Bromholm did not.

It has been suggested that Henry's greatest benefaction to Walsingham was the devotion to the shrine which he instilled in his eldest son.[53] Perhaps this was indeed why Edward believed that it was Our Lady of Walsingham who had saved him from death as a young man when part of the ceiling of a room in which he had been playing chess collapsed.[54] The pattern of his recorded visits as king, however, suggests an attachment which intensified in his later years. On his arrival back in England after his father's death he and Queen Eleanor went not to Walsingham but to Bury, in accordance with a vow which they had made in the Holy Land.[55] His first recorded visit to Walsingham took place in March 1277, when he was there on Palm Sunday. Like his father on so many occasions, he moved on within a few days to Bromholm, which however received little attention from him subsequently. He paid another visit to Walsingham in January 1281, but is not recorded there again until in September 1289, returning from Gascony, he went with Eleanor to Walsingham, 'to fulfil his vows' . He was there again for the same purpose in late 1292.[56] Thereafter his visits to Walsingham were more frequent and sometimes lengthy, as when in February 1294 he stayed there for most of two weeks before moving on, more briefly, to Bury.

In the winter of 1296–97, after a successful campaign in Scotland, Edward's itinerary incorporated stays at several notable shrines. He spent much of November 1296 at Bury, where he received the nobles who were accompanying John, count of Holland and Zeeland, to England for his marriage with the king's daughter Elizabeth. They proceeded to Ipswich to solemnise both Christmas and the wedding. The bride and her brother then returned to Windsor to await the king, who wished to perform a pilgrimage to Walsingham. His itinerary in fact shows that having left Ipswich on 10 January he went by way of Harwich, briefly Bury again, and Castle Acre, arriving at Walsingham very appropriately for the feast of the Purification (2 February) 1297. He stayed there until the 8th and then paid short visits to Ely and St Albans before arriving at Windsor on the 19th or 20th of the month.[57] He visited Walsingham in each of the years 1298, 1299, 1300 and 1302; on what proved to be his last visit, in 1305, he again managed to be present for the Feast of the Purification. He sent an image of himself to the shrine as his father had done to Bromholm, and numerous other benefactions besides.

Was this simply personal piety or, because Edward was a king, was the personal political? Focussing on royal visits and oblations to one particular shrine carries with it the risk of isolating attachment to one cult or another from the wider picture to which it belongs. Edward's itinerary shows that, not unnaturally, his visits to Walsingham, like his father's, were preceded or followed by a visit to Bury and very often also to St Albans. As he himself might well have said, he was a busy man, and isolated journeys for pious purposes, which for his lesser subjects might represent a holiday from the workaday routine, cannot often have been a practical possibility for him. His pilgrimages had to be integrated into a schedule which served many other purposes, and they had to carry weight as public demonstrations of royal *pietas*.

Edward had learned that part of his trade at his father's side, and some at least of his pilgrimages were family affairs. The journey made by the king and queen, with their five daughters and their infant son, to celebrate the Feast of the Translation of St Thomas at Canterbury in July 1285 has been reconstructed from a wardrobe account.[58] They went by water from Westminster as far as Chatham, where they all made their offerings at the then splendid church of St Mary. Payment was also made there for the burning of wax candles of a total length equal to the combined heights of the royal family. At Canterbury offerings were made at all the principal holy places in the cathedral and elsewhere in the town; like his father before him, Edward remembered St Adrian and St Mildred at St Augustine's Abbey, and the rest of the family followed suit. After leaving Canterbury the royal party traversed Kent and Sussex and offered at the shrine of St Richard at Chichester, where the king also gave alms to a guitarist whom he found playing at the shrine.

It was on this tour that Edward presented four images (of St Edward and the pilgrim, and of St George and his horse) to the shrine of St Thomas. This opulent gift can be taken as evidence not merely of the king's devotion to the saint, but of what may loosely be described as the royal policy of bringing into association emblems of different cults which were of importance to the monarchy. Henry III had made much of the statue of St Edmund at Westminster, and Edward's gift to Canterbury now imported the Confessor and the soldier saint into the presence of St Thomas. Perhaps the king thought that the martyr should reciprocate by performing a small service for him; in the following year he sent a wax image of a sick gerfalcon to be offered at St Thomas's altar, presumably either in thanks for or in hope of a cure. This gesture seems less idiosyncratic if it is recalled that Becket had in fact effected several cures of hawks in the very early years of his cult.

Edward's visits to Canterbury were numerous, and only a few of them can certainly be identified as having taken place simply in transit to or from the Continent. [59] In several years he made more than one visit, notably in 1299, when he was there in May, July and September. St Thomas was not in the front line of defence against the Scots, but the discovery of a Scottish royal crown in John Balliol's luggage when he passed through Dover on his way to France enabled Edward to confiscate it and offer it in July at the saint's altar. The king was back in September to be married to Margaret of France before the shrine of the martyr.[60]

The mere fact that the king was bodily present at a place where there was a noteworthy shrine cannot automatically be taken to mean that worshipping there was the sole or even chief purpose of his visit. The position of Canterbury between London and the coast, or of St Albans on a major road out of London to the north, made it highly likely that kings, like any of their subjects who were professionally mobile, would frequently pass through and indeed make overnight stays there. The same could be said of Waltham, which was a common royal stopping-place out of London on the road to East Anglia, particularly for Henry III; the veneration of the Holy Cross may have been a consequence as much as it was a purpose of the journey. The kings had a principal residence at Winchester and went there frequently; there is no reason to suppose that they went there primarily in order to venerate St Swithun or the other saints of Winchester, although they doubtless often did so. The Winchester annalist appreciated this point when he reported that in January 1276 Edward and the queen came to

Winchester, 'that is, to the castle', for the first time since his return from the Holy Land; but on the following day 'he came to the monastery of St Swithun by reason of prayer and reverence for the saints'.[61] The same point can be made with reference to royal visits to Worcester. We know of the devotion to St Wulfstan which John expressed on his deathbed, but the Worcester annalist only takes note of his visit in 1207.[62] He undoubtedly did reverence to the saint on other occasions, but there is no direct testimony to it. Similarly, Henry III was a frequent visitor to Worcester, but there is little evidence that he showed special favour to Wulfstan, although we know that he offered a pallium to his altar at St Albans when he paid his surprise visit there in 1256.

Edward I had reason to give more pointed attention to St Wulfstan. The problems of Wales frequently brought him to the west midlands, and he is recorded at Worcester on numerous occasions between 1276 and 1283 and again between 1291 and 1295. He celebrated Christmas there in 1281 and Pentecost in 1282. Only some of these visits are mentioned by the Worcester annalist, and it is not always indicated that the king paid any special attention to St Wulfstan.[63] For example, in 1278 it is simply recorded that he met Llewellyn at Worcester. Another event, noted earlier in the year by the same annalist, may supply a little more context for this meeting, whether or not the Welsh prince was aware of it. At Easter, Edward and Eleanor had been at Glastonbury where 'the lord king had the tomb of Arthur opened, many people did not know why. He had the bones gathered together and fittingly deposited in the treasury of the monastery until he could have them more honourably bestowed'. The demonstration of royal patronage was unequivocal, as it had not been when the remains were first 'discovered' in 1191, and there can be little doubt that it all had to do with the assertion of authority over the Welsh.[64]

The king was at Worcester again in 1281, but the description of his visit in November 1283 is for the first time explicit: 'King Edward, having subjugated all Wales, came to Worcester on pilgrimage (*gratia visitandi*) to St Wulfstan, for whom he felt a special love'. The royal accounts reveal generous oblations on this occasion to the relics of Wulfstan and Oswald.[65] Another royal visit to Worcester in November 1291 is again simply noted by the annalist, but Edward was careful to enlist the patronage of St Wulfstan during the next few years, and not only against the Welsh. On 16 February 1293 a royal clerk brought offerings to the shrine because the king was in haste to cross to France, and the chapter decreed on the same day that three weekly masses of St Wulfstan should be celebrated until the king had safely returned to England.

In November 1294 Edward again passed through Worcester on his way to Chester to punish the rebellious Welsh and heard a mass of St Wulfstan. The most notable of his pilgrimages took place the following year:

> On the 20th day of July the king and his people came early to Worcester by boat; that day he had vespers solemnly sung, and on the morrow a mass of St Wulfstan, and he offered a brooch worth eleven marks to St Wulfstan and one of 100 shillings to St Oswald, and two noble hangings to the altar. After mass the king knelt before St Wulfstan in the presence of the prior and the chanter, and said 'How can I repay the blessed Wulfstan for all that by his holy prayers he has conferred on me? This small thing I vow, in the presence of God and his saints, that in the fulness of time I shall pay for the support of three monks and two candles to burn before the saint.'

It took the king a few years to keep his promise, but in the meantime he sent more offerings to the shrine, including 'a gold ring and nine candles for the tomb and fourteen *solidi* in silver' when he landed in Dover in May 1295 after making a truce with Philip IV of France. At last, in April 1301, he came once more to Worcester with his pregnant queen and, 'mindful of his former vow', conferred the church of Worfield on the convent in fulfilment of it. His presence at Worcester is not recorded again, but in 1307, in the final months of his life, he was exerting considerable pressure on the bishop and chapter of Hereford to consent to the appropriation of the church of Lindridge to the prior and convent of Worcester in order to fulfil promises he had made to St Wulfstan.[66]

Edward's dealings with St Wulfstan are representative. We know enough about only some of his frequent visits to St Albans or to Bury to be sure that paying homage to the saints was the purpose of his visit. St Albans could easily be visited from the favoured royal residence at Langley. The younger Edward and his household made a lengthy stay at Langley and St Albans at Christmas 1294, with devastating results for the markets in the surrounding area; according to the Dunstable annalist the prince's household officers took all the provisions there were to be had for miles around, without payment, and extorted additional supplies from local traders. By contrast, the king's conduct, when he spent Christmas at St Albans the following year, was exemplary.[67] Edward sometimes visited Bury when he was *en route* elsewhere, often to Norwich, as he did in November 1278 when he and the queen attended the consecration of the restored cathedral. It is clear, however, that he went to some trouble to enlist both St Alban and St Edmund in his great causes.

In February 1285 Edward came to Bury with the queen and three of his daughters 'to fulfil vows made to God and the saint in his Welsh war'.[68] In 1284–85 the king was contributing to the making or remaking of the patronal shrines of both St Edmund and St David.[69] In 1292 he attended the feast of the translation of St Edmund with a resplendent entourage, including apparently both his son and daughters and the counts of Flanders and of Holland, before going on to Walsingham.[70] In March 1294 he came to Bury 'with great devotion', but only for one night.[71] It was remarked that in November 1296, after victory over the Scots, Edward came to Bury and held a parliament, but did not stay at the abbey, which gave offence. Nonetheless he kept the Feast of St Edmund there and feasted the convent, and Rhys ap Gryffyd submitted to him on the feast-day itself, for which the king gave due thanks.[72]

Later in his reign it was against the Scots that Edward needed most help. The most memorable accounts of his visits to St Albans and Bury come from the years of military activity in 1299–1300. The abbot of St Albans was among the guests at Langley at All Saints in 1299, when Edward, on his way north to invest Stirling, stopped there to celebrate the feast with the queen and other notables including the bishop of Norwich and the count of Savoy. On the following day, All Souls, the king came to St Albans, staying only for one night. The next morning he heard mass and with all his nobles prostrated himself before the martyr while a special canticle of St Alban was sung with the king's approaching expedition in mind. Then, as the large congregation fell silent, Edward explained the purpose of his visit to them:

> I have come devoutly hither for this reason, to seek licence and aid of the glorious martyr Alban and humbly to beg from this convent and people the benefit of their prayers. I must go to Scotland to suppress the arrogant presumption of my enemies the Scots, and I have no idea whether I shall succeed or whether I shall return.

At once all present promised their prayers and special masses and daily devotions. The king then set off towards Scotland with greater confidence.[73]

This was not all; after another three weeks the queen, Margaret of France, came to St Albans with her stepson the young Edward. She was received with great solemnity and made opulent offerings, and proceeded to stay for three weeks, even informing the king that she would like to spend Christmas there. On reflection she decided to go to Windsor instead, but before departing she entered the chapter and humbly sought membership in the fraternity of the abbey. She was, one chronicler observes, 'truly religious and devout in the divine services'.[74] It was not long before she, and the king, were at St Albans again. Edward himself spent Christmas at Berwick, but he was back at Windsor in late January 1300, preparing to organise a further Scottish offensive. He visited Canterbury in February and made a prolonged stay at Westminster in March. Meanwhile he had ordered his notables to assemble at St Albans to celebrate Easter with the royal family.[75] His presence at St Albans is recorded from 6–15 April.

He then proceeded to assure himself of the assistance of another of his principal patrons. On 9 May he came to Bury 'in order to dedicate his life to the blessed martyr with deep devotion. Never had he appeared more gracious to the church and convent'. He directed his justices not to infringe the privileges of the church, and expressed his confidence that the saint would be with him in Scotland in 'flashing armour'. A few days after he had left the abbey he sent back his standard so that a mass of St Edmund might be said over it and all the relics in the abbey touched to it. The itinerary shows that the king proceeded to Walsingham: the young Edward of Caernavon, who had been admitted to the fraternity of the abbey, stayed behind for several days, eating a monk's allowance of food, before hastening to join his father.[76]

Obviously the Scottish enterprise also meant enlisting the saints of the north, above all St Cuthbert and St John of Beverley. Edward did not venture to the north east of his kingdom until August 1280, when he went to Yorkshire for the first time in his reign. At various times after that he is recorded at Knaresborough and Tynemouth (where of course there were castles), at Ripon and at Beverley, in all of which places notable saints were there to be venerated if the king was so minded. In September 1280 he visited Durham for the first time as king, and in January 1284 he went specially to York in order to participate personally in the translation of St William's relics to a new shrine behind the high altar.[77] Carlisle too possessed religious as well as strategic significance for him. The cathedral had by this date obtained possession of the sword with which Becket had been murdered, and in 1297 Robert Bruce swore fidelity to Edward on this potent relic. Edward naturally made several visits to the city, and on the last, in the year of his death, bestowed the advowson of Castle Sowerby on the canons out of devotion to the Virgin and the relics of St Thomas.[78]

During the campaign of 1296 the banner of St John of Beverley was carried into battle against the Scots, and in September, at Berwick, the king granted gifts and privileges to both St Cuthbert and St John. He visited Durham briefly on 5 October, and Beverley on the 14th.[79] In 1298 he visited St John again in early June, before making his way to Roxburgh to find his army duly assembled at the appointed time.[80] In 1301, the banners of both St John and St Cuthbert were carried into battle against the Scots.[81] Edward was by now sufficiently well-informed to be able to tell the pope, in May 1301, that King Athelstan had invoked St John against the Scots, with miraculous success which was remembered every week in the church at Beverley.[82]

While the king's itinerary reveals a pattern that was broadly determined by the exigencies of war against the Scots, it also accommodated displays of devotion that were themselves part of the military and political agenda. The royal family as well as the king himself had a role to play in this public propitiation of the saints. Queens both accompanied their husbands on state visits to shrines and carried out independent pilgrimages. The newly-wed Margaret was employed in November 1299 to follow up her husband's lightning visit to St Albans, while on other occasions queens carried out veritable pilgrimage tours on their own account, which may have reflected not only their piety but their relative abundance of leisure. Unsurprisingly perhaps, this was a favourite occupation of widowed queens. In 1243 Pope Innocent IV authorised Isabella, the queen mother, to enter Cistercian churches *orationis causa*, accompanied by ten respectable women. It was probably in the context of this same tour that a reference occurs in January 1244 to a cope offered by the king's mother at St Thomas's shrine.[83] The Tewkesbury annalist noted that Queen Eleanor came to the abbey 'for the first time' in 1236, while in October 1257 she visited St Albans after a severe illness during which she had had herself 'measured' and vowed an offering to the martyr.[84]

Given that queens (before Elizabeth Woodville in the fifteenth century) were invariably of non-English and often of French birth, their homage to the saints of their adoptive kingdom may have had an additional public relations value on which increasing stress was laid when relations with the French were strained. Henry III and Eleanor of Provence called not only upon St Edmund but on St Thomas when she was pregnant with the young Edmund.[85] It was reported that Margaret of France invoked Thomas of Canterbury during her labour in 1300; coins which had been laid upon her belly were sent to be placed on the martyr's altar at Canterbury. The claim that the infant (another Edmund) refused a French wet-nurse was perhaps excessive.[86] Thanksgiving for the birth of children provided an unimpeachable pretext for pilgrimages such as Queen Philippa's to St Albans in 1341 after the birth of Edmund of Langley.[87] Only the potential political importance of the babies concerned differentiated such pilgrimages from those undertaken by mothers (and fathers) of much lowlier rank.

Although the styles of kingship represented by Henry III and Edward I in some respects look different, not least because of Edward's warrior image, pilgrimage, the very public display of reverence to saints who were either bound up with the history of the monarchy or were important regional patrons or both, played a conspicuous part in the timetables of both kings. That normally remained true for their successors both warlike and unwarlike, but there was some room for individual variation. Pilgrimage was a physical, active form of piety and, above all in the form of the supreme pilgrimage to the Holy Land, it met the need felt by warriors through the ages to call down divine assistance on their enterprises and fitted well into their chivalric self-image. When he delivered, or reported, summary judgements on the warrior kings Edward III and Henry V, the chronicler Thomas Walsingham noted that Edward was 'devoted to God, always making pilgrimages and venerating and honouring the ministers of the church', while Henry was 'frequent in pilgrimages'.[88] The less warlike King Edward II, who disappointed in other respects, seems to have been overshadowed as a pilgrim by his wife, Isabella of France. He did however visit Canterbury at least sixteen times during his reign, and is also known to have visited St Albans on a number of occasions, which would not have been difficult given his liking for the royal residence at Langley. On the eve of Palm Sunday in 1314 he offered there a gold cross inset with jewels and relics, and commended himself, the queen and his son to the prayers of the brethren. It was on this visit that he made a grant towards the completion of work on the choir, in fulfilment of what he knew his father's intentions to have been. He was back in August 1315, a year of dearth and famine, when sufficient bread could scarcely be found to sustain his household.[89] His first recorded visit to Walsingham also took place in 1315, although he had some years earlier made a generous grant to the house of licence to acquire lands and rents in mortmain, this, significantly, at the instance of Queen Isabella. She accompanied him on his visit in October 1315 and seems to have outdone him in the generosity of her oblations. He was certainly not the frequent visitor to the shrine that his grandfather or his father had been or that his son would be. In 1326, the last full year of his reign, he may have felt the urgent need of the succour of the Virgin, however, for he was at Walsingham for the Feast of the Purification.[90] Within a shorter space of time than he would have wished, he himself was to be an object of pilgrimage.

Before and after she disposed of her husband, Isabella was an enthusiastic pilgrim. In 1321 she was on her way to Canterbury when the wife of Bartholomew de Badlesmere refused her entry to Leeds Castle, and Edward took punitive action.[91] In December 1322, when she was planning a pilgrimage tour of the kingdom, Edward issued letters patent directing sheriffs and other officials to provide carriage for her goods and harness and necessaries for her household at her expense.[92] Late in 1326, when she returned with her son from France to inaugurate the final crisis of her husband's reign, she advanced on Bury with her supporters 'as if on pilgrimage'.[93] She remained an enthusiastic pilgrim and collector of relics during her thirty year long widowhood, which ended only with her death in 1358; she may well have felt that she had a good deal to repent at leisure. She spent much of her time at Castle Rising in Norfolk, which made frequent pilgrimages to Walsingham easy, but she dreamed of more extravagant ventures. In 1359 the pope authorised the bishop of London to publish the absolution she had received for her failure to fulfil a vow to go to the Holy Sepulchre.[94]

Edward III upheld many of the observances that would have been familiar to his grandfather and even his great-grandfather, as indeed we might expect. At least in the early years of his reign he visited Bury, St Albans and Walsingham with reasonable frequency, as they had done. He was at Bury and Walsingham in September 1328, at St Albans in January 1329 and again in January 1331, at Bury in late May of 1331 and at Walsingham in late June.[95] An unexpected visit to Canterbury in September 1332, when the prior of Christ Church was absent, required heroic efforts from the sub-prior to provide fit hospitality.[96] Edward visited both Bury and Walsingham in August 1333, presumably as part of the pilgrimage which a chronicler described him as undertaking after he had (temporarily) settled the affairs of the Scots, leaving Edward Balliol apparently in control of the kingdom: 'with a small household he went on pilgrimage to the holy places of England to which his devotion led him'.[97] In 1334 the king was at Bury in July and went to Walsingham in October, immediately after a short stay at St Albans. He was at Walsingham again in both 1335 and 1336.

If he was unable later in his reign to conduct domestic pilgrimages as often as he might have wished, Edward could and did send regular oblations, especially to Walsingham and other Marian shrines. He was also regular in offering to St Edmund and of course to St Edward, while his continuing embroilment with the Scots dictated that, like his grandfather, he remembered the saints of the north. He normally visited Canterbury every year, which might mean offering not only to St Thomas and the other holy places in the cathedral but to St Augustine, St Adrian and St Mildred at St Augustine's. Edward attended the translation of Thomas Cantilupe of Hereford in 1349 and made one other known pilgrimage to the shrine, in 1353.

War with France disrupted the pattern of the king's domestic pilgrimages, but it also provided a new context for the public advertisement of royal and English piety. During a turbulent sea-crossing from France in March 1343, Edward made many vows and promises of works of piety. Having landed safely at Weymouth, he went to London to greet the queen and then set out 'on foot' to Canterbury. Next he went to Gloucester and Walsingham, 'and other holy places', on horseback this time, but modestly escorted, as in 1333 (*cum mediocri familia equitando*). The tour lasted until Passion Sunday, when he joined the queen, still with a modest entourage, to celebrate Easter at Havering-atte-Bower in Essex.[98] The inspiration for this multiple pilgrimage seems obvious enough; giving thanks for deliverance from the perils of the sea was a common motivation for pilgrims all over Christendom. Yet, because kings were kings, and because Edward was at war with France, it is also tempting to see it as a propaganda move aimed at English 'public opinion': the king was to be seen on the road, with his 'modest escort', acknowledging that his fate was in the hands of the Almighty. The inclusion of his father's burial-place in this pious itinerary is especially interesting. Gloucester received one of five golden ships which the king presented that year to favoured churches, visually echoing his new coinage which showed him aboard a warship: the victory of Sluys in 1339 had prompted this form of propaganda. Two of the other ships went to Canterbury, to St Thomas and to the Lady chapel which was a favourite object of Edward's benefactions, one to the Virgin of St Paul's and one to Walsingham.[99] Only a few years later, Gloucester Abbey was to be adorned with the great east window which was in effect a Crécy war memorial (and in which Edward II is most probably depicted).

Edward visited Glastonbury with Queen Philippa in 1331 and some years later, in June 1345, granted John Blome of London permission to dig for the remains of Joseph of Arimathea at Glastonbury, which John informed him he had been divinely directed to do. The promotion of Joseph was an important episode in Glastonbury's ongoing multiplication of cults, and was of course linked to the Arthurian interests which had already attracted Edward I and were certainly congenial to his grandson.[100] If this represented an effort to enhance the prestige and mystique of one of England's ancient holy places and indeed of the kingdom, Edward's apparent indifference to such shrines as Reading Abbey, Hailes and Bromholm, the homes of relics of foreign provenance, has been seen as supporting evidence of the 'nationalistic' colouration of his piety.[101] Already in the thirteenth century, however, there is little evidence of much royal interest in Reading, and Bromholm seems to have lost much of its appeal for the monarchy after the middle of Henry III's reign. As for Hailes, Edward I visited it four times; on the last occasion, in March 1301, it was to attend the funeral of his cousin Edmund of Cornwall, the son of the founder. Edward II seems to have been there only once, early in May 1326, when he was taking refuge in the west country. The third Edward's indifference may therefore be less noteworthy than it might appear; Bromholm's fashionable heyday had passed, while that of Hailes had yet to come.

The king was sometimes accompanied by his eldest son when he visited shrines before departing on his expeditions overseas. In the summer of 1346, before the Crécy campaign, the prince went to Bury and Walsingham and later joined his father at Canterbury. They undertook another such tour in 1355, when the prince offered at Walsingham, and again in 1359; in France in 1360 they went together to Pontigny.[102] French hostages in England were sometimes licensed to make pilgrimages to Walsingham and Canterbury, and in 1360 King John II himself, on his way back to France in the company of the Prince of Wales, paused at Canterbury to make offerings both to St Thomas and the image of the Virgin in the crypt, so beloved of both Edward III and his son. When in October 1364 Count Louis of Flanders came to Dover to negotiate terms for the projected marriage of his daughter to Edmund Langley, it was indispensable that he should visit Canterbury in the company of the king's sons, returning to Dover on the following day.[103]

The personal attachment of the Black Prince to Canterbury is graphically expressed to this very day in the presence of his tomb and funeral achievements, not far from the now empty site of the martyr's shrine, although that was not the prince's own choice of burial place. Filial piety helped ensure that Richard II fulfilled what he would probably anyway have seen as his royal obligations to Canterbury, which he visited in 1382, 1384 (when like so many of his predecessors he is known to have offered at a number of holy places in the cathedral), 1392 and 1393, when his various offerings are again recorded and he attended a requiem mass for his father. It has however been suggested that Richard moved in the course of his reign from the style of religion which his parents transmitted to him to a more personal, inward piety which reflected the trends of the time.[104] He differed from his predecessors, not excepting Henry III, in large part precisely because he belonged to a changed religious environment. At the same time, he was at least as devout a believer in the religion of the monarchy as any of them. His regard for St Edward and St Edmund (both portrayed in the Wilton Diptych) would have been intelligible to his forbears, as his Marian piety would also have been, certainly to Edward III. St Edward the Martyr, another royal Anglo-Saxon saint, also attracted his devotion, and in 1397 he gave the monks of Reading Abbey a year in which to restore the tomb of his predecessor Henry I: only on this condition would he confirm their privileges. He also devoted a great deal of effort to the cause of obtaining the canonisation of his great-grandfather Edward II, whose tomb at Gloucester he visited on several occasions.

In May and June 1383 Richard and his queen performed just such a pilgrimage tour as so many of his predecessors had done, to Walsingham, Bury and Ely, where one of his courtiers experienced a notable miracle through St Etheldreda's intercession.[105] He seems never to have undertaken a similar tour again, a fact which might perhaps be taken to symbolise his hypothetical departure from old models. His other known pilgrimages combine the fulfilment of old obligations with the pursuit of new, or at least revived, fashions. He visited York in 1392 and, as at Canterbury, was a generous benefactor to its rebuilding programme. In March 1394 he was received at St Albans with a solemn procession.[106] He undertook a number of tours in the west country, for example in 1306 and 1398, which took in not only Gloucester, but places such as Tewkesbury, Evesham and Worcester which had long boasted notable relics. More novel was his personal encouragement of two cults, which, together with that of St David, were proclaimed as general feasts of the English church by the authority of Archbishop Walden of Canterbury in April 1398 and in 1416 by Henry Chichele.[107] Richard visited Lichfield for the first time in 1387 and from then on took a great interest in the cult of St Chad. In 1398 he visited St Winifred's shrine at Holywell, as Henry V would do almost twenty years later. All this devout activity had a melancholy finale. In 1399, on the point of crossing to Ireland, the king told his council that he wanted first to go on pilgrimage to Canterbury, but he felt he could not entrust his person either to the city of London or to the county of Kent. The archbishop of Canterbury personally guaranteed the king's safety and escorted him to the shrine and back under a heavy armed guard of men from Chester.[108]

Richard's adversary and eventual usurper, Henry Bolingbroke, earned a reputation as crusader and pilgrim in Prussia and the Holy Land during the early 1390s.[109] It is his son, Henry V, however, who has displayed the warrior image to the eyes of posterity. Henry strategically associated himself, as prince and as king, with regional cults both old and new. He went on pilgrimage to Canterbury in both 1403 and 1407, and, in accordance with an earlier vow, also visited a new saint, John of Bridlington, who was supposed to have prophesied that the throne would come to the House of Lancaster.[110] He is also known to have performed a pilgrimage to St Winifred. According to the chronicler Adam of Usk he made the journey on foot from Shrewsbury (where the saint's relics were venerated) to Holywell (which marked the site of her martyrdom).[111]

Returning to England after Agincourt, late in 1415, Henry landed at Dover and proceeded to Canterbury: 'and to meet him came the archbishop of Canterbury and all the monks in procession; and he alighted at the portal of St Thomas's church; where he offered his prayers, kissed the relics and made his offering'. Arriving at London, he went to St Paul's and adored the Holy Cross, the tomb of St Erkenwald and the high altar 'with great devotion and oblation', before going on to Westminster. This was all very much to be expected.[112] In 1421 the king took his new French wife on a pilgrimage tour of the kingdom (having purged her household of all French personnel except three noble waiting-women and two maids). In the course of this tour he visited both Beverley and Bridlington, and went on with Katherine to a number of other places including Lincoln, Walsingham and Norwich. He then kept the feast of St George at Windsor according to his usual custom.[113]

Canterbury and Walsingham seem to have maintained their status in the fifteenth century as shrines to which the kings were responsive whatever their personal characteristics, while St Albans has been described as 'fashionable' in the later fourteenth century.[114] An early fifteenth-century abbey chronicler was certainly able to recite a litany of distinguished visitors. In 1423 Humphrey, duke of Gloucester, spent Christmas at St Albans with his wife, Jacqueline of Hainault, and was followed during 1424 by Henry Beaufort, bishop of Winchester, and the earl of March. Humphrey of Gloucester arrived again in 1426 from a parliament at Leicester and went on to Barnet, while Henry Beaufort too was there again in 1427, as was the bishop of 'Chester'.[115] In June 1427 Queen Joanna, the widow of Henry IV, came St Albans 'from Walsingham, Norwich, Peterborough and various other places on pilgrimage', before going on to stay at Langley, as members of the royal family often did. Humphrey of Gloucester kept Christmas at the abbey again that year, and at Easter 1428 the young king and his mother were 'honourably received' there. Later in the year, the earl of Warwick was taken ill while approaching St Albans and was laid up there for six weeks, paying for everything *optime*, as the chronicler is careful to record. The countess of Westmoreland arrived on St Margaret's Day (20 July) while on a tour of 'several holy places'. Henry Beaufort, newly made a cardinal, was received with great pomp in 1428, with 'the new organs braying'; he blessed the people and offered at the shrine, where on the following day he heard three masses, before visiting the nuns of Sopwell and going on to have lunch with Queen Joanna at Langley. Humphrey of Gloucester was just passing through when he stayed for one night in late August on his way to settle a feud between the earl of Huntingdon and the duke of Norfolk.[116]

It might well be asked how many of these visits constituted 'real' pilgrimages and how many opportunistic indulgence in the abbey's hospitality. The earl of March in 1424 certainly behaved like a pilgrim. He stayed for only one night, offering a noble to the martyr, and also a sapphire ring which he directed should be fixed to the shrine. Queen Joanna's visit is explicitly described as a pilgrimage, by the use of both the adverb *peregre* and the descriptive phrase *causa devotionis*, and the countess of Westmoreland too was clearly on a pilgrimage tour. Similarly, Henry Beaufort came in 1427 *causa peregrinationis et devotionis*, whereas the bishop of 'Chester' (a former abbot of St Albans) was revisiting old haunts for what we might now term a retreat or at least a holiday (*gratia solatii et recreationis*). Humphrey of Gloucester was cultivating a very special relationship with the brethren, for he was to be buried in the abbey, in the magnificent tomb which still overlooks the martyr's shrine. The duke's patronage, however, was informed by the critical spirit that his humanistic interests had perhaps inculcated, for a century after his death Thomas More related the story of how he once unmasked a bogus cure of blindness, claimed by a beggar who was hoping to do well out of the crowds of people who were at St Albans because Henry VI was there.[117]

Whatever the precise motive of their visit, such notables would be received by the brethren in solemn procession, and they and members of their entourage might be received into the abbey's prayer fraternity. If this particular chronicle reads somewhat like a fifteenth-century court circular, the fact remains that many of the highly-placed persons whose movements are recorded regarded themselves as pilgrims, even if they were transacting other business in the course of the same journey. In this respect they in fact differed little from pilgrims lower down the social scale, who might well combine trade with pilgrimage. Royal 'pilgrimages' could, however, be burdensome if they resembled extended hotel stays. The young Henry VI's advisers in effect dumped him on the abbey of Bury St Edmund's for a period of four months, from Christmas 1433 to St George's Day 1434, it seems as a means of economising on household expenses. Even this had a positive outcome, in the form of John Lydgate's illuminated manuscript of his *Lives* of St Edmund and St Fremund of Dunstable, subsequently presented to the king, which commemorated his visit.[118]

Henry later visited Bury in four successive years between 1446 and 1449. 1448 can be identified as an exceptional pilgrimage year for him, in that it included a sortie into the north of the kingdom.[119] He was at Canterbury in March, but his large-scale journeying was concentrated into the second half of the year. He went from Westminster to Waltham Abbey on 6 June and spent the night of the 13th at Walsingham, proceeding via Norwich to Bury, where he stayed from 19–21 June. While at Bury, he also visited its dependency, the Marian shrine of Woolpit. Returning via Waltham to Westminster, he set off on a tour of the west country which took him *inter alia* to Shaftesbury, Glastonbury, Bristol and Malmesbury. Setting off again from Westminster early in September, he reached York on the 20th and stayed there for a few days before proceeding to Durham, where he was a pilgrim to St Cuthbert. He arrived on 26 September and stayed until the 30th with the bishop in the castle, attending first vespers, the procession, the mass and second vespers on St Michael's Day. He was at Beverley on 9 October on his way south, and at York again between the 13th and the 15th.

At Lincoln on 17th October he wrote a letter describing his reactions to his Durham visit:

Wee greet you hartly well, letting you witt that Blessed be our Lord God we have been right merry in our pilgramage, considering iij Causes, one is how that the Church of ye province of Yorke and diocesse of Durham be as nobill in doing of Divine Service in multitude of Ministers and in sumptuous & glorious buildinge, as anie in our Realme. And also how our Lord has radicate in the people his faith and his Law, and yat they be as Catholicke people as ever wee came amonge and all good and holy, that wee dare say, yat i Commandement may bee verified right well in them, *Diligunt Dominum Deum ipsorum ex totis animis suis et tota mente sua* (They love the Lord their God with all their hearts and all their minds). Alsoe they have done unto us all great hertly Reverence and Worshipp, as ever we had, with all great humanity and meekness, with all Celestiall, blessed and honourable speech and blessinge as it can be thought and imagined, and all good and better than wee had ever in our Life, eaven as they had been *caelitus inspirati* (heavenly inspired). Wherefore we dare well say, it may be verified in them ye holy saying of ye prince of ye Apostles, St Peter when he sayeth, *Deum timete. Regem honorificate. Qui timent Dominum et Regem honorificant cum debita Reverentia* (Fear God. Honour the King. Who fears God and the King gives honour with due reverence.) Wherefore ye Blessing yat God gave to Abraham Isack and Jacob descend upon them all &c.[120]

If this letter expresses a certain ingenuous enthusiasm, it also suggests that Henry was as well aware as any earlier king that the purpose of a royal pilgrimage was not only to give the king an opportunity to show reverence to the saints but to give his public an opportunity to do honour to him. Proceeding south, he visited St Albans on 31 October. After a period commuting between his principal residences in the London area, he was at Canterbury again in December before returning to Windsor for the Christmas season.

In 1449 Henry performed an East Anglian circuit which recalled old royal times: he was at Ely on 25–26 August, Walsingham on the 28th and 29th, Norwich on the next two days, and then Bury on 2–3 September, again going to Woolpit. He visited St Albans frequently, both earlier and especially later in his reign. He is recorded there in 1437, in three successive years 1450–52, in 1455 and again in successive years between 1458 and 1461. In 1455 the monks had reason to be glad that he was not, according to his usual custom, staying in the abbey when the first battle of St Albans erupted. Indeed, they attributed this unusual behaviour to the intervention of the martyr. The duke of York found the king in a tradesman's house and reverently brought him to the shrine, while his savage northerners despoiled the town.[121] Of Henry's other visits his Easter pilgrimage in

1459 is the most vividly described, in terms designed at least to hint at his Christ-likeness:

> near that time at which our Lord Jesus came to Jerusalem on an ass to celebrate that Pasch with his disciples, there also came our Lord King to the monastery, with his dukes and earls, barons and knights, and various other nobles and household servants.

On leaving he gave his best robe to the convent, which they then pawned. Among other pleasantries on this occasion the king asked that his obit should be celebrated by the brethren.[122]

It has been said that Henry's supplanter Edward IV was not noted for his patronage of learning or religion.[123] He is supposed to have had a personal devotion to the Virgin's mother St Anne, which was confirmed by a miracle at Daventry in 1471, at the climax of his struggle with the earl of Warwick. The manner in which this is described if anything reinforces the impression that Edward was a casual pilgrim. While the king was hearing mass, the saint suddenly opened the doors which concealed her image and then closed them again. This reminded the lackadaisical monarch that he had in fact previously vowed to make his prayer and give his offering to the next image of her he should see.[124]

The gossip that reached the Pastons in Norfolk occasionally informed them of pilgrimages Edward had made or intended to make. Their local interests were such that they were most likely to hear about the pilgrimages of the great to Walsingham, which was fashionable and attracted visitors of rank. Sir John Fastolf in 1456 knew that the duke of Norfolk was going to Walsingham on foot from Framlingham. Edward IV was rumoured to be coming to Walsingham in 1461, and in 1466 was certainly there on 21 and 22 June; he had previously been at Bury. He and the queen were expected at Walsingham again in late May 1469. The political upheavals of 1471 were followed by an epidemic which sent many people off on pilgrimage; in September the king and queen were reported to be riding to Canterbury, while the duke and duchess of Norfolk were going on foot to Walsingham. Edward was expected again at Walsingham in October 1475 on his return from France.[125] After 1478, however, he moved little beyond the vicinity of London. He left a memento of his presence at Canterbury in the form of the stained glass of the north-west transept, installed around 1480, which depicts him with his wife and children.

Whatever other continuities or discontinuities there may have been between the Yorkist and Tudor regimes, the royal predilection for Walsingham was maintained and even intensified under the first Tudors. Henry VII, who needed all the supernatural backing he could get for his dubious authority, was a noted devotee and frequent visitor. Early in 1487 he came to seek the Virgin's help against the rebellion of Lambert Simnel and returned after the battle of Stoke to give thanks. In 1505 he brought his son Henry to visit the shrine with him. In his will he desired that an image of himself should be set up at St Thomas's shrine at Canterbury to match the one that had already been sent to Walsingham.[126] Like Edward IV, Henry and his wife honoured St Anne: in 1486 he visited her chapel at Brislington near Bristol in 1486, and did so again with Elizabeth of York in 1502, when the queen offered 2s. 6d.[127] The royal couple also offered to the Holy Rood at Boxley, demonstrating not only their own piety, but also a continuing awareness of the royal need to be alive and responsive to the currents of devotion which were animating their subjects in different parts of the kingdom.[128]

Whatever counter-currents of criticism of pilgrimage were running, it would have been hard to imagine during the reign of the first Tudor king that the monarchy was soon to endorse them. The will of Katherine of Aragon remembered Our Lady of Walsingham, and for the greater part of their married life her husband seems to have shared in this devotion. Henry himself came to Walsingham on 19 January 1511 to give thanks for the birth of a son almost three weeks previously.[129] A host of notables displayed their devotion to Our Lady for as long as they were able to do so. In April 1513 the lord admiral, Sir Edward Howard, reported on the bravery of Arthur, Lord Lisle, the illegitimate son of Edward IV, who in great peril in action near Brest had vowed not to eat flesh or fish till he had seen Our Lady of Walsingham. Later in the year Katherine told the king that she was praying for his soul and his safety, and that she proposed to go to Walsingham 'that I promised so long ago to see'.[130] Henry's ambassador to the emperor, Sir Robert Wingfield, plaintively requesting his recall in 1515, expressed his intention of bearing his now white beard to Walsingham 'an God give me life', and Cardinal Wolsey made a well-publicised pilgrimage to the shrine in 1517.[131]

Early in the reign, Henry VIII was to be found making offerings in different parts of his kingdom, just as his predecessors had done. In the late summer of 1510, for example, offerings were recorded to a number of shrines in Hampshire, Dorset and Wiltshire, including St Osmund at Salisbury and Our Lady at Southwick.[132] Much later, it seemed still to be business as usual when in September 1524 Wolsey was informed that the pope had granted a brief of plenary indulgence to the king and queen on condition of annual pilgrimage to Walsingham, Bury or Canterbury, with power to share this boon with twenty others.[133] That some of the king's subjects were vociferous in their criticism of pilgrimage did not, at this moment, seem to threaten the upheavals that were soon to come. Henry made regular payments to Walsingham, and also to St Thomas at Canterbury, which dramatically ceased after March 1538.[134] If the Virgin's failure to deliver a live male heir to the throne helped to seal the fate of her shrine among many others, the responsibility was not hers alone. In the spring of 1518 Katherine had also sought the aid of St Frideswide of Oxford in the same doomed quest.[135]

No later pilgrimage by an English king can easily be compared with Henry II's self-abasement at Becket's tomb in 1174, for no English king ever found himself in a like situation. The pilgrimage activities of Henry III, Richard II and Henry VI, all personally devout, display both broad continuities and equally striking shifts of emphasis which reflect changes in the religious atmosphere around them. Similar conclusions might be drawn from a comparison of the warrior kings Edward I, Edward III and Henry V. Edward IV's Canterbury pilgrimage in the troubled year of 1471, exactly three centuries after the pilgrimage began, showed the world that the king was still supplicating the deity, both as an individual and on behalf of his people, for relief from present troubles. That was an ancient purpose of royal pilgrimage; but the years wrought changes in the setting in which it was performed.

7

Unofficial Pilgrimage

The Fourth Lateran Council in 1215, as we have seen, prohibited the un-licensed veneration of relics. During the remainder of the century a number of English diocesan synods reinforced this prohibition, but also added to it, in terms which echoed much earlier decrees. The synodal statutes of the bishop of Bath and Wells in 1258 repeated the Lateran prohibition and added that 'stones, wood, trees or springs are not to be venerated as holy on the pretext of any dream or illusion, since by this means we believe great perils have arisen to the souls of the faithful'. Walter Cantilupe of Worcester in 1240 had published a similar prohibition, referring to magical practices and identifying places in his diocese where there was a particular problem. He forbade, on pain of withdrawal of the sacraments, 'superstitious worship of springs and assemblies of people at [North] Cerney and at a spring near Gloucester ...' Bishops of Winchester and Exeter issued similar if more generalised decrees in the course of the century. [1]

It is unlikely that we know about more than a tiny fraction of the popular cults of this dubious type (from the official point of view) that undoubtedly flourished, mostly on a small and localised scale. What we do know has more to do with springs than with trees and stones, which is hardly surprising in view of the curative and purifying properties of water, which played an important part in many cults of unquestioned respectability. A tincture of Becket's blood in a phial of water, the water in which Cuthbert's relics, Dunstan's walking-stick or Ecgwin's arm had been washed, water in which dust or chippings from a tomb had been mixed, all had curative powers. According to some Lollard heretics, however, the veneration of wood and stones was effectively flourishing in late medieval England, for that was all that the images of the saints and the crucifix in fact were.

Many holy wells were frequented, as they had long been, without giving rise to scandal. In 1200 Eustace, abbot of the Cistercian house of Flay in Normandy and a follower of Fulk de Neuilly, came to England to preach moral reform and Sunday observance. He arrived at the village of Wye in Kent, where, according to the chronicler Roger of Hoveden, 'he blessed a spring in which the Lord infused such grace that whoever drank of it rejoiced that they had received their health'. When a woman who was both possessed by a demon and enormously inflated by dropsy came to Eustace for help, he sent her to drink at the spring, where she vomited forth two enormous black ruffians (*buffones*) who then turned into huge dogs and finally asses. Understandably surprised, the woman ran after them in an effort to catch them, 'but a certain man who had been appointed to look after the spring sprinkled water from it between her and the monsters, which immediately rose into the air leaving behind them a foul smell'.[2]

There are a number of interesting ambiguities in this account. Was the spring already a flourishing concern when Eustace arrived? If so, did he cannily decide to Christianise an un-Christian devotion by conferring a blessing on it? Was the man who guarded the spring Eustace's appointee, or had the post already been created by local initiative? What exactly were his functions: to prevent magical or other improper practices, or simply to collect offerings; to serve the infirm with drinks of water or to help them to immerse themselves in it? Eustace, while instructing the woman to drink from it, is supposed to have referred to the *natatoria fontis de Wy*, which seems to imply bathing. The spring – or at least what tradition has identified as the spring – is still to be seen, marked on the Ordnance Survey map as 'St Eustace's Well'. It is a short walk from Wye, and one can imagine it as the goal of a small local pilgrimage. It is now largely obscured from view by trees and bushes; a handrail leads down to it and a flat stone juts a short way out into the water as if to serve as a seat or perhaps the resting-place of a jug or cup.

Adjoining the parish of Wye to the west are the parishes of Eastwell and Westwell, both lying on the ancient trackway known, somewhat misleadingly, as the Pilgrims' Way. At Eastwell the now ruined church of St Mary stands a little way from what the map calls 'Plantagenet's Well'. In 1543 it was reported that 'There is an image of Our Lady at Estwell, yet standing, whereunto was continual oblation in times past of money; which image had also a coat fixed with pence.'[3] A band of springs runs westwards to Maidstone, where the Kent County Council offices occupy an area called Springfield, where the waters were associated, as in many places in England, with St Anne. From Maidstone the band continues to Otford where the archbishops of Canterbury had a residence. Here a legend grew up that Thomas Becket himself had caused the spring near the church to flow. Like others, this retained its fame and its efficacy down to modern times, 'when children were sent to bathe their grazes there, and hop-pickers took bottles of its waters back to London at the end of the season', while St Edith's Well in the adjacent parish of Kemsing was still considered good for bad eyes early in the twentieth century.[4]

To assume that St Eustace's Well, or any of these other holy wells which

were frequented either in the medieval period or more recently, was venerated continuously from the days of Kentish paganism would be to assume
a great deal too much. From the standpoint of this book, however, the
significance of such cults is rather different. Whether we believe in unbroken
continuity, recollection and revival, or innovation, their existence in
Kent and virtually everywhere else in England in the medieval period tells
us a great deal about the character of popular religion and, very often,
its accommodations with the attitudes of higher ecclesiastical authority.
Sometimes new devotions of this kind sprang up, or came to light, and
accommodation did not always prove possible.

At the end of the thirteenth century Bishop Oliver Sutton of Lincoln had
to deal with two unlicensed cults centring on wells in his diocese. The earlier
to come to his notice concerned the so-called well of St Edmund near the
church of St Clement at Oxford. This had apparently been identified as the
spot where Edmund of Abingdon, while a student at Oxford, had experienced
a vision of Christ. A number of sites claimed miracles on the strength of
some association with Edmund, but Oliver Sutton took a dim view of this
one: he believed that miracles had been fabricated in order to attract a
considerable number of people to the spring, and the whole episode smacked
of 'pagan error', not to say heresy. The bishop instructed the archdeacon
of Oxford to see that sentence of excommunication was proclaimed in all
the churches under his jurisdiction against any who should henceforth visit
the site *causa venerationis*.[5] This action notwithstanding, the problem was
bequeathed to Sutton's successor, John Dalderby, who in 1304 addressed
himself to the archdeacon once more in terms which suggested he had
already tried to deal with it at least once. He wanted to target not only those
who went to the spring for the wrong reasons but those who incited them
to do so and who, even after previous prohibitions, continued to receive
offerings and to do business in candles and other merchandise. The archdeacon was to proclaim the bishop's new sentence not only in the churches
of Oxford and the archdeaconry but at the spring itself; he was also to
summon any whom he found to be guilty to appear before the bishop.[6]

In 1299 Oliver Sutton had taken a very similar line in response to the
reported veneration of a spring in a field at Linslade in Buckinghamshire.
Here too people were coming 'by reason of pilgrimage', healing miracles
were being fabricated and offerings made. The finger of suspicion, in this
instance, pointed firmly at 'those who have the governance of the parish
church' and their motive was 'cupidity'. The bishop stated the principle
that 'no profane place is to be frequented by the people by reason of
veneration on account of the audacious assertion of miracles which have
not been approved by the church'. The archdeacon of Buckingham was to

proclaim excommunication on those who persisted in going to the spring and was also to summon the greedy vicar of Linslade before the bishop to answer for his faults. It has been suggested that there was some connection between the cult and the weekly market and annual fair which had been granted to the lord of the manor, William Beauchamp, in 1251.[7] People from eastern England who frequented the more considerable fairs of St Ives would have been familiar with such a juxtaposition.

Bishop Sutton may have possessed enough circumstantial information to convince him that there was imposture and chicanery involved at Oxford and Linslade, but he also had orthodox suspicions about the unlicensed veneration of natural objects on his side. A degree of nervousness on the subject is suggested by the contemporaneous story of one of Thomas Cantilupe's clients, a Yorkshire girl who in about 1288 had been lamed in an accident near Stamford as she set out with her father on a pilgrimage to Compostela. Her condition deteriorated, but it was ten years or more before she was brought to Hereford. During the intervening period she was reduced to begging in London. One day she bathed her foot in the spring at St Clement Dane's, but the reporter of her eventual cure was anxious to make it clear that this was 'not out of any devotion which she had to a well or stream, but because as a beggar she had no other medicament with which to clean her wounds'.[8]

Wells and springs were clearly not always treated as suspect. William Worcester and John Leland noted a great many on their tours in the later fifteenth and mid sixteenth centuries respectively. In Cornwall and Wales they were particularly numerous. St Nectan carried his own head to a well (at Hartland in Devon) which, William Worcester reported, still bore the marks of his blood. As here, and in the stories of St Alban and St Winifred, wells were often associated with martyrdom by beheading. William Worcester also observed that there was 'a very fine spring of water' in the crypt of the chapel of St Mary beneath the shrine of St Edmund at Bury.[9] St Rumwold's Well at Brackley in Northamptonshire had rather different asociations, for the saint was supposed to have preached at it within a few days of his birth, while a stone at the bottom of St Cedd's Well at Lichfield was reputedly the one on which Cedd had stood while praying immersed in the water.[10]

In May 1464, Bishop Bekynton of Bath and Wells received a report from the prior of the hospital of St John at Bridgwater that healing miracles were occurring at St John's Spring on the land of the parish church of Wembdon, which was appropriated to the hospital. In the last few days, although not previously, there had been

a great concourse of people thirsting to drink the water thereof and in fact drinking it and making their offerings there in honour of the Virgin Mary and St John the Baptist, and ... now there is a concourse there every day and many people who have suffered for many years and are quite distrustful of the physicians are daily relieved of their sufferings and restored to health when they drink the water of the spring and make their offerings there.

The bishop's response was simply to order an investigation. If what the prior reported was true, particulars of the cures were to be submitted.[11] The prior was being very circumspect: there was no concealment of what was happening, and therefore, no reason for the bishop to suspect him of illicit profiteering. That simple fact may go far to account for Bekynton's measured reaction. It might also be suggested that the bishops of the suggestively named diocese of Bath and Wells had more reason than most to be familiar with the curative powers of springs. In 1449 Bekynton himself had taken steps to prevent the public mistreatment of men and women who were using the hot springs at Bath and who were stripped of their modest garments by irreverent onlookers as they tried to enter the waters.[12] The springs were in use in the twelfth century, when William of Malmesbury said that their 'sulphurous' odour was difficult to cope with until custom mitigated the initial revulsion.[13] The leprous monk Elias of Reading pretended to be setting out for Bath when in fact he intended to go to Canterbury. A few years later, in about 1180, Bishop Reginald built a hostel for the use of visitors to the springs, on which Leland commented in his description of the spa in the mid sixteenth century.[14]

Questionable devotions could of course arise from other causes. Oliver Sutton's attention was directed to two other disquieting cases in the diocese of Lincoln during the 1290s. In August 1298 he learned that people were being attracted to the church of Great Crawley by news of some rather ill-defined phenomena (it is not clear whether visions or miracles, or both, were being claimed). He directed the rural dean of Newport Pagnell to go in person to the church with the local clergy and investigate how, why, when and at whose instigation this had all begun. If error or 'superstition' were uncovered, he was to take the necessary steps, employing ecclesiastical censure.[15] The bishop's information may have been incomplete; perhaps he did not know enough even to express the suspicion that the clergy of Great Crawley were responsible for these goings on, which by analogy with other incidents would seem likely. Possibly the fact that whatever was happening was happening in or at a church, a consecrated building, was a *prima facie* reason for caution, since the possibility of authentically miraculous phenomena could not be automatically dismissed. Either fuller information or dogmatic assumption excluded the possibility that this could apply to events in a 'field' at Oxford or Linslade.

Earlier in the decade Bishop Sutton had been presented with another problem which had its delicate aspects, since it involved, at least indirectly, one of the greatest men in the kingdom. In April 1296 he had been informed, as he told the archdeacon of Buckingham, that 'certain people' were presuming, without ecclesiastical authority, to celebrate the divine office publicly in the oratory in Edmund of Cornwall's newly built manor-house at Hambleden. Not only that, but 'superstitious figments and occurrences' (he would use exactly the same language two years later with reference to Great Crawley) were taking place which were attracting pilgrims, and miracles of healing were being claimed. Here too the bishop made the point that this was 'a place altogether profane', that is, not consecrated ground. His response had been to go personally to Hambleden to establish that the report was true, which it was. With all due regard for the earl's 'zeal and honour', this could not be tolerated. The archdeacon therefore was to proclaim that mass was not to be celebrated in the oratory in the earl's absence and to prohibit the pilgrimages. Here again Sutton used language which he would echo when dealing with the well at Linslade three years later: the people were not to venerate a place by reason of miracles which had not been approved by the church. The bishop's minimum demand was that the pilgrimages must cease. In August 1296, and finally in March 1297, the earl was permitted to have mass celebrated in the oratory 'as long as the flow of people to it on the pretence of miracles is altogether at an end'. [16]

What does not emerge from any of these references is the fact that the earl had built the oratory to the honour of God and Thomas Cantilupe, for whom he was an enthusiast. Hambleden was Cantilupe's birthplace. At the inquiry into the bishop's sanctity held in 1307, his nephew William Cantilupe testified that 'he had seen in the aforesaid place the *signa* of various miracles, which God is said to have performed through the said Lord Thomas'. [17] It is not stated when he had seen them, so there is no way of telling whether Sutton's attempts at repression in 1296–97 had been successful or not. The bishop of Lincoln's apparent attitude, and his noteworthy failure to mention the apparent cause of the miracles, may reflect either a keen sense of propriety or what he took to be a difficult situation. As he said, this was unlicensed veneration in an unconsecrated place. He doubtless knew also that Cantilupe had died out of favour with the archbishop of Canterbury, John Pecham, and that he was not yet even an official candidate for canonisation. He also knew, however, that Cantilupe was doing miracles at Hereford, and he himself had issued a testimonial to his sanctity in September 1294. [18]

Sutton might have been forgiven for feeling that he was somewhat put upon, and that too many people in his admittedly large diocese were too quick to follow whatever devotional carrot was dangled in front of them. Other cases had different causes and different outcomes. Supposedly miraculous images could be particularly problematical. In April 1313 Archbishop Greenfield of York published a ban on the veneration of an image of the Virgin Mary which had been newly set up in the parish church of Foston-in-the-Wolds in the East Riding. The image had attracted a great concourse of the 'simple', 'as if', Greenfield said, 'there was more holiness in it than in other similar images'. The archbishop professed to be worried about the risk of idolatry, as he doubtless was, but there was another sub-plot involved. Greenfield noted that a conflict about the image had arisen between the prior and convent of Bridlington and Joanna, the widow of Thomas Poynton.[19] He does not say what this was about, but we know, from an inquest taken a little later, that the image had been bought by Thomas Poynton in Scotland and installed by him in the church of Fraisthorpe, a dependency of the parish church of Carnaby, which lies somewhat south of Bridlington, and was appropriated to Bridlington Priory. It was evidently still at Fraisthorpe in 1310, when the canons of Bridlington came to an agreement with the vicar of Carnaby about the division of the offerings which had quite suddenly started to be made to it. Thanks to the mediation of 'mutual friends', it had been agreed that the vicar would take one-third of the takings and the priory, as rectors of Carnaby, two-thirds.[20] Joanna Poynton, however, evidently regarded the image as private property and by 1313 she had sold it to Robert Constable, rector of Foston, who had taken it to his church. The prior of Bridlington was now disputing the validity of this transaction. From the point of view of the disputants it was not the propriety of devotion to the image but the ownership of the rights in it that was at stake. Archbishop Greenfield, vainly trying to focus attention on the issue of propriety, directed his officials to forbid the pilgrimage and the offering of money or other things to the image, either at Foston or 'in any other place where it may happen that it is moved'. Meanwhile the usual sort of enquiry into the origins of the devotion was to be set up.

A year later the archbishop was again instructing his official to prohibit pilgrimage to the image, which was now at Bridlington. Still concerned about idolatry, he referred on 20 February 1314 to his earlier mandate, which, although it had been duly published, had failed to have the necessary effect. Again he mentioned disputes between 'different people' on account of the image. The prohibition was to be repeated throughout the East Riding and especially at Bridlington itself. The inference that the canons had not merely appropriated the image but were promoting recourse to it is unmistakable; the 'simple' were only part of the problem. The party in dispute with the canons was now the rector of Foston, Robert Constable, who only three days later, on 23 February, was granted two years' leave of absence 'to pursue the business of his church'.[21] The rector had already taken his grievance to the royal court, complaining that the prior and a host of others had 'broken his doors and houses at Foston', assaulted him and carried away the image and other goods of his; a commission of oyer and terminer was issued on his complaint on 25 September 1313.[22] The resultant inquest, which is the source of much of our information, established the story so far and found that the sheriff of York had sent officers to Foston 'with sufficient warrant' to recover the image.[23] The prior of Bridlington had successfully obtained possession, but Archbishop Greenfield's interdict still lay upon the veneration of the image. His death early in December 1315 eased the pressure. The prior of Bridlington now humbly asked that the 'interdict' should be lifted, and on 6 January 1316 the dean of Dickering was directed to cite Robert Constable to show cause why this should not be done. The issue of idolatry was not mentioned; from the point of view of the administrators of the vacant diocese this was a bit of unfinished business that could with advantage be cleared up.[24]

The Foston (or Fraisthorpe) Madonna was not a unique case. In 1306 Bishop Ralph Baldock of London had ordered the archdeacon of Essex and the vicar of Prittlewell to conduct a similar investigation at Ashingdon in Essex. Here a miraculous image, which is not further described, was attracting an 'innumerable multitude of the people', who, the bishop feared, were attracted by the presumed miracles rather than by 'ordered devotion'. He was the more concerned that the faithful should not be misled precisely because he thought it important that churches and the saints whose images they contained should be properly venerated. His addressees were to go to Ashingdon, carefully examine the 'form and quality' of the image, and consult both local clergy and respectable layfolk in order to find out who had first promoted the devotion and how and why the flow of people to the image had started so quickly. At all events the pilgrimage was to be brought under control, and no 'new veneration' permitted until higher authority had given its approval; offerings already made were to be sequestrated. The use of ecclesiastical censure was authorised to enforce these directives. [25]

There is, then, evidence that some bishops in the early fourteenth century were seriously concerned about the propriety of pilgrimages to images which caught the popular fancy. More commonly disputes arose about issues of property, either in the image itself, as at Foston, or, more commonly still, in the offerings which were made to it. These disputes could be between the rectors of a church and the vicar actually in charge of it, as had been the case at Fraisthorpe in 1310, or they could be between clergy and laity, as when in 1254 Robert Anketil, rector of the church of Saltwood in Kent, complained to the pope that the parishioners of the chapel of St Leonard at Hythe were claiming for themselves the offerings made by pilgrims to a certain crucifix containing holy relics. This crucifix had been given to the chapel by a benefactor who specifically declared that the offerings, and any gifts and legacies made to it, were not to go to the rector or his ministers. The pope unsurprisingly upheld the rector's rights in face of this wilful subversion of the proper order. [26] Here there is specific reference to 'pilgrims', although it is hard to suppose that they were coming from very far afield.

Such disputes probably more commonly turned on the offerings routinely made by locals. In 1310 Archbishop Greenfield of York had to deal with the insubordination of the parishioners of Newark, who were appropriating not only the offerings of the faithful at the altars of the Virgin and St Laurence and at the cross in the parish church but also those made at funerals and churchings, placing their own locked collecting-boxes in the church in order to do so. [27] Such cases were not all that uncommon. On 13 February 1318, Adam Orleton of Hereford asked his official to enquire into the offerings made to the image of the Virgin at the church of Madley. A few days later, the leading parishioners acknowledged that, except by special grace, they had no right to the oblations which were deposited in a collecting-box which stood at the feet of the image, and which had for some time been disbursed by the laity on the building of the new chancel of the church. [28]

The involvement of the laity in the management of parish churches or dependent chapels might be fraught with difficulty, but in none of these instances did anyone involved suggest that the veneration which produced the contested offerings was in itself improper. On the contrary, in 1309 Walter Stapeldon of Exeter commanded the parishioners of Ilfracombe, on pain of a fine, to provide for the parish church, within a year, an image of the Virgin 'as befitting and beautiful as they then had in the chapel of the Blessed Virgin'. [29] There are some scattered hints of an ongoing dispute between the parishioners and a succession of rectors of Ilfracombe in which this image, or perhaps a successor to it, may well have played a leading part. In 1443 the pope was informed that the parishioners had built a cemetery chapel in honour of St Mary the Virgin 'de Thorn' where she had worked many miracles and attracted many alms and oblations. Fearing that the rector would appropriate these, they had obtained from the papacy an agreement that the fourth part of the offerings, and also legacies and donations, should be converted to the fabric and ornament of the church, provided that the parishioners matched the amount out of their own pockets. The rector objected to this arrangement, and the pope ordered that it should be annulled if on investigation his arguments were upheld.[30]

There is no specific reference here to an image, nor is it clear that the cemetery chapel mentioned by the pope was the 'chapel of the Virgin' mentioned over a century earlier by Bishop Stapeldon, but wonder-working Virgins were usually images, and there is other evidence that the laity regarded the cemetery as their territory. In 1384 Bishop Brantyngham directed that no fairs, markets or other business dealings were to take place there. He had been informed that

> many people from different parishes, flocking to the parish church of Ilfracombe and its cemetery, conduct various business deals and a market in the church and cemetery on Sundays and feast-days and, not afraid to create uproar there, brazenly and wrongfully impede the celebration of the divine office in the same.[31]

If people from the surrounding locality were indeed flocking to the cemetery, the offerings at the chapel may well have benefited. It was not perhaps an unexpected consequence that in 1385–86 Bishop Brantyngham had to order an investigation into the pollution of the cemetery by bloodshed (again, not an uncommon occurrence).[32] In 1390 the parishioners were rebuked for withholding offerings from the rector, as well as for burying the body of one Thomas Fisher within the church, against the rector's will.[33] Whatever the personal issues that may from time to time have been involved here, it is possible that we can dimly discern, as one of the sub-plots in the conflict between rector and people, the struggle to control a local pilgrimage to an image of the Virgin which may have acquired a miraculous reputation.

If rebellious layfolk were one problem, subordinate clergy, the vicars or chaplains put in to serve a church on behalf of its rectors, could be another, and were often provided for in advance. When establishing a perpetual chantry in the chapel of East Haddesley in 1313, Archbishop Greenfield specifically provided that the serving priest was to render all the usual oblations faithfully to the rector of the mother-church, Birkin, which was some way distant; he could however keep any offerings which might be made by outsiders (*extranei*) who happened to come to the chapel 'by reason of pilgrimage or devotion'. The distinction here was between offerings from locals, over whom the mother church retained its parochial rights, and those made by outsiders, which the rector of Birkin was prepared to concede to the chaplain as one of his perquisites.[34] The situation of East, now Chapel, Haddesley on what is today a major road (the A19) to York, suggests that as a wayside halt it may in fact have attracted modest oblations.

More often, as in the case noted earlier of Woolpit in Suffolk, all such offerings were specifically assigned to the rector. Dispute, or at least debate, arose when a pilgrimage developed suddenly and unexpectedly, as it did at Fraisthorpe in 1310.

Images, miraculous or not, may have been reaching a new peak of popularity early in the fourteenth century. If that is so, one possible explanation is that, thanks to the workings of both lay and clerical patronage, parish churches and subsidiary chapels all over the country were becoming more richly furnished than they had ever been before with images and other paraphernalia. The layman Thomas Poynton had brought the Madonna to Fraisthorpe and the priest Robert Constable had then bought it for Foston; the parishioners of Ilfracombe had obtained an image of the Virgin for a chapel they evidently regarded as peculiarly their own, and the bishop of Exeter wanted them to be equally generous to the parish church. References to images, new or old, multiply at this period, and many congregations were probably being confronted with images and crucifixes which were outside their previous experience and seemed disturbingly lifelike. In producing an art designed to humanise the divine and engage the sympathies of the onlooker the contemporary Tuscany of Giotto, Duccio and their followers was symptomatic, rather than exceptional, in Europe. Great monasteries were more likely than parochial patrons, urban or rural, to buy in the international art market,[35] but by the fifteenth century testamentary bequests amply demonstrate the hold that images, probably often of provincial workmanship, had on the affections at least of those Christians who were prosperous enough to leave a will.

The propensity to attribute miraculous powers to the crucifix, like the veneration of images of the Virgin, typified one of the strongest strains in late medieval piety. Both could arouse the same difficulties as the veneration of other types of image, most basically the danger of confusing the image with its spiritual prototype and attributing the nature and powers of the one to the other, a mere object. Furthermore, the question that Archbishop Greenfield asked about the Foston Madonna, why this particular image should be deemed holier than another, was pertinent. It was a question that was taken up later in the century and in the next by the Lollards, but often it was not even asked (or was asked very quietly) and the real issue was who had property in the image. The evidence of indulgences is sufficient to show how many such cults flourished everywhere.

Similar problems arose (or failed to arise) with respect to the veneration of the relics of individuals. That hundreds of persons were venerated in medieval England without the benefit of formal canonisation is clear. Unofficial cults could even be imported from abroad. There is evidence for the veneration of the 'servant-saint' Zita of Lucca (d. 1278) in the mid fourteenth century in London, and her cult was reinforced when the Hospitaller Sir John Langstrother brought a relic of her from Lucca itself to the commandery of Eagle in Lincolnshire in 1446. She came to be known in England as 'Sithe', or sometimes 'Citha': Alison Hudson of York in 1509 said in her will that she owed pilgrimages to St Sithe of Eagle and to other saints, which John Hudson would perform for her. Zita's popularity in several areas of the country is attested not only by mentions in wills but by images of her on painted rood screens and in other media, where she often appears alongside other virgin saints of a much older vintage, such as Katherine or Margaret. She also acquired a reputation as a defender against death by drowning, which helps to account for her presence in bridge chapels, as at Ripon. This acceptance of a 'modern' Italian saint, who had been a housekeeper in life and performed homely miracles, into the company of the martyrs is suggestive of a devout mentality in which neither historical awareness nor the distinction between 'official' and 'unofficial' saints was of much importance compared to the meaning a saint or saints might acquire for a particular devotee. Neither Katherine nor Margaret had ever been canonised, after all, but they were familiar figures, and their legends and attributes and the traditions that had accumulated around them shaped devotion.[36] Zita became well enough known as a finder of lost keys for harassed housewives to attract the opprobrium of Lollard preachers, as Sir Thomas More knew later.[37]

Not only were unofficial cults numerous, in a few cases they received conspicuous marks of favour from those in authority. Into a special category came individuals, such as Thomas Cantilupe or Osmund of Salisbury, who were venerated in the hopes of an official canonisation which took a long time to come. For some, such as Archbishop Winchelsey of Canterbury, Thomas, Earl of Lancaster, or King Henry VI, moves were made, with official support, to obtain canonisation, but without result. For others yet again, veneration was entirely informal and in principle open to condemnation, even when the supposed saint and his devotees were persons of some standing. In 1341 Bishop Grandisson of Exeter intervened to investigate what turned out to be a bogus miracle, a cure of blindness, allegedly performed in his own cathedral. It had been hailed by the ringing of the bells on 13 February 1341. Grandisson gave strict orders that this was not to happen again, nor were public prayers or any solemnities to be performed in honour of anyone who had not been canonised by the Holy See. His investigations revealed that the supposed beneficiary, John Skinner, had been induced to simulate the cure in order to relieve his own poverty.[38] It is possible that the supposed miracle was staged at the tomb of Bishop

Berkeley who (as we saw in an earlier chapter) enjoyed a modest cult at the cathedral for a period in the fourteenth century. Grandisson's disapproval may have helped bring it to an end. Not for the first time or the last, the custodians of a shrine stood accused by their bishop of profit-mongering. Grandisson prohibited the censing of the tombs of his predecessors in the choir, 'unless any of them should be canonised'.[39] He was acting in a manner to support Thomas More's argument, nearly two centuries later, that bishops had no vested interest in pilgrimage and no reason not to suppress malpractice if they suspected it.

This was not the invariable result. Episcopal permission, it seems, was often tacit rather than explicit: bishops intervened to prevent, or to attempt to prevent, devotions only if they had some special reason to disapprove of them or if (like Grandisson) they were rigorists by disposition. A number of informal cults indicate popular willingness to find sanctity among the parish clergy. Master John Schorne was the outstanding example. Rector of North Marston in Buckinghamshire, he died in 1315. He was principally famous for having conjured the devil into a boot, and was also associated with a healing spring, good for the gout, which he had helped to discover. His cult is attested by testamentary bequests and by numerous pilgrim souvenirs, both from North Marston itself and from St George's Chapel, Windsor, where his relics were taken by the bishop of Salisbury, with papal permission, in 1478. The bishop simultaneously obtained the rectory of North Marston from Dunstable Priory, so that he also controlled what now became the secondary shrine. Within a few years, the remains of Henry VI joined Master John's at Windsor, and together they enjoyed considerable popularity. It has been remarked that the persistence of Schorne's cult until the Reformation, despite the absence of a written life or record of his miracles, made him exceptional among unofficial saints.[40]

Other parish clergy enjoyed local celebrity. In 1396 severe damage was done to the church of Keyingham in the East Riding during a storm. The tomb of a former rector, Philip Ingberd (d. 1325), began to exude oil and it came to be believed that his prayers had saved the church from further damage. As the Meaux chronicler reported, 'miracles then began to happen through the merits of Master Philip and the people flocked there from all sides in his praise'. Instituted to Keyingham in 1305, Philip was supposed to have seen the execution of Thomas of Lancaster in a vision while a woman was confessing to him, and also to have seen a servant of his rewarded in heaven for charity to a poor man. An Oxford scholar, he apparently never resided in his parish, but posthumously at least he established a presence; a cross and a well of 'St Philip' were also remembered locally.[41] Somewhat resembling Ingberd in that he was a man of learning, but better known over a wider area, was Richard Caister, vicar of St Stephen's Norwich from 1402 to 1420, whose cult flourished sufficiently, like Master John Schorne's, to prompt a modest pilgrim-badge industry.[42] Richard was a man of 'radical views', whom the local populace (in an area which produced a good crop of Lollards) were willing to regard as a saint. Only a little later, the veneration of the heretic priest Richard Wych, after his execution on Tower Hill in June 1440, may be evidence of popular confusion and credulity (the vicar of All Hallows Barking confessed to encouraging it). It may also represent either an endorsement of religious radicalism or simply a widespread willingness to recognise victims of violent death as martyrs.[43]

Not the least interesting local cult of a parish priest erupted at Whitstone in the north east of Cornwall, a few miles west of the River Tamar and the border with Devon.[44] In the late summer of 1361 Bishop Grandisson was deeply perturbed to learn that the late rector of the church, Richard Buvyle, who according to different accounts had either been killed by his enemies (*aemuli*) or had committed suicide, was popularly regarded as a saint, with the result that:

> All the inhabitants of the region round about, and many outsiders, flock on pilgrimage to the place where it is said he was first buried, and make solemn offering, and every week, on Saturday evening and all night, keep vigils there; so that victuals and other goods for sale are brought to the place and distributed as if at a market. On this pretext feasting and drinking and improper get-togethers take place and many unlawful and shameful acts are perpetrated, which it is not fitting to describe.

The bishop instructed John Milys, his commissary in the vacant archdeaconry of Cornwall, to publish a ban on the pilgrimage, but also to investigate the alleged miracles, acknowledging the theoretical possibility that they might be authentic.

On 27 October Milys duly reported on the investigations he had conducted in the church of Week St Mary, a few miles west of Whitstone, naming the witnesses, lay and clerical, whom he had examined. He had directed several of them to appear before the bishop on 15 November, and was particularly keen that Lavyna Stolloke of Whitstone, the first person known to have received a cure, should be summoned; it does not seem that he had himself interviewed her. She had been lamed for a month by an enormous swelling on her foot when, hearing that Buvyle's body was going to be moved, she came to the graveside in Easter week 1359, to pray for the soul of the dead rector. When she had recited the Paternoster and the Ave Maria she was cured. If there had been any earlier miracles, or premonitory signs such as lights above the grave, Milys seems not to have been told about them; nor is it clear whether the assemblies in the cemetery had already begun when this first reported cure took place. It is unclear, therefore, why the decision had been taken to move the tomb into the church. Further miracles occurred at the original burial place in June 1359, but that does not necessarily mean that the body had not been moved by then; certainly the new tomb inside the church existed by June 1360, and six of the ten recorded miracles took place there.

Milys supplied the bishop with a schedule of the miracles of which he had been told. Someone locally may have kept some kind of memorandum of the miracles as they occurred, but names and dates were remembered rather unevenly. The following table shows where the beneficiaries came from, approximately how far they had come, and when and where they were cured.

The pilgrim	Place of origin	Date and place of cure
Lavyna Stollok	Whitstone	Easter week 1359; at the original burial place
Child of William Ludlow	Launcels (6 miles NNW)	Unspecified; the original burial place
A Cornishman	unspecified	'Around Holy Trinity' (16 June) 1359; original burial place
Johanna Gyffard	Hartland, Devon (16 miles N)	Saturday 21 June 1359; original burial place
A smith	Winkleigh, Devon (26 miles ENE)	Unspecified; at the new tomb in the church
A woman	Northam, Devon (29 miles NE)	'Around St John the Baptist' (24 June) 1360; in the church
A woman	Clovelly, Devon (18 miles N)	'Around St Peter ad Vincula' (1 August) 1360; in the church
A man	Bodmin (30 miles SW)	Saturday 26 June 1361; in the church
A man	Woodford in the parish of Plympton (40 miles SE)	'Around the Feast of the Assumption' (15 August) 1361; in the church
Thomasia, wife of Arnulf Coke	Great Torrington, Devon (25 miles NE)	12 September 1361; in the church

The late rector drew his clients from a remarkably wide area. The most local of the beneficiaries, Lavyna Stollok apart, was the child from Launcels. Whitstone at the present time stands on a principal north-south road between Launceston and the north Devon coast; perhaps some of Richard Buvyle's pilgrims were on their way to or from another shrine, such as St Petroc's at Bodmin or St Nectan's at Hartland, or engaged on some other business. Those from Hartland, Clovelly, Northam and Great Torrington, it should be noted, were all women. The woman from Northam was deliberately brought to Whitstone in search of a cure, at a date (June 1360) which suggests that word of the late rector's sanctity and his reburial in the church had spread throughout the region. Bound and chained, this woman was raving mad, tearing with her teeth at the candles in the church and trying to throw down and break the images. Some of the jury whom John Milys had empanelled said that they had subsequently seen her come *compos mentis* on pilgrimage to the church. Bishop Grandisson objected to the vigils and associated merry-making which were still taking place in the cemetery on Saturday nights; Johanna Gyffard of Hartland came there on a Saturday in June 1359 and was cured 'around midnight', and there was at least one other recorded cure on a Saturday. What became of this cult is not apparent; there seems to be no further reference to it in Grandisson's register or in those of his successors.

Two other aspects of the cult of Richard Buyvle are worthy of comment. On the available evidence, the first cure performed at his tomb was that of a local woman who, it was said, had come to pray for his soul. It has already been commented that bishops sometimes granted indulgences for prayers for deceased persons, and sometimes it was specified that they should go to the tomb to do so. The word 'pilgrimage' was not usually applied to such pious expeditions, but there were exceptions. In December 1312 Richard Kellawe, bishop of Durham, wishing to encourage prayers for the dead, especially while their memory was fresh, offered an indulgence to any who should go *peregrinationis causa* to the church of St Alkmund in Bliborough, Lincolnshire, and pray for the soul of Walter, late rector of that church.[45] It would be intelligible if, when the faithful were invited to make 'pilgrimages' for such a purpose, occasional confusion should arise in their minds about the precise reasons for which the indulgences were being offered. Those most likely to respond to the invitation were presumably local people and they would therefore be in a position to know something about the reputation of the deceased. At Durham, offerings at the tomb of the priest John Warton are recorded in several years between 1456 and 1538; they fell steeply in value after 1459, when 102s. were received, but in 1513–14, when his tomb attracted only 15d., Warton was, for the first time in the surviving records, designated 'saint'.[46] Had he been spontaneously acclaimed as a saint from the beginning, or did his 'cult' originate simply in offerings made for the benefit of his soul?

Richard Buyvle, according to Bishop Grandisson, had either committed suicide or been killed by *aemuli*. It seems, on the face of it, unlikely that a suicide would be credited with sanctity, but a victim of murder was quite another matter. Many objects of unofficial cults, in England as elsewhere in medieval Christendom, were victims of violence. It is sometimes difficult to know what claims to personal holiness, if any, they had apart from the attribute of supposed martyrdom. Within this category, some of the most conspicuous were figures of political significance, but it is not easy to draw a neat line around the category. Some saints, especially if their credentials were disputed, could become issues in local politics posthumously, if they had not been in life. Sometimes we are at a loss to know what the significance of such cults was, for simple lack of evidence. This seems to be the case, for example, with Simon of Atherfield on the Isle of Wight, who has been neatly described as 'a martyr to his wife'. Simon was apparently murdered by his wife Avicia, who was burned for the crime in 1211. The accounts of the bishop of Winchester's manor of Calbourne, taken at Michaelmas 1211, include an amount of £7 12s. 1d. received in offerings at Simon's tomb. It is not entirely clear where this burial place was; Atherfield had no church of its own and was dependent on Brightstone, a parish in the bishop's patronage. It may well be that the bishop wanted to suppress the cult, and he was in a very good position both to do so and to appropriate the offerings that had already been made. No more is heard of it, and we are unlikely to become any the wiser about the circumstances of Simon's death and the reasons why the Waverley annalist used the word *martirizatus* to describe him.[47]

Even more mysterious are the origins of a somewhat more enduring cult which in the early sixteenth century was attracting testamentary bequests to the parish church of Newington, near Sittingbourne in Kent. In October 1350 Edward III granted the abbot of Lesnes a small plot of land on the highway at Newington so that he could build a chapel 'at the cross where Robert le Bouser was killed'.[48] The cross itself was presumably the one associated with Becket, which had been erected to mark the spot where he had stopped to confirm local children on his last journey between London and Canterbury in 1170, and where miracles subsequently occurred. The chapel that the abbot of Lesnes (the proprietor of Newington) intended to build in 1350 was going to be dedicated to St Mary and Holy Cross, but from the beginning it evidently contained a tomb, which was presumably that of the mysterious Robert. The base of it is still to be seen in the parish church of Newington, and it looks very much like a shrine: it is surrounded by deep recesses, one of which, unusually, is pierced right through the depth of the tomb-base. Local belief was that suppliants used to crawl through this aperture to obtain the maximum proximity to the holy relics within. By the end of the fifteenth century, the chapel was ruinous, and around 1500 the tomb was taken into the parish church. 'St Robert' is mentioned in a number of local wills in the early sixteenth century, including one bequest for a pilgrimage from the neighbouring village of Upchurch.

Who Robert le Bouser was, and when and how he died, we seem unlikely ever to know. We cannot even be sure that he was the victim of human violence rather than of an accident involving a horse, perhaps, or an over-turned cart. Given Newington's location, he may well have been a pilgrim, passing along the high road from London to Canterbury or, possibly, if he died in 1350, to Dover on his way to Rome for the Jubilee. Whether the building of the chapel, with its respectable dedication, but also with Robert's handsome tomb within it, was a ploy on the part of the abbot of Lesnes to exploit local belief in the sanctity of a pilgrim or other traveller who had met his death at a place hallowed by association with Becket must also remain obscure, although the abbey of Lesnes had numerous financial problems at the time. If Robert was indeed a pilgrim, it is conceivable that someone had had the idea of emulating the cult of William of Perth at nearby Rochester. William had been on his way to the Holy Land in 1201 when he was murdered, and he furnishes a good example of what might be termed a semi-official cult. Bishop Laurence of Rochester on a visit to Rome in 1256 sought his canonisation, but there is no evidence of a formal process, let alone of canonisation. The cult was, however, respectable and occasionally enjoyed royal patronage. Here too a chapel was built on the site of William's murder.[49]

One distinctive category of real or alleged victims of violence who at-tracted veneration consisted of the boys who were supposedly ritually murdered by Jews. The earliest of these was William of Norwich, whose reputed murder occurred in 1144. The popularity of his tomb in Norwich Cathedral experienced considerable fluctuations. It was at its greatest in 1150–51, when a substantial majority of devotees were local people, in the sense that they lived within fifty miles of Norwich. As the years went by the miracles declined in frequency and the average distance travelled by beneficiaries increased, as if William was losing his lustre, through sheer familiarity, in the eyes of those who lived nearby. The record of offerings at the cathedral is very incomplete for the thirteenth century, but it seems that the refurbishment of the tomb in 1305 excited some interest. William took on a new lease of life later in the century. The Norwich guild of pelterers (furriers) adopted the supposed saint, who had been an apprentice skinner, as their patron. An annual procession of guild members to the shrine, headed by a boy who represented the 'glorious martyr', gave the cult publicity which seems to have helped to extend its fame beyond the confines of Norwich.[50]

There were numerous other such 'martyrs'. Jocelin of Brakelond related that the 'holy boy Robert' was martyred at Bury in 1181. He was buried in the abbey church and 'there were marvels and many signs among the people, as I have written elsewhere': this account unfortunately does not survive.[51] The Winchester annalist reported the crucifixion of a boy by Jews in that city in 1232 and Matthew Paris a similar incident at London in 1244. Matthew's phrasing is a little guarded: many people said that the Lord had worked miracles through the boy, and the canons of St Paul's solemnly interred him near the high altar, although there was no appearance of the stigmata on the body.[52]

More detailed attention was given by the Burton Annalist to 'Little St Hugh' of Lincoln, 'martyred' on 31 July 1255. The body was evidently lying in the parish church when the miracles began: a blind woman received her sight on touching it, and other cures followed. The cathedral clergy thereupon came in solemn procession, with tapers, crosses and incense, to take possession of the martyr. At this point one of the canons objected, simultaneously raising issues of propriety and interest. He was the rector of the parish church from which the body was being removed; the child, he said, had lived in the parish from birth to death and should not be taken away. His 'audacious' objections were disregarded, and Little St Hugh was interred in the cathedral, close to the tomb of another uncanonised saint, 'the most holy father Robert [Grosseteste]'. The cult had an early royal witness in the shape of Richard of Cornwall who came 'on pilgrimage' to St Robert: several miracles were performed in his presence, whether by Little St Hugh or by the late bishop is not made entirely clear. The earl was subsequently instrumental, for financial reasons, in protecting the Jews who had been imprisoned on suspicion of complicity in the murder. The Dominicans too made themselves unpopular by intervening to protect the Jews.[53]

Among the miscellaneous adult victims of violence who enjoyed a brief cult, one may have owed something to anti-Jewish sentiment. The imminent departure of Richard the Lionheart on his Holy Land crusade in 1190 was marked by the outbreak of antisemitic violence in many parts of England. The goods of Jewish traders were plundered at Stamford fair in Lent (always a dangerous time for Jews living in a Christian society). One of the perpetrators made off to Northampton, only to be murdered there by the person to whom he had entrusted his takings. The murderer cast the body outside the town walls and took flight when it was discovered and identified. It was not long before the 'simple', as William of Newburgh called them, began to attribute miracles to the dead man. At first people came from neighbouring areas and then from 'different regions', all expecting to behold miracles and to offer prayers at the tomb of the 'new martyr'. The prudent laughed at this spectacle, but it was gratifying to the clergy who profited from the superstition. Eventually the matter was brought to the notice of Bishop Hugh of Lincoln, himself destined to be an officially authenticated saint. Hugh intervened promptly, coming in person to the spot, dispersing the *insignia* which had been assembled by the efforts of 'the simple and the greedy' and forbidding any further veneration on pain of excommunication. Thanks to his prompt and firm action, this particular work of the deceiving spirit was soon a thing of the past.[54]

We are not told precisely why the populace regarded the nameless robber as a martyr. There is no explicit indication that they knew that he had been involved in anti-Jewish activity, which, in the current atmosphere, might conceivably have been sufficient to invest him with the aura of a Christian hero. What other rumours about his character, or the reason for his killing, may have circulated we cannot know, nor whether it was simply sufficient for him to have died an unjust and violent death. The usual (although not quite invariable) response of the ecclesiastical establishment to such episodes was hostile, but, as the story just recounted reveals, local clergy might well not be averse to encouraging 'the simple' in their enthusiasm. What such stories certainly seem to reveal is the omnivorousness of that enthusiasm. This emerges also in the story of William fitz Osbert, called Longbeard, who was executed in London by the justiciar Hubert Walter in 1196. William of Newburgh is again our fullest source for this episode, but other accounts were written, at varying length, by Ralph Diceto, canon of St Paul's, Gervase of Canterbury, Roger Hoveden, Roger of Wendover and a little later Matthew Paris.[55] Mostly hostile to 'Longbeard', they vary in ways which will repay a brief examination.

William fitz Osbert was an educated and eloquent man who became one of the ruling magistrates of London. He seems to have been well known to Richard I, and in 1190 he was one of a party of Londoners who went on the crusade. While on the outward sea voyage he and a companion experienced a vision of St Thomas Becket, who assured them that he, St Edmund and St Nicholas had been divinely appointed guardians of the ship.[56] As one of the magistrates of the city, Longbeard took up the cause of the poorer citizens against the oppressions and malpractices of the rich. Newburgh gives a précis of one of his speeches, in which he described himself as 'the saviour of the poor'. To Ralph Diceto his crimes included the unpardonable one of agitation against the canons of St Paul's. Longbeard went overseas to the king to plead his cause, and, emboldened by what he took to be Richard's support, became more aggressive in his activities on his return. Hubert Walter at this point demanded that he should give hostages for the preservation of peace and fealty to the king, which he did. He always went about under guard, so the justiciar awaited a moment at which he could be taken by surprise and sent an armed posse to arrest him. Of these Longbeard killed one and wounded another, and took refuge in the church of St Mary-le-Bow with a few companions and, Newburgh cannot resist adding, his inseparable concubine. He expected the citizens to rise in his defence, but they did not. Eventually he was smoked out, seized and executed. For all his hostility, Newburgh does not go to the lengths of Diceto (followed by Wendover) in claiming that Longbeard set fire to the church himself; like Gervase, he leaves the responsibility unclear. Roger of Hoveden has no doubt that it was on the justiciar's orders that the church was fired, and he adds the detail that the monks of Christ Church Canterbury were ill-pleased, as St Mary's was appropriated to them.

William of Newburgh gives the only full account of the sequel; Gervase refers to it more briefly and Matthew Paris rather obliquely. A kinsman of Longbeard who was a priest got hold of the chain with which he had been bound and laid it on a fever patient, who suppposedly soon recovered. When this miracle was publicised, 'the senseless people' adopted the belief that Longbeard had died for piety and justice and began to venerate him as a martyr. The gibbet on which he had died was stolen away and secretly honoured, and the earth around where it had stood, as if consecrated by his blood, was dug out to quite a considerable depth for the making of remedies. Among the many who flocked to the spot were people from many parts of England who happened to be in London on business, and the 'multitude' kept overnight vigils there. Frantic to discredit the pseudo-martyr, Newburgh quoted the usual trustworthy witnesses to the effect that the dead man had confessed before his execution that he had polluted the church by intercourse with his concubine, and that when his enemies had launched their final attack he had denied Christ and called upon the devil to save him. Hubert Walter proceeded against the priest with ecclesiastical censures, sent soldiers to disperse the 'rustic multitude', and posted an armed guard on the spot to drive off the inquisitive. Within a few days, the popular excitement had calmed down.

This *cause célèbre*, widely reported by the chroniclers as we have seen, was sufficiently well-remembered to give rise to some later reflection, as Matthew Paris's version of it indicates. Interestingly, the St Albans chronicler disregards the hostile account given by his predecessor Roger of Wendover. He does not directly refer to the alleged miracles, but concludes :

> Thus William called the Bearded was ignominiously put to death by his fellow citizens for the assertion of truth and in defence of the cause of the poor. Wherefore, as it is well known that the cause makes the martyr, he may justifiably be reckoned among the martyrs.

Described thus, Longbeard's case seems to foreshadow those of Simon de Montfort or Thomas of Lancaster, who were hailed as martyrs for the common weal. One wonders if his crusading history contributed to his reputation or whether, if the story of his vision of St Thomas was well-known, it helped to associate him with a more famous martyr for the 'truth'. Was it relevant that he had been driven out of sanctuary? There was clearly some anxiety about this among the chroniclers; it had to be shown that he had not taken legitimate sanctuary because (leaving aside the concubine) he had fortified the tower with arms and provisions.

The immediate and obvious context for fitz Osbert's 'martyrdom' was provided by local political tensions in London. There may have been other such incidents. In August 1279 the bishop of Worcester, Godfrey Giffard, learned that one William de Lay had been dragged from the churchyard of SS. Philip and James at Bristol and executed on the orders of Peter de la Mare, the constable of Bristol Castle. On 21 August, the bishop sentenced the guilty parties to do public penance and with their own hands to restore the body (and head) to the church for burial. From the bishop's point of view this was, first and foremost, a case of violation of sanctuary. One of the accused testified that he had at one point had the fugitive by the feet, while the rest of his body was in the churchyard, but fled because of the clamour of the people. Peter de la Mare admitted responsibility and said that his orders for the detention of William de Lay had been given for the safety of himself and his adherents. What William's ostensible offence had been we are never told.

The bishop, however, was already interested in other aspects of the case. The rector of St Mary's, when questioned, claimed ignorance of the authorship or dissemination of 'a certain libellous song' about which Giffard had enquired, but said that he had heard of miracles done by the dead man. He admitted that his brother Richard had 'recited' these miracles. They must therefore have begun while William's body was, presumably, still at the castle. Two days later, by which time he had clearly been reinterred as directed in the churchyard from which he had been snatched, the bishop instructed the archdeacon of Gloucester and dean of Westbury

> to inquire in the town of Bristol if any had wickedly gone to the body of William

de Lay, next the church of the Apostles Philip and James, as to a saint, asserting that he was a martyr, or who had presumed to compose a song about him, or recited a composition, or related it in public, and especially concerning the authorship of a certain libellous song written on and fixed to a certain board and to punish the rectors of Blessed Mary in the Market and of the Apostles Philip and James, and others who stirred up scandal and errors in the town of Bristol by reason of William de Lay deceased.

There are a number of familiar ingredients here, such as the complicity of local clergy in the attempt to create a cult, and as usual a number of unanswered questions. Precisely why the dead man was hailed as a martyr eludes us. It is tempting to suppose that the incident was in some way connected with the ongoing disputes between the townsfolk and the constable, who claimed an arbitrary portion of every cargo which was landed in the port of Bristol.[57] Was the public clamour which put one of the miscreants to flight caused by popular resentment of the violation of sanctuary, or by William's local popularity, or perhaps by the constable's unpopularity? Of whom was the offensive song libellous? That it was posted up on a board for the public to read (and perhaps learn by heart or copy) is an interesting detail.

Some of these stories give us glimpses of how popular cults (whether or not they received official sanction) were promoted and serviced. One thinks of the *custos* of the spring at Wye; the candle-sellers who plied their trade by St Edmund's Well at Oxford; the *insignia* with which the dead robber was honoured at Northampton; the selling of victuals and other goods in the churchyard at Whitstone during the Saturday vigils; the interest taken in William Longbeard by traders visiting London; the 'recitation' of William de Lay's miracles by the brother of one of the interested parish clergy and the composition of a song, or songs, about him. Such features did not confer legitimacy on a pilgrimage, but they were equally characteristic of those which were legitimate and those which were not. When Henry III established a fair in London at the feast of Edward the Confessor and prohibited the holding of any other during the same period, he was high-handedly attempting to utilise the same attractive power of commerce which helped give wider publicity to the cult of William Longbeard and may have attracted pilgrims to the spring at Linslade while the market was on.

Even when every bishop's register, every will and every chronicle have yielded up their evidence, it will remain uncertain how complete a record we can ever compile of the myriad popular cults which flourished once upon a time in England, however briefly and obscurely. What has been considered here is a small and arbitrary sample, but it is apparent that the anxieties expressed by Archbishop Greenfield of York or Bishop Baldock of London about the veneration of images, or by Bishop Grandisson of Exeter about honours done to uncanonised persons, were not felt universally or consistently by the ecclesiastical authorities, still less acted upon in such a way as to confine popular veneration within the bounds of a strict and narrow legality. It was said earlier that not all pilgrimage was undertaken in the hope or expectation of miracles, but it is equally true that, wherever and whenever miracles were reported, a pilgrimage, even if only for a short time, was highly likely to result. The ambiguity of the miraculous in the eyes of authority came uppermost when it was associated with dubious cults. An awareness that miracles (especially *in vita* miracles) might be fabricated was embodied in the formal canonisation process, which insisted on proof of holy life and subjected miracle stories to at least a measure of scrutiny. Claims for 'many miracles' were of course made in corroboration of the powers of an approved holy personage or the holiness of an approved shrine, but they could also be made on behalf of bogus saints and quasi-pagan water-cults. The faith that was meritorious when the source was authentic became mere ignorant credulity when it was not.

Among cults which never received formal authorisation, but did receive differing degrees of popular and sometimes official support, there is a loosely definable category which were beyond any doubt political, because of the circumstances of their origin or the rank of their objects or both. In many respects they displayed characteristics common to cults of other and less controversial kinds, but they had a special power to concern, and often to agitate, the kings of England.[58]

Throughout much of recorded history, rulers have struggled to repress the belief that opposition to their authority can claim the support of religion. The kings of England were conspicuous examples, notably during the later middle ages. The special circumstances which had given importance to King Harold and to Earl Waltheof passed with the years, but others took their place. An implausible and evanescent cult sprang up around Henry II's son, the Young King, when he died prematurely in 1182, and there was an unseemly squabble over his body between the cities of Le Mans and Rouen. Not all the English chroniclers relayed the reports of miracles, but one who did, William of Newburgh, was sceptical: 'certain people ... broadcast the rumour that the sick were being cured at his tomb, meaning, that is, either that he had had a just cause against his father, or that he had pleased God mightily with his final penitence'.[59] 'Justice' was the key word, and one who either fell victim to unjust violence, or died for the sake of justice, might be accorded the title of 'martyr'. Matthew Paris, as we have seen, thought William fitz Osbert merited the title because he had died for 'truth' and in defence of the poor. Matthew also said, elaborating slightly on the account he had received from Roger of Wendover, that Peter the Hermit, who had unwisely prophesied John's deposition and was hanged with his son at Wareham in 1213 on the king's orders, 'was seen as a martyr and a declarer of the truth'.[60] There seems, however, to be no record of miracles.

The kings had the additional misfortune that rebellion, or at least resistance, was frequently given a sanctified colour by the support it received from certain of their bishops, not least certain archbishops of Canterbury. What originated as the defence of the 'liberty of the church' in the immediate post-Gregorian epoch, when Anselm of Canterbury clashed first with William Rufus and then with Henry I, had by the thirteenth century become a more inclusive insistence on the king's obligation before God to provide good governance, in which the privileges of the church as an institution were seen alongside the rights and 'liberties' of the king's subjects generally. This was no dramatic or perverse development. The royal coronation oath presented the defence of the church as an inseparable part of the king's duty. Thomas Becket was, officially, a martyr for the rights of the church, but he was also, or could be seen as, the opponent of tyranny and the defender of good custom. Forty-five years after Becket's death, the involvement of another archbishop of Canterbury, Stephen Langton, in the process which produced Magna Carta took the development a stage further, while Thomas himself continued posthumously to stand up for liberty in some unexpected and entirely secular ways. Early in 1241 a priest of London had a vision of the late archbishop destroying the new walls of the Tower, which, as a good Londoner, he regarded as prejudicial to the city. On 23 April, Matthew Paris reported, they duly fell down. [61]

In the two centuries after Magna Carta, the kings of England were intermittently confronted both by bishops who founded a reputation for sanctity in part on their efforts in defence of justice and good government, and by martyr-rebels who died a violent death and menaced them from beyond the grave. Edmund of Abingdon was involved in an early stage of Henry III's difficulties with his baronage; Robert Grossesteste was a personal friend of Simon de Montfort (which did no harm to Simon's own saintly reputation); and Thomas Cantilupe was also associated with the baronial 'reform' movement as Simon de Montfort's chancellor. When in 1267 the cardinal-legate Ottobuon Fieschi summoned the the 'Disinherited', the rebellious adherents of the now dead Simon de Montfort, to return to their obedience to Henry III, they replied by invoking 'the faith they had learned from the holy bishops Robert [Grosseteste], Edmund and Richard [of Chichester], and other Catholic men'.[62] Robert Winchelsey of Canterbury later tried to resist Edward I's assaults on clerical liberties, and was actually suspended from office in February 1306. Restored in January 1308, after

Edward's death, he was subsequently identified with the movement that imposed reforming Ordinances on Edward II in 1310. On Winchelsey's death in 1313, the leader of the baronial opposition, the future 'martyr' Thomas, earl of Lancaster, was an enthusiastic proponent of his canonisation.[63]

It was once suggested that the Capetian kings of France needed to 'profiteer justly', that is to achieve a government which was effective from their own point of view without seeming to their subjects unduly oppressive or exploitative. Their brothers of England from John to Edward II (not excepting Edward I) recurrently failed to strike that balance, nor did they bring off the monarchic coup that was achieved in France when, in 1297, Louis IX himself was canonised, to become and remain a royal icon even after his direct line ended thirty years later. To Henry III and his successors, the sainted defender of the English monarchy was the more remote figure of the Confessor, and perhaps also St Edmund, whom as we have seen they also greatly revered. Henry III discovered that personal piety did not exempt a king who was variously seen as weak, greedy, untrustworthy and incompetent from the counter-claims of a higher spiritual loyalty. His second translation of the Confessor to a resplendent new shrine at Westminster in 1269, even while the cult of Simon de Montfort flourished, could be seen as an affirmation not merely of his own piety but of the supposedly unchallengeable authority, moral and political, of the monarchy – or, indeed, of monarchy *tout court*.

The chronicles reveal a widespread, though not quite universal, understanding of the death of Simon de Montfort at the battle of Evesham in 1265 as martyrdom.[64] It was agreed that he was savagely dismembered, and this in itself may have contributed to the popular view. The Annals of Oseney related how some of his adversaries, not satisfied with his death, objected to his burial in consecrated ground. They had him exhumed from the tomb in which he had been placed at Evesham and

> thrown into a remote spot, a place well-hidden and unknown except to a few down to the present day. But God is the most merciful founder of all and redeemer of the faithful, who will reveal the merits of His servants who have shed their blood for the honour of His name and the laws of their country, and succumbed to the swords of the many, to the eternal praise and glory of His name.

The message – and the association of God's honour with the defence of the laws – is hard to mistake, as it is when another chronicler puts the words 'Truly, as I believe, I shall die for God and justice' into Simon's mouth, and describes his killers as 'martyring' him and tearing him apart. To the Waverley annalist, Simon had suffered martyrdom 'for the peace of the country, the reform of the realm and of mother church'.[65]

The longest and most extravagant report was carried by the chronicle of another Cistercian abbey, Melrose in the Scottish borders, but was probably derived from a Franciscan source. This account attributed miracles also to Simon's comrades, such as Hugh Despenser (also entombed at Evesham) and included a long and tedious comparison of Simon with Simon Peter (who was, however, conceded to be the superior). Enormous stress is laid on evidence of holiness in Simon's life. It is regarded as highly significant that he wore a hair shirt. The mere fact that this was known to be so was sufficient to cause 'grave and religious men' , while he yet lived, to anticipate his future sanctity: they would, they said, 'quite as willingly visit his tomb, for the purpose of their praying to God, as they would go to Jerusalem for the same purpose'. The hair shirt was also a point of resemblance to Becket, as was Simon's death in a just cause:

> There were others who said that if, at the time when they were speaking, Simon had fallen for the sake of right (as he afterwards did) they would quite as readily have gone to his sepulchre, there to pray to God, as to the great shrine of the holy martyr Thomas, in which he reposes at Canterbury, endowed by God with many miracles and adorned with precious stones. The remark which they made in their conversation with each other was not devoid of sound reasons; for no less did Simon die in a just struggle for the lawful rights of the realms of England than Thomas had formerly done for the lawful rights of the church in England. Each of them had died in his own day, clothed in the penance of haircloth – a penance which sooner than any other leads a man to God – that so they might put on incorruption through means of the penance thus voluntarily assumed by God's inspiration.[66]

This somewhat tortuous insistence that Simon's credentials were substantially established before he died betrays either the unease about the sufficiency of a merely political martyrdom which seems also to be observable in the later case of Thomas of Lancaster or the simple belief that a martyr in death must automatically have been a saint in life. As with Becket and others, the ruminations of religious professionals about the nature of Simon's sanctity do not necessarily tell us why he was regarded as a saint by the people who flocked to Evesham and experienced miracles. The Lanercost chronicler said that pilgrims came by night, because Simon's enemies obstructed their access by day. The buildings subsequently erected at Evesham proved that they were successful in making their offerings; even if men were silent, the stones proclaimed Simon's sanctity.[67]

Were these pilgrims demonstrating solidarity with the cause for which the earl had died, or knowledge of and belief in his personal holiness, or both? Analyses of the miracles collected at Evesham between 1274 and 1279 have shed a little light on these important questions, although as usual it is hardly possible to give definite answers in the absence of clear statements by the pilgrims themselves. There were 198 cures, involving 333 people and 273 place-names. The probability that 60 per cent of Simon's pilgrims were peasants, because they are not credited with any other rank, does not necessarily mean that they were indifferent to his political significance, since there is good evidence for peasant participation in the baronial revolt; but equally it does not actually prove that individuals were specifically going to pay homage to him as to a rebel leader. One might speculate that once the cult was launched, and for as long as it thrived, members of the local population would go to the shrine with their problems just as local populations went to shrines everywhere. There was a high proportion of inhabitants of Worcestershire among Simon's clients, as one might expect, and a lesser but still substantial take-up in the adjacent counties of Herefordshire, Gloucestershire and Warwickshire. Leicestershire and Oxfordshire, contiguous to these on the east, were also well represented. What is more striking is that twenty or more cures were reported by inhabitants of Kent and Northamptonshire, both areas strongly implicated in the baronial revolt.[68] In addition, named followers and connections of Simon himself received cures.

Simon received one known pilgrim who did not experience, or perhaps need or expect, a miracle. This was Robert de Vere, earl of Oxford, an adherent of the reform who suffered very considerable hardship as a result, but was eventually restored to his estates and title. A fragmentary household account reveals that he visited Evesham in September 1273. (Henry III, we may note, had been dead for almost ten months.) At Evesham, the earl participated in what were clearly the established pilgrim rituals. At the shrine itself he was 'measured' and spent fifteen pence on two and a half pounds of wax to his measure. This does not necessarily mean that he was in need of a cure. Edward I and the entire royal family donated money for candles made to their united measure when they visited St Mary's Chatham in 1285, but it is not apparent that any of them, let alone all of them, were ill; such offerings were often what might be termed *ex gratia* payments into the saint's account. The earl then went to the spring, which had (almost inevitably) been discovered on the battlefield and where cures were effected, and offered 2*d.* in alms.[69]

Simon de Montfort's cult was impressive while it lasted, but quickly and quietly ebbed after about 1280. An oblique testimony to his memory comes from the story of a mad Cornishman, who in 1290, urged by his friends to have recourse to Thomas Cantilupe of Hereford, 'stupidly' replied, 'I think that he's the same kind of saint as that Simon de Montfort is, whom you called a saint too, who is buried at Evesham'. Thomas appeared to him in a vision and cured him, saying mildly, 'Friend, don't go on making mock of the servants of God with your foolish speeches'.[70] If Simon's cult was starved of nourishment by Edward I's success and shrewdness in implmenting key elements of the baronial reform programme, one might argue *a posteriori* (if not with entire confidence) that while it lasted it was above all a political cult, or at least that it depended on a leadership from above which faded away in the new reign. The Melrose chronicler noted that the liturgical celebration of St Simon was unlikely to achieve official recognition while Edward I lived.

At all events, the outcome contrasts with what happened in the longer term to the equally political cult of Thomas, earl of Lancaster, executed after the battle of Boroughbridge on 22 March 1322. Here we do not have a miracle collection to analyse, but we do have scattered evidence of various types to prove the existence of a cult at Pontefract which lasted down to the Reformation.[71] From the beginning, miracles were reported both at the place of the earl's execution and at his tomb in Pontefract Priory. A blind priest dreamed that his sight would be restored at the place of execution and when it duly was he went to give thanks at the tomb. A drowned child was brought back to life at the tomb itself. Thomas also rapidly established his power to effect long-distance cures: a Gascon who was suffering from a repulsive flesh-eating affliction received a cure and came to Pontefract to give thanks. Hugh Despenser, it was said, denounced these miracles as heresy and sent word to the king to take action. The messenger, passing by the place of the earl's death, paused to defecate upon it, but he lived, briefly, to regret it, for 'a strong flux' came upon him before he had reached York, and he 'shedde all his bowailles at his fondement'. Understandably perturbed by this news, Hugh Despenser urged the king to order the closure of the church doors, although this was against all the liberties of holy church, and for four years afterwards, that is for the rest of the king's reign, 'myght no pilgrime come unto that holy body'.'[72] This simply meant that pilgrims resorted to the place of execution instead. In the course of 1323 Edward II ordered the constable of Pontefract Castle to go there 'and prohibit a multitude of malefactors and apostates from praying and making oblations there in memory of the said earl, not to God, but rather to idols, in contempt of the king and contrary to his former command'. Two of the constable's servants were killed as a consequence of his attempted intervention. A guard was subsequently set on the place.[73]

The king rapidly found that he was dealing with a many-centred phenomenon. St Paul's in London also became the scene of miracles, which took place near the tablet which Thomas had set up there 'in remembrance that the king had granted and confirmed the ordinances made by St Robert

Winchelsey and by all the great and wise persons of England, to the great profit of the whole realm'.[74] According to the Westminster chronicler, the tablet showed Thomas in arms: he described the miracles and almsgiving and the iniquities of the king in equally enthusiastic language. The king instructed the bishop of London to take steps to prohibit assemblies at this *tabula*, where, he had been informed, 'statues, sculptures or images of various people, among them the likeness of Thomas once earl of Lancaster, our enemy and rebel, are depicted'. Vainly Edward appealed to propriety: Thomas was not a canonised saint. He used strong language to express his suspicion that the bishop was conniving at these outrages for the sake of gain, and to remind him of his duty.[75]

As if all this was not enough, miracles were also being claimed at Bristol on behalf of Henry de Montfort and Henry of Willington. They had been subjected to a degrading death, drawn by horses and hanged, and their bodies then suspended from gibbets as examples to anyone else who was meditating crimes against the monarchy. In the circumstances, this merely provided grisly icons for popular veneration. In a letter written at Skipton on 2 October 1323 the king complained about a group of named malefactors, headed by Reginald de Montfort, who

> maliciously fabricating fraudulent causes with which to alienate the affection of the people from us and move the said people against us, have several times gone to Bristol, to the places where the bodies of the said enemies and rebels remain hanged, and there faking miracles, have created and proclaimed figments of idolatry, and caused them to be created and proclaimed by others.[76]

These miscreants had also resisted the king's servants with armed force.

Archbishop Melton of York was inevitably caught up in these events. In August 1323 he ordered the officials of the archdeacons of York and Cleveland to put a stop to the devotion, professing a concern not only for theological propriety but for public order, as there had been homicides and other injuries at the place of the earl's death. With the deposition of Edward II at the beginning of 1327, however, Melton found himself living in a different world. Solicited by the earl's brother and successor Henry to urge the pope to enquire into his miracles, he duly did so on 24 February. The hordes of pilgrims, who four years previously had been condemned not only for disloyalty to the king but for their disregard of canonical decorum, now became presumptive evidence for Thomas's sanctity.[77] A few days later the new young king wrote in similar terms, and he made renewed efforts in March 1330 and April 1331.[78] The pope did not respond, and thereafter Edward, firmly established on his throne and emancipated from the tutelage of those who had put him there, had no further need to pursue the matter.

He showed no hostility to the cult, however: in September 1332 he renewed his protection to the collectors who were going about the kingdom on behalf of the priory of Pontefract raising money for building works at the church itself and also in hopes of erecting a chapel on the spot where the earl was beheaded.[79]

Thomas's cult endured, whereas Simon's did not. Why was this? It would be hard to say that it was because Thomas had better character references. Simon's personal piety, whether or not it really mattered to his transient reputation as a saint, seems to have been impeccable. The Chester chronicler Ralph Higden gave measured consideration to the character evidence for and against Thomas. The best that could be said was that he gave alms, honoured religious men and died in a just cause. More circumstantially, it could be argued that those who persecuted him (notably Edward II himself, although this is not stated) met unpleasant ends. On the other hand, it was said that, as a married man, he neglected his wife in favour of innumerable *mulierculae*, did to death those who offended him even slightly and gave protection to fugitives from religious orders and transgressors of the laws. The claim to martyrdom could be impugned by pointing out that Thomas was in flight when apprehended and went unwillingly to his death. In the end it was the offerings at the place of execution and the miracles (or the appearance of miracles, *miraculorum simulacra*) which told. Higden seemed inclined to defer judgement to future generations.[80]

Like Earl Simon's, Thomas's tomb doubtless attracted visits from, or on behalf of, individuals who acknowledged some debt of *pietas* towards his memory. Humphrey de Bohun, earl of Essex and Hereford, who died in 1361, stipulated in his will that a man should go to Pontefract and offer forty shillings on his behalf. Humphrey's father had died at Boroughbridge as an adherent of Thomas; perhaps his memory was also jogged by the news that in 1359 blood was seeping from the earl's tomb.[81] The dissemination of the cult is attested, among other evidence, by the making of souvenir badges in Thomas's honour.[82] The information that, on the eve of the Reformation, his hat and belt were used at Pontefract as remedies for headaches and the perils of childbirth suggests that by then the cult had bedded down as a source of assistance to a regional population in the trials of life.[83]

The fortunes of Edward II and Thomas of Lancaster continued to be intertwined after both their deaths. Higden reported that when Edward himself died, it was publicly debated in just the same way whether he was a saint. It was appropriate in this context to reaffirm the orthodox view that no amount of ill treatment, nor a vile death (if these were merited by the subject's crimes), nor abundant offerings or miracles, proved sanctity unless accompanied by evidence of holy life.[84] The chronicler of St Peter's

Abbey at Gloucester claimed that three neighbouring west country monasteries, St Augustine's at Bristol, Kingswood and Malmesbury, refused to
accept Edward's body for burial for fear of reprisals from the king's widow
(and mother of the new king) Isabella and her lover Roger Mortimer.
Gloucester got its reward for receiving him, for

> within a few years there was such a resort of the common folk (*plebis frequentatio*)
> that the city of Gloucester could scarcely hold the multitude of people flocking
> from various cities, towns and places of England, with the result that within six
> years of becoming abbot [John Wigmore, 1329–37] built the transept of St Andrew,
> as it now appears, from its foundations to completion, out of the offerings offered
> there.[85]

In the absence of detailed miracle stories it is impossible to give more
precision to the chronicler's description of the pilgrims as *plebs*. The evidence
for pilgrimage to Edward II would, however, seem to be as concrete, in a
literal sense, as the Lanercost chronicler took the evidence for pilgrimage
to Simon to be: just as Evesham had been enabled to undertake substantial
rebuilding, so now was Gloucester. These facts are suggestive. It would be
hard to find evidence of Edward II's popularity, let alone of his reputation
for saintly character. He was, however, an anointed king, who (it was
generally believed) had died in highly suspicious and unpleasantly violent
circumstances. It does not follow that the three cults, of Earl Simon, Earl
Thomas and King Edward, are all to be explained in the same terms and
that neither 'justice' nor personal character had anything to do with any
of them, but there must at least be a faint suspicion that what was earlier
called the omnivorousness of popular enthusiasm for new saints and miracles was implicated in all three.

There is little evidence that Edward III took any special measures to
promote his father as a saint. His inclusion of the tomb at Gloucester in
the pilgrimage-tour he undertook in 1343 in thanksgiving for his deliverance
at sea may have represented a tacit endorsement of the cult or merely a
demonstration of filial piety. It is striking, however, that in 1347 the bishop
of Rochester felt entitled to send a penitent 'to King Edward at Gloucester'. [86]
Richard II devoted considerable effort to a campaign for the canonisation
of his great-grandfather, especially after 1385, but he clearly did not invent
the cult out of whole cloth. Not only Richard's personal convictions but
the circumstances of his reign may have reawakened in his mind, and
others, the threats and promises of political canonisation. [87] Thomas Walsingham reported that Simon Sudbury, archbishop of Canterbury, murdered
by the rebels in 1381, did miracles.[88] In 1384, rumours sprang up around a
Carmelite friar who was arrested and murdered in custody after accusing

John of Gaunt of conspiring to usurp the throne. It was said that the hurdle on which his body was drawn put out shoots and leaves, that a blind man was healed by it, and that 'a great light' shone over the friar's grave.[89]

With the death of Henry of Lancaster in 1361, the title and the estates (including Pontefract) had passed to the royal house itself, in the person of John of Gaunt. In the last decade of his reign, and the duke's decline, Richard was giving way to fear and suspicion of the house of Lancaster, now effectively headed by Henry Bolingbroke, the future Henry IV. Thomas Walsingham related that in 1390, in the midst of Richard's efforts to secure the canonisation of Edward II, 'St Thomas of Lancaster was canonised'.[90] What exactly he meant by this seems never to have been fully explained; but it is quite possible that not only the king's attempt to create a new and official monarchic cult but his assaults on the Lancastrian interest had breathed renewed political life into Thomas's memory. At a much later crisis in Lancastrian fortunes, the imprisonment of Henry VI in the Tower in 1465, the tomb at Pontefract was once again reported to be oozing blood.[91]

In 1396 Richard himself was at least temporarily terrified by the threat that another political cult might be raised up against him. He had nightmares after the judicial execution of the earl of Arundel, and his disquiet was augmented by talk that the populace reputed the earl a martyr and were making pilgrimages to his tomb. It was being said that his head had become miraculously reattached to his body, a story which, as Richard may well have known, recalled the legend of St Edmund and perhaps also of Earl Waltheof. On the tenth day after the earl's burial the king had a investigation conducted by night in order to assure himself that this was not the case. Not content with the outcome of this post mortem, he ordered the Augustinian friars with whom Arundel was buried to take down the *insignia* which had been put up around the grave and hide the burial place beneath the paving. The chronicler Adam of Usk firmly believed that the earl was a saint and said that 'his body, although then irreverently buried with the Augustinians in London, is now most gloriously venerated with the utmost reverence and frequent offering from the people'.[92]

Richard's own mysterious end helped promote rumours among the disaffected that he was not really dead. He himself did not become a martyr in the cause of 'legitimism', but Henry IV almost managed to create one when, in 1405, he had Archbishop Scrope of York executed with other rebels. The cult that promptly erupted at York affords an interesting comparison with those already discussed.[93] Initially, the king tried to suppress it, but he was (or was advised to be) judicious in his proceedings. A five-point directive to the York authorities laid it down that miracles were not to be publicised, nor were people to be encouraged to adore the archbishop; they were by no means however to be deterred from praying for his soul. Three named clerks of York were to be deputed to explain to those who wanted to make offerings that they should do so not at Scrope's tomb but at St William's shrine or some other *locus devotus* within the church. If wax or other things, or gold and silver, were deposited in defiance of this prohibition they were to be removed by the *custodes* and applied to the uses of the church as they saw fit. Thomas Arundel, archbishop of Canterbury, in association with Thomas Langley, chancellor of the kingdom and also treasurer of York, gave discreet support and urged caution: all must wait upon the will of God, which would be manifested in due season. A little later, the king's son John, as constable of England, directed Thomas Garton, one of the three named clerks, to remove the wooden enclosure that had been made around the tomb and see to the erection of a more substantial barrier of stones and logs to prevent 'the foolish crowd' from paying their devotions.[94]

It was not long, however, before Henry IV himself, evidently breathing more easily, relaxed these restrictions, and offerings to Scrope were accepted and channelled into building work. Early in the reign of Henry V, at much the same time as the new king gave Richard II and his queen honoured burial at Westminster, all royal opposition was withdrawn and an official *custos* of the tomb was appointed. It was receiving substantial offerings, superior to those received by St William: £73 8s. in 1415, £150 in 1419. In the 1450s Scrope took on a new lease of posthumous life as a Yorkist saint. The legend that Henry IV had been smitten with leprosy in punishment for the execution was remembered, and Edward IV himself referred to Scrope as a martyr 'for the right of our ancestry whose estates we now have'. Like Simon de Montfort and Thomas of Lancaster before him, Scrope was honoured also at the place of his death, where a chapel was built. In 1462 a possible canonisation was under discussion at York, which prompted a canon of Ripon to leave money in 1467 for a new shrine.

Nothing came of these projects, but inventories taken early in the sixteenth century of offerings around the tombs of St William and of 'Master Richard Scrope' show that the late archbishop had been comfortably assimilated into the devotional round at York.[95] Both shrines were adorned by a motley collection of objects, including jewels and jewelled belts and models of body parts (breasts, heads, hearts) as well as of whole bodies. Scrope had received the tribute of two images of cows, one larger and one smaller, and also a great many ships. New acquisitions in 1509 included 'ankers and hukes', a silver horse and a silver image of St George on horseback, silver legs and feet, hearts and teeth, and miscellaneous items of jewellery and other precious knicknacks. In their different ways, the ships and the teeth suggest with particular vividness that Scrope was now enacting a role which had little to do with the precise circumstances of his death. Once again the canonised and the uncanonised saint worked harmoniously side by side. After initial attempts at repression, the Lancastrian kings had learned to live with this cult and it persisted, for the most part, quietly.

Half a century later they acquired a martyr of their own. The honours paid to the dead Henry VI at Chertsey Abbey were naturally embarrassing to Edward IV and to Richard III, who in 1484 had the body removed to Windsor for safe-keeping. To Henry VII the cult was no longer an embarrassment, and in correspondence with a succession of popes, he put forward plans, not destined to be fulfilled, both for the late king's canonisation and for his removal to the mausoleum of the monarchy at Westminster. It was at Windsor that the cult achieved its greatest popularity, attested by numerous miracles, by the making and marketing of pilgrim-badges which have been found over a wide area of the country, and by testamentary bequests.[96]

To ask whether Earl Simon, Earl Thomas, Edward II, Archbishop Scrope or Henry VI deserved to attract pilgrims is less important than to ask why they did. All cults required promotion. However unusual the circumstances in which these particular cults began, the motives of many of those who promoted them, including the actual proprietors of the shrines, for example the monks of Gloucester, would innately have differed little from those of other promoters, especially with the passage of time and the abeyance of any risks that may initially have attended the enterprise. Were these 'saints' in any way differentiated in the minds of pilgrims themselves from other saints, official or unofficial, to whose shrines they or their neighbours also had resort? Was the actual act of pilgrimage to Thomas of Lancaster or to Henry VI a political demonstration, or were their shrines simply identified as new places where solace of body and mind could be obtained? The same questions, as we have already seen, could be asked about pilgrims to Thomas Becket, especially in the early days of his cult. We need to know what the word was on the street, in the fifteenth century as in the twelfth, and we do not know enough. The miracle stories themselves tell us little; they are, for the most part, miracles like any others. That some of them had the effect of convincing and converting sceptics is not evidence this was what the beneficiaries of the miracles themselves had in mind when they went to the tomb or called upon the martyr in prayer; such stories were told about many saints, by no means all of them politically controversial.

All of these men died (or were believed to have died) a violent death. As we have seen, that seems sometimes to have helped to attach a reputation for sanctity to some very inconspicuous individuals; but these individuals were far from inconspicuous. In every case, large numbers of contemporaries would have known enough about them and the circumstances of their deaths to believe that they had been the victims of injustice and even of sacrilege, for Edward II, Scrope and Henry VI had all been anointed. Simon de Montfort's miracles suggest pointers, rather than conclusive answers, to the questions just propounded. An analysis of Henry VI's extant miracles leads to similar results.

There are surviving records of 174 miracles, a few of them no more than chapter-headings, and some of them undated summaries, giving few useful particulars. In many of these instances no place of origin is given for the *miraculé*, which does not help when we try to plot Henry's constituency on the map, and although some early miracles may be concealed among these, there is little or no record of the wonders he must have performed while still buried at Chertsey. That there was pilgrimage to him there, and a great deal too much for Edward IV's liking, is clear from the measures the king took to prevent it. A proclamation issued in May 1473 against vagabondage and mendicancy by bogus pilgrims (and bogus university students) may well have been aimed at Henry VI's devotees, although in fact it echoed the policy of Richard II's government nearly a century before in the wake of the Peasants' Revolt. Henry VII himself would make a similar proclamation in 1493.[97] In the eyes of the secular authorities, it would seem, pilgrimage was less likely to be illegitimate because of its objects than because of the motives of the participants.

Henry's recorded miraculous activity was concentrated in two principal periods, first, from 1484 to the early 1490s, and then in 1498–99. As Henry VII pressed on with his plans for his predecessor's canonisation and translation to Westminster, miracles which had occurred several years before were investigated in several parts of the country. It was not infrequently decided that they could not be verified, often doubtless because witnesses could no longer be found. The miracles themselves exemplified the late medieval norm, in that the vast majority of them occurred at a distance from the shrine, as a result of prayers and vows and occasionally visions. These vows were often accompanied by the old custom of selecting a coin to offer to the saint and 'bending' it to mark it for that purpose and no other; many clients were also 'measured'. Some cures however still took place at the shrine itself, and cripples left their crutches in evidence.

The Windsor miracles however only give us a partial view of Henry's popularity. There were regional centres of devotion to him. In October 1479 the archbishop of York complained to his official that many people of the diocese were coming to venerate a statue of the late king that had been set up in the cathedral itself and making offering to it 'although his body is buried not there but elsewhere'. If this was offensive in itself, the insult to Edward IV was clearly also very much on the archbishop's mind.[98] York remained an important centre, and there was veneration also at Ripon and Durham. Offerings were being made to King Henry at Hereford Cathedral in the 1490s, while in East Anglia there were shrines at Ely and at Yarmouth. These facts may help to account for the seemingly lopsided provenance of the pilgrims who came to Windsor, which in the end conforms to the common pattern by being broadly regional.[99]

The majority of Henry's Windsor clients came from southern England. If we look at 137 miracles whose beneficiaries can be placed, it transpires that some were reported from the west, from Shropshire, Worcestershire, Wiltshire, Somerset and Dorset, and that there was a little interest in Devon and Cornwall; but no cures were reported from Herefordshire or Gloucestershire, one from Cheshire and only one from Wales proper, from Montgomery. There were two apiece from Westmoreland and Lancashire, but no miracles at all were collected from Cumberland, Northumberland or Yorkshire. Further south, there were four Cambridgeshire miracles, three of them at Cambridge itself (not counting the deliverance of a Hammersmith man from unjust execution). Lincolnshire and Norfolk, however, produced only one miracle apiece, and one of the two that can be credited to Suffolk may in fact, thanks to scribal confusion, belong to Sussex. Several of Henry's clients invoked him together with the Virgin, and a Somerset man who was delivered from the gallows at Salisbury said that he intended to make a pilgrimage of thanksgiving to Walsingham. In the midlands, a good showing was made by Northamptonshire, with six miracles, and there were three from Leicestershire, but only two each from Nottinghamshire and Rutland, one from Warwickshire and none at all from Derbyshire. The poor showing of Herefordshire, the north east and East Anglia may, as we have seen, owe something to the availability of subsidiary shrines in those regions.

If we add together the cures claimed by natives of Oxfordshire, Berkshire, Hertfordshire, Essex, London and Middlesex, Kent, Sussex, Surrey and Hampshire, they total eighty of the sample of 137. Even within this block, different areas contributed unevenly. London and Middlesex together accounted for sixteen, as did Kent single-handed; Sussex contributed twelve (possibly thirteen) and Essex ten. Berkshire, Buckinghamshire and Oxfordshire together mustered thirteen. The strong Kentish showing is interesting in view of the fact, noted earlier, that over two hundred years earlier pilgrims from the same county had gone in relatively large numbers to Simon de Montfort at Evesham. Both Kent and Essex, it is worth noting, also sent strong contingents of pilgrims to Thomas of Lancaster in the year after his death.[100] A large proportion of Henry's Kentish clients came from within a few miles of Canterbury. It could be that their own day-to-day familiarity with pilgrimage stimulated their appetite for new cults; or perhaps they were just restive by nature. One native of Higham required unique treatment from Henry VI. As a result of his heretical beliefs (which included rejecting pilgrimage) he suffered severe burning pains all over his body. The king restored both his physical and his spiritual health.[101]

Did Henry's cult, wherever it was fostered, have a political message for the generality of its devotees? We know little about the very early years of the cult, when its political edge may have been at its keenest, but the accession of Richard III may well have resharpened it. One of Henry's two recorded cures of cases of the King's Evil (scrofula) involved a snub to Richard, for the parents of the afflicted child rejected advice to take her to be 'touched' by the reigning king.[102] On a few occasions, Henry seems to have performed miracles for members of families who had some kind of connection with him. The daughter of the Sussex knight John Devenish got a plum stone stuck in her nose, and her mother saved her by invoking Henry. The mother was a daughter of Thomas Hoo, whom Henry had ennobled as Baron Hoo and Hastings. In 1484 Henry saved Richard Beys, a servant of a member of the Stourton family, when he was condemned to death by a packed jury at Salisbury. If his master was one of the Stourtons of Maiden Bradley in Wiltshire, they too had been ennobled by the late king. Another Sussex client, Thomas Stapleton, was severely wounded in the intestines in an attack by personal enemies, and underwent drastic surgery, but he appealed to Henry when a mysterious visitor reminded him that his father had died fighting for the king.[103]

It might be possible to tease out more such connections, but the general aspect of the miracles argues that Henry simply did for his clientele the things that needed doing, as Earl Simon had done and as Thomas of Lancaster and Archbishop Scrope surely also did. His interventions covered the usual run of afflictions, including blindness, plague and epilepsy, and a large number of rural accidents involving agricultural implements and loaded waggons. A priest at Brighton got trapped with another man in a well from which they were trying to remove two dead ducks, for fear that the ducks would pollute the water supply; an unfortunate Oxfordshire man got buried under an enormous pile of peas and beans.[104] Children were always getting drowned and suffering other mishaps in play. Henry, like other saints, rescued them; yet all the while, like so many others, he remained uncanonised.

This was not for want of good intentions. In 1504 Julius II authorised Henry VII to remove his predecessor's body from Windsor to Westminster, both for the late king's greater honour and for the profit of the abbey (although the translation was not in fact effected). The pope also followed in the footsteps of Innocent VIII and Alexander VI by commissioning a number of English bishops to undertake an investigation of the miracles.[105] Henry VII could not pre-empt a formal canonisation process, but his accession effectively transformed the environment of Henry VI's cult. Unofficial, in strict terms, it remained, but it ceased to be even potentially subversive, and in a religious climate dominated by devotion to the Virgin and the person and attributes of Christ, it achieved an impressive popularity, as witnessed not only by the miracles but by wills which mention King Henry's tomb. The partnership into which Henry entered at Windsor with another uncanonised saint, John Shorne, is striking testimony to the fluidity of the boundary between the official and the unofficial.

8

The Pilgrim's Voice

Our descriptions of medieval pilgrims come from almost every kind of interested party except the pilgrims themselves. Given that a majority of ordinary pilgrims were probably illiterate, this is all but inevitable. Pilgrims and what they did were for the most part described by members of a literate (and numerate) minority who were professionally identified with the saints and the churches which constituted pilgrimage destinations.

Among the various types of documentation thus created, the records of offerings at shrines, which naturally survive most often from the larger churches, occupy one extreme of objectivity. Although these are obviously of the greatest value, not least in making possible some idea of the popularity of shrines and altars over a period of time, the ordinary pilgrim as an individual does not feature in them; his penny or his candle are subsumed into the mass. At an opposite extreme stands the miracle story, examples of which survive from every century of the medieval epoch and have provided the bulk of historians' evidence for the study of pilgrimage. Sometimes these are presented as as if in the pilgrim's own words. In addition to addressing occasional explanatory remarks to the reader, William fitz Stephen sometimes tries to evoke the reality of the pilgrim's presence in the most amiable and gossipy fashion: 'Brother William returns to hear what news the people are bringing. And behold! two women, one of them married, the other not yet ready for a husband.' The young girl, through her father, then tells in direct speech how she was put to the study of letters at the age of five and suffered an accident playing with her schoolfellows, while the older woman waits with matronly modesty for her husband to speak for her. Next, a clerical pilgrim tells his own story, beginning 'You ask, brother William, who I am, from where and why I have come'. [1] There was less room for this quasi–verbatim mode of reporting in the more formal collections made with canonisation in view, but the same eagerness to convince the reader (or hearer) of the reality of the experience is, naturally enough, often in evidence.

Miracle stories, then, bring us face to face with pilgrims, their names, often their places of origin and social status or occupation, sometimes their ages. Yet they can hardly be seen as a straightforward account of what the generality of pilgrims either expected or experienced. Above all, they served a purpose, or several interlocking purposes. They were, in the first place, a record in a quasi-legal sense. Even if their standards of proof were not ours, respectable churchmen claimed to require trustworthy evidence that what had occurred was really a miracle: it was common for witnesses to be produced to testify that the beneficiary had really been suffering from the condition that had now been cured. The development of formal canonisation procedures placed increasing emphasis on verification. A good many of the miracles attributed to Henry VI were reckoned to be unproven or unverifiable when investigated some years after they occurred. The record had to conform to what were currently taken to be scientific standards of truth, while at the same time interested clergy had every reason to believe in miracles and to encourage others to do so.

This was not necessarily a discreditable aim. Miracles, and the pilgrimage and offerings they might encourage, meant not only revenue but faith and respect for the church as the institution which proclaimed and validated the saints, as well as for particular churches which possessed particular relics, and miracle stories undoubtedly document a part of an ongoing interrelationship between church and people. There was, ideally, an equilibrium between the clerical custodians of shrines and their clients, a joint investment in a basic belief system and the practices that were built upon it. This also implied investment in the financial sense: outlay (by clergy and also by lay patrons) on buildings, decoration, hospitality, which met with and was itself partly dependent on the offerings of the faithful. Observing this interplay, contemporary critics such as the Lollards accused the one group of cynical profiteering and the other of ignorant gullibility. Some modern observers have been prone to agree with them, which is probably not so much a mistake as a partial view, in both senses of the word, of how the minds of those involved actually worked.

Depending on the purposes for which they were primarily intended, as evidence for canonisation, as edifying reading or as material for preaching, miracle stories needed to carry conviction within the framework of cultural norms and expectations. We can take it that we possess the names, ages and places of origin of many pilgrims and that we can accept as real many of the circumstantial details of their lives which are relayed to us. There seems little reason to doubt that the problems and afflictions from which suppliants sought relief, their daily tasks and occupations and living conditions, were often accurately described. There is valuable information about practices which were familiar to all those involved with pilgrimage: the drawing of lots to choose between shrines, the 'measuring' of sufferers, the offering of specially reserved bent coins, and so forth. Miracle collections also however tend to include stock items which were endlessly repeated in different collections, such as the almost obligatory success of saint B in conferring a cure which saint A had failed or refused to perform. It is such features that most sharply remind us that these stories originated not with the clients but with the promoters of the shrines. They are bound to be defective as records of the subjective experience of the lay pilgrim, because, while that is what we might like them to be, it is not in fact what they were intended to be. Miracles, to those who recorded them, served larger purposes. As they had done for Gregory of Tours and Pope Gregory the Great at the end of the sixth century, they testified to the continuing activity of God in the world, and were therefore a stimulus to faith; they also of course advertised the merits of particular saints and particular shrines, which was scarcely less to the point as far as their custodians were concerned.

Furthermore, miracles were only a small part of pilgrim experience; pilgrims may have believed in them, but most probably never witnessed one, whether at the shrine or away from it. Even in an age when the official attitude to what constituted a miracle was more liberal than that of the modern Catholic church, let alone that of the modern Protestant or sceptic, they were still unusual events at all but moments of the most extraordinary collective excitement. The changing relationship between shrines and miracles, mentioned in an earlier chapter, must also be remembered. Already in the late twelfth century Becket was performing many miracles at long range, and this has been identified as a growing late medieval trend. It has been remarked that the miracles submitted for the pope's consideration when the first canonisation process was initiated in behalf of St Osmund of Salisbury in 1228 centred on and around the tomb, but of the second batch of thirty-three miracles, collected in the forty years down to 1424, only six occurred at the tomb itself.[2] Suppliants invoked the saint wherever they happened to be, and might perform a pilgrimage of thanksgiving afterwards, although sending an offering by the hand of another was often a possible alternative. Later in the fifteenth century Henry VI's miracles confirm the trend. If pilgrims experienced miracles, it was increasingly likely to have been elsewhere than at the shrine.

Pilgrimages carried out after a miracle had occurred, rather than before, raise interesting questions of psychological interpretation. It is far from uncommon for entirely secular-minded individuals at the present day, in moments of danger or crisis, to make an inward resolution which might be paraphrased something like this: 'If I get through this, I will be a better person/never lose my temper again/give a large sum to charity, etc.' The vow of pilgrimage, in the culture of medieval Christianity, discharged a similar function (as indeed it still sometimes does, and not just for committed

Christians, today). For such cures or escapes to be recorded as miracles, they had to be reported as miracles; and while an individual who was deeply moved by his or her experience may well have sought out the shrine authorities in order to tell the story, this seems most likely to have happened when bishops or other interested parties were actively soliciting such testimony and an atmosphere was created in which large numbers of people became prepared to interpret what had happened to them as miraculous.

This is not for one moment to deny that the propensity to explain the unexpected as miraculous was more prevalent in this pre-modern culture; but it is an interesting fact that the only two late medieval Becket miracles of which we have specific record occurred at the shrine itself. In 1394 Richard II wrote to congratulate Archbishop Courtenay on a miracle which God had recently worked for 'a foreigner, as though for the purpose of spreading to strange and distant countries the glorious fame of his very martyr aforesaid'. There are no further particulars. In 1445 a crippled native of Aberdeen who had made his painful way south was cured at the *feretrum*, having made a vow of pilgrimage at a Scottish shrine (perhaps Our Lady of Seton) where he had unavailingly sought a cure.[3] Was Becket really rendering no miraculous assistance to any Englishmen or Englishwomen in the fourteenth or fifteenth century? Chaucer would have us believe that he was, and many people still came to him and remembered him in their wills, but we have no itemised record.

Miracle stories often in fact claim that pilgrims went to Canterbury as elsewhere simply 'to pray' and then, perhaps, witnessed or experienced unexpected marvels; while such a journey, undertaken out of pure devotion, might lay the foundations of belief for a future miracle, as it did for some of Thomas Cantilupe's clients. The slightly convoluted wording of one of Henry VI's miracles inverts the same relationship: the abbess of Burnham came to Windsor, 'prompted no less by a miracle than by devotion', to testify to the cure of a young boy.[4] 'Devotion' by itself would have been a sufficient and intelligible motive for her pilgrimage, but as it happened she had another. 'Devotion' was a broad and only loosely definable category; fictional though she may be, Chaucer's Wife of Bath, who had been to the Holy Land, Rome, Santiago, Cologne and Boulogne, suggests how broad, not to say elastic, it may have been for those who were sufficiently prosperous and energetic.

From the twelfth century on, devotion was increasingly (though by no means exclusively) focussed on indulgences. It may not have been deliberate ecclesiastical policy to encourage the faithful to seek indulgences rather than miracles, but the church did at least know that it could deliver the former on request. That too has attracted unfavourable comment from sceptical modern observers, who have not only frequently been irritated by or un-comprehending of the theology of indulgences, but have seen late medieval pilgrims as caught up in an absurd inflationary spiral, endlessly pursuing more and more stupendous quantities of remission. It seems harsh to criticise medieval Christians for taking steps to avoid the appalling pains of Purgatory, given that they were convinced that they deserved them and were likely to incur them, but that too is beside the present point, which is to ask whether we do, or can, in fact know why ordinary individuals went on pilgrimage and how the practice of pilgrimage fitted into their lives.

On 19 September 1373 a group of twelve men gave evidence at a inquest held at Malmesbury. They explained how it was that they remembered that Walter, son and heir of Bevis fitz Waryn, was born and baptised at Box, near the Somerset border, on the Feast of the Assumption in 1349. 'This they know', they said, 'because the church is dedicated to the honour of the Assumption, and they were there on that day in one company as pilgrims, and saw how Walter de Paveley, the heir's godfather, lifted him from the sacred font.' It is not clear either from what distance or why this little group had come on their 'pilgrimage' . Perhaps there was a modest indulgence available at Box on its chief feast day; possibly they were *en route* elsewhere, perhaps to Glastonbury via nearby Bath. Still to be seen at Chapel Plaster, a little over a mile east of Box, are a fifteenth-century hospital and chapel, thought to have served pilgrims to Glastonbury.[5] We know these pilgrims' names: John Brimylham, Richard Parfet, William Kaynesham, Thomas Mowle, Henry Umfray, William Heyr, William Anesse, Walter Ameneye, Adam Hurdle, Peter Davy (charmingly recalling that other company who went to Widdecombe Fair), Robert Clyverden and Thomas Clyve. In 1373 they all claimed to be aged fifty or more, so at the time of their pilgrimage they would have constituted a company in their mid to late twenties, joined together in a pious late summer excursion. They witnessed no miracle but remembered a social experience.[6]

The inquisitions post mortem, which supply this information, have so far been published in calendared form for the period from the middle of the thirteenth entry to the early years of the fifteenth, and also for the reign of Henry VII. These inquests were most often held to establish whether the heir or heiress to a free tenancy was of sufficient age to enter into his or her inheritance. Witnesses were asked to remember events which had typically taken place twenty-one years or more before the date of the inquest, fourteen years or more if the heir in question was female. They make available a wealth of incidental information about many aspects of social life apart from pilgrimage. The first record to contain information relevant for our purpose dates from 1297 and refers to the birth of an heiress in

1283; one of the witnesses remembered performing a pilgrimage to Santiago at around that time.[7] Between 1297 and 1405 a total of twenty-eight witnesses recalled pilgrimages to English shrines; the pilgrimages themselves had been performed between 1278 and 1382, twenty-one of them to Canterbury.

This may not sound like a very large number of references, but many of them are not to single pilgrims but to parties, like the twelve who went to Box in 1349, and a number of other considerations need to be taken into account before we can assess their quantitative significance. There were many more records of pilgrimages to shrines outside England. One group of Cambridgeshire witnesses, giving evidence in 1308, remembered how in 1284 they had set out for St Andrew's and had their staves and purses consecrated in the same church, on the same day (23 November) that the heir had been baptised.[8] These hardy souls apart, well over a hundred witnesses remembered pilgrimages to continental shrines, either by themselves or by kin or persons known to them. There are ninety-nine records of pilgrimage to Compostela, and smaller numbers of witnesses remembered journeys to Rome (eleven) and the Holy Land (sixteen). In 1309 one individual recalled that Edmund, son of Roger de Coleville, had been so named in 1288 because his father had been on pilgrimage to St Edmund of Pontigny and vowed to give his son the saint's name.[9]

These figures are important as another reminder that English pilgrims who went only to English shrines lived side by side with men and women who made much longer devotional journeys. It seems a fair assumption that most people who went to Rome, Santiago or the Holy Land also visited English shrines. The witnesses at one Lincoln inquest, held in May 1354, included one man whose son, now aged twenty-one, had set off for the Holy Land in the previous February, another who had been to Santiago in 1333, and another who had in the same year begun a series of annual pilgrimages to Canterbury.[10] Andrew Plaitour of Aldbury in Hertfordshire remembered how in May 1334 he had been greeted at St Albans by 'many of his neighbours' as he returned home from Santiago.[11] Did they then together visit the shrine of the protomartyr by way of thanksgiving? Was the returned pilgrim identified as an especially suitable godfather when two months later he sponsored John de Noers at the font?

It would hardly be possible to deduce from a total of about 160 mentions of pilgrimage in a period of just over a century a plausible order of magnitude for pilgrimage undertaken by the English population as a whole, at home or abroad. In fact, the total is quite impressive evidence for the popularity of pilgimage if one reflects how very restricted a sample it represents. We have this evidence only because some of the men who were impanelled as witnesses at inquisitions post mortem had gone on pilgrimage, in

England or elsewhere, somewhere around the time of the birth of a certain heir or heiress. Doubtless many other witnesses had gone on other pilgrimages at other times which it was not relevant to mention, while many English pilgrims must have gone through life without giving evidence at these inquests, if only because they were female, clergy, or males of lowly or unfree status. The sample consists solely of law-worthy laymen, who sometimes mentioned women as pilgrims (notably to the Holy Land), but overall give the impression that in their experience pilgrimage was a largely masculine activity. The twelve who went to Box in 1349 described themselves as 'one company', and on other occasions too several men are named as having set off together; in some instances the possibility that there were women with them cannot be excluded, as when a Warwickshire man recollected having gone to Canterbury with a party of 'neighbours' in 1332, but if so they are never named.[12] Women certainly went on pilgrimage, even if they were in a minority over long distances, so our sample, which as noted also excludes clergy, is not only an unknowable fraction of the total of male pilgrims but gives us no guidance at all as to how many female English pilgrims there were.

With all their deficiencies, these records have unique value in that they give us a more matter of fact view of pilgrimage performed by ordinary people than it is easy to get from many other sources. Their character is such that they give no more than clues to interesting issues like motivation, but even here they are not entirely mute. There may have been special reasons for pilgrimage to Rome or the Holy Land, but there seems no good reason to suppose that motives for going to English shrines differed essentially from motives for going to Santiago, even if the journey to Galicia was obviously a more arduous and momentous undertaking than any domestic pilgrimage. Simon de Stedeham of Sussex recalled in 1321 that he had gone to Rome 'to obtain indulgences' in 1300; this was, of course, the year of the first Roman Jubilee.[13] Two men from Kent said that they had gone to Santiago in 1343 'for the amendment of their lives', but such explicit moralism is very rare; the reference might conceivably be to a penitential pilgrimage.[14] Pilgrims to English shrines say nothing about either collecting indulgences or 'amending their lives', although John Curteys, who set out barefoot from Bedfordshire to Beverley in February 1351, was undertaking a markedly penitential exercise, whether voluntarily or involuntarily we are not told.[15] A faint hint of another kind of motivation might be gleaned from the recollections of Edward Brond in 1405: asked to testify that Fulk de Gray was of age, he recalled that he had been at Canterbury with the heir's father when his mother gave birth to him in 1382.[16]

Vows are the only motives for pilgrimage to which specific reference is made. Such vows may sometimes have been made out of pure devotion, but, in some instances at least, they followed the experience of a cure or other deliverance from trouble. A Yorkshireman who went to Canterbury in 1336 did so because of a vow made in sickness.[17] At Ascensiontide in the previous year a small party set out from Lincolnshire to Canterbury in fulfilment of a vow made when they had been in danger of death during a thunderstorm while returning from the assizes at Lincoln.[18] Another Lincolnshire witness, Thomas Blaunkeney, remembered that he had served as clerk at the baptism of Robert Bate on 6 December 1332 and that at Easter in the following year, when he was about twenty, he had made the first of his annual pilgrimages to Canterbury. This presumably implied some sort of vow, but the motive for it is not explained.[19]

No English pilgrim refers specifically to indulgences offered at English shrines. It is probable that they were too much taken for granted to be memorable, unlike individual vows made in time of difficulty or danger. There are occasional clues as to possible motives in the departure dates which pilgrims remembered. Easter was one of the favoured times for pilgrimage, to judge from our small sample. Four of the witnesses who remembered Canterbury pilgrimages said that they had gone at that season, while a group who set out from Rutland on 15 March 1360 may have intended to be there for Easter, which that year fell on 5 April.[20] One difficulty in the way of knowing how long these pilgrimages took is that the witnesses only name their principal and ultimate destination, but they are quite likely to have stopped at other shrines, or indeed transacted other business, in London for example, on the way. Departures for Canterbury in late June, of which five are recorded, suggest that the pilgrims in question may have aimed to arrive in time for the feast of Becket's translation on 7 July and therefore to obtain the appropriate indulgences.

The only other shrines mentioned by witnesses are those of Thomas of Lancaster at Pontefract, Thomas Cantilupe at Hereford and the Virgin at Walsingham. An Essex witness recalled that he had gone with Sir Hugh de Nevill to Hereford, apparently some time around 1312, certainly before Cantilupe was canonised.[21] William Levere of Leicester, who in 1333 went to Earl Thomas at Pontefract, was another Easter pilgrim. Thomas neither was nor would be canonised, but William's pilgrimage fell in a period of active promotion of his shrine, when collectors were going about raising money for building at Pontefract.[22] The first of three references to Walsingham is to a pilgrimage undertaken from Northamptonshire in April 1339, while a witness from Essex remembered going there in March 1351, perhaps for the feast of the Annunciation, and another from Gloucester went in October 1352.[23]

On the showing of these witnesses, English pilgrimage had a somewhat seasonal character. No one remembered a departure to any English destination between November and January; by contrast, sixteen of the ninety-nine Santiago pilgrimages mentioned began in those months. February, especially around the Feast of the Purification on the 2nd, was a favourite departure time for those going to Santiago, and is mentioned as such twenty-seven times. The March-April period was generally popular with pilgrims; in England there was at least some hope of better weather, while for those going to Galicia it offered a compromise between the harshness of winter and the heat of summer. In addition, it was appropriate to go on pilgrimage in Lent and to mark Easter by visiting a shrine. Few pilgrims remembered setting out for Santiago in June or July, whereas in England the Feast of Becket's translation was a big attraction at just that season.

Often, although not invariably, the ages of the witnesses were recorded, and although some seem to have been a little vague about this, and suspiciously fond of saying that they were forty or fifty, it is possible to establish at least a rough age profile of this exclusively masculine sample. By and large it seems that pilgrimage was a young man's game, but a comparison between the forty-eight pilgrims to English shrines whose ages it is possible to estimate at least roughly and the ninety-six comparable Santiago pilgrims reveals two somewhat different profiles.

Age	English shrines	Santiago
Under 25	16	21
25–34	24	44
35–44	8	25
45–59	–	5
59 or over	–	1
Totals	48	96

The overwhelming predominance of men under thirty-five among the 'English' pilgrims hardly needs emphasising, nor does the total absence of pilgrims aged more than forty-five. Just as striking is the relatively much more important part played in the Santiago pilgrimage by men between thirty-four and forty-five, who constituted more than a quarter of the total. It is interesting to speculate on possible reasons for these differences. Was the journey to St James regarded as a more serious penitential exercise, appropriate to men who had survived their young manhood and should now be beginning to plan for their eternal retirement? Had these same individuals done their stint of English pilgrimage earlier in life?

The Yorkshireman who vowed an Easter pilgrimage to Canterbury in 1336 was about forty and was on the old side at that period. A generation later, however, he might have looked a little less exceptional. A couple of parties which set out around 1370 consisted of people older than the previous average. A party of three from Luton who were returning from Canterbury in April 1371 when they heard of the birth of William Ferrers were aged thirty-three, thirty-six and thirty-seven, and another trio, from Dunster in Somerset, who went there in February 1378 consisted of two men aged perhaps just under forty and another of twenty-nine.[24] Between them these two little groups accounted for half the eight pilgrims in the 35–44 age-band recorded in the entire period: another was the Cambridgeshire man noted above, Edward Brond, who went in October 1382, aged about forty.

It is hard to know what significance to attach to such small figures, and it has to be acknowledged that few references to pilgrimages to any destination English or foreign are made in inquests taken after about 1382; that is to say, few pilgrimages performed after 1360 are mentioned at all. English pilgrimage to Santiago became difficult for much of the later fourteenth century because of strained relations with the kings of Castile and the civil wars in the kingdom in the 1360s, and the English government was renewing its efforts to impose controls on all movement of men, horses and valuables outside the country, but this does not explain why domestic pilgrimage, as reflected in our small sample, also slowed to a mere trickle after about 1360, nor why the few pilgrims who are mentioned should have been slightly older than the previous average.

Whether or not pilgrims ever thought they might witness miracles when they set out for St Thomas's shrine, they probably more often experienced mundane and sometimes unpleasant accidents, which may well have been one reason why they remembered the journey so many years later. John le Clere from Staffordshire went to Canterbury in 1315, very likely for the Feast of the Translation, but on his return he fell ill and made a will, which he still had in his possession in 1336; its date enabled him to pinpoint the time exactly.[25] At Easter 1332 a group from Alcester in Warwickshire encountered one of the occupational hazards of the pilgrim when they were attacked by robbers and severely wounded on what the scribe rendered as 'la Bleo', surely a reference to the still heavily wooded tract of country known as Blean Forest, north west of Canterbury.[26] The year 1337 seems not to have been lucky for Canterbury pilgrims. Roger de Holbeche fell ill on his way back to Lincolnshire during the summer and lay at London for a fortnight. John Cause broke his left arm on his way back, and William de Hyllyng, who was only about seventeen and had gone with his father, broke his right leg.[27] In the summer of 1381, a party returned to Houghton Conquest in

Bedfordshire to find that all their barns had burned down, accidentally as they apparently believed, although 1381 was a year in which barns tended to burn down for non-accidental reasons.[28]

The very few references to pilgrimage that are to be found in the published inquisitions of the reign of Henry VII are worth noting because the witnesses went to a quite different selection of shrines. A Somerset man remembered going to Our Lady of Cleeve in his own county in 1467; witnesses at two different Norfolk inquests had been to St David's in 1481; a man from Cambridgeshire began a pilgrimage to St Michael's Mount in Cornwall in January 1482 and a York witness remembered setting out, also in January 1482, for St Ninian in Scotland. Another witness at the same York inquest had clung to the tried and trusted, for he had gone to St Thomas in Kent.[29]

Pilgrimage, then, was a memorable event. For longer-distance pilgrims in particular, the preparations necessary before departing may have been as memorable, in a very precise sense, as the pilgrimages themselves. John le Clere was able to date his Canterbury pilgrimage in 1315 by the will he made when he fell sick on his return, but several Santiago pilgrims made wills before they left which they were still able to refer to years later. Perhaps it was out of awareness of age or infirmity that Elizabeth Wilson of Gisburn made her will in 1508 before departing for Canterbury or perhaps it was a journey such as she had never undertaken before. At all events, the will was not proved for another four or five years.[30] Wills made before departure to English shrines are not common, but those which contain bequests for the performance of pilgrimages for the sake of the testator's soul, to English or overseas shrines, are valuable evidence for the historian of pilgrimage, even though they usually refer to pilgrimages intended rather than to pilgrimages actually performed. They have the advantage that they were made by women as well as men, and by clergy as well as layfolk. The observations which follow, it must be stressed, are made on the basis of a small selection of published wills; many more exist in archives and private collections and are coming to light all the time.

Here too the nature of the record is shaped by the setting in which it was made. When this was the deathbed (which was not always the case), the mental state of the soon-to-be-deceased was obviously influential, but wills were not free-form documents which expressed nothing but the testator's personal fancies. Social, familial and ecclesiastical pressures went into their making; there were bequests, to local churches for example, which it was all but obligatory to make. Only a small proportion of wills include bequests for the performance of pilgrimages, and it therefore seems reasonable to assume that these reflect a real choice on the part of the testator, which, as far as one can tell, no one was forcing him or her to make. Alongside those which actually use the word 'pilgrimage' or some equivalent phrase, however, we can reckon others which required an offering to be conveyed to some favoured shrine or image beyond the testator's immediate neighbourhood. Not the least valuable feature of wills is the insight they sometimes give into an individual's mental map of shrines, even if we may not know exactly how that map had come to be drawn. What light then do they shed on the value attached by men and women to pilgrimage and on their knowledge of the shrine landscape? The word 'value' in this context in fact has a double meaning, since testators often specified exactly how much was to be spent on the pilgrimage.

The most common motive for such bequests was the simple belief that the performance of one or more pilgrimages on the testator's behalf would be of assistance to his or her soul in Purgatory, and not infrequently also to the souls of previously deceased spouses, parents or other kin. The will of Gerald Braybooke, knight, proved before the archbishop of Canterbury on 11 July 1429 was comprehensive:

> I wol and ordeyn that thre prestes be hired to goo on pilgrimage for me, oon to Jerusalem, an other to Rom, the thriddere to Seynt James in Galice and to Seint Michelles Mount in England for the whiche pilgrimage I assigne £1 and more yf hit needeth. And here charges sullen be that they saye hir masses every day whanne they be disposed and may have place, tyme and leyser to do it and to prey in speciale for my soule, my fader and moder soules, my auncestres soules and for al cristen soules, and also to saye every day *Placebo* and *Dirige* and comendacioun, but the gretter nede lette hem.[31]

There are a number of typical features in this will, among them the inclusion of an English shrine, which presumably had personal meaning for the testator, alongside the major international shrines, and the recognition that the priests who were to carry out the pilgrimages might be prevented, by bodily indisposition or other causes, from saying a daily mass. A not dissimilar proviso appears in the will of Walter Doleman of Merston in Sussex in 1449, who wanted five pilgrimages to be perfomed for him, for which he proposed to pay (or rather that his executors should pay) widely different amounts.[32] Two of the pilgrims were to be priests; one of them was to go to Rome and, if he could, sing thirty masses, or as many as he could, at the Scala Celi just outside the city. This was already a favoured choice with English testators: in 1383, John of Guildford, 'panterer' of London, wanted masses said for him at the chapel of the Blessed Mary called 'Scala Celi'.[33] Walter Doleman had perhaps been advised that his envoy might not be able to celebrate all the intended masses there. This priest was to have ten marks, whereas the one who went to Santiago to perform a mere five masses was to have only five. Walter also wanted three pilgrims, who were presumably to be laymen, to go to English shrines and make offering for him. One was to be at Walsingham on the day of the Assumption and to have ten shillings, another was to have five shillings to go to St Thomas of Canterbury on St Thomas's Day (presumably 29 December), and another a mere five groats to be at Sion Abbey 'at Lammesse [Lammastide, 1 August] next after my pasyng owte of yis world when pardon is used yer to be had'. All three were to offer one penny.

The Roman Scala Celi, favoured by Walter Doleman, bred more accessible English namesakes which obtained generous indulgences and themselves attracted bequests. Thomas Brooke of Rustington in Sussex in 1516 left money for four 'trentalls of masses', of which one was to be said at Scala Celi at Westminster.[34] In 1528 the Somerset knight Sir George Speke displayed a permissive faith in the efficacy of secondary shrines, desiring mass to be said for him for a year 'at Scala Celi in Oxforth or ellsewhere, whersoever Scala Celi be'.[35] Ralph Balington, rector of Hickling in Nottinghamshire, was even less informative when in 1521 he bequeathed fifteen shillings for a trentall to be sung 'for my soule and all Crystyne soules at Scala Coeli in England'.[36]

Similarly St James drew bequests both to Santiago de Compostela and to substitutory shrines in England. John Perfay, draper of Bury St Edmunds, in 1509 left money 'to the making' of St James's church at Bury and wanted a pilgrimage done for him to Santiago. The 'honest priest seculer' who was to undertake it was also to go to 'our Lady of Park' at Liskeard in Cornwall and to St Michael's Mount, which suggests that the testator envisaged him taking ship to Galicia from a port in the south west. In 1504 John Bawde of Woolpit, a dependency of Bury and an important regional shrine of the Virgin, was proposing to go to Santiago. It transpires from the will he made with this in view that he had installed a tabernacle of St James in the north aisle of the church of Woolpit and he now left money for various embellishments of it: the 'stool' which he had made was to be 'coloured and garnished with scallops and other signs of St James'. He also left a black girdle with silver ornaments to the image of Our Lady.[37]

It seems a reasonable presumption that pilgrimages to Jerusalem, Santiago or Rome were generally believed to be of superior value. Despite the evident pulling power of such shrines, however, some testators who could presumably have afforded otherwise expressed an exclusive attachment to their native land. Thomas, earl of Arundel, was invalided home after Harfleur and died, at the age of thirty-four, only a few days after he made a new will on 10 October 1415, which included a number of pilgrimage bequests:

Item, I ordain and will that William Ryman or someone else shall go in my name with all possible haste after my death, on foot from London on pilgrimage to St Thomas of Canterbury, and that two other pilgrimages shall be made, by him or another, on foot from Arundel to St Richard of Chichester, on account of various vows which I made to fulfil personally, offering to St Thomas 20s. 8d., and, for the fulfilment of these pilgrimages, I will that as much should be expended for the labour and expenses of the said William or another, in going on my behalf and in giving alms on the way there and back, as I would have spent if I had performed these pilgrimages in person, according to the judgement of my executors. Item, I ordain and will that because of a vow which I made to St John of Bridlington when I was there with the lord king as now is, when he was prince, that every year of my life I would take or send five marks to the said St John, that the arrears due, together with the reasonable costs of whoever is going to go there on this business shall be paid and discharged as soon as possible.[38]

Henry V's dying companion in arms had no thought of foreign shrines; his attachments were local, national and personal. The cult of St John of Bridlington, where he had gone with Prince Henry, was new in his time. Half a century earlier Humphrey de Bohun, earl of Essex and Hereford (d. 1361), had expressed his personal concerns in a somewhat different manner. He desired his executors to appoint a chaplain 'of good condition' to go to Jerusalem for the sake of his soul and those of his father and mother, saying masses wherever he could along the way. Humphrey also wanted 'a good and loyal man' to go to Canterbury, and another such to Pontefract, forty shillings of silver to be offered in each place.[39] As noted earlier, his father had died at Boroughbridge in 1322, fighting with Thomas of Lancaster.

As this will and Walter Doleman's both indicate, testators might specify the qualifications, professional, moral or both, of the pilgrim or pilgrims who were to act on their behalf. Ordinary laymen acting on behalf of the deceased could convey offerings and hear masses, thus, it was evidently believed by some, earning indulgences both posthumously and vicariously for the dead man. Priests could say masses in favoured holy places at home or abroad. In 1463 another man of high rank, Humphrey Stafford, earl of Devon, played an interesting variation on this theme. He willed that Master Nicholas Goffe and Master Wattes, the warden of the Grey Friars of Exeter, should 'for the salvacion of my soule goo to every parisshe churche in Dorsetshire, Somersetshire, Wiltshire, Devonshire and Cornewalle and to say a sermon in every chirche in towne and other'.[40] One supposes that the preachers were mindful of their obligation wherever they went to request prayers for the soul of the dead man.

Often the testator named the individuals who were going to act for him. When money was left to named persons to carry out a pilgrimage, they were often friends or neighbours who had presumably intimated that they would do it and were to be paid for their trouble, as when in 1510 Robert Harryes of Ticehurst in Sussex left Robert Hope and John Bele 26s. 8d. to go 'to blessed Mary of Walsingham, St Thomas the Martyr of Canterbury, to the blood of the Lord Jesus at Hailes and Master John Schorne'. [41] Money was not the only currency in which such persons might be recompensed. William at Wood of the village of Upchurch in north Kent said in 1504 that another William at Wood and Thomas Rider were to have ten shillings and four bushels of wheat for going to Walsingham and on a number of very local pilgrimages on his behalf, and one Richard Brown was in 1514 to have 'a mark for his labour, and my best gowne, or else 6s. 8d. with the mark', when he went to the Holy Blood of Hailes for another Kent testator, Simond Gaunt of St Margaret at Cliffe. [42]

The explicit requirement that a son or a wife was to carry out the duty implies a sense of familial obligation and quite possibly affection. There was a pilgrimage tradition, and perhaps an accumulation of obligations, in the Kentish family of Culpeper. Thomas and Nicholas Culpeper, father and son, died within six years of each other, in early 1429 and early 1435 respectively. On 30 January 1429, Thomas added some pilgrimage bequests to earlier wills. His son was to go 'in his own person' to Norwich to offer to 'the holy vicar' (that is, Richard Caister); he was also to go personally to Canterbury and offer to St Thomas. Nicholas's own will, made in August 1434 and proved in January 1435, left four marks to his wife Elizabeth to complete 'my promised pilgrimages to the Blessed Mary of Walsingham and to Canterbury'. He had presumably undertaken the Norwich pilgrimage for his father, and the Canterbury pilgrimage he now wanted Elizabeth to perfom may have been one he had vowed on his own account. [43]

Sometimes wives were given the option of performing the pilgrimage themselves or hiring another to do so: thus the York butcher John Cowper in 1518 willed that his wife Margaret 'or another' should go for him

to oure Lady of Burgh [Peterborough?], to our lady of Kirlell [Carlisle], to Kynge Henry of Wyndesour and to the Roode of Dancastre at the brigge end, after my dethe, if I do it nott, nor cause it to be done, before my dethe. [44]

This wording is a reminder that it was also possible to arrange for a vicarious pilgrimage in one's own lifetime. A different kind of confidential relationship was implied when Edward Storey, bishop of Chichester, in 1502 left five marks to his chaplain, Nicholas Taverner, to go on his behalf to our Lady at both Southwick and Walsingham, and to St Thomas of Canterbury. [45] Benedict, minister of the church of St David's, in 1433 said that Master Henry Wells and Dom John Sutton were to have £10 to go on his behalf to Bridlington, Beverley and Walsingham, and was anxious that the money should be released to them 'so that they can fulfil my purpose with all possible speed after my death'.[46] This concern to reap the benefits of the pilgrimage as soon as possible was frequently expressed.

When mere hirelings were envisaged, the testator may have been more concerned that the pilgrimage should be performed than by whom. Walter Doleman of Merston, already mentioned, probably expected his executors to be able to hire at London, perhaps from a pool of professional pilgrims. In 1531 John Benett of Raunds in Northamptonshire wanted 'a honest man' to be found to go to Walsingham for him, leaving a total of 13s. 4d. which was to cover the pilgrim's daily wage as well as the alms and offerings he was to disburse.[47] To stipulate for a man of good character was presumably to express the belief that the duty could only be carried out efficaciously, or at all events would be carried out more efficaciously, by someone capable of representing the deceased in a suitable posture of repentance and contrition. In 1516 John Longe of Croft desired the priest William Gibson and his successors to make pilgrimages for him to Rome, Compostela 'or any oder pilgrimage when he or they be disposyd, so that he or they be vertuouse and goo in good intent'. Another Lincoln testator, Thomas Quadring, late of Careby, was similarly more concerned about the personal and professional qualifications of the hireling than about where he went; he wanted 'an honest priest' to be paid twenty marks 'to thentent that the same prest shall go diverse pilgremmages to holly sayntes when my executors or my next kynnesmen then shall thynke most best'.[48]

Testators might lay down other conditions which they deemed would enhance the spiritual value of the pilgrimage. The earl of Arundel had wanted pilgrimages to Canterbury and Chichester performed on foot; Hugh Peyntour of London in 1361 wanted them undertaken 'with naked feet', to various shrines in Canterbury and also to Walsingham.[49] The amounts to be laid out were not exactly proportional to the distance involved, as forty shillings was to be paid for the Walsingham journey and only twenty to the Canterbury pilgrim. Walter Doleman eighty years later envisaged the same two to one ratio for pilgrimages undertaken to these destinations from London.

Few of the bequests so far mentioned specifically state that the testator had ever been on pilgrimage or had even thought of going, but it was far from uncommon for money to be left to carry out pilgrimages which he or she had promised and failed to perform. Sometimes the intention seems to have been conceived only in the testator's last illness. The will of John de Copildik, knight, proved before Philip Repingdon of Lincoln on 3 May 1403, included in the codicil the stipulation that 'some man should be hired for the pilgrimage to Jerusalem for his soul and the forgiveness of his crimes, if he himself shall be unable to perform that pilgrimage during his life'. The will was dated only 3 April; John Copildik was perhaps being optimistic about his chances of recovery.[50] In 1516 Richard Peke simply referred to 'pilgrimages not done' and left money for road-mending in Wakefield, including 3s. 4d. 'wher itt is moost nede, by the descrecion of Sir William Joys preste, to ament a fowl holle abowt the bridge', where stands one of the few surviving bridge chapels in England, itself a goal of pilgrims.[51] Roger de Wandesford of Tireswell in Nottinghamshire in 1400 recalled specifically that he had promised to visit the 'glorious confessors' at Beverley and Bridlington when 'I was in serious danger of the waves of the sea and almost drowned between Ireland and Norway'.[52]

Women, it has been seen, were often deeply involved in the business of carrying out their husband's wishes as to pilgrimage. Their own bequests often took the form of garments or jewellery left to their chosen shrines rather than of money for pilgrimages so called. The shrines in question were often Marian, as when Dame Catherine Hastings in 1507 left 'To our lady of Walsingham my velvet gown. To our Lady of Doncastre my tawny chamlett gown. To our Lady of Bell Cross my blak chamlett. To our Lady of Hymmyngburgh a piece of cremell and a lace of gold of Venys set with perle'.[53] Bequests of beads occur in a number of wills. Lady Anne Scrope of Harling left 'beads of gold laced with crimson silk and gold' to four shrines, Walsingham, Our Lady of Pew at St Stephen's Westminster, St Edmund and St Thomas. In 1520 Alice West left 'my best belt' to St Wilfrid at Ripon and beads to our Lady of Doncaster, while Agnes Constable of Withernwick in 1521 bequeathed garments to Our Lady at Beverley and Hull, beads to St John of Bridlington and a silver heart to 'St John's head'.[54] It is not unreasonable to suppose that Agnes had in her lifetime visited all these shrines, as Bridlington, by far the furthest of them from Withernwick, is only about twenty-one miles away. Such legacies implied pilgrimage at least in the sense that someone had to make the journey to convey the offering to the shrine. Lady Margaret Aske used more explicit language when in 1465 she requested 'that a man be hired to go on pilgrimage to St Ninian in Scotland at my expense and offer there on my behalf a gold ring with a diamond in it'. She also wanted a pilgrim to go to Canterbury and offer to St Thomas '1 gold saluz'.[55]

Men also bequeathed jewellery. William Mauleverer in 1498 left a diamond ring 'that King Richard gave me' to Our Lady of Walsingham.[56] Members of the upper nobility sometimes made opulent bequests, of jewels, cloth or images, to a range of shrines. John, earl of Warenne, in 1347 bequeathed jewels and plate to Our Lady of Walsingham, St Thomas of Canterbury,

St Richard of Chichester, St Alban, St Edward, St Edmund and St Cuthbert.[57] A century later, wills made by Richard Beauchamp, earl of Warwick (d. 1439), and his second wife, Isabella, may bear witness to different personal tastes, shifts of fashion, or both. The earl is commemorated still by the chantry chapel in St Mary's Warwick, with his splendid effigy at its centre, but it seems to have been his earlier intention to have such effigies of himself made and distributed to the shrine of St Alban, 'to the honour of God, Our Lady and St Alban', to the shrine of St Thomas of Canterbury, to Bridlington and to the shrine of St Winifred at Shrewsbury, thus combining devotions old and new. St Winifred's cult, as we have seen, was receiving marks of royal favour from Richard II's reign onwards. The earl's intention that 'a goodly tomb' should be made for his first wife at Kingswood in Gloucestershire connected him also with a prominent Marian shrine. Countess Isabella's will, made in the year of her husband's death, included several bequests of images to Our Lady, at Walsingham, Tewkesbury, Caversham and Worcester, and she also willed substantial quantities of cloth to St Winifred.[58]

Probably, if not certainly, these highly-placed personages had patronised these shrines in life. A personal attachment may be made perfectly clear, as when Richard Fowler, chancellor of the duchy of Lancaster, in 1477 desired that

> the aisle of St Rumwold's church [at Buckingham] where I am to be buried, be finished at my cost, and that a new tomb or shrine for the said saint, where the old is now standing, be made curiously with marble, in length and breadth as shall be thought convenient by my executors, consideration being had to the room; and upon the same I will that there be set a coffin or chest, curiously wrought and gilt, as it appertaineth for to lay the bones of the said saint, and this all to be done at my cost and charge.[59]

St Rumwold, a Mercian child saint whose legend has been modestly described as 'quite incredible', was enjoying considerable popularity in late medieval England, most notoriously perhaps at Boxley Abbey in Kent where there was a famous animated statue of him.

Wills are, therefore, informative about the range of shrines with which people were familiar either by personal experience or by hearsay. On the one hand, they reveal intensely local attachments; on the other, the striking popularity of a few major shrines. The same testator frequently combined both, as a number of Somerset wills illustrate. In 1487 Thomas Chokke bequeathed sums of money (he does not speak of pilgrimages as such) to numerous churches including the hospital of St Mary 'Rounceval' at Charing Cross, St Mary de la Grace at St Paul's, St Etheldreda and St Mary of Bethlehem (the famous 'Bedlam', another London hospital); to St Mary of Walsingham, St Henry the King, Master John Schorne; and to St Mary Redcliffe, Bristol, and 'St Anne', clearly the chapel at Brislington just outside Bristol which was a major centre of her cult.[60] John Wadham was wider-ranging still in the choices he made in 1501, putting first his desire for a pilgrimage to Santiago. He wanted pilgrimages to be made for him 'to St Jamys, to Hailes, to Master Schorne, to Walsingham, to Canterburye, the rood of Northdore at Pawlis, to our Lady of Pewe, to king Harrye, to Sainte Brownewill, to Bysshope Lacy'. The local attachment here was to two Devon saints, Edmund Lacy, bishop of Exeter (d. 1455) and St 'Brownwill' , who is presumably Beornwald of Bampton. John Wadham may himself have been a pilgrim of some note, if he is the same man who made a will in August 1473 before his intended departure for the Holy Land.[61]

In 1532 James Hadley wished his negligence in making pilgrimages during his lifetime to be repaired by the making of offerings as follows:

> To our blessed Lady of Clive 5s., St Saviour of Porlock 5d., St Culbone 3d., St Saviour of Taunton, Bradford and Bridgwater each 5d., to St Jophe 3d., blessid King Henry of Windsor 3d., Maister John Shorne 3d., Holy Blode of Hayles 5d., Our Ladie of Walsingham 3d., St Thomas of Canterbury 5d.[62]

There is no doubt that, to judge by the size of the offering proposed, St Mary at Cleeve Abbey was closest to James Hadley's heart, but his threepences and fivepences were shared between shrines which few outside Somerset would have heard of, and others which almost everyone in late medieval England knew. 'St Jophe', for a Somerset resident in 1532, is most plausibly identifed as Joseph of Arimathea, the latest jewel in Glastonbury Abbey's crown. A codicil to another Somerset will of similar date, that of Sir Richard Place, vicar of Kingston, proved in 1534, stipulated for a pilgrim to offer 3s. 4d. to St Joseph, accompanied by alms of 5d. to poor people. There followed a number of other requests for west-country pilgrimages:

> likewyse to our lady of Cleve and there to offer xx 1d. and in almes v d. – also to the cross of Chaldon [Dorset] xx d. and in almes v d. – also our lady of Petye in Sydbery [Sidbury, Devon] xx d. and there to delyver v d. – and to Bysshope Lacy there to offer xx d. and to delyver in almes v d ... 63

This basic pattern naturally took on very different local or regional colourations. The list of intended pilgrimages in the 1472 will of William Ecopp, rector of Heslerton, began with the more southerly 'national' shrines (the crucifix at the north door of St Paul's and Thomas of Canterbury) and worked north, via Walsingham, St Etheldreda of Ely and St Mary of Lincoln, to a large number of northern saints and churches:

to St Thomas of Lancaster, St Saviour of Newburgh, the Blessed Mary of Scarborough, St Botulph of Hackness, the Crucifix of Thorpbasset, Blessed Mary of Guisborough, St John of Beverley, St John of Bridlington, St William of York, Blessed Mary of Jesmond, Blessed Mary of Carlisle, and St Ninian in the church of Candida Casa in Galloway.[64]

Wills suggest that Canterbury and Walsingham were to a remarkable degree the common property of English pilgrims. A testator who was prosperous enough to think of a number of pilgrimages was likely to include either or both. John Benett of Raunds in Northamptonshire, who wanted pilgrimages performed to a large number of churches in his own county, gave priority to provision for Our Lady of Walsingham. An inhabitant of the east midlands was in principle well-placed to look both ways, like William Boston, chaplain of Newark, who in 1466 left 26s. 8d. for a priest to go to Bridlington, Walsingham, Canterbury and Hailes on his behalf.[65] In 1528 Thomas Walter of Cransley in Northamptonshire similarly wanted pilgrimages done to Walsingham, Our Lady of Lincoln and to Hailes. [66] The national appeal of Walsingham, aided by a position which was accessible both from north and south, is beyond doubt, but the pulling power of St Thomas of Canterbury in the far south east, over 300 years after his martyrdom, is in some ways even more noteworthy.

There were clearly broad regional divisions within which the interests of most individuals remained largely confined. This helps substantiate the conclusions suggested by analyses of the origins of pilgrims as revealed in miracle collections. By the end of the fifteenth century, testators dwelling in the southern half of the country might well include one or several of Canterbury, Walsingham, the Holy Blood of Hailes, King Henry of Windsor and Master John Schorne. John Pyel, citizen of London, in 1379 wanted a pilgrimage done to St John of Beverley, as well as to Walsingham, Canterbury and Lincoln, but, at least among the published wills that I have examined, there are no Sussex or Somerset legacies which echo this intention or the earl of Arundel's devotion to John of Bridlington.[67] The exchange of compliments between north and south was generally limited. When Richard Wilflit, mariner of Hull, in 1521 looked far afield, it was far to the east; he made provision for two offerings, one to be taken to Walsingham and the other to 'the holy bloyd of Welslayk', Wilsnack in Prussia.[68] At least occasionally, however, Yorkshiremen thought about the Blood of Hailes, as John Pigott, knight, did in 1488, when he willed a total of thirty shillings for pilgrimages to Our Lady of Doncaster and of Walsingham, to Hailes and to St Thomas of Canterbury.[69] King Henry of Windsor appears among the pilgrimages, noted above, that the York butcher John Cowper wanted his wife to attend to in 1521; perhaps his attention had been

drawn to the sainted king by the popular image of him which stood in
York Minster.

For the humbler testator, the availability of images and 'lights' as substitute
goals of pilgrimage made it possible to pay homage to a saint without straying
too far afield. John Schorne, the wonder-working rector of North Marston
whose relics were taken to Windsor in 1478, attracted a great many bequests,
but not all were for pilgrimages either to North Marston or to Windsor.
Richard Easingwold of Islip in Northants in 1508 desired burial at Binham
Priory, Norfolk, 'before the holy image of maister John Shorne'. [70] In 1507
Edward Symond of Ashford in Kent wanted his wife Margaret to go to King
Henry and John Schorne at Windsor for him; but another Kentish testator,
John Soute, rested content with a bequest of 20d. to Schorne's 'light' in
Faversham church.[71] John Soute's modest horizons contrast with those of
the widow Thibaude Evyas who in 1478 wished to be buried at Faversham,
but willed jewellery not only to St Richard at Chichester but to the shrines
of St John at Amiens and the three kings at Cologne. [72]

Without making too many assumptions about the relationship between
the pilgrimages men and women may have performed during their lifetimes
and those for which they left bequests, wills suggest that there were two
major incentives for voluntary pilgrimage. First, there were obligations
expressed in the form of a vow or promise. We are only occasionally
informed about the circumstances in which these obligations were entered
into. Although moments of personal danger, sometimes at sea, and presumably also from illness, clearly often prompted them, some may well have
arisen purely from a devotional or nostalgic impulse, as the earl of Arundel's
vow to John of Bridlington perhaps did. Secondly (and this was not necessarily entirely separable), there was the desire to earn remission, in the form
of indulgences and their posthumous extensions, from the pains of Purgatory. Personal and family relationships also helped to determine who went
on pilgrimage where and when. This is of course to leave to one side
journeys undertaken in a purely holiday spirit and also the involuntary
pilgrimages that were sometimes imposed as penance.

Many pilgrimages, clearly, resulted from the making of vows, and many
more should have done, had the men and women involved not sought
absolution from vows they subsequently regretted or discovered they were
genuinely unable to perform. It is easier to find evidence of dispensation
from undertakings to perform the major overseas pilgrimages, because this
was reserved to the pope, and many such dispensations are to be found in
the published calendars of entries in the papal registers. Many a local English
pilgrimage must have been quietly exchanged for 'other works of piety'.
Occasionally, however, an English bishop was called upon to mitigate the

rigours of a vow made in an excessive fit of enthusiasm. John de Drokensford of Bath and Wells thus addressed Sybil of St Martin in August 1320:

> Under terror of death you have vowed rashly to eat no flesh or fish pending your pilgrimage to our Lady of Walsingham, an abstinence beyond weak powers. In pursuance of the canonical rule, viz., that a vow is saved by substitution of a better thing, we now substitute abstinence from beef, enjoining fish diet, with alms to ten poor, until the day of pilgrimage.[73]

Terror of death also accounted for the comprehensive pilgrimage vow of John de Holderness of Danbury in Essex, who informed Edward III in 1367 that, while in grave danger on the sea while returning from the Holy Sepulchre, he had vowed to visit in pilgrimage 'all the shrines of the saints in the king's realm, which vow he devotedly intends to fulfil with continuous labour as soon as possible, God willing'. He asked for the king's special protection on his person and goods, a precaution which was not normally made for domestic pilgrimages; this however was likely to be an exceptionally long one.[74] Otherwise, it was rare for pilgrimages made by individuals within England to require the attention of either bishop or king. From the pilgrim's point of view, the short duration of English pilgrimages made it unnecessary to appoint attorneys as he or she would probably do if going abroad, which removed one reason for recourse to the royal government. The latter was most likely to become involved when crimes or disorders involving pilgrims occurred or were thought likely to do so, and an exceptional case-history occasionally emerges from the royal records.

On 2 April 1364 Edward III issued a pardon to a suspicious character called Philip Cryhere, who had lately been held in the royal prison at Hertford, 'indicted of exortions'. He obtained his keeper's licence to make a pilgrimage to Walsingham, and on his way back was set upon by Robert Rolf of Waltham and others; we are not told whether they had been the victims of his 'extortions' or whether they were simply highway robbers. Philip killed Robert in self-defence and had now been indicted for his death and for gaol-breaking, although he had gone to Walsingham with permission. The king pardoned him on all counts.[75] Whatever the rights and wrongs of this case, it indicates that pilgrimage was sometimes at least regarded as a valid pretext for letting a prisoner out of confinement, as Edward himself did when he extended permissions to the French nobles who were held hostage in England for the ransom of John II to make visits to Canterbury or Walsingham. In April 1334 Brother William de Irreby, prior of St Guthlac at Hereford and for years an opponent and thorn in the side of Bishop Adam Orleton, was detained in the prison of the bishop of Worcester and was granted the latter's permission (rather reluctantly, one surmises) to be absent until the feast of St John the Baptist (24 June) on pilgrimage. This may either have been an authentic cry for spiritual help or a stratagem on William's part to get out of confinement at least for a while; in October of the same year he was consigned to the care of the abbot and convent of Gloucester, of which he was a monk, since he was destitute in prison. [76]

Bishops, like kings, were only occasionally concerned with domestic pilgrimage. Sometimes they imposed sentences of penitential pilgrimage on individuals, but their principal reason for interest in voluntary pilgrimage was to encourage it through the grant of indulgences. Less commonly, they intervened to prohibit pilgrimages they thought improper. When they granted leave of absence to parish clergy to go on pilgrimage, it was almost invariably pilgrimage overseas. This clearly does not mean that members of the clergy did not go on English pilgrimages, rather that it was less necessary to make formal arrangements to cover for their absence. There were exceptions: the vicar of Bridgwater was licensed to be absent for a fortnight while he went to Canterbury in early October 1318, and in June 1340 Dr Hugh, perpetual vicar of Henbury in the diocese of Worcester, obtained leave of absence both to go to Walsingham and to visit parents and friends. This may have been a more leisurely trip, as the bishop specified that his church was to be properly provided for.[77]

Curious biographical details occasionally emerge from the registers. In 1329 Adam Orleton as bishop of Worcester was dealing with the case of Alice Grene of Droitwich, who was accused of having ceased to live matrimonially with her husband John de Gaysham of Bletchingley in the diocese of Winchester. He had moved to Bletchingley after the marriage, which had taken place at Droitwich. Alice stayed with him for a few days while she was making a pilgrimage to Canterbury and returned to Droitwich with his good will. Now, although willing to receive and obey him as her husband, she said that 'for fear of death and disinheritance' she dared not live with him at Bletchingley. Her Canterbury pilgrimage, and indeed the mysterious domestic melodrama in which she was embroiled, are known to us only because her marital affairs came to the bishop's attention. Pilgrim or not, she was to be summoned by the dean of Droitwich to answer on certain articles 'touching the health of her soul'. [78]

Other incidental references to pilgrimage sometimes emerge from sources such as court records; but for an adequate picture of English pilgrimage from the point of view of the pilgrim we would require the letters, diaries and autobiographical writings characteristic of an age when pilgrimage had ceased in England. What does not exist cannot be manufactured, but we must use what little in these categories we have. As it happens, it amplifies our scanty picture of female participation in pilgrimage.

Margery Kempe of Lynn, it must be said, cannot safely be taken as an 'ordinary' pilgrim, and this is not just because of the geographical range of her pilgrimages, which few individuals and certainly few women can have equalled. She went to Jerusalem, to Compostela, to Rome and Assisi, to Wilsnack and Aachen. We know this because we have her autobiography, and we have her autobiography because she was an aspirant religious professional, who sought the company, counsel and approbation of other religious professionals, priests, friars and anchorites, and through them felt the influence of some of the major spiritual writings of the later middle ages. As a result, we know that, although the desire to give thanks and obtain indulgences played a part in motivating her pilgrimages, as they did for thousands of others, they also formed part of her determined quest for the intimate visualisation of the person of Jesus, whether in the places of His birth, ministry and death in Palestine, or in images, relics and His presence in the sacrament wherever she went. Devotion to the sacrament and to the person of Christ, and techniques of vivid mental imaging of the incidents of His life and death, were themes in contemporary spirituality and not Margery's unique property. [79]

Margery's first pilgrimages, which took in York, Bridlington and other unspecified places, were undertaken with her husband to give thanks for her recovery from the prolonged illness which followed the birth of her first child. As she put it, she 'was mevyd in hir sowle to go vysytyn certeyn places for gostly helth in as-mech as sche was cured, and myght not wyth-owtyn consentyng of hir husbond'. [80] Her vocation was taking shape, but this journey, in form and motive, must have looked entirely conventional: her husband not merely consented but accompanied her. Later she went to Canterbury at least once in his company; ominously, however, he was so embarrassed when she was rebuked by the monks and others for her excessive weeping that he 'went away fro her as he had not a knowyn hir'. [81] Thereafter, with his consent, she went to the Holy Land without him. Her behaviour always created problems for her with her fellow-pilgrims, of which one of the most serious, from a practical viewpoint, was that she often found herself alone in situations where, as she was only too well aware, a single woman needed, and was expected to have, an escort. The exchanges she records with the hostile 'doctor' who questioned her on a later visit to York are of interest as shedding some light on the position of the female pilgrim who travelled without her husband.

She had already aroused suspicion by prolonging her stay in York when she was brought before the 'doctor'. His first question was why she had come, to which she replied 'to offyr her at seynt William'. He then asked whether she had a husband, and whether she had any 'letter of record'. She replied that her husband had given her his verbal permission to come, and asked why the doctor demanded such a letter of her and not of 'other pilgrimys that ben her, wheche han no lettyr no mor than I have'. The inference to be drawn from this is presumably that there were other female pilgrims present who were alone in the sense that no husband or other male relative was with them. If Margery was right in implying that no questions were being asked of them, we may conclude that this was regarded as perfectly normal behaviour, unlikely to arouse concern so long as accepted norms were not transgressed.[82]

Margery was in close touch with new fashions in pilgrimage. When she returned to Bristol from her pilgrimage to Santiago, she went to the Holy Blood of Jesus at Hailes Abbey, where she received absolution and 'had lowde cryes & boystows wepyngs'.[83] Hailes was only now coming into its own as a major pilgrimage centre, aided by the indulgence granted by Pope John XXIII in 1413. It was probably in 1434 that Margery went to the newly built Bridgettine house of Sion, to the west of London, for the Lammas Day indulgence which, as we saw earlier, attracted a bequest from a Sussex testator in 1449. Here the memory of the Passion awakened in her 'plentivows teerys of compunccyon & of compassyon'.[84] This was not the first Lammas Day indulgence Margery had obtained, for she had been at Assisi years before for the Indulgence of the Portiuncula, while her interest in the Bridgettine convent may well have been stimulated by memories of her visit to Bridget's own house at Rome and her conversations, through an interpreter, with the saint's servant.[85] It is hardly to be supposed that, living where she did, she did not have frequent opportunities to go to Walsingham and also Ely, but both are mentioned once only: she and her husband were arrested near Ely on one occasion when returning to Lynn, and she went much later 'to offer to Our Lady' at Walsingham when she escorted her widowed German daughter-in-law to Ipswich, where they took ship for Stralsund.[86] It was this journey which led her to the shrine of the Holy Blood at Wilsnack, and to Aachen on her way home.

Margery knew about the canonisation of John of Bridlington, but says nothing specific about pilgrimage to him, although she went to Bridlington with her husband on her first pilgrimage tour. Perhaps it was then that she met John's confessor, William Sleightholme, who subsequently became one of her confessors also.[87] She visited Beverley after a later consultation with Sleightholme at Bridlington, but again she makes no explicit reference to performing a pilgrimage. The unimpeachably orthodox John of Bedford was (she was told) on her trail, and she was arraigned, not for the first time, before the archbishop of York in the chapter house at Beverley. This was late in 1417: the duke had himself been at Bridlington that year with his cousin, Thomas Beaufort.[88]

William Sleightholme was later believed to do miracles, but Margery's closest personal contact with a reputed saint was with Richard Caister of Norwich, the 'holy Vikary', as she calls him, of the church of St Stephen. Christ Himself sent her to consult Caister about her visions, incidentally bearing the message that the vicar was 'a chossyn sowle of myn', and she won the holy man's steadfast support.[89] She endorsed the view that he was a saint by visiting his tomb, not long after his death in March 1420, to pray for the sick priest who for seven years had nourished her spiritual life at Lynn by reading classics of devotion to her. She behaved at Caister's tomb as she usually did: she 'fell down boistows sobbyngys, wepyngys and lowde cries besyden the grave of the good Vikary'. Margery here was overcome by the awareness that she had personally known the saint, but the bystanders, as always, tried to cut her down to size with the observation 'We knew hym as well as thou'. Certain priests who knew her ways were present and prudently took her to a tavern for a drink.

It was immediately after this that in another Norwich church, which she does not name, Margery beheld a *Pietà* ('a fayr image of owr Lady clepyd a pyte') and was immediately put in mind of the Passion. It was not that reaction itself, but the intensity of it, her weeping and crying out, that were unwonted. A priest testily said to her 'Damsel, Ihesu is ded long sithyn', thus expressing the reactions of *l'homme moyen spirituel*, which Margery elicited wherever she went: everyone knew the proper boundaries of response to the apparatus of religion, holy places, images, the sacrament itself, and she constantly overstepped them. Her riposte to the irritable priest was calculated to irritate him further: 'Sir, hys deth is as fresch to me as he had deyd this same day, and so me thinketh it awt to be to yow and to alle Cristen pepil.'[90]

The essential oneness of Margery's devotional responses is well-illustrated by her description of her miniature pilgrimage to a church of St Michael 'too mile' from Lynn, which has been identified as that of Mintling. She went at the invitation of two priests and they took a couple of children with them. When she had prayed, she was overcome with devotion and made as much noise weeping and sobbing as she would have done if she had been in a crowd of people; she was well aware of the charges of exhibitionism which were levelled against her. On the way home she met some women with children in their arms, none of them, unfortunately, male; Margery was afire to have the image of the Christ child embodied before her eyes.[91]

As a pilgrim, Margery was not inventing unheard of responses to what she saw and heard but realising them with an uncomfortable thoroughness which, in the eyes of most clergy and laity alike, went beyond what was needful. Her emotional reaction to the Norwich *Pietà* was extreme, but the clergy relied on less extreme versions of this reaction as on a basic prop of their influence over society. When images like the Foston Madonna, discussed earlier, attracted pilgrims, even without official approval, individual reactions not unlike Margery's were most probably at work. In the Holy Land, and indeed on all her pilgrimages, Margery was doing what she believed the place and the occasion demanded of her. That she should have been suspected of Lollardy may seem ironic to modern students who have read Lollard sarcasms against pilgrimage and image-worship; in a later age and a different religious culture she might have been accused of 'enthusiasm' or of hysteria, as indeed she has been. She is a good guide to the devotional possibilities of pilgrimage, if not to the experience of the average pilgrim, male or female.

A striking feature of Margery's pilgrimages, however, is that they do not seem to have been rooted in family concerns, as they were for many female pilgrims, and indeed for many men. The evidence of hundreds of miracle stories over a lengthy period supports this contention, particularly so far as fertility, the safe delivery of babies and the cure of children's illnesses and injuries are concerned. Margery struggled mightily to escape from sexual relations; with the exception of one son, we see her children only as the cause of post-partum depression and increased yearnings for celibacy. This one son, after a life of lechery and vanity, submitted to her influence and 'went many pilgrimagys to Rome and to many other holy placys to purchasyn hym pardon' as a sign of his reformation.[92]

The scanty evidence of fifteenth-century private letters occasionally amplifies our knowledge of pilgrimage as a response to the ills of adult family members. In the autumn of 1479 there was sickness both in England and in Calais, where the merchant George Cely was living and working. On 8 November William Maryon, a close associate of the Cely family, wrote to George from London. The news that George had been ill had reached his parents at their home at Aveley in Essex, and they had been consumed with anxiety until they received a letter from him on All Hallows' Eve. Both George's brother, the younger Richard Cely, and his mother had had 'a lytell fette' of sickness too. In this troubled time, the old couple resorted to trusted measures. On 11 November Richard Cely the younger wrote to George to tell him that their parents, still 'hevy', 'goys a pillgrymage dayly for yow'.[93]

Where could the Celys have gone on a daily pilgrimage from Aveley? One possible answer is Pilgrim's Hatch, now on the northern edge of

Brentwood, which was one of the innumerable secondary shrines to St Thomas which dotted the English landscape. It lay about ten miles north of Aveley, and both were on the approach to the Thames crossings that were well used by Canterbury pilgrims.[94] If the elder Celys had two comfortable horses to ride, Pilgrim's Hatch and back would certainly not have been beyond their reach in a day. Whether this was what they had had in mind when they had tried to coax their son home in the previous July is not clear. William Maryon told George that his father and mother wanted him to come to them in Essex and not go to London 'and for to be mery ther wyt them thys hervest and so for to do youre pylgrymage'.[95]

The elder Celys might be described at this stage in their lives as semi-retired; at all events it seems that Richard the elder was free to participate in the daily pilgrimage. When men in the prime of life were fully engaged in business, their womenfolk may well have taken on the responsibility of seeking celestial assistance in the trials of life. Of course, they had tasks of household management to attend to; their leisure was by no means complete. They were not, however, taken from home as often or as long by the demands of law, politics, warfare or business, and they could therefore plan to integrate local pilgrimages into their domestic schedule. These points are well illustrated by the letter Margery Paston wrote to her husband John in September 1443. He had been ill and, like the elder Celys, Margery and his mother Agnes had been in low spirits until they heard he was better. They had taken practical measures to assist. Agnes had ordered 'another' image of wax, of John's weight, to be sent to Walsingham (presumably she done so already on a previous occasion) and had also sent four nobles to the four orders of friars at Norwich so that they might pray for him. For Margery's own part, she had promised to go on pilgrimage to Walsingham and to St Leonard's in Norwich on John's behalf.[96]

The Paston family had close connections with both nearby Bromholm and Walsingham but, although Bromholm, close to Paston, was a family mausoleum, it is not mentioned as a goal of pilgrimage. John Paston was encouraged in his benefactions to Walsingham by William Yelverton, who assured him that Our Lady would requite him for them.[97] The other shrines frequented by the family and people known to them were St Leonard's at Norwich and the image of the Virgin at Ipswich; when the later Margery Paston told Sir John Paston on 10 February 1489 'I have fulfyllyd myn pylgremage, thanke it be God', it is a reasonable guess that it was to one of these places that she had gone, perhaps to Walsingham for the Purification.[98]

A certain division of labour is apparent here. Women kept the home fires burning, while grander gestures, if made at all, would be made by one of the men. The Paston women did occasionally stray beyond East Anglia.

In September 1465 the younger John, an enthusiast in all things, wrote from Norwich to his mother, who was at London, urging her to visit the Rood of the north door at St Paul's and also St Saviour's at Bermondsey, and to take his sister Margery with her 'to pray to them that sche may have a good hosbond or sche com hom ayen'. 99 It was John who announced on 22 June 1470 that he proposed to set off during the next week on foot from Norwich to Canterbury.100 Three years later he was off to Santiago, taking ship from Yarmouth to Calais; if he proposed to go on from there by ship, he may have been aiming for the major feast of the year, St James's Day on 25 July. Sir John Paston's original reaction to his younger brother's announcement that he was going to Santiago was, in effect, that he would believe it when he saw it.101 There may however have been method in John's enthusiasms. 1470 was a Jubilee year at Canterbury, celebrated with unprecedented solemnity, and he probably hoped to obtain a plenary indulgence; 1473, similarly, was a Santiago Holy Year, that is one in which St James's Day fell on a Sunday and lavish indulgences were available.102

The pilgrimage activities of royalty and the nobility naturally attracted the notice of the Pastons and other observers. Among the great ladies with whom Margery Kempe came into contact, in about 1413, was Joan Beaufort, countess of Westmoreland, who apparently approved of the strange enthusiast from Lynn who at least had in common with her a taste for devotional exercises. Fifteen years later, a widow since 1425, the countess arrived at St Albans on St Margaret's Day while engaged on a summer tour of holy places; 'a woman devoted to God', according to the St Albans chronicler, she had another twelve years of widowhood to beguile.103 In October 1476 Elizabeth Stonor told her cousin William that she had tried to get an opportunity to speak with the king's sister, the duchess of Suffolk, in London on a matter of money, 'but trwly sche was very besy to make hyre redy ffor she is redyne to Cauntyrbery as thys same day, and sche will be here ageyne as on Satyrday next comyng, for so sche told me hyr selff'. 104

Exactly two years later, Elizabeth herself was preparing to go on a pilgrimage from London, which may perhaps have been connected with a recent illness of her own or with the commemoration of her father, whose 'dirge' she had just attended. She told her husband that were it not for the pilgrimage she did not care 'how sone I were with you at Stonor', for she was weary of London; she begged him not to forget to send her horse for her on the following Saturday. As she was writing on Monday 5 October, she did not expect to take more than four days over the pilgrimage; perhaps it was to St Albans, with which the Stonors had some connection, but it may have been to Canterbury.105 The Stonor men seem not to mention pilgrimage at all; their Paston counterparts show more awareness of it.

The Worcester Pilgrim: conjectural reconstruction of the pilgrim whose grave was discovered in 1986. (*Helen Lubin*)

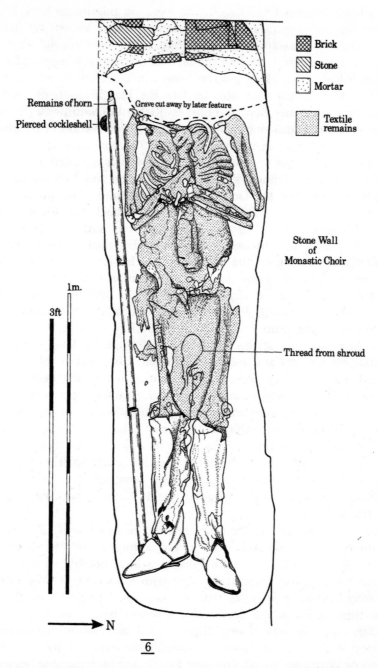

Brick

Stone

Mortar

Textile
remains

Remains of horn

Pierced cockleshell

Grave cut away by later feature

Stone Wall
of
Monastic Choir

1m.

3ft

Thread from shroud

N

6

The Worcester Pilgrim: plan of the grave and its contents. (*Helen Lubin*)

Two late medieval Englishmen who went on pilgrimage have been discovered for us by entirely different means; one is known by name, the
other is not. Archaeology has contributed in miscellaneous ways to the
history of pilgrimage: revealing the lay-out of shrines subsequently altered
or demolished, uncovering pilgrim-tokens in graves, riverside excavations
and elsewhere. Rarely does this lead to the identification of individuals.
The Southampton merchant and burgess Richard of Southwick (fl. 1268–90)
is known from documentary sources, but the preservation of rubbish from
the stone-built house in which he lived in Cuckoo Lane reveals not only
a great deal about his prosperous life-style, which included a taste for the
wines of southern France, playing board-games and keeping an African
monkey as a pet, but the fact that he (or someone in his household) had
gone at least once to Canterbury and brought back two souvenir ampullae.[106] The anonymous Worcester pilgrim lived and died two centuries
later.[107] His grave was discovered in 1986 during excavations at the base of
the south-east tower of the cathedral which were carried out to help
ascertain the state of its foundations. At an earlier date the grave had been
unwittingly damaged, so that the head of the skeleton (and perhaps a
pilgrim hat) was missing. What remained indicated a man just over 5 feet
7 inches in height, who was probably over sixty when he died. In earlier
life he had been robust and muscular, although he later suffered from
arthritis and his legs and feet were swollen. Examination of the skeleton
revealed features which were consistent with his having been a doughty
walker. Most intriguing of all was evidence in the right hand, arm and
shoulder that he had exerted a great deal of pressure on just such a staff
as the magnificent specimen of ash wood which was buried with him.
This had a double-pronged iron spike at one end and bore traces of a
horn tip at the other, to which the pierced cockle-shell which was also
found in the grave may once have been attached. Also preserved were
substantial remains of a pair of good quality leather boots dating probably
from the 1490s.

There are problems in the interpretation of this burial. The balance of
probability is that the man was indeed a pilgrim in life, since he was
deliberately buried in that garb. Was he a local notable who was known
to have been a great pilgrim, or a pilgrim who died at Worcester? The
anatomical evidence suggests that he was not capable of much walking
at the time of his actual death, and it would have been unusual for an
outsider, unless he was of very distinguished rank, to receive burial in the
cathedral itself; there is however considerable evidence for the burial of
citizens of Worcester there. The dyer Robert Sutton requested burial before
the image of St James, of whom he was a great devotee, but he must

have died before 1457, which seems a little early for the archaeological evidence. One interesting, but entirely unverifiable, possibility is that he was a servant of the cathedral, who may have undertaken pilgrimages on the community's behalf. The cockleshell may, but does not necessarily, signify that he had been to St James, for it is not a scallop, which was more strictly the emblem of the Santiago pilgrimage. There are therefore a lot of unanswered, and perhaps unanswerable, questions about the Worcester burial: but the probability is that it preserves for us much of the appearance of a late medieval English pilgrim.

The very miscellaneous types of evidence that have been considered here are broadly complementary in the picture they give of the range of shrines patronised by a wide variety of people. They reveal both the powerful attraction of the local and familiar and a striking level of awareness of a few nationally (and internationally) important shrines. Such insight as they give into motivation is reasonably consistent. In these respects the inquisitions post mortem harmonise with the other sources but, however valuable in themselves, they would if read alone totally obscure from us the role of women in English pilgrimage. It remains one of the important virtues of miracle collections that women figure so prominently in them. Even if the temptation to see pilgrimage solely or even primarily as a quest for the miraculous should be resisted, there is no gainsaying that without the details they provide our picture would be not only less colourful, but in important respects more limited, than it is.

9

Pilgrims in a Landscape

In November 1347 Richard Brayleigh, dean of Exeter Cathedral and also parson of the church of Colaton Ralegh a few miles to the east, addressed a complaint to the king which elicited the usual instructions for a commission of oyer and terminer to establish the facts of the case and take the appropriate action. The dean's complaint was that a group of named people, headed by Peter Ralegh, knight, had

> come armed, contrary to the statutes of the peace, to the chapel of St Theobald, Colaton, annexed to his said church, and by grievous threats demanding. nay extorting, toll and other unwonted customs from men coming to his chapel for the cause of pilgrimage and devotion and veneration to St Theobald, to do oblations and other works of devotion, and from others selling victuals in the cemetery and sanctuary of the chapel and in the fee of the church of Colaton, have by force prevented those and others who would have come as pilgrims from doing their oblations and other pious works and have carried away his goods and assaulted his men and servants, whereby he has lost the profit and emolument of the said oblations and the service of his men and servants for a great time.[1]

We owe this snapshot of a small local pilgrimage to the fact that it had been overtaken by what may have been either a feud between local notables or simple brigandage on the part of Peter Ralegh and his henchmen. Disputes over the emoluments of local churches were far from uncommon, and the fact that there was apparently a more than usually flourishing traffic in pilgrims and offerings to St Theobald at Colaton raised the stakes. In May 1347, only six months before the dean made his complaint, he had entered into an agreement wth Robert, the perpetual vicar of Colaton, whereby he was to receive the major and minor tithes and also the oblations made at the chapel of St Theobald.[2] This was the usual arrangement, which allocated pilgrim offerings to the rector of the church, leaving the vicar only with an agreed stipend. It meant that the dean retained responsibility for upkeep. A previous dean, Henry of Somerset, had left both the church and the chapel in a grievous state of disrepair; in 1307 both were roofless, and a grange and dovecote also needed a lot of work.[3] By 1347 the necessary work may have been done; the dean was clearly aggrieved not only at the breach of the peace and the violation of ecclesiastical space but at his loss of profits.

Fleetingly, at least, we hear this dignitary's voice raised in protest, and we can perhaps also visualise his adversaries, the ringleader a man of some local consequence. Almost invisible in the background are the people who were both the victims of Peter Ralegh's violence and the source of the dean's profits: not only the nameless pilgrims to this modest shrine, but the victuallers who made a probably equally modest living ministering to their needs in the very cemetery and sanctuary of the chapel, as the dean said. Bishop Grandisson of Exeter later objected strongly to festive gatherings in the cemetery of the church of Whitstone in Cornwall, and the desecration of cemeteries by blood shed in fights was not all that unusual, but the dean seems in his own interest to have been accepting, not to say encouraging, the use of the ground by pilgrims to St Theobald and local traders.

In their small way the victuallers and their customers at Colaton Raleigh remind us that the generality of pilgrims travelled with money in their purse and were therefore potential customers. The association of shrines with markets and the grant of fairs on and around major feast-days is the clearest possible indication that this was so. A major fair took place alongside the shrine of St Ivo in Huntingdonshire; the priest of the church at Linslade may have been tempted to promote a holy well at his church by the existence of a local fair. In an equally humble mode, Liverpool traders might be offered indulgences at the chapel of St Mary 'on the quay'. Merchants could be pilgrims and pilgrims merchants. Wherever shrines, licit or illicit, came into being, sellers of wax and other material for offerings, of souvenirs and foodstuffs, sprang into life, in obedience to the law enunciated by a modern humourist: 'Wherever two or three are gathered together, there will be someone else trying to sell them something hot in a bun'.[4]

There were penniless pilgrims and those who made a life's work of it, as well as those who hired themselves out for pay to perform pilgrimages on behalf of others. One such person may have been the William de Nesham, simply described as a *peregrinus*, who in 1335 received royal protection: he had come from the Holy Land, returning thither after a few months, and was dependent on alms for his support.[5] Pilgrims in fact sometimes gave alms to other pilgrims, and pilgrimage was often associated with almsgiving along the way. Penitential pilgrims were sometimes directed to give alms as they went, and testators left directions that pilgrimages performed on their behalf should include almsgiving. Thomas Becket took action on behalf of would-be pilgrims to his shrine who were deprived either of their means to make the pilgrimage or of the alms they had intended to give. His notable generosity, in safeguarding his pilgrims' money or even providing it, prompted William fitz Stephen to speculate that this was because he had been offered so much money during his lifetime that he had been unable to spend it all.[6] Occasionally he took drastic action, as in the case of a poor woman who wanted to sell the wool from her handful of sheep to provide her *viaticum* for her Canterbury pilgrimage. They were appropriated by a rich man of Nottingham who unwisely refused to restore them and was struck dead.[7]

These stories paint a picture of a road shared by the affluent and the less affluent. Richard, chaplain to the sheriff of Devon, had vowed to give alms to every pilgrim he met along the road who asked in the name of the martyr, and instructed a servant to provide him with a quantity of small change for the purpose; but he soon exhausted the farthings, which obviously represented the going rate, and was resigned either to breaking his vow or having to give a whole penny to the next petitioner. Five more pilgrims approached him before he got to Canterbury and five halfpence, which had not been there before, were discovered in his purse. Ralph, sub-prior of St Augustine's, had a similar experience when he went on business to Rochester, taking five shillings with him for expenses, some of which was duly laid out on shoeing horses, fodder and other necessaries. Encountering Canterbury pilgrims along the way, as he might well expect to do, he also gave three halfpence in alms. Returning to the monastery, he counted out what he had left and found the five shillings intact, plus three halfpence, in recompense for his generosity.[8] Other types of charity to pilgrims were rewarded, as when an unnamed man who had given hospitality to sick Canterbury pilgrims was released from unjust imprisonment.[9] Refusal of such charity, on the other hand, brought punishment. The wife of a knight who was brewing outside her house near Abingdon one day refused a drink to five pilgrims who begged it for the love of Thomas, using abusive words which expressed her view (quite probably widely held by respectable people) that they were good-for-nothings, *trutanni*. She of all people really should have known better, for the martyr had saved her own son (or, at least, her husband's son) from a mill-race. She was punished when her best barrel, containing the best beer, began to leak copiously.[10]

Some miracles were demonstrations of Becket's power rather than remedies for indigence. As William fitz Stephen put it, he 'not only healed the bodies of those who called upon him, but preserved their baggage and their travelling expenses, acting the part of overseer and steward'. A pilgrim from the vicinity of Bury St Edmund's bought some gloves at Sudbury in Suffolk, giving a penny and receiving a halfpenny in change. So tiny was the coin that it slipped through his fingers and rolled away, causing him to say jestingly, 'St Thomas's pilgrim has lost his halfpenny'. When he took out his purse at Rochester to pay for food he discovered the missing coin, which of course was then earmarked, as the saint doubtless intended, for an offering. When the companion of the abbess of Polesworth lost the money which she had intended to offer at 'the shrines (*aediculas*) which have been constructed along the wayside in honour of the martyr' (interesting testimony to the speed with which these were set up), she found it untouched in the road.[11] Another story concerns the return rather than the outward journey. A pilgrim fell victim to a cutpurse, an occupational hazard of the crowds at shrines, and his wife had to beg two halfpence to cover the cost of bread and their journey home. On the way home he heard a rattle in the ampulla of the martyr's water which he had around his neck and investigated, thinking it was caused by a fragment of the tin of which the vessel was made. When he poured the water out (clearly into another container) he poured four pennies out with it.[12]

Different pilgrims undertook their journeys under different, often self-imposed, constraints. A man and his wife who were on their way to Canterbury came upon a pilgrim, evidently walking, who was exhausted. They offered to put him on their ass, or donkey, but he was determined to complete the journey on foot. When the man asked his wife (clearly the keeper of the purse) whether she had anything she could give him, she replied that she had some farthings set aside to give to the poor, and produced one. When the poor pilgrim opened his hand, it had turned into a piece of silver.[13] A pilgrimage performed voluntarily on foot was especially meritorious, not least when the pilgrim was a person of consequence, but it was not the norm for the moderately affluent. Chaucer's company all had mounts of varying quality – the Wife of Bath an ambler, the Ploughman a mare, the Reeve 'a ful good stot'. Of the Knight we are told simply that 'his horse was good'; but the unfortunate Nun's Priest had to make do with a 'jade', which according to the ever outspoken Host, was 'bothe foul and lene'.

Some pilgrims who were even worse off than the Nun's Priest had little alternative to walking, although the genuinely incapacitated had to find other means. Miracle stories sometimes highlight the restored walking capacity of a once crippled pilgrim. Alditha Page came from Staffordshire to Thomas Cantilupe's tomb at Hereford in April 1290 and was so completely cured of a severe and prolonged debilitating condition that 'together with the others who came to the tomb by reason of devotion, she was able to complete the whole day that is usual for pilgrims of this kind, walking on her own feet, with the help of the servant of God'.[14] The phrasing implies a rough standard measure that a party of pilgrims expected to be able to achieve in a day. Cures were not always so complete, however, that the beneficiary could cover even quite short distances entirely unaided. The family of the crippled Margaret Honymer, who lived only about three miles to the west of Hereford, delayed the pilgrimage she wanted to perform for two months, both to accumulate money and to await finer weather. They brought her on a horse and left her at the shrine; gradually she was cured and was able to cover part of the distance home on foot: 'she walked where the way was flat and elsewhere rode'.[15]

As a category, pilgrims shared the protection of the law with merchants and other peaceful travellers; they also shared the same roads and basic amenities. Pilgrims were most likely to follow roads which were – literally – viable for broader economic reasons, rather than to create roads which existed for no other purpose.[16] Common sense, however, suggests that there were reciprocal processes at work here. A flourishing pilgrim traffic must have augmented the need for infrastructural support along the way and created additional incentives for the provision of goods and services, precisely because the generality of pilgrims were not barefoot and penniless. The favoured routes to Santiago may have been shaped by needs other than those of pilgrims alone, but there would have been little reason for thousands to go to Santiago had it not been for the shrine of St James. The description in the twelfth-century *Pilgrim's Guide* of the marketplace in front of the church at Compostela is a reminder of how many items, apart from specific pilgrimage souvenirs, the pilgrim might need or want to buy: his shoes might be worn out, or a water-bottle might need replacing.[17] Descriptions of the Roman Jubilees also leave us in no doubt that traders and inkeepers, as well as churches, profited from the presence of pilgrims and, equally, suffered from their absence.[18]

Rome and Santiago and the roads to them were merely the most conspicuous European examples of a phenomenon which was many times repeated on a smaller scale. The fact that in most European towns and cities the church was an extensive landlord and had important investments in the business premises which serviced pilgrimage, including taverns and shops, strengthened the ties which bound monastic communities and cathedral chapters into an economic nexus. The livelihood of many of the inhabitants of Canterbury, Bury, St Albans or Glastonbury must have been affected by the flow of pilgrims and its seasonal fluctuations. Indeed, the fortunes of churches could often be profoundly influenced by their relationship to the road network, whether or not they were themselves major or minor shrines.

An interesting example of this relationship is provided by Birkenhead Priory, which was founded in the middle of the twelfth century in what at the time was a quiet spot.[19] Liverpool, just across the Mersey, became a borough in 1207, but its church did not achieve parochial status until the late fourteenth century. The problems of Wales were attracting increased royal attention in Edward I's reign, with obvious consequences for the west midlands and the adjacent north west. The priory received royal visits in 1275 and 1277, and it is at about this time that the famous Mersey ferry, whenever it actually originated, is first mentioned. In 1284 the monks complained to the king that the public road to the ferry ran through their grounds and they received permission to protect their premises 'with a ditch and hedge or wall', as long as the road was diverted into a more suitable place.

The priory's relationship to the ferry did not remain passive for long. In 1310 the community petitioned Edward II for some relief from the burdens of hospitality that the proximity of the ferry imposed on it, since there were no market-town facilities nearer than Chester. In 1317–18 the king granted the prior and convent licence to erect houses on their ground for the lodging and entertainment of travellers. It had been represented to him that, when the weather obstructed the crossing, the men of Chester, wishing to cross over to the county of Lancaster, 'in great numbers turn aside to the said priory'. It therefore received licence not only to build suitable houses but to place men in them who 'may buy and sell, without hindrance, victuals for the sustenance of the persons about to cross the arm of the sea'. By 1330, when Edward III confirmed these earlier licences, the prior and convent were complaining about extortionate practices by Liverpool ferrymen (as the people of the Wirral had earlier done) and the king granted them the right themselves to run a ferry for men and horses, taking reasonable toll. Their involvement in the Liverpool economy was clearly growing. By 1346 they possessed a burgage plot and a granary or warehouse there, and in 1350 the prior himself and a fellow-monk were accused of assault and theft during the market. A few years later, the escheator of Cheshire claimed the ferry on behalf of his lord the Black Prince, and during the subsequent hearings alleged that the prior and monks were making exorbitant charges for the use of it. They charged 2d. for a man with a horse, loaded or unloaded, and a farthing for a man on foot, but on market day (Saturday), a man had to pay a halfpenny (*obolum*) or a penny if he had a load.

The priory's involvement was initially described in terms of the north-bound traffic across the Mersey; it is not clear whether it also offered hospitality to travellers in the other direction who were weatherbound or otherwise unable to get on to Chester or elsewhere in the day. It seems unlikely, and it is certainly not stated, that there was any substantial number of pilgrims among these travellers in either direction, although there must from time to time have been some, for example to St Werburga at Chester, but it is equally hard not to think that the priory church would have hoped to attract offerings from passers-by, just as the chapel of St Mary on the Liverpool side hoped to do. It is an intriguing detail, and one that may not have escaped the notice of its visitors, that the priory church was dedicated to St James, the greatest of pilgrim saints, and that the conventual seal depicted him in his usual pilgrim garb; very probably there was an image of him so arrayed somewhere on the premises.

Canterbury and Winchester look rather different from Birkenhead or Liverpool. Both had been provincial capitals of Iron Age peoples and subsequently Roman cities; both may have contained shrines of importance from an early date, perhaps even before Christianity. In his consideration of the 'Old Road' which links the two (more recently, if misleadingly, known as the Pilgrims' Way), Hilaire Belloc speculated, almost a century ago, that both owed their prominence to their positions in the hinterland of coasts on which there were several possible landfalls: accidents of wind or current might drive a ship to Rye or Dover, Sandwich or Reculver, but Canterbury was an identifiable rendezvous not too far away from any of these.[20] The building of Watling Street from Dover to London by the Romans put Canterbury firmly on their map. In a more localised fashion, during the early Anglo-Saxon period, the settlement remained central to the kingdom of Kent. Canterbury has been seen as the hub of a network of early churches and cults, a local pilgrimage centre long before Becket.[21] Similarly, Watling Street north of London enmeshed what would become St Albans in the major communications network of the Roman province and of the future kingdom of England. The roads, as such, were not created by Christian pilgrimage, but as Abbot Leofstan of St Albans perceived when he undertook improvements on Watling Street in the reign of Edward the Confessor, pilgrims and merchants alike used them. Mention of the 'Old Road' or Pilgrims' Way to Canterbury, or of Watling Street, draws attention to another important truth: that shrines, particularly shrines of importance, were approached by a number of routes, and certainly not just by the 'royal', 'public' or Roman roads, which sometimes lay too low for comfort in dirty weather, especially as their original surface deteriorated. Wherever they could, pilgrims used well-worn tracks which were passable and as secure as possible.

The present-day walker along the Pilgrims' Way, much of which now coincides with a long-distance footpath, the North Downs Way, will pass the handsome thirteenth-fourteenth century church of Boughton Aluph, not far north of Wye and some ten miles from Canterbury. A brick south porch with a large fireplace was added to it on the south side, perhaps in the sixteenth century, and it was the local belief that this was used by pilgrims, 'who gathered here in the warmth until there were enough of them to brave the robbers who haunted King's Wood'.[22] King's Wood, which begins about a mile further on from Boughton Aluph, is today haunted, at the right seasons, by bluebells or at worst pheasant-shooters rather than by robbers, but the walker who continues along the Way will get a good impression of what conditions may have been like for the medieval pilgrim. The broad and well-defined track under the trees is perhaps better kept up now than it was in the middle ages, but weather and season must have made a considerable difference to the ease and speed of a pilgrim's progress. The surface of such a path bakes hard in dry weather, but can be slippery and dotted with puddles, some of them sizeable, especially in the winter. Even where the surface has been mended, for the benefit of Forestry Commission vehicles rather than of walkers, a thick slurry of mud collects from the raised banks and is churned up by horses' hooves (and the wheels of vehicles). As the modern walker well knows, horses quickly destroy the going for pedestrians on such a path, and pilgrims on foot must often have cursed them. We hear of sick pilgrims being pushed or pulled in carts, and these must have suffered from bad going and simultaneously made matters worse for those coming after them.

Although probably less well-shod and well-nourished than the modern recreational walker, the medieval pilgrim may have been hardier and more accustomed to walking in his daily routine, so it does not seem unreasonable to assume that some at least could average between two and three miles an hour over such a path, as the average modern walker will, depending on the state of the going, the energy and fitness level of the individual and the amount of time taken for rest and refreshment. The equestrian pilgrim should approximately have doubled this rate of progress, while the available hours of daylight would also have affected the distance that could be achieved in a day by both pedestrians and equestrians. Pilgrims who went to Canterbury for the Feast of St Thomas on 29 December, and those who went for the Feast of the Translation on 7 July, will have experienced very different going and have been able to make very different speeds. At best, a party on foot may have taken an hour and a half or more to negotiate the perils of King's Wood and emerge to the welcome sight of Chilham Castle.

It is possible to make very rough calculations of what daily distances pilgrims are likely to have been able to cover, winter and summer. Occasionally we are given sufficient detail about a pilgrim, or intending pilgrim, to enable us to confirm these estimates. The pilgrim from Bury St Edmunds who paused to buy gloves at Sudbury, and who was probably riding, reached Rochester on the third day afterwards. This was a distance of about sixty miles; the exact distance would have depended on which of the available ferry services across the Thames from Essex to the Kent shore he chose to use. It is not stated at what time of year he was travelling. On 22 June 1470 John Paston the younger announced his intention of going on foot from Norwich to Canterbury. Still at Norwich on the 25th, he expected to be at Canterbury in a 'sevennight', that is, by Monday 2 July. If he meant what he said, he was reckoning to cover a distance of about 160 miles at a rate of about twenty-two miles a day. He hoped to be back at London by the 7th; he does not say how long he intended to stay in Canterbury but, at the same rate of going, three to four days would have sufficed for the sixty-two miles.[23] John was fond of extravagant gestures, but he had the long hours of midsummer daylight in his favour and his estimates were not beyond the reach of possibility. The larger the party, however, the slower the overall rate of progress, as a party axiomatically travels at the speed of its slowest member, especially if it takes prolonged breaks for refreshment. The first overnight stop out of London for Chaucer's pilgrims and others was at Dartford, only fifteen miles distant. They started at first light, but the pace was clearly leisurely. The Host stopped the party only two miles out, at a brook known as the Watering of St Thomas, where they drew lots to determine the order of the story-telling. Presumably their going pace must have been affected by the need to keep together to hear the speaker. The Knight and the Miller had both told their tales by the time the party was approaching Deptford, about five miles out, at 'half-wey prime', that is, at about half past seven in the morning.

For such a party, coming directly from London, Blean Forest on the approach to Canterbury was a hazard corresponding to King's Wood on the Old Road; a group of pilgrims from Warwickshire were set upon and robbed at 'la Bleo' in 1332.[24] At Boughton under Blean, five miles from Canterbury, Chaucer's pilgrims were overtaken by the Canon and his Yeoman, both riding hard in their eagerness to catch up with 'this merry company'. The Canon's professed motive for joining them was his love of 'dalliance', but, since there were so few miles left for that, one might suspect that the pair were also glad of the extra security. Three miles further on, at Harbledown, 'under the Blee, in Canterbury Weye', the Host was jocularly alarmed to see that the Cook was nodding off and lagging in the rear of the party: 'A theefe myghte hym ful lightly robbe and bynde'.[25] Robbers were and remained a danger on all roads, and long stretches of lonely and wooded road were the worst. Another blackspot on the high road from London was at Shooter's Hill, which remained a byword for robbers into the seventeenth century. It is thought to have been here that a certain Fretus in the 1170s constructed a *xenodochium* or hostel for pilgrims, 'seven miles from the city of London'; he dedicated the eastern part of the hill, 'where robbers threatened the lives of travellers', to the martyr. After a while he began to think of moving elsewhere, because of the lack of water, but St Thomas obviously judged that there was a need for the hospital in this particular spot, and Fretus was directed in a dream where to dig a well.[26]

A majority of Kent's medieval hospitals were built along Watling Street.[27] This does not mean that they catered only, or even primarily, for pilgrims, but the increased traffic generated by the shrine at Canterbury, especially after the translation of Becket's relics in 1220, put additional pressure on existing facilities. It does not seem coincidental that the Maisons Dieu at Dover and at Ospringe just outside Faversham, were founded in the immediately following decade or so, respectively by Hubert de Burgh and Henry III, who soon took over the patronage of the house at Dover. There was no separate or special accommodation for pilgrims, at Dover, at Ospringe, or at the Eastbridge hospital, still to be seen in Canterbury. Pilgrims had to share a single hall with the sick and destitute. The revised statutes of the Eastbridge, approved by Archbishop Stratford in 1342, make it plain that 'poor sick pilgrims' were to be received in preference to the healthy, who could only be accommodated for one night. Lepers had to go elsewhere, but other sick were to be received. If they died, they were to be given burial in the cathedral cemetery, in the place allocated of old for the purpose. There were only twelve permanent beds, which were to be attended by a honest woman of at least forty years of age, so even at full stretch the hospital could hardly have catered for flocks of pilgrims.[28] The poor able-bodied pilgrim either had to move on elsewhere or make other arrangements; a pilgrim both able-bodied and possessed of means would anyway have been expecting to stay in one of the city's inns, and the noble would certainly have done so, or rented lodgings.[29] According to a papal indulgence in 1363, the Eastbridge catered 'for the poor, for *Romipetae*, for others coming to Canterbury and needing shelter, and for lying-in women'.[30]

At both Ospringe and Dover superior accommodation was available for important people. Royal visits to Ospringe were frequent, and the captive King John II of France may have stayed at the hospital as many as three times. On his way back to France in the company of the Black Prince in 1360, he stayed at the Maison Dieu in Dover after making his offering at Canterbury.[31] A papal indulgence granted to the house in 1497 still described it as a place 'in which many pilgrims travelling to and from the tombs of the apostles Peter and Paul and the Roman curia and also St James of Compostela resort and in which they are charitably received and given all necessary hospitality'.[32] Hospitals often gave priority to their liturgical functions and to provision for the sick and indigent, but it was far from uncommon for them to own inns nearby for the accomodation of pilgrims and other travellers, as Walter Suffield's foundation of St Giles at Norwich did.[33]

It was commonplace for bishops and other benefactors to assign revenues to monasteries or cathedral chapters on the pretext of the burdens of hospitality. At the end of the thirteenth century Archbishop Winchelsey complained that, for lack of facilities, *viri religiosi* who visited Canterbury sometimes had to seek accomodation dishonourably with laymen of the town.[34] There seems to be little evidence, however, that these communities in general put up any but the most important pilgrims (and of course business visitors), who would be lodged in the guesthouses revealed on many late medieval plans. The abbey of St Albans, a day's journey north from London along Watling Street, offered a great deal of this kind of hospitality and invested in it: Abbot John II (1236–60), for example, built a new hall for guests.[35] For all the important pilgrims that St Albans Abbey attracted, many other people merely passed through the town on business. In 1484 Thomas Hethnes, landlord of the George at St Albans, was licensed by the abbot to have mass said in 'the oratory or chapel' on his premises if great men and other guests came accompanied by their chaplains.[36] It was with the critical eye of one who knew all about inns and innkeepers that an earlier abbey chronicler noted the great fire at Walsingham after Easter in 1431 which destroyed four *hospitia*: 'no mortal person knows by whose agency or how this disaster occurred, unless it were vengeance because their inmates extorted such excessive and unjust charges for food from the pilgrims who came there'. He says nothing about the beds, and does not make it clear whether he thinks the vengeance was human or divine.[37]

St Albans was notorious right down to modern times for the sheer number of inns it contained. In 1884 the landlord of one of them, the Harrow, wrote a piece of doggerel verse which at a rough computation listed ninety-two, including mere beer-houses. Even if not all of these (the Garibaldi for example, or the Cricketers) had necessarily had a lengthy history, under those names at least, the figure is not beyond the reach of medieval possi-bility, if is is true that there were ninety-five or more taverns recorded at Glastonbury in the period. The imposing three-storeyed facade of the George and Pilgrim at Glastonbury is a reminder of the intimate involvement of local ecclesiastical landlords in the urban economy: it was built by Abbot Selwood around 1450.[38] Similar developments took place at Gloucester, where the surviving New Inn was built by the monks around 1457. Another intended for pilgrims stood on the site of the present Fleece Hotel, while Abbot Richard Kidderminster of Winchcombe in the reign of Henry VII built the George, which still stands, for visitors to St Kenelm.[39] There were such establishments wherever there were pilgrims, such as the one John Leland noted at Cleeve Abbey in Somerset: 'on the south side of it is a goodly ynne al of stone, a late usid for pilgrimes'.[40]

It is probable that private householders also supplemented their income by providing food and lodging for pilgrims, as people dwelling along the roads to Rome did, especially in Jubilee years. In 1261 John le Champeneyes claimed that he had killed Roger le Worth of Bintree in Norfolk in self-defence when a quarrel involving some other people had erupted while he was staying with his mother in Roger's 'house' while on a pilgrimage to Walsingham.[41] It is not easy to tell whether Roger was running an inn or simply taking in paying guests. One of Becket's early pilgrims, the dropsical knight Robert of 'Bromtune' (perhaps Brompton in Middlesex) was return-ing from Canterbury when, shaken by the jolting of the cart in which he was travelling, he turned aside to the village of Newington (on Watling Street), where he obviously found both food and somewhere to sleep.[42] It has been suggested that it was at Newington that Chaucer's Pardoner wanted to stop and have a drink and a snack when the pilgrims were between Rochester and Sittingbourne. At all events, there was what he called an 'alestake' somewhere along that road.[43] Henry Bolingbroke, returning from Calais to prepare for his Prussian crusade in the early summer of 1390, was able to buy 'wine of Rochelle' at Newington and on another occasion to hire horses there as far as Rochester.[44] These scraps of evidence suggest that the inhabitants of a modest settlement on Watling Street could at least supplement their income by meeting the wants of pilgrims and other travellers.

It was one of the many points of Lollard criticism of pilgrimage that it involved unseemly expenditure on tapsters and 'hostellers', who, it was clearly believed, provided services other than alcoholic beverages for their customers. In the prologue to The Tale of Beryn, the pilgrims have no sooner arrived at Canterbury and put up at the Chequer of the Hope than the tapster is showing the Pardoner her empty bed and lamenting the loss of her husband.[45] Pilgrims may sometimes in fact have occupied a privileged position as drinkers. Bishop Roger Martival of Salisbury (1315–30), renewing an offensive of his predecessor Giles of Bridport, wanted the archdeacon of Dorset to take action against the parochial festivities known as 'common potations' and 'scotales'. The 'common potations' were defined as gatherings of more than ten people of the parish where the beer was being sold, or in the taverns of neighbouring parishes, or even within their own homes, 'for the sake of drinking'. Viatores peregrini and merchants attending fairs and markets were however exempted from the bishop's strictures. Peregrini here looks like an adjective, and rather than specifically denoting pilgrims is probably being used to distinguish 'outsiders' from the native parishioners whom the bishop wanted brought under control; but a group of pilgrims travelling together would, it seems, have been officially at liberty to form a drinking party. [46]

The hazards of pilgrimage were those of all travel, including brawls in taverns, and its infrastructural requirements, from board and lodging to road and bridge upkeep, were correspondingly similar. Road and bridge mending had long been regarded as meritorious charitable work, and English bishops sometimes granted indulgences in respect of it. Bridge chapels, sometimes attended by hermits, received testamentary bequests and might themselves be visited by pilgrims, for whom they were often obvious wayside halts: the one at Wakefield is probably the finest of the few survivors. Leland noted 'Ther is also a chapel of Our Lady on Calder Bridge wont to be celebrated *a peregrinis*'. At Rotherham too there was 'a chapel of stone wel wrought' on 'the fair stone bridge' by which he entered the town.[47] Fords and ferries also required attendance. One ford that was naturally much used, by pilgrims and others, was at Dartford on Watling Street, where, as the place-name indicates, the River Darenth enters the Thames. The 'hermit of the ford' here is documented first around 1235 and continued to exist until at least 1518, a century after the Darenth was bridged. There seems to have been a subsidiary market in Canterbury pilgrimage souvenirs at Dartford, run by the brethren of the Holy Trinity hospital, who had a stall in the parish church. In an inquisition taken on the death of Edmund Woodstock, earl of Kent, in 1429, the Dartford ferry was described as yielding 13s. 4d. yearly, with 40s. from tolls, and the existence of a quay was noted.[48]

If Dartford was the first stop out of London for those travelling by road, Gravesend, further along the Thames and passed on the south by Watling Street, was the first for those coming by water. Water transport was used extensively for the carriage of goods in medieval England, but there seems to be little direct evidence of the use of inland waterways by pilgrims to English shrines. Edward I and his family, however, went by water as far as Chatham on their Canterbury pilgrimage in 1285. In 1293 it was complained that the boatmen of London, of Gravesend and of the manor of Milton, which is now part of Gravesend, were making exorbitant charges for their services: they were exacting a penny for a foot passenger to London where they had once taken a halfpenny, and they could not deny it.[49] Undoubtedly, boatmen made a living ferrying pilgrims, and of course others, across the Thames proper and across the estuary. These crossings were made at a number of places. On his arrival from Gascony in August 1289, Edward I called at Canterbury and made his way thence, via Maidstone and Rochester, to Cliffe on the Hoo Peninsula. From there he crossed by boat to South

Benfleet, proceeding to the castle at Rayleigh and thence to Bury St Edmunds and Walsingham.[50] This was by no means the only occasion on which the king availed himself of the Thames ferrymen: in April 1294, for example, he was at Chelmsford on the 2nd, Tilbury on the 4th and Chatham and Gillingham on the 6th, whence he proceeded, after a stay of several days at Dover, to spend Easter at Canterbury.[51]

Over a century earlier, many of Becket's pilgrims from Essex and East Anglia avoided the digression via London by using one of these Thames ferries. Those who made a living ferrying pilgrims (and their horses) to and fro were integral to this traffic. Two early pilgrims from Essex who made the crossing were disconcerted to discover that their *pyxides* of the martyr's water had completely dried up. The 'carrier' (*vector*) who had conveyed them, both going and coming, himself had a supply in his hut (*tugurium*) on the bank of the river, and from this his customers' containers were miraculously replenished.[52] It has been suggested that the ferry service most used by Canterbury pilgrims ran from West Thurrock on the Essex side to a promontory on the Kentish side north of Swanscombe: a road running from the promontory down to the main London road is still called Pilgrims' Road. At both West Thurrock and East Tilbury churches with twelfth-century features, now quite isolated, stand close to the riverside, perhaps suggesting that their use was once bound up with the ferry traffic.[53]

It was obviously not just for the benefit of pilgrims that an eye was kept on these services, or that Rochester Bridge (rebuilt in stone after 1381) was built and maintained, but pilgrims were among those who from time to time were drowned crossing the Medway by ferry when the bridge was broken, which happened no fewer than nineteen times between 1277 and 1381.[54] Their needs were emphasised when in 1366 Edward III directed that the inhabitants of Strood, on the London side of Rochester Bridge, should be made to do something about the state of the roads in their town, 'through which is the common passage of magnates, pilgrims and others visiting the shrine of St Thomas of Canterbury and returning therefrom'. The going through Strood was obviously tough, as it must have been in many other towns as well, since 'for lack of paving and through the negligence of the inhabitants [it] is so deep and heavy for horse and foot that great peril may arise therefrom'. Every inhabitant was therefore to be made responsible for paving the road in front of his tenement.[55] Pilgrims would have been among those who should have benefited when Richard II regulated the cost of the hire of 'hackneys' on the road from London via Rochester and Canterbury to Dover.[56]

The features of this particular complex of roads and waterways, into which a major pilgrimage route was integrated, would be hard to parallel very closely elsewhere in England, not least because of its nearness and openness to London on the one hand and to continental Europe on the other. Road networks and provision for pilgrims in many other parts of the country would however be worthy of study, in Devon and Cornwall for example, or in Yorkshire. By the fifteenth century, York, Beverley, Bridlington and Pontefract formed a rough parallelogram of flourishing shrines, within which and around which clustered a host of others, at Hull and Scarborough, Selby and Hemingbrough and elsewhere. Some of the roads which traversed this region rested in part on Roman foundations, like the main road from York to the Humber, which was joined at Market Weighton by the road to Beverley and Hull. The Meaux chronicler refers to 'the high road to Beverley' and to 'the royal road which leads from Beverley to the hospital of Routh' (about four miles away). This led north east from Beverley to Bridlington and thence by the coast to Scarborough. At Routh it ran less than a couple of miles north of Meaux itself, so there was perhaps good reason for the monks to think that a beautiful new crucifix, well advertised, might attract interest. [57]

Like Canterbury, Hailes Abbey in Gloucestershire drew people along established routes which long antedated the pilgrimage. The reformer Hugh Latimer wrote in 1533: 'I dwell within half a mile of the Foss-way, and you would wonder to see how they come by flocks out of the west country to many images, but chiefly to the blood of Hayles.' This has been taken to imply pilgrims coming from the south west via Cirencester, who would have had a choice of turnings off the Fosse Way in order to get to Hailes.[58] Another ancient road, the Icknield Way, could serve pilgrims to a variety of destinations. It intersected with Watling Street at Dunstable, and led on through Royston, Newmarket and Swaffham towards Walsingham; there were serviceable turnings for both Ely and Bury St Edmund's off this road. The approaches to Walsingham were dotted with hospitals, wayside chapels and subsidiary shrines, the most famous of them being the 'Slipper Chapel' at Houghton St Giles, where the pious, Henry VIII among them, stopped to take their shoes off and complete the journey barefoot.[59]

Pilgrims and pilgrimages left their mark on urban toponymy in a number of places. In Newcastle, Leland noted 'Pilgrim's Gate' (demolished in 1802), while 'Pilgrim Street', first mentioned in 1272 and still in existence, albeit transformed, was a principal medieval thoroughfare through the town. There were numerous hospitals in medieval Newcastle, including the Maison Dieu mentioned by Leland. In 1564 reference was made to 'the great innes on Pilgrim Street', and one of these was known in Henry VIII's reign as St Cuthbert's.[60] It is plausible to suppose that pilgrim traffic passed south through Newcastle to St Cuthbert's shrine at Durham and beyond, and north to St Andrew's, which attracted some English pilgrims. In the seventeenth century the earliest historian of Newcastle believed, however, that the gate, the street, and the Pilgrims' Inn were all named for pilgrims to the shrine of Our Lady at Jesmond, a very short distance outside the gate to the north east and now itself part of Newcastle.[61]

At the end of the eleventh century Margaret of Scotland left what was to be a permanent imprint on the map when she provided a free ferry and lodgings for pilgrims crossing the Forth, as the names Queensferry and North Queensferry recall.[62] Much traffic to shrines on or near the east coast, from St Andrew's to Walsingham, came by sea, as it also did to Southampton, where 'Pylgrymesgate', opening off the north end of West Hithe where the galleys docked, marked the point of entry for many French and Spanish pilgrims, who would then take the land route to Canterbury; this may well have been judged easier than trying to beat on through the Channel to Dover or Sandwich.[63] The existence of this other major route to St Thomas naturally helped nourish subsidiary shrines, among which, certainly from the perspective of any foreign pilgrim, Winchester's would have been numbered. Two Marian shrines close to Southampton were noted by Leland, at Netley Abbey, on a creek 'out of the mayne haven', and Southwick Priory, which 'is a good bigg thorough fare but no celebrate market'.[64]

English pilgrims were of course compelled to take ship when going to foreign shrines (or to venerate St Lide on his island in the Scillies) and seafaring men often had occasion to call upon the Virgin and the saints. It was natural that ports should develop shrines of their own. St Anne's shrine at Brislington, just outside Bristol, attracted mariners, and the commanding situation of St Mary Redcliffe, on rising ground close to the harbour at Bristol, suggests that this, the parish church of the Cabots and other prominent merchant families, must have done likewise. Around the year 1200 an elaborate north porch was built on to the church, with a relic chamber and niches for statues. Later in the century, this was enclosed in a sumptuously carved outer porch with doors to east, north and west, as if to facilitate exits and entrances.[65]

Road, bridge and hospital upkeep were pious works, as was pilgrimage itself; yet an activity which brought out onto the public highway large numbers of common folk, who otherwise might have had little pretext or excuse for absenting themselves from home, had the potential to worry those in authority. This began to become noticeable in the later fourteenth century. For the better part of a century, during much of which they had been at war with France, the kings had sought to impose controls on the movement of pilgrims and other travellers overseas, with possible losses of money, horses and manpower in mind. Ships, also, might be needed for the royal service, and could not always be spared for taking pilgrims to Galicia. Pilgrimage within England, however, had not seemed to be problematical apart from isolated incidents. The various disasters of the mid and later fourteenth century brought about some shift in attitudes, although it certainly did not result in a consistent disposition to discourage popular pilgrimage.

During the Peasants' Revolt in 1381 bands of rebels 'arrested' pilgrims on the road to Canterbury, regardless of their social status, and compelled them to swear that they would preserve fealty to King Richard and the commons and that they would never accept a king called John, this out of fear and hatred of John of Gaunt.[66] These were extraordinary times and the immediate emergency soon passed; but in 1388–89 parliament expressed growing concerns about labour shortages and vagabondage by enacting a statute to prevent begging by persons who were 'able to serve and labour'. They were to abide in their localities unless they could produce testimonial letters justifying their movements. The statute included the stipulation that 'all of them that go in Pilgrimage as beggars and be able to travail, it shall be done as of the said Servants and Labourers, if they have no Letters testimonial of ther Pilgrimage'. The same applied to scholars of the universities that went begging. It was further laid down that

> no Servant or Labourer, be he Man or Woman, shall depart at the end of his Term out of the Hundred, Rape or Wapentake where he is dwelling, to serve or dwell elsewhere, or by Colour to go from there in Pilgrimage, unless he bring a Letter Patent containing the cause of going and the Time of his Return, if he ought to return, under the King's Seal.[67]

This statute was echoed in somewhat different circumstances in 1473. In 1471 Edward IV had finally surmounted the challenges to his tenure of the throne. The earl of Warwick, 'the Kingmaker', was killed with other enemies of the Yorkist king at the battle of Barnet in July, and Henry VI was soon disposed of. Almost no sooner had all this been achieved than plague erupted. Pilgrims were among those who brought news of it to the Pastons in Norfolk and perhaps indeed helped to spread 'the most universall deth that ever I wyst in Ingelonde', as John Paston called it on 15 September. Later in the month, 'the Kyng, and the Qwyen, and moche other pepell, ar ryden and goon to Canterbery, nevyr so muche peple seyn in Pylgrymage hertofor at ones, as men seye'.[68] Edward, not the most assiduous of pilgrims, had many reasons to demonstrate his piety and propitiate the deity by joining in supplication with his subjects, themselves agitated by the troubles of the times. Soon, however, he was confronted by the beginnings of a popular pilgrimage to the burial place of the late king at Chertsey Abbey.

The language of his directive to the sheriffs of London in May 1473, even if inspired by this unwelcome spectacle, was generalised, and contains strong echoes of Richard II's statute:

> Forasmuch as as this day many persons being strong of body to service in husbandry and other labours feign them to be sick and feeble and some ... in going of pilgrimages and not of power to perform it without alms of the people ...

The thrust, as before, was ostensibly against mendicancy and not against pilgrimage undertaken by respectable people with money in their purse. The guilty parties were further accused of 'sowing seditious language whereby the country people be put in great fear and jeopardy of their lives and losses of their goods'. Once again, an intending pilgrim 'not able to perform it without begging' was to have 'letters testimonial under the great seal'. [69]

Twenty years later, Henry VII, who, whatever else may have been worrying him, was not concerned about pilgrimage to Henry VI, returned to the theme:

> The kynge our soverayne lord is informed that full heynes murdres, robries, thefte, decaye of husbondrye and othir enormyties and inconveniences daily increase within this his realme to the greate offense unto God, displeasour to his highnesse, hurt and impoverisshing vexacion and trouble of his subgjetts by the mean of idelnesse and specially of vagabundes, beggers able to werk and by faitours; summe excusyng them self by colour of pylgrymages ... [70]

These broadsides do not help us to quantify the problem, if problem it was, of mendicant pilgrimage. They have nothing to say about the pilgrim who was able to pay his way, but comprehend the indigent pilgrim in the same condemnation as a number of other social types who were regarded as workshy and fraudulent. That there was always an undercurrent of suspicion, not to say disdain, of pilgrims who claimed alms, as of 'the poor' generally, may perhaps be inferred from stories such as that of the knight's wife near Abingdon who refused a drink to five Canterbury pilgrims and told them, 'Be off, *trutanni!*' In its context, like other stories of grasping innkeepers who refused to extend charity to pilgrims, the story was simply underlining the obligation to honour the pilgrim's intentions and the risks of failing to do so; but it suggested also that all the world did not necessarily love a pilgrim.

10

Penitents and Critics

In July 1491 Isabel Dorte of East Hendred in Berkshire admitted before the bishop of Salisbury, Thomas Langton, that she had openly spoken

> ayenst worshipping of ymagies of seynts and pilgramage doying, shewing that no man shuld wourship no stokkes nor stonys ne nothing made or graven with mannys hand understandyng and felyng in my mind that it wer better to give a poor bitynel or lame man a peny than to bestowe their mony in pilgre goyngs and wurshippyng the immagys of sentys, for man is the very ymage of godde which ought all only to be wurshipd and no stokky ne stonys.

Isabel was not alone in her views. Among other heretics arraigned at Ramsbury on different dates in 1491, Thomas Tailour of Newbury had affirmed his ridicule of those who went to St James, for 'seynt Jamys had no fote to come ayenst them no hand to welcom theym neither tonge to speak to theym, so reprevying the wurshipping of ymages and all odir holy peregrinacions'. William Carpenter endorsed these opinions and, like Isabel, believed 'that it were better to geve a poreman a peny to them adding hereto that offerynges be made but only for the availe and lucre of the pristis and not for soule helthe'. Alice Hignell, also of Newbury, was very satirical about images: why could the Virgin Mary not blow a cobweb off her face? Why did St Martin stand up there in the cold and not come down and sit by the fire? Harry Benet of Speen, one of a group who abjured their heresy in the parish church of St John at New Windsor on 28 January, said that he 'wold never goo a pilgremage but onys' and had often reproved those who 'wold spend their money in pilgremage doyng seing thei might better spend hit at home'.[1]

Isabel Dorte's views were typical, but her punishment was not. She alone of this cluster of heretics was sentenced to perform a pilgrimage: 'during the next year if she lived in East Hendred [she] was to go on pilgrimage in the manner of a penitent to St Mary of Colethorpe or if she lived in another village was to make a pilgrimage to the nearest shrine of St Mary'. By contrast, the satirical Alice Hignell was not to go more than four miles from Newbury without the bishop's licence, a restriction frequently imposed on heretics. One may well wonder whether Isabel's inward disaffection was going to be assuaged by her penance. In her own person she represents two classes of individual whose perceptions of pilgrimage (as distinct from mere unfortunate experiences in the course of pilgrimage) were negative, or likely to be: the penitential pilgrim and the critic of pilgrimage.

Penitential pilgrimage was, we have already seen, ancient and not necessarily involuntary. In the traditions of early Irish monasticism, to cut oneself off from all that was comfortable and familiar and embark on what might be endless wanderings for the Lord's sake was a penitential exercise in the most general sense, a form of ascetic discipline and purification of the sinful self rather than of purgation of one particular sin. From that tradition grew the practice of imposing pilgrimages, which sometimes effectively amounted to exile, as penance or rather punishment for a variety of offences. This practice spread over Europe with the influence of Irish and then English missionary monks between the sixth and the eighth centuries, but by the early ninth century there were signs of a feeling, among the high-minded men who shaped Carolingian policies, that this mode of correction of faults conflicted with the purpose of creating a more orderly society in which the individual Christian was securely located within a disciplinary structure of parish and diocese (or religious community). The Council of Châlons in 813 expressed anxieties on this score: was it not preferable for a penitent to discharge his penance under the supervision of his own priest? There was also concern about more general issues like the mistaken belief that the mere act of going on pilgrimage was sufficient to discharge the sinner of the burden of his sin. [2]

This is not the place to recapitulate the development of the penitential system in the medieval west. It is sufficient to indicate that while pilgrimage continued to be used as penance it was increasingly hedged with bureaucratic safeguards. The change in atmosphere is perhaps symbolised by the declining popularity of one miracle story, which was told to the credit of St Swithun, St Aldhelm and St Ivo among other saints: a wandering penitent, painfully constricted by iron bands around his person, goes from shrine to shrine until at last the final chain is spectacularly shattered before the shrine of the most potent saint. In later centuries, exploding fetters were increasingly replaced by testimonial letters. From the mid thirteenth century on, the inquisition of southern France imposed pilgrimages, both major and minor, on repentant heretics; they were told where to go, and required to bring back a certificate of performance from the church authorities at their destination. This was a precaution used by other authorities, lay and ecclesiastical, which imposed penitential pilgrimages.[3] The secular courts of many of the cities of late medieval Flanders did so, operating with lengthy lists of approved destinations which included some English shrines. Canterbury, unsurprisingly, was the most commonly named, but Walsingham, Beverley, Bury St Edmund's and Hereford also featured in several lists, together with a number of other places in the east of England which were doubtless familiar to the Flemish through their trading connections, such as Yarmouth, Peterborough and Louth, and also the shrines of the Virgin at Salisbury, Lincoln and Oxford.[4]

English bishops seem to have been discreet in their use of long-distance pilgrimage as penance. The sense that it was preferable to keep delinquents under close supervision was probably uppermost in their minds, particularly if they were deemed likely to spread a contagion of misconduct or misbelief, as the bishop of Salisbury obviously believed Agnes Hignell of Newbury might do. Pilgrimage featured in the repertoire of available penalties, as one of a number of bodily austerities which were regarded by many bishops as morally preferable to money fines as punishment for certain offences. In 1282 John Pecham of Canterbury commissioned the official of the bishop of Worcester to carry out 'corrections' in the archdeaconries of Worcester and Gloucester, strictly forbidding him to impose monetary penalties for crime, but rather to use 'pilgrimages, whippings and other penances of that kind'.[5]

During his long episcopate Hamo de Hethe of Rochester (1319–52) used pilgrimage more than many, but the geographical range of the destinations he employed was limited and the distance and arduousness proportional to the nature of the offence.[6] Only once did he order a penitent to go outside England, when John Mayde was sent to Santiago in 1325 for the heinous offence of adultery with his godmother. Other sexual offences incurred pilgrimages beyond the confines of Kent. Henry Elham, knight, guilty of adultery, was enjoined in 1321 to make annual pilgrimages in each of six years to Canterbury, Hereford, Bury and Chichester; he had also to offer a three-pound candle at Rochester itself annually on the feast of St Andrew and on top of this to give annual alms of 20s. for six years to the poor of the parishes of Stone, Kingsdown and Wrotham.[7] As so often, we are unlikely to know whether he actually had to carry out the sentence, as the bishop reserved the right to moderate it. In at least two instances, much later in Hamo's episcopate, we know that the culprits in cases of clerical incontinence bought off the pilgrimages, to Canterbury and Walsingham, that were imposed on them. In a more complicated case, in March 1332, Simon de Buntingford, chaplain and farmer of the fruits of the church of Ryarsh, admitted various defects in connection with his farm but, charged also with living in adultery with Ellen de Butynford in the rectory house, replied ambiguously that he had never done so in the jurisdiction of Rochester. Failing to purge himself, he was ordered to make pilgrimages to

St Thomas of Canterbury and St Thomas of Hereford, offering a prescribed amount at each shrine and bringing back certificates of performance.[8]

A woman guilty of slander was treated with some severity. Sybil, wife of Geoffrey le Brevetour of Rochester, in 1327 admitted wrongly accusing Joan, wife of William of Gillingham, of adultery with a monk of Rochester, and was sentenced to go three times to Canterbury and once each to Chichester and Bury, as well as offering a candle at the altar of St Andrew at Rochester.[9] The penalties for adultery were normally harsh. Simon Heyroun of Woldham in 1320 had to go every year for seven years to Canterbury, and three times each to Hereford, Bury and Walsingham within the same period; like John Mayde he also had to perform an act of charity, in his case feeding the poor every Friday during the seven years. Another male adulterer had to visit St Thomas, St Edmund and Our Lady of Walsingham on foot, while the woman was whipped three times around the church and the marketplace.[10] William Covel, who was guilty of repeated adultery, only had to go to Canterbury and Rochester, but he had to be barefoot and naked but for his breeches.[11] Mere fornication tended to be punished only with local pilgrimage unless it was 'habitual', in which case sterner measures were called for: William Usher in 1347 was sent to Walsingham and also to King Edward at Gloucester, bringing back some 'sign' of performance in either case.[12] Bishop Hamo was evidently prompt to make use not only of the newly canonised Thomas of Hereford but of the more contentious figure of the late king.

Hamo also occasionally imposed miniature pilgrimages for offences which concerned him in his capacity as lord of the manor. Disturbing the peace, 'violating the liberty' of the church, or poaching in my lord's park at Halling, sent various 'penitents' simply to Rochester Cathedral. Just as voluntary pilgrimage could be essentially local, so some of the penitential pilgrimages imposed by bishops were essentially public penances, to be carried out within the locality. In imposing such punishments the bishop might or might not use the word pilgrimage to describe them. While it was not uncommon for a bishop to require the penitent to visit his own cathedral, he might equally well prescribe a circuit of other local churches and market-places (especially perhaps when the diocese was large and the cathedral far distant from the offender's dwelling-place). It was also possible for the bishop's own cathedral to be part of such a circuit, as when in February 1343 Ralph of Shrewsbury, bishop of Bath and Wells, instructed William le Bret to stand barefoot and bareheaded in the cathedral of Wells on Ascension Day next with a taper of one pound weight in his hands, and to do likewise at Bath, Taunton and in his own parish of Saundford.[13]

Two different considerations may have weighed with bishops and their law officers when imposing such sentences: on the one hand, proportionality to the offence; on the other, the positive desirability of humilating the offender before a local public. This is well illustrated in the penance imposed by Ralph of Shrewsbury on the ringleader of a group of miscreants who had set upon the bishop and his entourage in the churchyard at Yeovil while he was conducting a visitation in 1349. The other guilty parties were ordered to stand bareheaded in the church at Wells, each with a taper in their hands, but the ringleader had to do so in the church at Yeovil itself three times on Sundays and feast-days, while the celebrant expounded the cause of his punishment in the vernacular. He was in addition to be paraded through the market-place there on the three days of the next market and also through the churches of Wells, Bath, Glastonbury, Bristol and Somerton. Finally, he was to visit St Thomas the Martyr 'in a penitential manner'. [14]

Bishops and their officials presumably each worked with their own scales of severity of both offence and punishment. Robert Rede, bishop of Chichester, in March 1404 imposed penances on two men of Arundel for violating sanctuary and on another for entering the bishop's liberty and taking a horse away. The first two incurred the more severe penalties: in addition to going on foot to St Richard at Chichester, they were to be beaten four times through the church of Arundel. The horse-thief was to be content with one kind of fish on three days of the week, Fridays apart, until Easter, and to go to Chichester on the feast of St Richard 'or on another occasion when it pleases him' and offer there. The bishop described both penances as pilgrimages. [15] John Waltham of Salisbury (1388–95) imposed pilgrimages to Canterbury as punishment for the offence of farming churches to laymen, while the 'bailiff errant' at Netherhampton, guilty of adultery, and the chaplain of Motcombe, a fornicator, had to go as pilgrims to the nuns' church of Kington St Michael and offer 20s. Another chaplain who had merely been absent from the bishop's visitation had to go to the cathedral and offer 15d. In a class of his own among Waltham's penitents was William Ramsbury, 'a virtual layman' and unlettered, who had been preaching heresy and sexual libertarianism in order to populate the earth, and also dishonouring the sacrament all over Wiltshire. He was to go to Rome, if he had the means, to receive the Jubilee indulgences in 1390. [16] William was a harbinger of troubles to come for several of Waltham's successors at Salisbury and for other English bishops besides.

The conditions that might be attached to a penitential pilgrimage were very various. Henry Woodlock of Winchester in May 1308 passed a suspended sentence on Robert Urry, one of a number of people who had been molesting the vicar of Arreton on the Isle of Wight. He was to go both to Canterbury and to Bury by Michaelmas, without drinking wine on his way there, but on his way back he could drink what he liked. [17] A later bishop

of Winchester, William Wykeham, in 1369 had to mitigate 'certain absti-
nences' which Elizabeth Juliers, countess of Kent, had 'specially vowed' to
perform by way of accompaniment to a pilgrimage to St Thomas of Canterbury. The pilgrimage itself was a penance for Elizabeth's fault in
remarrying without licence, after she had taken the veil of widowhood.
Apparently she had embraced her penance too enthusiastically and added
her own conditions to it.[18] Personalities who were easily moved to both
pious and less pious impulses accounted for many vows and also for many
penances and substitutory benefactions.

One of the most elaborate descriptions of a penance which contained a
pilgrimage element is to be found in the register of Archbishop Wickwane
of York, who had an ongoing battle on his hands againt violators of his
rights at Beverley, including poachers in his park there. On 31 October 1281
he directed the dean of Beverley to receive 'patiently' a group of named
penitents, lay and clerical, if they should present themselves to him before
the church of St John on the following Sunday, 2 November, the day after
All Saints. They were to be barefoot, clad only in their shirts, without girdle
or head-covering, and with suitable candles in their hands. They were at
once to set out for York, passing through the villages of Bishop's Burton,
Market Weighton, Hayton and so on as far as Stamford Bridge. The dean
was to follow them personally to Burton, which marked the limits of his
jurisdiction; thereafter he was to appoint a servant to follow them to see
that they conducted themselves penitently. Two priests who had evidently
been implicated in the offence were to follow the others, more decently clad
since the archbishop had compassion for their order, carrying rods in their
hands and explaining along the way why it was that they were thus going
as penitents. The dean was authorised to suspend this penance if any of the
offenders should prove to be old or infirm, lest perils ensue which the
archbishop wanted to avoid, while the punishment of a woman who had
also been involved was reserved to the archbishop's discretion. Wickwane
himself was going to be unavoidably absent when the penitents arrived at
York, but the dean of Christianity on 2 November duly received his instructions to go to the church of St Nicholas when he was notified of their
approach and bring them by way of the Ouse Bridge and the public highway
to the cathedral, following them with 'rods of discipline'. He was then to
administer 'discipline' to each one in front of the church and proceed with
the necessary rites when they had solemnly offered their 'lights' within.[19]

The walk to which this group of penitents were committed was of some
thirty-three miles, to be undertaken 'barefoot', in Yorkshire, in early November. It was longer and more arduous than many so-called pilgrimages;
Wickwane does not, as it happens, apply that word to it, although he might

have done. This was but one salvo in an ongoing struggle between the archbishops and the men of Beverley. In 1310 William Greenfield was again imposing penances for poaching in the park there. These were actually to be discharged at Beverley, except that the two chief culprits were within seven days to go on foot and clad in woollen garments to the shrine of St William at York, to make humble and devout offering.[20] Whatever the deterrent effect of this kind of penance, it is hard to think that it endeared the church to the offenders, especially perhaps when imposed not for what the laity would normally have agreed were moral offences, but for infringements on what they persistently tended to regard as mere seigneurial rights like any others.

However much such resentments may ultimately have contributed to the unpopularity of the church and its privileges, it is not immediately obvious that they had much influence on the popularity or unpopularity of pilgrimage as such. Where that is documented, it seems to have sprung from different and quite specific origins. By the time Thomas Langton of Salisbury was exacting abjurations from Lollards in Berkshire in 1491, their heresy was a century old. The chronicler Thomas Walsingham reported with reference to the period around 1389 that 'the heretics preached that pilgrimages should not be done, and especially to Walsingham and the cross of the north door at St Paul's in London, for there was nothing of the spirit there, but rotten stumps, crawling with worms, by which the unskilled multitude were deceived and forced into manifest idolatry'. As a monk of St Albans, Thomas was professionally sensitive to such imputations, even if the cults for which his own monastery was famous were, historically, centred on relics rather than on the images which were currently so abundant and so fashionable. He pointedly reported miracles which occurred at St Albans itself, at Ely, Cambridge and at a cross erected on the public road at Wymondham, 'as we think to support those who believe piously and to refute the heretics'.[21]

There was an ancient and respectable tradition of criticism of pilgrimage, or at least of reservations about it, and pilgrimage had never been a requirement of the Christian faith, even if one may suspect that it sometimes became a social imperative.[22] The concept of human life as itself the essential pilgrimage was an old metaphor, much used by monastic and mystical writers of the twelfth and thirteenth centuries who insisted on the superiority of the cloistered, inward quest for the heavenly Jerusalem over the mere physical journey to the earthly Jerusalem. A series of ecclesiastical councils and moral broadsides had over the centuries sought to enforce as a rule of conduct the view that the cloistered religious had chosen the better part, the heavenly and not the earthly Jerusalem, and these principles were reiterated by the English ecclesiastical authorities in the later medieval period. At the end of the twelfth century William Longchamps as papal legate tried to legislate against the 'wandering' of monks to St Thomas and St Edmund, although Abbot Samson of Bury regarded this as an infringement of his power over his community, and just over a century later Archbishop Winchelsey was complaining that the monks of Canterbury, not content with their own incomparable relics, were going to the new St Edmund at Pontigny and the new St Thomas at Hereford. Pilgrimage vows were no defence, for they were invalid without the consent of the superior. 23

The greater anxiety was however reserved for nuns. In 1298 Boniface VIII decreed a general restriction on the mobility of nuns in the decree *Pericoloso*. Archbishop Melton of York logically interpreted it as implying a ban on pilgrimage by female religious, and in 1318 sought to enforce it on the inmates of Nun Appleton, with imperfect success. He wanted them to commute their vows of pilgrimage by saying as many psalters as it would have taken days to complete the pilgrimage.24 In 1344 Hamo de Hethe of Rochester similarly tried to stop the nuns of Malling from 'wandering around the country on the pretext of pilgrimage or of visiting your friends'.25 In 1417 four Swedish Bridgettine nuns had made a vow to visit St Thomas of Canterbury while they were at sea, on their way to England to enter the new convent at Sion, but found that they were for various reasons unable to perform the pilgrimage and asked Henry Chichele of Canterbury for dispensation. He was only too happy to oblige, quoting the well-established principle that 'all opportunity for wandering about should be denied to women who are professed in a religious order'. 26 One suspects that the presence of Chaucer's Prioress on the road to Canterbury, even if the portrait is gently satirical, would not, in practice, have raised too many eyebrows: she had clearly exercised her authority and given herself permission to go. The Monk, we are explicitly told, thought little or nothing of any rule that would confine him to his cloister. The anchorite or anchoress, although they were supposed to be dead to the world, enjoyed a more ambiguous status. In 1401 Boniface IX licensed Emma Schermann, a recluse at Pontefract, to remove herself from her present cell 'on account of the tumults and clamours of the people in the said place' and to establish herself in a new one, which she was to be free to leave annually, without anyone's permission, 'for the purpose of visiting churches and other pious places and of gaining the indulgences granted there'. 27

Even if the rules against pilgrimage by professed religious were unevenly enforced, the idea underlying them, that Christian perfection was not necessarily best sought by such means, exerted an increasing influence beyond the cloister. A version of this idea, adapted to the circumstances of the laity, became part of the repertoire of some popular preachers in the thirteenth and fourteenth centuries. Monastic writers had already insisted that the duty of an abbot to his monks, of a ruler to his people, should keep them at home; such counsels translated readily into the duty of ordinary folk to attend first to the needs of their families and neighbours. The availability of the Body and Blood of Christ Himself in every church merely strengthened the case against gadding about after relics or images. Anxieties about idolatry were very old, and the belief that pilgrims behaved badly away from home and came back no better than they went were also commonplaces. So far from being innovators, in these respects at least, the Lollards can be seen as one outgrowth of a long tradition, just as the supreme devotional classic of the fifteenth century, *The Imitation of Christ*, with its austere view of pilgrimage, was another. Given the supreme reality of Christ on the altar, what of greater value could possibly be obtained by making journeys to shrines? Such an argument pointed not necessarily to an abandonment of devotional cults but to their pursuit in the pilgrim's home environment. Here literacy obviously opened new doors, even if only for relatively few as yet. In the next century Erasmus gave a fresh twist to the argument in favour of domestic responsibilities with his image of the *paterfamilias* performing his pilgrimage by going from room to room of his own house seeing to the welfare of all his family.[28]

By 1400, however, a number of long-term developments had contributed to make an ancient and popular custom into a structural necessity as well as a habit which it was questionable to challenge. Indulgences were hardly new, but a lot of English churches, great and small, had availed themselves of papal generosity, especially in the later fourteenth century, to obtain them. Both papal and episcopal indulgences were usually available to persons who merely subscribed to the upkeep or rebuilding of the church, or other good cause, in question. That the scope and conditions of the remission offered by indulgences were misunderstood, at least by some, seems probable. A curious incident took place in 1370 when Simon Sudbury, bishop of London (and fated to die, as archbishop of Canterbury, at the hands of the rebels of 1381), fell in with a party of pilgrims who were going to Canterbury for the Jubilee indulgence. He aroused great indignation when he told them it would do them no good, and what was interpreted as disrespect to St Thomas ultimately cost him his life, or so some believed.[29] It seems more likely that the bishop was referring obliquely to the necessary state of contrition which alone would make the indulgence valid than that he was impugning the credentials of the saint himself.

That pilgrims both misbehaved and misunderstood what they were about was certainly believed by some of Sudbury's contemporaries. William

Langland in *The Vision of Piers Plowman* satirised souvenir-hunting pilgrims who did not know who or where Truth was, work-shy pseudo-hermits who went off to Walsingham with their whores in tow, or Greed personified and his wife, the fraudulent alewife, who thoughtlessly swore to go to Walsingham and Bromholm to get remission of their guilt, although Greed had no idea what the word 'restitution' meant, and pleaded illiteracy in extenuation. Greed and his like believed that it was sufficient just to go to a shrine. Langland also reflected the rather different concerns of royal government about the possible disruptive effects of unregulated popular pilgrimage in an age of war, demographic slump and social unrest.[30] To control vagrancy was one thing, however; to undermine the principles on which pilgrimage was based was quite another, which the kings themselves, devout pilgrims as we have seen, were hardly likely to do.

The eighth of the Twelve Conclusions of the Lollards, which were fixed to the door of Westminster Hall during the sitting of parliament early in 1395, began: 'The eighth conclusion needful to tell to the people beguiled is that pilgrimage, prayers and offerings made to blind roods and to deaf images of tree and of stone, be near of kin to idolatry and far from alms deeds'. The image of the Trinity was the worst of all. God commanded 'alms deed' to the needy, for they were the true image of God; God did not say, 'Let us make a piece of wood or a stone in our image and likeness' but 'Let us make a man'. If the 'rood tree', nails, spear and crown of thorns were to be adored in church, 'then were Judas's lips, if anyone could get them, a wonderful great relic'. The doubts thus expressed about the propriety of adoring the instruments of Christ's sufferings, the Cross in particular, were far from new, but had been largely quiescent since the twelfth century.

> But we pray thee, pilgrim, us to tell when thou offrest to saints' bones enshrined in any place, whether relievest thou the saint that is in bliss or the poor alms hoouse that is so wel endowed? For men be canonised, God wot how, and for to speak more plainly, true Christians suppose that the points [the cause] of that noble man that men call St Thomas were no cause of martyrdom.[31]

The two principal thrusts of this broadside were against idolatry and against the financial aspect of pilgrimage, seen as a diversion of funds from charitable and human purposes to the supposed uses of saints who, being 'in bliss', had no need of them. The criticism of Becket may be due equally to the facts that his was the most popular shrine in England and that he was seen as having died to secure clerical privilege and in opposition to royal authority. These beliefs found almost instant echoes in the testimony of individual Lollards who were arraigned before the bishops, and continued to do so for a century and more down to the Reformation.

Criticism of the actual conduct of pilgrims was central to the criticisms made by some Lollards. Summoned before Archbishop Arundel in 1407, William Thorpe averred that he did indeed believe that there were true pilgrims: they were 'travelling towards the bliss of heaven' and keeping God's commandments, and every virtuous thought, word and action was a step along the way. Non-metaphorical pilgrims, however, were typically ignorant of the commandments, of Pater Noster, Ave Maria and Creed; they spent or misspent money 'on vicious hostelers, which are oft unclean women of their bodies', offering what should go to the poor 'to rich priests who have mickle more livelihood than they need', and neglecting their needy neighbours at home. They borrowed, or even stole, money in order to go. They were accompanied by 'men and women that can well sing wanton songs' and even bagpipers, so that on arrival in a town they made more noise than the king with all his heralds and minstrels. If they were away for a month, such men and women would be 'great janglers, tale-tellers and liars' for six months afterwards.[32]

The all-but inevitable response of the ecclesiastical authorities to the Lollard challenge was to affirm the necessity of believing in the validity of pilgrimage and the proper veneration of images with greater force than had hitherto been thought necessary or even desirable. In 1409 Robert Hallum of Salisbury registered the mandate of the bishop of London to publish the constitutions against Lollardy which had been drawn up at Oxford and confirmed at the convocation of Canterbury meeting at St Paul's. These included a prohibition on all 'disputing' on the articles of the faith, 'especially concerning the adoration of the cross, images, saints and pilgrimages, and no one is to question their authority'.[33]

In 1412 William Mundy, a chapman of Wokingham, was arraigned in Hallum's court. His erroneous beliefs included 'that all who go on pilgrimage to St Thomas of Canterbury or to the cross of Boxley or to the priory of Bridlington or other such places are cursed, because he did not believe that Thomas archbishop of Canterbury was a saint in heaven, even though he was called such on earth'. William's theoretical grasp of general principles may have been a little weak, because he also said 'that he did not know whether it was permissible to make pilgrimages or not'.[34] His choice of shrines to stigmatise was an interesting one. Thomas, we have seen, was a prescribed object of abuse; John of Bridlington was newly canonised and doubtless therefore in the news; and the monks of Boxley were currently promoting their Holy Rood with some energy.

Sir John Oldcastle, socially the most conspicuous of these early Lollards, was examined before the archbishop of Canterbury in September 1413. His views on the respect that was to be paid to images were expressed with some caution, but he trenchantly maintained the opinion that salvation followed infallibly on obedience to the 'just precepts' of God and was otherwise sought in vain, even were one to travel to every corner of the world. He who obeyed God's commands 'cannot perish, even if he never in his life goes on pilgrimage, and never goes to Rome, or to Canterbury, or to Compostela, or anywhere that the common people are accustomed to go'. Oldcastle was bidden to assent to the view that pilgrimages were 'useful and necessary'. [35] Similarly, when Robert Chapell, a chaplain of the diocese of Rochester, abjured in the court of the archbishop of Canterbury in 1416, he was required to affirm 'that pilgrimages to the relics of the saints and other holy places were not prohibited nor to be rejected by catholics but are useful for the remission of sins and are rightly to be commended by the approval of the holy fathers'. In addition,

> the veneration of images of Christ or of any of the saints, whether placed in church or elsewhere, is not prohibited, nor, in the manner which the holy fathers command, does it lead to idolatry, but such images are extremely profitable for the salvation of the Christian people for this reason, that they call to mind the merits of the saints whom they represent and their appearance excites and invites the people to devotion and prayer. [36]

The implication that pilgrimage was all but obligatory, to which the authorities evidently felt themselves driven in response to subversion, may well have aroused a little unease in some quarters. In the middle of the century Reginald Pecock, bishop first of St Asaph's (1444) and then of Chichester (1450), mounted an eloquent and interesting defence of images and pilgrimage.[37] He was reluctantly prepared to concede that a given individual might choose to abstain from pilgrimages because of the abuses they brought in their train, although he wished such a person to be very sure of his facts. He did insist, however, that the church might intervene to prohibit that person from speaking out against the practice.[38] Both Pecock and Thomas More, in the corresponding parts of his *Dialogue concerning Heresies* (1529), written when Lutheran criticism was beginning to turn the Lollard trickle into something more like a flood, were keenly aware that the issue of images was at the heart of the matter.[39] Both endorsed the long-held belief that images were not merely useful to the illiterate, but possessed a superior affective power over what was merely heard or read, a power to stir the emotions and stimulate the memory. Both, also, were insistent that idolatry was not a real problem. The man (or woman) in the street had far too much sense to confuse the image with its prototype. Confronted with the objection that silly women professed a preference for Our Lady of Walsingham or Our Lady of Ipswich, More argued that they knew perfectly well that neither was actually Our Lady who stood by the Cross at the Passion.[40]

In 1313 Archbishop Greenfield of York had wondered why the Madonna venerated at Foston should be regarded as holier than any other image. A century later, such questions were coming to be associated with people of whose views, one imagines, Greenfield would hardly have approved. In these changed circumstances, Pecock identified the belief that all places were equally holy as having been particularly harmful to the popular use of images and the practice of pilgrimage.[41] The comment is an interesting one because it suggests that, on the information available to him, Pecock believed that Lollard criticism had had an impact. It is also interesting that when he quoted the Lollard 'argument' on this point, as the fourth of the fifteen he had to refute, he suggested, like Thomas Walsingham, that the heretics singled out two particular shrines to exemplify the evils they were attacking: 'Wherfore it is vein wast and idil forto trotte to Walsingham rather than to ech other place in which an ymage of marie is, and to the roode of the north dore at London rather than to ech other roode in what ever place he be.'[42] Of the importance of Our Lady of Walsingham there can be no doubt, and testamentary bequests furnish evidence of the popularity of the cross at the north door of St Paul's.

For Pecock, there was an easy answer to the question why certain images were to be regarded as holier than others: it was because God so willed it and had worked miracles through them. Thomas More echoed this view. There was evidently a fine balance to be struck between the wide availability of images and an indiscriminate egalitarianism which deprived any one of them of any special value it might be believed to possess. Pecock in fact favoured the multiplication of images, of Christ and the Virgin in particular, because of the absence of bodily relics. Images could of course fulfil their function as what he called 'rememoratif signes' without being miraculous, but individual Lollards who came to trial seem to have been generally given to a blanket condemnation of images. If no image was holy, then all were negatively equal in that respect. John Claydon, arraigned before the arch-bishop of Canterbury's court in 1415, simply said 'that images are not to be sought in pilgrimage nor should Christians bend the knee before images or kiss them or venerate them in any way'. Thomas Granter, priest of London, appearing before the same court in 1428, thought it more profitable 'to abide at home and beat the stools with their heels for it was, I said, but tree and stone that they sought'.[43]

The Lollard belief that money was ill-spent on pilgrimage can look like social and economic criticism, and to a degree it was. Different criticisms were sometimes integrated into a single polemic, as when one preacher attacked the silly woman who made an expensive pilgrimage to 'St Sithe' (Zita of Lucca) in order to find her lost keys, abandoning simple faith in the ability of Our Lord, the Virgin and the saints to help:

> as bi comune custome, and a wife lose a key of valewe of three pens, anon she wil hete to seke seynt Sithe and spende a noble or ten schilyngis in the iurney, and not onus in the yeer visite the lest bedrade Cristis quicke image by hir with a dragth of dryng. Allas! what avowe is this, to waste so myche good in veyn pilgrimage for a thing lost of so litil valewe?

The 'wife' in question was ignoring not only common sense and logic, but the poor man at her door, the true image of Christ, to whom she denied even 'a draught of drink'. [44]

The malign role of images was central to many of these arguments. In the first place there were the simple facts that many images were fraudulent and that offerings to them only enriched their already wealthy owners. There was also the finer point that the ordinary poor man was a fitter object of benefaction because a truer image of God or of Christ, a view which drew strength not only from the account of the creation of Man in Genesis but from Christ's own declaration that acts of charity to one's needy neighbour would be rewarded as if performed for Him personally. Pecock aggressively denied that the ordinary human being was in fact the true image of Christ. A true image, he claimed, must both closely resemble its prototype and be designed for that purpose and no other. A mere man only qualified as an 'image' of Christ if he hung on the cross during the performance of a mystery play. [45] The belief that the poor were fitter objects of benefaction than shrines and images had a perhaps predictable vitality. It was specifically refuted in 1535 by a Franciscan preaching at Herne Bay in Kent on Passion Sunday. At the last gasp of English pilgrimage, he maintained that

> whoever offered one penny to St Thomas's shrine, it was more meritorious than to give a noble to poor people; for one is spiritual and the other corporal. They come 200 miles, he said, to that blessed shrine and when they see the goodly jewels, how they think in their hearts 'I would to God and to that good saint I were able to give such a gift'. And by such good thoughts thousands of souls were saved. [46]

The friar's contemporary, Thomas More, believed that there was enough money and to spare both to relieve poverty and to beautify churches; much more was wasted on things of absolutely no value (an argument which strikes a chord nearly five hundred years later). [47] As for the simple woman who claimed that St Sithe had miraculously restored her keys, More evaded the attack by querying the restricted concept of miracle that, he believed, the critics entertained. He instanced the conception and birth of a healthy child to a couple who were married in St Stephen's Walbrook, 'which is not gretely famous for any myracles, but yet merely in saynt Stephen's day it is somwhat sought unto and vysyted with folkes devocyon'. The birth of a healthy child served to illustrate his point that wonderful things, which no one identified as miracles, were happening all the time. [48]

The majority of Lollards who appeared before episcopal courts seem to have played variations on a limited number of themes. This is in large part because they had to respond to a fixed range of questions, but occasionally the rather stereotyped form of the record allows an individual voice to be heard. There are some good examples among the records of the trials of East Anglian heretics in the court of the bishop of Norwich between 1428 and 1431. Simple rejection of images, and affirmation of the belief that the money spent on pilgrimage was better spent on poor people, were commonplace. The forthright Hawisia Moon roundly declared that 'all pilgrimage going servyth of nothing but oonly to yeve prieste good that be to riche and to makke gay tapsters and proude ostelers'. Some of the accused elaborated a little on their reasons for not venerating the cross: Edmund Archer said that 'every suche crosse is the signe and the tokene of Antecrist', and William Bate of Seething believed that 'no maner of worship shuld be do to the crosse whiche Crist deyed upon'. [49]

Occasionally the metaphor of life as pilgrimage reappears in Lollard confessions. Thomas Bagley, who appeared before the archbishop of Canterbury in 1431 and refused to abjure, struck a loftier note than most:

> I believe that every traveller is a pilgrim on earth; the end of his pilgrimage ought to be the celestial fatherland, to which those who observe the commands of God and attend to works of mercy are on the right way. But there are many who wander around various places, putting their hope in images, making their vows to them, asking the dead for life, beseeching the infirm for health, seeking help on the journey from that which cannot walk; such people I say are displeasing and not pleasing to God, because they put their hope in images rather than in God and thus gravely offend God in the sin of idolatry; therefore I have advised those who thus go forth on pilgrimage to avoid the sin of idolatry by seeking the living image of God and extending helping hands to his nature. [50]

Bishop Pecock numbered among his opponents those who appealed to the power of the scriptural word as the sole source of Christian authority: books were best. This was ironic, as this had been the orthodox view proclaimed by the ecclesiastical hierarchy earlier in the middle ages. Pecock clearly understood that pilgrimage involved a high degree of visual experience, and that it was precisely that which gave it much of its instructive power. The reverse association, of true belief with the written word, is hinted at in the trials of several Lollards. The chaplain John Yonge, late of the parish of the Holy Cross of the Temple in Bristol, was examined at Muchelney in October 1449 after a year's detention. He denied that pilgrimages were meritorious or necessary, asserting rather that 'every step of the pilgrims turns them towards sin.' In abjuring, he had to forswear 'English bokes of errours and heresyes'. In other respects, however, he was conservative: he debarred women from preaching and believed in the priestly power of transubstantiation.[51] In 1472 Thomas Tymbre of Lydney in Gloucestershire admitted to believing 'that the images of the saints are not to be venerated, pilgrimages to the tombs and relics of the saints not to be done, and that it is permissible for laypeople to have books of Holy Scripture translated into the English language and to read them'.[52] He was one of a group at Lydney who professed similar beliefs. Pecock's criticism of the heretical position focussed not on the permissibility of the possession of vernacular books, but on their effectiveness. The word was not only less accessible than the image, because books and people who could read them were few, but less memorable and less communicative even to those who could read. In this view a pilgrimage was not merely a journey to venerate an image, but an opportunity to see images and learn from them, as he said, the people of London did when they flocked to St catherine's College by the Tower on the saint's annual feast day. All the books about St catherine that existed in London were of little account in comparison.[53]

Occasionally a heretic singled out particular shrines for disapprobation, as William Mundy had done in 1412. John Skylan at Norwich said that 'no pilgrimage shuld be do to the Lefdy of Falsingham, the Lefday of Foulpette and to Thomme of Canterbury, ne to noon other seyntes ne images'.[54] A different regional bias was naturally displayed by Thomas Cole, arraigned with his wife Agnes at Wells on 18 January 1460. He declared:

> I have affermed and openly sayde ayenst pilrymages, as too the Trinite of Bath and other places, and have seyde that it is but wast to offre to the syed Trinite, and that I wother wherfor pilgremages serve, and in especial, in tyme of Translacioun of Seynt Osmunde I affirmed and seyd that I wolde that the weyes to Salesbury ward, on the whiche the people went on pilgremage were ful of bremmell [brambles] and thornes as eny wode is to lette theym to go thidre. Also, I have affermed and seyd ayenst the worshippyng of ymages and in dyvers wises uttered langage evils ownyng to the erys of wel disposed Cristen people.[55]

Thomas Cole was under pressure not merely to comply with the directives of ecclesiastical authority but to accept the social consensus. He had with his own eyes seen (and disapproved of) his fellow countrymen flocking to Salisbury to venerate a newy-canonised saint; he had uttered language offensive to such devout people. His is interesting testimony to the publicity which such events as St Osmund's translation received in Salisbury's wider neighbourhood.

Whether the criticisms of the heretics can help to account for the observable decline in the offerings at the major English shrines in the fifteenth century is a teasing question. It would be easy to jump to conclusions: there is the decline; there are the criticisms. The difficulties, however, are equally obvious: how is one to prove that the people who failed to come, failed to give or simply gave less were doing so because of an ideological shift against pilgrimage? How influential, in short, were the critics?

There were, in fact, several cults, such as those of Henry VI and Master John Schorne, which, whether or not they were new, seem on varied evidence, such as testamentary bequests and finds of pilgrim badges, to have been flourishing over a fairly wide area of England at the end of the fifteenth century. Promising careers such as that of Bishop Edmund Lacy at Exeter may have been denied their natural development by the Reformation. Some major churches maintained their income, or at least tried to do so, by 'diversifying'. One examination of the Hereford accounts has suggested that in addition to a continuing diversification of cults which attracted offerings, devotion to Thomas Cantilupe continued at a respectable level. With an income of about £10 a year, Cantilupe, while not in the first division of sixteenth-century English shrines, could be classed with the Holy Blood of Hailes, if below the image of St Mary in Worcester Cathedral at £40 and far below Our Lady of Walsingham at £260, these being the values recorded in the 1535 *Valor Ecclesiasticus*. Receipts may however have been dropping in the 1520s and in 1532 the cathedral authorities were worried about the level of pilgrimage.[56]

The Ripon accounts furnish a picturesque example of diversification.[57] Images proliferated in various parts of the church with their annexed collecting-boxes: among many others, there was a *Pietà*, an image of Henry VI and one of the lately popular pilgrim saint Roche, which was first mentioned in 1502–3. Already before the end of the fourteenth century, the canons were hiring out 'St Wilfrid's burnynge iron' to be used (for a fee) in the branding of cattle. In some years in the late fourteenth century this expedient brought in nothing, and in 1392–93 the return was only 18*d.*, but in 1396–97 the figure soared to 12*s.* 8*d.*, only to fall back to 8*d.* in 1399–1400. By the early sixteenth century the annual sum received usually surpassed £5; in 1520–21 (the last recorded figure) it was 107*s.* It was explained in 1503–4 that the chapter conceded the use of the *ferrum* 'to all the faithful of Christ to sign their beasts for the better preservation of them from the murrain and the diseases which afflict them'. In this same year there was a new attraction, St Wilfrid's 'Pokestone', which has been supposed to have been a 'charm stone' that was immersed in water to make cures for man and beast.

Cromwell's commissioners, touring religious houses in 1536 in search of damaging information, discovered many more such ingenious expedients, especially in the north. Among the most popular items which were rented out to local people were girdles, frequently but not solely associated with the Virgin, which were used to help in pregnancy and childbirth. Meaux Abbey possessed a 'girdle of St Bernard' which was so used, and another Yorkshire Cistercian monastery, Rievaulx, employed the girdle of St Ailred for similar purposes. At Chester, St Werburga's girdle was in demand, and at Pontefract Thomas of Lancaster's belt was good for lying-in women and his cap was used for headaches, as St Guthlac's bell was at Repton. In certain circumstances (such as childbirth) the prophylactic relic had to be made available in the domestic setting, in others the petitioner could go to the shrine, as women went to the nuns' church of Arden, not far from Rievaulx, to offer to an image of St Bride or Brigid, an ancient protectress of animals, 'for cows lost or sick'. Carlisle Cathedral, which still possessed the sword with which St Thomas was martyred, also advertised a girdle of St Bride. Not all these cults were exclusively local. The commissioners found that Kentish men were accustomed to go to Bury St Edmunds and 'to carry thence *triticum panxillum* (wheat) and wax candles which they light at the end of the field while the wheat is sown, and hope from this that neither tares nor other weeds will grow in the wheat that year'.[58]

It would be easy to dismiss these contrivances as a meeting of superstition with profiteering, as Lollards and Protestants did. The profits were not always very impressive, however, and such customs arguably had other purposes. The double movement to and from the shrine represented the continuance of an ancient tradition. For centuries the relics of the saints had been brought out from their resting-places in times of trouble for the local community, to avert plague, fire, flood or drought. In the sixteenth century these humble relics, which seem to have been much used for the relief of individual problems, had the similar effect of establishing and maintaining bonds between the shrine custodians and the wider community.

Much of this book has been devoted to local, short-haul pilgrimage. Even if is true that pilgrimage to the cathedral shrines and the great old abbeys such as Bury and St Albans was in decline, or at least was reaping a lower return, it would not necessarily follow that that there was less pilgrimage overall. It may simply have been directed to a greater variety of local destinations, like the northern shrines of the Virgin enumerated by William Ecopp of Heslerton in his will in 1472. No one of these perhaps ever equalled the pulling power that Becket had at his height, but collectively the lesser shrines may well have accounted for a great deal of energy and a respectable quantity of offerings.[59] The proliferation of images and indulgences noted earlier could point towards that conclusion, as did the observations and experiences of the reformers in the 1530s and 1540s, who certainly were not solely occupied in stripping great shrines. Such localised devotion might also shade easily into the belief, agreeable to high-minded orthodox preachers, that devotion, like charity, began at home. A great deal of evidence vividly documents the attachment of men and women on the eve of the Reformation to their local churches, and to their involvement with them in life and in death.[60] Some pilgrimages which had once attracted a wide public dwindled into small affairs of strictly local concern. In May 1537 the duke of Norfolk reported to Cromwell from Bridlington that the shrine of St John was 'of small value' and that the best course would be to let the local people have it, so that their oblations could 'come to the Kynges profite'. He observed also that Bridlington 'standythe in a faire corner of the shire adioynynge to the see, where no resorte is of strangers except such as dwellyth abowte the same that comyth to the market there'. Richard Pollard, writing a few days later, commented on the poverty of the people around Bridlington, although he had been able to find a great deal more silver, and some gold, about the shrine.[61]

Already in the mid fifteenth century, Bishop Pecock thought that Lollard criticism had had a negative impact on pilgrimage and hoped that his arguments would help to reverse the trend. One convicted Lollard early in the sixteenth century claimed that he had been deflected from an intended local pilgrimage by the persuasive language of a more senior heretic. William Baker of Cranbrook in Kent was one of several witnesses to the conversation and influence of Edward Walker of Maidstone, one of the five defendants arraigned before Archbishop Warham in 1511–12 who refused to abjure. Baker was not made of such stern stuff, and on 15 May 1511 recanted a range of heresies including disbelief in the sacrament of the altar and rejection of pilgrimage and image worship. Labour and money spent in pilgrimage, he had been prevailed upon to believe, 'ys but lost and doon in vayn'. He had not thought this before he joined in discussions, on May Day twelve years before, in Edward Walker's house in Maidstone. As a result, although he had been 'mynded to goo and offer to the roode of grace', he changed his mind 'and went not thider but gave his offeryng to a poore man'.[62]

Erasmus was aware of the prevalence of this view. According to his fictional *alter ego* Ogygius, St James was suffering from the 'new doctrine which is spread through the world'; even those who bothered to visit him gave less than formerly, 'saying that the money may be better spent upon the poor'. For her part, the Virgin was relieved no longer to be bombarded by absurd and sometimes improper requests, but it had all gone too far, and instead of being clad in gold and jewels and frequent changes of raiment she was 'scarcely covered with half a petticoat, and that eaten by the mice'.[63] The Virgin may have felt neglected, but pilgrimage to Walsingham seems still to have been fashionable among the leaders of English society on the eve of the Reformation and its popularity ensured that it would attract much of the intermittently vociferous abuse of heretics. In 1528 two Colchester men were accused of having declared that it was 'mysavoury to go on pilgrimages to Walsingham, Ipswich or elsewhere, for it is idolatry; [the images] cannot help themselves and therefore cannot help another.' In July of the same year, it was reported that Richard Fox, the parish priest of Steeple Bumstead, had held forth in the house of John Darkyn about the evils of idolatry, saying to the householder, 'Ye make a vow or a behest to go in pilgrimage to Oure Lady of Ipswich, or Walsingham, or to Canterbury and there by a candle of wax think ye do well.' To this Darkyn replied, 'Yea. How say you?', to which the subversive priest made no reply.[64] This sort of talk may have seemed wearily familiar and possibly no more seriously threatening than it had been, although there was now a new theological label that could be attached to it and a new source of intellectual inspiration for at least a few of the critics. In June 1528 the bishop of Lincoln reported that he had both Lutherans and the sweating sickness in his London house. He himself was proposing to make a pilgrimage to Walsingham. [65]

Essex dissidents may have focussed their attacks on the Virgins of Ipswich and Walsingham. The pilgrimage to the Rood of Grace at Boxley Abbey, from which William Baker of Cranbrook had been deterred, could scarcely have been more local, and there were inhabitants of Boxley itself among those examined before Archbishop Warham. For some years to come, the weight of authority was behind the Rood. Warham himself wrote to Wolsey in May 1524, referring to the pilgrims who came to Boxley 'from all parts of the realm' and the many miracles it performed; he was therefore reluctant to put the abbey under an interdict because of the abbot's debts to the king.[66] Yet within a generation of William Baker's recantation, the Rood had been exposed as the centrepiece of a profitable fraud and destroyed in so well-publicised a manner that it has been suggested that no other single incident did as much to discredit image and pilgrimage with the general public.

The story of the unmasking of the Boxley Rood was entertainingly told by the ferociously Protestant William Lambarde in 1570. [67] Having given a bare account of the foundation of Boxley in the twelfth century, he remarks:

But if I shoulde thus leave Boxley, the favourers of false and feyned Religion would laugh in their sleeves and the followers of Gods trueth might justly cry out and blame me. For, it is yet freshe in minde to bothe sides and shall (I doubt not) to the profit of the one, be continued in perpetual memorie to all posteritie, by what notable Imposture, Fraud, Iuggling and Legierdemain, the sillie lambes of Gods flocke were (not long since) seduced by the false Romish Foxes at this Abbay.

The reader is thus forewarned not to expect a dispassionate account. Lambarde recites the legend of the coming of the Rood to Boxley. An English prisoner of war in France, lacking other means to obtain his ransom, manufactured an ingeniously articulated crucifix, which

> not onely matched in comelynesse and due proportion of the partes the best of the common sort: but in straunge motion, variety of gesture and nimbleness of joints, passed al other that before had been seene, the same being able to bow down and lifte up it selfe, to shake and stirre the handes and feete, to nod the head, to rolle the eies, to wag the chaps, to bende the browes and finally to represent to the eie both the proper motion of each member of the body, and also a lively, expresse and significant shew of a well contented or displeased mind ...

Lambarde describes the uses the monks allegedly made of this remarkable image. 'If you minded to have benefit by the Roode of Grace', you had first to be shriven by one of the monks, and you were then put to the trial of the image of St Rumwold, by the common sort called Grumbold, 'the picture of a pretie boy Sainct of stone'. The supplant had to prove his (or her) purity of heart by lifting the statue; if he could not, he had to be reconfessed, 'for it was to be thought that you had concealed somewhat from your ghostly Dad'. The statue had a heavy stone base, but it could easily be raised up by a mechanism worked by the foot of the custodian, that is if the pilgrim had made a satisfactory offering. 'To such as offered faintly' it remained immovable. Lambarde goes on to sketch a circumstantial picture of the consequences:

> In so much, as many times it moved more laughter than devotion to beholde a great lubber to lift at that in vainne, which a young boy (or wench) had easily taken up before him. I omit, that chaste Virgins and honest married matrones, went oftentimes away with blushing faces, leaving (without cause) in the mindes of the lookers on, great suspicion of unleane life, and wanton behaviour: for feare of whiche note and villannie, women (of all other) stretched their purse strings and sought by liberall offering to make S. Rumwalde man their goode friend and favourer.

Whether Lambarde here is drawing on authentic testimony, or painting

an imaginative picture, his conclusion as to the motive of all this makes
sense:

> without treble oblation (that is to say) first to the Confessour, then to Sainct
> Rumwald, and lastly to the Gracious Roode, the poore Pilgrims could not assure
> themselves of any good, gained by all their labour. No more than such as goes
> to Paris-gardein, the Bel savage, or Theatre to beholde Beare baiting, Enterludes
> or Fence play, can account of any pleasant spectacle unlesse they first pay one
> pennie at the gate, another at the entrie of the Scaffolde and the thirde for a
> quiet standing.

The exposure of these contrivances by Cromwell's commisioner Geoffrey
Chambers (which Lambarde does not narrate, although he regards it as a
story still well-known) led to the denunciation of the Rood and its public
burning at St Paul's Cross on 24 February 1538.[68] How many other examples
of the kind were there? Bishop Pecock (who does not specifically mention
Boxley) was familiar with popular beliefs that images did miracles, or spoke,
or heard what was said to them or sweated.[69] He evaded the issue of
imposture by resort to a favourite argument to which he gave a more
general application: erroneous beliefs might be held about images, frauds
and fabricated miracles might sometimes occur, pilgrimages might give rise
to misbehaviour, but all this was to say no more than could be said about
any human activity, and of itself was no reason to abrogate pilgrimage or
the veneration of images. Here again More took a similar line.

Few of these images are described. Aside from the Lollards' contemptuous
generalisations about 'stocks and stones' we get little idea of medium and
style. Comments made earlier about the reception of images in the fourteenth
and fifteenth centuries are relevant here. In successive ages new artistic forms
have had the power not merely to shock but to impress with a unprecedented
'truth to nature'. In the eleventh century Bernard of Angers had reacted
uncomfortably to the new generation of images, such as those of St Gerald
of Aurillac or St Foy of Conques, which to him looked like an invitation
to idolatry. The image of St Gerald, he remarked, seemed to the peasants
who adored it to see and hear them.[70] The early figured crucifixes, such as
the cross of Gereon now in Cologne Cathedral, must have had a comparable
impact. Pecock and More were confident that the common man did not
confuse image with prototype, but they also, rightly, believed in the superior
power of images as a means of communication, and this in fact depended,
not just on psychological verities which seem to apply to most human beings
in all ages, but on the fact that most of their contemporaries saw few works
of art and did not pigeonhole them in the detached or unthinking fashion
which is possible in the age of photography, colour printing and the mass

media. Margery Kempe may have been unusually suggestible, but it is hard to think that she was alone in her emotional response to an image of Our Lady of Pity.

Such images were everywhere in England on the eve of the Reformation, nor were they easy to eradicate. In 1539 Cromwell's servant William Goldwell remarked that they still survived in many churches; they were objectionable not least because they did not represent an authentic story from scripture, 'yet to these images the people have much mind'. Goldwell also mused on some information which had been sent to Cromwell about the continued existence of a crucifix in a chapel in the north aisle of the parish church at Ashford in Kent. There was a collecting-box before it and a 'table' bearing words such as 'honour' and 'reverently' which Cromwell's informant, the priest Henry Broderick, had erased and the priests of the church had reinserted. Goldwell remarked that in his experience such free-standing crucifixes excited more 'fashions of idolatry' than those which stood on the roodloft over the entrance to the chancel.[71]

It seems highly probable that many of the miracles which were attributed to such images and crucifixes were not old-style miracles of healing, but phenomena (in the strict sense of that word) of precisely the kind that the monks of Boxley were accused of fabricating: blinking, nodding, smiling, weeping, sweating. If healing miracles could be generated from psychosomatic causes, so much the more could subjective reactions help to produce such kinetic wonders, and clearly the custodians of some shrines at least were not averse to helping the process along. The monks of Boxley (and others) may simply have overdone things and sought to guarantee effects which might have been more safely left to imagination, atmosphere and clever lighting. Erasmus portrays Ogygius entering into the spirit of the thing at both Santiago and Walsingham. 'When I made my offering', St James 'appeared to smile and slightly bend his head, and at the same time bestowed this scallop shell'. This certainly suggests contrivance. At Walsingham, when Ogygius had been shown the relic of the Virgin's milk and addressed a pious prayer to it, 'the holy Milk seemed to leap a little and the Eucharist shone somewhat brighter'. Now was the moment for the attendant to proffer the little slab on which he collected the offerings.[72]

In the 1530s criticisms of pilgrimage, which were in essence already familiar to Pecock, took on new life in the polemic of preachers, such as Hugh Latimer, whose moment seemed to have come. A Cambridge graduate who had fallen foul of authority during the 1520s, Latimer stirred up a hornet's nest with his preaching at Bristol in Lent 1533, which, according to one of his opponents, gave great offence to the people. He himself commented sardonically that Dr Edward Powell, dean of Salisbury, who preached against him, had difficulty in deriving pilgrimages to Master John Schorne, Walsingham and St Anne in the Wood (that is, at Brislington outside Bristol) from St Matthew's Gospel.[73] Bishop Pecock had opposed the claim that pilgrimage was nowhere enjoined in scripture with the counter-argument that it was nowhere forbidden in scripture; he had also, as we saw earlier, objected to the heretical criticism of the veneration of one image rather than another. In his Convocation Sermon, delivered in the summer of 1536, Latimer returned to this old charge: 'Do you think that this preferring of picture to picture, image to image, is the right use and not rather the abuse of images?'[74] In fact, as the event would show, for the more radical reformers, an image had only to exist to be an incitement to idolatry and abuse; a series of steps led from the abolition of pilgrimages by statute in 1536 and the stripping of shrines to the destruction even of some images to which (local people claimed) there had never been any tradition of pilgrimage or offering.

Latimer became bishop of Worcester in 1535. In his Convocation Sermon, preached in the summer of the following year, he spoke of the possibility of imposture in respect both of images and of relics. Whether or not they were fraudulent, people consumed time, effort and money in seeking them out. At the very least, pilgrims were guilty of excess, and he thought people and clergy alike to blame for the indiscriminate use of vows. He cited old legislation which inhibited women, especially, from making vows without the consent of their husbands and the advice of their priests, and concluded that to enforce this directive would be to abolish pilgrimage: 'For they that restrain making vows for going of pilgrimage restrain also pilgrimage, seeing that for the most part it is seen that few go on pilgrimage but vow-makers and such as by promise bind themselves to go.' It was his belief, also, that 'this the common people of England think to be going on pilgrimage, to go to some dead and notable image out of town, that is to say, far from their house'. That the appeal of going 'out of town' (even if in fact it was not all that far) was the appeal of a change of scene, a holiday, is implicit rather than explicit, but he went on to complain of 'the solemn and nocturnal bacchanals, the prescript miracles that are done upon certain days in the west part of England'.[75] The abolition of pilgrimage would clearly serve to restore both theological propriety and a wholesome social discipline. That there was particular anxiety about the conduct of women wandering about away from home is unsurprising. Censorious preachers drew attention to the paradox that shrines of the Virgin provided female pilgrims with opportunities for the most unvirginal conduct: 'at her pylgrymages be made many a foul metynge'. One, as reported by Thomas More, advised husbands either to go with their wives to Our Lady of Willesden or to keep them at home. This was not the only testimony to the bad reputation of this shrine.[76]

The doomed shrines and objects were innumerable, although some attracted more notice than others, none more than the Rood of Boxley and the Holy Blood of Hailes. If the Rood represented the fraudulent image which attracted pilgrims, the Holy Blood represented the fraudulent relic. In 1533 Latimer had marvelled 'to see how the pilgrims come out of the west country ... chiefly to see the Blood of Hayles'. His objection to the pilgrimage was more far-reaching than the belief that the relic itself was bogus:

> And they believe verily that it is the very blood that was in Christ's body, shed upon the mount of Calvary for our salvation, and that the sight of it with their bodily eye doth certify them, and putteth them out of doubt, that they be in clean life and in state of salvation without spot of sin, which doth bolden them to many things. For you would wonder, if you should commune with them both coming and going, what faiths they have: for as for forgiving their enemies, and reconciling their Christian brethren, they cannot away withal; for the sight of that blood doth requite them for the time.[77]

This was, in essence, the criticism that Langland had made of the theological ignoramus Greed.

The last abbot of Hailes, Stephen Sagar, was Cromwell's man. Early in 1538 he expressed cautious and politic scepticism about the authenticity of the relic. Because it had been reputed miraculous for so long, it was shown to those who asked for it, but he was reluctant to continue the exhibition in case he should be accused of having 'renewed' it with drake's blood. He swore that he had never done so, and that an old monk who had been custodian of it for nearly forty years would say the same. A commission of enquiry was appointed, and the results emboldened Sagar to ask for the permission Cromwell was only too eager to give, to do away with the relic and its shrine, 'every styck & stone'. Latimer was among those who examined the Holy Blood, pronouncing it to have 'a certain unctious moistness', and the official word, publicised at Paul's Cross in a sermon by the bishop of Rochester on 24 November 1538, was that it was in fact 'honey clarified and coloured with saffron'.[78] Erasmus would not have been surprised: Ogygius at Walsingham acknowledged that the Virgin's milk, which was enclosed in crystal, was dried up, as was only natural since it was fifteen hundred years old: 'You would say it was ground chalk, mixed with white of egg.'[79]

As bishop of Worcester, Latimer became closely acquainted with one of the leading representatives of another important class of objects of devotion. The Virgin Mary had for centuries had an important presence at Worcester

Cathedral, and in recent years her image received 'phenomenal offerings', of money and wax, from pilgrims.[80] In June 1538 Latimer expressed the hope that Cromwell

> will bestow our great Sibyll to some good purpose *ut pereat memoria cum sonitu.* She hath been the devil's instrument to bring many, I fear, to eternal fire; now she herself, with her old sister of Walsingham, her young sister of Ipswich, with their other two sisters of Doncaster and Penrysse [Penrith], would make a jolly muster in Smithfield. They would not be all day in burning.[81]

In July of the previous year Thomas Emans had been accused of attempting to revive devotion to Our Lady of Worcester, who had been stripped of her accumulated finery, by entering the chapel, kissing the image and saying to the people, 'Ye that be disposed to offer, the figure is no worse than it was before and the lucre and the profit of this towne is decayed through this'. The latter point, at least, Latimer himself acknowledged. In October 1538 he reported to Cromwell on the poverty of his cathedral city: 'By reason of their Lady, they have been given to much idleness. Now she is gone, they be turned to laboriousness and so from ladyness to godliness.' Nonetheless, there was currently difficulty in maintaining the school, bridge and walls.[82] The fame of this particular image was sufficient for it to be mentioned, along with the Rood of Boxley and the Blood of Hailes, in an official defence of the Reformation which was circulated early in 1539. According to this account, the Lady of Worcester had been revealed, when her ornaments were removed, as 'the similitude of a bishop, almost 10 feet long'.[83]

Latimer had a checklist of the images of the Virgin which seemed to him most notorious; but there were many more which occupied the attentions of the reformers. John Husee reported to Lady Lisle early in 1538 on the removal not only of the Blood of Hailes but of Our Lady of Southwick, near Southampton, and St Saviour (at Bermondsey).[84] On 17 September 1538, Thomas Cromwell's emissary Dr London informed his master that he had just 'pulled down the image of our ladye at Caversham, whereunto wasse great pilgremage' and which was covered with silver plate. He had also 'pullyd down the place sche stode in, with all other ceremonyes, as lightes, schrowdes, crowchys, and imagies of wax, hangyng abowt the chapell, and have defacyd the same thorowly in exchuyng of any farther resortt thedyr'. Caversham, near Reading, belonged to the Augustinian priory of Notley, in Buckinghamshire, and a canon of Notley was warden of the church, taking the offerings for his living. According to Dr London, he exhibited some 'pretty relykes' to supplement the image of the Virgin, including 'the holy dager that kylled kinge Henry', an ingenious exploitation of the popular cult at Windsor, not far distant. London sent the unfortunate canon home to Notley and fastened the doors of the chapel. In another letter, he added the detail that, while he was at work, as many as a dozen people came in 'with imagies of wexe'. He discovered also that the canon had taken away with him 'the principal relic of idolatry in England', to wit, 'an angel with one wing that brought to Caversham the spear's head that pierced our Saviour's side upon the Cross'. London had taken steps to recover it.[85]

Whatever Dr London's estimate of the one-winged angel, Thomas Becket was in a class by himself. The shrine at Canterbury was demolished in September 1538 and its riches, which included the Regale, the great ruby given by Louis VII of France over 350 years before, were carted off to enrich the king. Dr Layton, one of the foremost of Cromwell's lieutenants, presided over the destruction. So much is beyond dispute, but the fate of Becket's remains is another matter, and the debate on this issue is still not closed.[86] An optimistic minority believes that they were in fact saved and hidden, as Cuthbert's were at Durham. Cuthbert disconcerted Dr Leigh and Dr Henley, as they set about despoiling his shrine, with the same weapon that had helped to assure him his reputation for sanctity, his bodily incorruption. Observing that his bones could not easily be 'cast down', because they were still held together by 'sinews and skin', the commissioners sent to London for further instructions, and the saint was subsequently reburied 'in the ground under the same place where his shrine was exalted'.[87] The majority view of Becket's fate is that his bones were exhumed and burned on Henry VIII's orders. This was being reported at Rome by late October 1538. The great reformer Philip Melanchthon, at about the same time, had learned that 'superstitious pilgrimages' had been abolished in England, that the monument of St Thomas had been destroyed and the image of Our Lady of Walsingham and others overthrown. The bishop of Tarbes, early in December, reported that the pope's nuncio was pressing for vengeance for the relics of both St Thomas and St Edward, although there was no reference to St Edward in the papal bull which in December repeated the allegation that Becket's bones had been burned and scattered.[88]

It was evidently perceived that the charge was a damaging one, and an official version of events was included in the defence of royal policy mentioned earlier. Here it was maintained that the body had simply been disposed of where it could 'cause no superstition'. All that had been burned was a head which had been separately exhibited, and which was judged to be surplus to requirements, as the authentic skeleton was complete with its head. If this head, which was 'but a feigned fiction', had been burned, 'was therefore St Thomas's burnt? Assuredly it concludeth not'. Other relics, such as St Swithun's, had been safely stowed away, secretly, 'as some say the body of Moses was hidden, lest the Jews should fall to idolatry'. If Becket was, in fact, subjected to a unique degree of savagery, it was not necessarily because his shrine was still, in 1538, uniquely popular, but because he himself represented everything that the king found most intolerable: resistance to the crown and loyalty to Rome.

We cannot certainly know how many of the English people welcomed these transformations, how many deplored and lamented them, and how many were largely indifferent. There were those who made so bold as to preach publicly that the current madness would pass and that the people should continue to venerate saints and perform pilgrimages as they had done in the past. In August 1538, sundry persons were questioned at Salisbury about rumours that an angel had appeared to the king and instructed him to perform a pilgrimage to St Michael's Mount, which Isabel Nowell, a widow of the town, had greeted with rejoicing as a sign that pilgrimages would soon resume.[89] Archbishop Cranmer was to discover in his own diocese in 1543 a rich mixture of iconoclastic Bible-reading radicalism, resolute conservatism and sheer perplexity on the part of clergy and laity alike.[90]

There are contradictory strands in the evidence, which may point to a greater variability, in and after the fifteenth century, in the religious behaviour of groups and individuals. The proliferation of images and indulgences might indeed suggest, as a recent examination of the figures for offerings at the 'cathedral shrines' has done, that the fourteenth century was the heyday.[91] Pilgrimage did not exist in a world of its own, and in the plague-ridden second half of the fourteenth century, peculiar economic circumstances combined to give many individual members of a reduced population greater purchasing power than they had ever had, together with very considerable anxieties about their future in this world and the next. The fifteenth-century decline in offerings at the major English shrines was gradual, but by the early sixteenth century it was moving in the reverse direction to the level of population, for that was recovering from the effects of the plague years. As an influence on this movement, hostile criticism, partly provoked by the very popularity of pilgrimage and the amount that was spent on it, may have been no more significant in the fifteenth century (though possibly no less) than a gradual accompanying shift on the part of many individuals towards more internalised styles of piety. Perhaps the half-way house was a growing preoccupation with the domestic, the local and the small-scale. How far, we may wonder, had the pilgrims come who must have been disconcerted to find Dr London demolishing the shrine at Caversham? We are of course fated never to know what further developments, what new cycle, might have begun had it not been for the needs and ambitions of Henry VIII. The critics were destined to obtain the upper hand, in dramatic fashion, but the speed and the scale of their triumph could probably not have been foreseen when Edward Walker, who had persuaded William Baker not to make his pilgrimage to Boxley Abbey, was relinquished to the secular arm in October 1511.

Notes

Notes to Introduction

1. For one recent reconstruction see J. Ravenglass, *In the Steps of Chaucer's Pilgrims* (London, 1989).
2. *The Tale of Beryn*, ed. F. J. Furnivall (*Early English Text Society*, extra series, 105, 1887).
3. M. Dillon, *Pilgrims and Pilgrimage in Ancient Greece* (London, 1997), p. xviii.
4. *The Book of Margery Kempe*, ed. S. B. Meech and H. E. Allen (*Early English Text Society*, 212, 1940), p. 200.
5. S. M. Bhardwaj, *Hindu Places of Pilgrimage in India: A Study in Cultural Geography* (Berkeley, 1973) pp. 158–59, 162.
6. *Selections from English Wycliffite Writings*, ed. A. Hudson (revised edn, Toronto, 1997), p. 87.
7. Quoted by J. Nicholls and J. Taylor, *Bristol Past and Present* (3 vols, Bristol 1881–82), ii, p. 124.
8. For a brief treatment of this subject see D. Webb, *Pilgrims and Pilgrimage in the Medieval West* (London, 1999), pp. 52–63.
9. On indulgences in general see N. Paulus, *Geschichte des Ablasses im Mittelalter vom Ursprunge bis zur Mitte des 14. Jahrhunderts* (2 vols, Paderborn, 1922); on the status of crusaders, J. A. Brundage, *Medieval Canon Law and the Crusader* (Madison, Wisconsin, 1969).
10. R. M. Serjeantson and H. I. Longdon, 'The Parish Churches and Religious Houses of Northamptonshire: Their Dedications, Altars, Images and Lights', *Archaeological Journal*, 70 (1913), pp. 46–47.
11. *CIPM*, 13, p. 358.

Notes to Chapter 1: Beginnings

1. For the subjects briefly treated in this paragraph and the next, see B. Cunliffe, *Roman Bath* (London, 1995); A. Woodward and P. Leach, *The Uley Shrines: Excavation of a Ritual Complex on West Hill, Uley, Gloucestershire, 1977–9* (London, 1993); A. Woodward, *Shrines and Sacrifice* (London , 1992); M. Henig, *Religion in Roman Britain* (London, 1984); C. Thomas, *Christianity in Roman Britain to AD 500* (London, 1981).

2. References are to the translation by Bertram Colgrave (Oxford, 1994), originally published with the Latin text of the *History* (Oxford, 1969).
3. Translated by M. Winterbottom in *The Ruin of Britain and Other Works* (London 1978). For the disputed dating of this work see the remarks of M. E. Jones, *The End of Roman Britain* (Ithaca, New York, 1996), pp. 43–47.
4. Bede, i, c. 7, pp. 18–19. Gildas' account is in *The Ruin of Britain*, pp. 19–20. Gildas also identifies two other Romano-British martyrs, Aaron and Julius of Caerleon, of whom nothing more is known.
5. Thomas, *Christianity in Roman Britain*, pp. 47–50, 180; W. Levison, 'St Alban and St Albans', *Antiquity*, 15 (1941), pp. 337–59; M. Biddle, 'Alban and the Anglo-Saxon Church', in *Cathedral and City: St Albans Ancient and Modern*, ed. R. Runcie (London, 1977) pp. 23–42.
6. Bede, i, c. 26, p. 41. It has been suggested that Bede wrongly identified St Martin's as the church used by Bertha: see Thomas, *Christianity in Roman Britain*, pp. 170–74, and, on continuity of Christian worship at Canterbury, N. Brooks, *The Early History of the Church of Canterbury* (London, 1984), pp. 16–21. See also R. Gem, ed., *St Augustine's Abbey, Canterbury* (London, 1997).
7. Brooks, *Early History of the Church at Canterbury*, p. 20.
8. Bede, i, c. 30, pp. 56–57.
9. N. J. Higham, *The Kingdom of Northumbria, AD 350–1100* (Stroud, 1993), p. 107, citing B. Hope-Taylor, *Yeavering: An Anglo-British Centre of Early Northumbria* (London, 1977).
10. T. M. Charles-Edwards, 'The Social Background to Irish *Peregrinatio*', *Celtica*, 11 (1976), pp. 43–59.
11. Bede, iii, c. 27, p. 161.
12. Bede, iii, c. 8, p. 122.
13. Bede, iv, c. 23, p. 210.
14. Bede, iv, c. 3, p. 178; v, cc. 91–10, pp. 247–51.
15. *Memorials of Saint Dunstan*, ed. W. Stubbs (*RS*, 63), pp. 10–11, 74–75.
16. Bede, v, c. 5, p. 180; c. 7, pp. 244–45.
17. Bede, v, c. 19, pp. 267–68.
18. The phrase is Clare Stancliffe's: 'Kings who Opted Out', in *Ideal and Reality in Frankish and Anglo-Saxon Society: Studies Presented to J. M. Wallace-Hadrill*, ed. P. Wormald, D. Bullough and R. Collins (Oxford, 1983), pp. 154–76.
19. *Bedae Venerabilis Opera*, iii (*Corpus Christianorum Series Latina*, 122), pp. 93–94. For a translation of this passage, see Webb, *Pilgrims and Pilgrimage*, pp. 28–29.
20. B. Colgrave, ed., *Eddius Stephanus' Life of St Wilfrid* (Cambridge, 1927). For another translation see *The Age of Bede*, ed. D. H. Farmer, revised edition (Harmondsworth 1983), pp. 105–82.
21. Bede, iv, c. 23, p. 212.
22. Bede, v, cc. 15–17, pp. 262–66.
23. This memoir, entitled *Hodoepericon*, was translated by C. H. Talbot in *The Anglo-Saxon Missionaries in Germany* (London, 1954). The translation has been

several times reprinted, most recently in *Soldiers of Christ: Saints and Saints' Lives from Late Antiquity and the Early Middle Ages*, ed. T. F. X. Noble and T. Head (London, 1995), pp. 141–64.

24. Bede, iv, c. 6, p. 183

25. Bede, iv, c. 10, pp. 188–89; iv, c. 19, pp. 204–5; c. 30, p. 230.

26. Bede, iv, c. 3, pp. 178–79.

27. A. Thacker, 'Lindisfarne and the Origins of the Cult of St Cuthbert', in *St Cuthbert: His Cult and his Community to AD 1200*, ed. G. Bonner, D. Rollason and C. Stancliffe (Woodbridge, 1989), pp. 103–22. For text and translation of the *Lives*, see B. Colgrave, ed., *Two Lives of St Cuthbert* (Cambridge, 1940); Bede's prose life is also translated in *The Age of Bede*, ed. Farmer.

28. *The Age of Bede*, pp. 95–96. Circumambulation is a common feature of pilgrimage cultures, as at Mecca and in Hinduism, and is known to have been practised at Irish hermitages: M. Herity, 'Early Irish Hermitages in the Light of the *Lives* of Cuthbert', in *St Cuthbert: His Cult and his Community*, especially pp. 53–56. A similar ritual was enacted by a youth from a neighbouring monastery whose paralysis was relieved when he put on the shoes in which Cuthbert had been buried.

29. See the essays in *Oswald: Northumbrian King to European Saint*, ed. C. Stancliffe and E. Cambridge (Stamford, 1995), especially A. Thacker, '*Membra Disjecta*: The Division of the Body and the Diffusion of the Cult'.

30. Bede, iii, c. 2, pp. 111–13.

31. Bede, iii, cc. 9–10, pp. 124–26.

32. A. Thacker, '*Membra Disjecta*', in *Oswald: Northumbrian King to European Saint*, esp. pp 102–3.

33. M. Henig, *Religion in Roman Britain*, pp. 43, 18–19, 169–70.

34. For a general account see J. Marsden, *The Fury of the Northmen: Saints, Shrines and Sea-Raiders in the Viking Age* (London, 1996).

Notes to Chapter 2: Saints and Conquerors

1. *GP*, p. 202.

2. *Vita Oswini Regis*, ed. J. Raine, *Miscellanea Biographica* (SS, 8, 1838), pp. 1–59.

3. *Inventio*, although often represented as an unexpected event prompted by divine signs such as visions, could be a carefully stage-managed and premeditated occasion, used to enhance the authority of the community, bishop, abbot or ruler responsible for it.

4. *GP*, p. 306; P. Hayward, 'The *Miracula Inventionis Beate Mylburge Virginis* Attributed to "the Lord Ato, Cardinal Bishop of Ostia"', *English Historical Review*, 114 (1999), pp. 543–73. There is a translation, based on a faulty text, in A. J. M. Edwards, 'An Early Twelfth-Century Account of the Translation of St Milburga', *Transactions of the Shropshire Archaeological Society*, 57 (1961–64), pp. 134–51.

5. D. W. Rollason, 'Lists of Saints' Resting-Places in Anglo-Saxon England',

Anglo-Saxon England, 7 (1978), pp. 61–93. The *Secgan* and other texts were published by F. Liebermann, *Die Heiligen Englands* (Hanover, 1889).

6. *The Peterborough Chronicle of Hugh Candidus*, ed. W. T. Mellows (London, 1949), p. 64.

7. S. J. Ridyard, '*Condigna Veneratio*: Post-Conquest Attitudes to the Saints of the Anglo-Saxons', *Anglo-Norman Studies*, 9, *Proceedings of the Battle Conference 1986*, pp. 179–206; A. Williams, *The English and the Norman Conquest* (Woodbridge, 1995), chapter 6; P. Hayward, 'Translation-Narratives in Post-Conquest Hagiography and English Resistance to the Norman Conquest', *Anglo-Norman Studies*, 21, *Proceedings of the Battle Conference 1998*, pp. 67–93 ; J. Crook, *The Architectural Setting of the Cult of Saints in the Early Christian West, c. 300– c. 1200* (Oxford, 2000), pp. 176–81.

8. *GP*, p. 322. He did not even wish to transcribe the names of the saints, for they had 'a barbarian ring (*barbarum quiddam strident*)'.

9. *Hermanni Archidiaconi Liber de Miraculis Sancti Eadmundi*, in *Memorials of St Edmund's Abbey*, ed. T. Arnold (3 vols, RS, 96), i, pp. 26–103

10. *Symeonis Monachi Opera Omnia*, ed. T. Arnold (2 vols, RS, 75);

11. *Liber Eliensis*, ed. E. O. Blake (*CS*, third series, 92).

12. See Hayward, 'Translation Narratives', and the further references given there. Several of Goscelin's lives were gathered together by J. P. Migne in *Patrologia Latina*, 155 (reproducing the texts already published in the relevant volumes of *Acta Sanctorum*). For the Sherborne connection, see C. H. Talbot, 'The Life of Saint Wulsin of Sherborne by Goscelin', *Revue Bénédictine*, 69 (1959), pp. 68–85.

13. R. W. Southern, *Saint Anselm and his Biographer* (Cambridge, 1966). When the monks of Glastonbury claimed to possess St Dunstan's relics, Eadmer asked sarcastically why they had not hired 'some foreigner, one of those experienced and knowledgeable men from beyond the sea, who would have invented some likely lie on such an important matter'. It is likely that he was referring to Goscelin (Southern, p. 232).

14. See the biographical outline and list of Osbert's works in *The Letters of Osbert of Clare, Prior of Westminster*, ed. E. W. Williamson (Oxford, 1929).

15. *Historians of the Church of York*, ed. J. Raine (3 vols, RS, 71), i, p. 452.

16. *Three Eleventh-Century Anglo-Latin Saints' Lives*, ed. R. C. Love (Oxford, 1996), p. 72. On this *Life*, see Hayward, 'Translation Narratives', pp. 73–77.

17. *GP*, p. 309; see also p. 174, with reference to St Edburga. Goscelin's life of Werburga is in *Patrologia Latina*, 155, cols 93–110.

18. *GP*, p. 27.

19. For observations on Dunstan's attitude to saints' cults, see A. Thacker, 'Cults at Canterbury: Relics and Reform under Dunstan and his Successors', in *St Dunstan: His Life, Times and Cult*, ed. N. Ramsay, M. Sparks and T. Tatton-Brown (Woodbridge, 1992), pp. 22145.

20. For a discussion and typology of eleventh and twelfth-century miracles, performed both at and away from the saint's burial place, see P.-A. Sigal, *L'homme et le miracle dans la France médiévale, XIe-XIIe siècle* (Paris, 1985).

21. Oswald himself was active in the manipulation of relics for the benefit of the religious communities with which he was associated: A. Thacker, 'Saint Making and Relic Collecting by Oswald and his Communities', in *St Oswald of Worcester: Life and Influence,* ed. N. Brooks and C. Cubitt (London, 1996), pp. 244–68.

22. *Historians of the Church of York,* i, pp. 452, 472, 475.

23. Eadmer, *Miracula Sancti Oswaldi Archiepiscopi,* in *Historians of the Church of York,* ii, pp. 41–59; Crook, *Architectural Setting of the Cult of Saints,* pp. 165–66.

24. Thacker, 'Saint-Making and Relic-Collecting', p. 255.

25. *GP,* pp. 163–64.

26. A very incomplete text was published, together with a later version by Goscelin, among Goscelin's works in *Patrologia Latina,* 155, cols 57–62. The missing portions were supplied by E. P. Sauvage, 'Sancti Swithuni Wintoniensis episcopi translatio et miracula', *AB,* 4 (1885), pp. 367–410. A new edition of Lantfredus and other early sources for Swithun is in preparation by Michael Lapidge. For the Anglo-Saxon shrine, see Crook, *Architectural Setting of the Cult of Saints,* pp. 163–64.

27. In a letter to the monks of Winchester introducing his account of the miracles Lantfredus further admitted that, although the fame of Swithun's miracles was diffused all over Europe, he knew of none that he had done in his lifetime: *Memorials of Saint Dunstan, Archbishop of Canterbury,* ed. W. Stubbs (*RS,* 63), pp. 369–70.

28. *Patrologia Latina,* 155, cols 65–66.

29. S. Ridyard, *The Royal Saints of Anglo-Saxon England* (Cambridge, 1988), pp. 111–14.

30. Edburga's life was later written by Osbert of Clare for the monks of Pershore, where some of her relics were taken later in the tenth century. It is printed in Ridyard, *Royal Saints,* pp. 259–308. Osbert suggested that Edburga and Swithun alternated between cooperation and competition in the performance of cures at Winchester. The translation, however, diverted 'innumerable' pilgrims to Pershore; a hundred cures were done there within a year. The nuns of Winchester lamented that the saint was not performing for them as she had once done, and went barefoot to Pershore to implore her not to desert them; as a result, God benevolently redressed the balance. According to William of Malmesbury, Edburga in his time was doing more miracles at Pershore than elsewhere: *GP,* p. 298.

31. William of Malmesbury later knew of Elgiva's wonder-working, which he himself celebrated in verse, and he also knew that she had been joined at Shaftesbury by her murdered grandson St Edward, by whose name the church came subsequently to be known: *GP,* p. 187.

32. Translated by F. Shaw, *Osbern's Life of Alfege* (London, 1999).

33. D. Rollason, 'Goscelin of Canterbury's Account of the Translation and Miracles of St Mildrith (BHL 5961/4): An Edition with Notes', *Medieval Studies,* 48 (1986), pp. 139–210. See also R. Sharpe, 'The Date of St Mildreth's Translation from Minster-in-Thanet to Canterbury', *Medieval Studies,* 53 (1991), pp. 349–54.

34. R. Gem, ed., *St Augustine's Abbey* (London, 1997) gives a succinct account.
35. A. Thacker, 'Cults at Canterbury'. All the *Lives* and other materials cited here are to be found in *Memorials of St Dunstan* (*RS*, 63). For the prayer see p. 440. On 'B', see M. Lapidge, 'B and the *Vita S. Dunstani*', in *St Dunstan: His Life, Times and Cult*, pp. 247–59.
36. *Memorials*, pp. 128–29; Thacker, 'Cults at Canterbury', p. 224.
37. *Memorials*, pp. 69–161. On Lanfranc's attitude to the English saints, see the concise summary by Crook, *The Architectural Setting of the Cult of the Saints*, pp. 178–81.
38. *Memorials*, pp. 130–32.
39. *Memorials*, pp. 134–36.
40. *Memorials*, pp. 136–38.
41. The related exchange of letters between Archbishop Warham and the abbot of Glastonbury is in *Memorials*, pp. 426–39.
42. Canterbury here was the biter bit, for Eadmer, who roundly condemned the pretensions of the Glastonbury monks, defended Canterbury's claims to the relics of St Wilfrid, allegedly brought there by Archbishop Odo, that is before 959, after the desolation of Ripon by the Danes: *Historians of the Church of York* (*RS*, 71), i, pp. 223–26. Raine reviews the controversy, pp. xliii–xlviii; William of Malmesbury was aware of it (*GP*, pp. 22, 244). As a precaution against counter-claims Eadmer said that Odo left *some* of the remains at Ripon. The abbot of Glastonbury in 1508 similarly conceded that Canterbury might still have the smaller bones of St Dunstan.
43. *Memorials*, pp. 83–84.
44. *Memorials*, pp. 421–22. It is equally to be inferred from this passage that the custom had fallen into disuse, which it might well have done in the uncertain period after the fire at Canterbury in 1067, when Lanfranc temporarily stored the bodies of his predecessors first in the oratory of the Virgin and then in the refectory.
45. *GP*, p. 317.
46. *GA*, i, pp. 12–18.
47. *GA*, i, pp. 38–39.
48. *GA*, i, p. 51. The Ely claim to Alban stemmed from the belief that Abbot Alfric had taken them there for safekeeping from the Danes when a fresh Danish invasion was feared on the death of Cnut; the St Albans claim was that he had only hidden them (*Gesta*, pp. 34–35). The disputes between Canterbury and Glastonbury about the possession of Dunstan's relics, and between Canterbury and Ripon over St Wilfrid's, are comparable.
49. *Memorials of St Edmund's Abbey*, i, p. 28.
50. *Memorials of St Edmund's Abbey*, i, pp. 49–50.
51. A. Thacker, 'Saint-Making and Relic-Collecting', pp. 258–59. The transaction helped Ramsey to strengthen its hold on a group of properties of which the manor of Slepe itself was the chief.
52. Goscelin's *Life* is in *Patrologia Latina*, 155, cols 79–90, but the text of the

miracles is incomplete. They are given in *Chronicon Abbatiae Rameseiensis*, ed. W. D. Macray (*RS*, 83), pp. lix-lxxxiv.

53. *Chronicon Abbatiae Rameseiensis*, pp. lxxi-lxxii.

54. *GP*, p. 320.

55. His activity was recorded in the history of the abbey which was probably compiled by Prior Dominic early in the twelfth century. Dominic wrote *Lives* of both St Egwin and St Odulf, and possibly also of St Wistan, and may have been the first compiler of the history of Evesham. All of these works were included in a manuscript compiled by Abbot Thomas of Marlborough early in the thirteenth century, and are published in *Chronicon Abbatiae de Evesham*, ed. W. D. Macray (*RS*, 29); see J. C. Jennings, 'The Writings of Prior Dominic of Evesham', *English Historical Review*, 77 (1962), pp. 298–304.

56. *Chronicon Abbatiae de Evesham*, p. 83.

57. *Chronicon Abbatiae Rameseiensis*, pp. 149–50; *Chronicon Abbatiae de Evesham*, pp. 36–38. Elfward became bishop of London in 1034 but retained control of Evesham.

58. *Chronicon Abbatiae de Evesham*, pp. 335–36, 55–65.

59. Dominic's *Life* was based on one written not long after 1000 by Byrhtferth, the monk of Ramsey who also wrote the *Life* of St Oswald: Thacker, 'Saint-Making and Relic-Collecting', pp. 260–61; M. Lapidge, 'Byrhtferth and the *Vita Ecgwini*', *Medieval Studies*, 41 (1979), pp. 331–53.

60. *Chronicon Abbatiae de Evesham*, p. 15.

61. *Chronicon Abbatiae de Evesham*, pp. 50–51.

62. The history of the church is summarised in the introduction to *The Waltham Chronicle*, ed. L. Watkins and M. Chibnall (Oxford, 1994). The apse had a simple ambulatory without radiating chapels, of a type rare in England, which left room for processions. 'Bubble' chapels, one of them for the cross, were added a little later in the century. In 1177 the secular canons of Waltham were replaced by Augustinians, as part of Henry II's reparations for the death of Becket.

63. See the essays by E. Cambridge and G. Bonner in *St Cuthbert: His Cult and his Community*, pp. 367–95.

64. For Cuthbert at Durham, see *Anglo-Norman Durham, 1093–1193*, ed. D. Rollason, M. Harvey and M. Prestwich (Woodbridge, 1994); V. Tudor, 'The Misogyny of Saint Cuthbert', *Archaeologia Aeliana*, fifth series, 12 (1984), pp. 157–67; Tudor, 'The Cult of St Cuthbert in the Twelfth Century: The Evidence of Reginald of Durham', in *St Cuthbert: His Cult and his Community*, pp. 457–67.

65. *GP*, pp. 323–24; *Liber Eliensis*, pp. 58–61.

66. E. G. Whatley, *The Saint of London: The Life and Miracles of St Erkenwald, Text and Translation* (*Medieval and Renaissance Texts and Studies*, 58 (Binghamton, New York, 1989). William of Malmesbury's references are in *GP*, pp. 142, 144.

67. D. Bethell, 'The Miracles of St Ithamar', *AB*, 89 (1971), pp. 421–37. Bede's brief references to Ithamar are in the *History*, iii, c. 14, p. 131; c. 20, p. 143.

68. *Historians of the Church of York*, i, pp. 239–60.

69. *Historians of the Church of York*, i, 261–347.

70. Bede refers to Aldhelm in the *History*, v, c. 18, pp. 266–67, treating him as a scholar rather than as a saint.

71. *GP*, p. 390.

72. *GP*, pp. 407–9.

73. *GP*, pp. 422–24, 433. Aldhelm's arm performed a miracle at Salisbury when carried in procession on Ascension Day.

74. *GP*, p. 430.

75. 'Goscelin's Account', pp. 186-87. It is not easy to be sure which church the merchant proposed to visit. The best candidate seems to be St Margaret's at Cliffe, although this is seventeen miles, not twelve, from Canterbury. The church gave its name to the settlement, which is mentioned for the first time in Domesday Book, shortly before the time at which Goscelin was writing. It belonged to the canons of St Martin at Dover, and was rebuilt around 1140 on a magnificent scale, with an elaborate west door and a spacious chancel. Rollason assumes that the merchant's destination was *on* Barham Down, and that it must therefore have been the church of Womenswold, the only one in that area dedicated to the martyr. The text seems to admit the possibility that the merchant was *crossing* (or dreamt he was crossing) Barham Down, and his path could equally well have led him on to St Margaret's. Womenswold is only about seven modern miles from Canterbury, so neither place quite corresponds to Goscelin's topographical indications.

76. Alan Everitt, *Continuity and Colonization: The Evolution of Kentish Settlement* (Leicester, 1986), p. 249, suggests that 'Behind the whole network of early church-dedications in Kent we must envisage a widespread tradition of local pilgrimage, originating with the death of St Augustine', and centred on Canterbury, which 'was not simply the political capital of the Kentish kingdom and the seat of the archbishop, but the focal point of a whole galaxy of indigenous cults and local devotional customs'.

77. N. Pevsner and E. Williamson, *The Buildings of England, Buckinghamshire* (2nd edn, Harmondsworth, 1994), pp. 749–50. The examination of the skeleton, the subject of an episode in the television series *Meet the Ancestors*, was reported in the *Guardian*, 27 January 2000.

78. *Councils and Synods: With Other Documents Relating to the English Church*, i, *AD 871–1204*, ed. D. Whitelock, M. Brett and C. N. L. Brooke (Oxford, 1981), i, p. 489.

79. G. R. and W. D. Stephens, 'Cuthman: A Neglected Saint', *Speculum*, 13 (1938), pp. 448–53; T. P. Hudson, 'The Origins of Steyning and Bramber, Sussex', *Southern History*, 2 (1980), pp. 11–29. Steyning was of some importance, and belonged to the kings of Wessex until Edward the Confessor gave it to the Norman abbey of Fécamp; Alfred's father Ethelwulf was first buried there.

80. See the numerous references in A. Everitt, *Continuity and Colonization*, and in K. P. Witney, *The Kingdom of Kent* (London, 1982).

81. *Councils and Synods*, ed. Whitelock, Brett and Brooke, p. 678.
82. *The Waltham Chronicle*, p. xxvii.
83. *GP*, pp. 321–22. The death and miracles of Waltheof were described by Orderic Vitalis, who was commissioned to write a verse epitaph for him: *The Ecclesiastical History of Orderic Vitalis*, ed. and trans. M. Chibnall (6 vols, Oxford, 1969–80), ii, pp. 320–23, 348–51.
84. *Opera*, ed. F. S. Schmitt (6 vols, Edinburgh, 1946–61), iv, p. 144.

Notes to Chapter 3: From Wulfstan to Becket

1. *VCH, Suffolk*, i, pp. 508–509.
2. For a general outline of the history of canonisation, see E. Kemp, *Canonisation and Authority in the Western Church* (Oxford, 1948); see also A. Vauchez, *La sainteté en Occident aux derniers siècles du moyen âge* (Rome, 1988), English translation by J. Birrell, *Sainthood in the Later Middle Ages* (Cambridge, 1997).
3. For these transitions see P.-A. Sigal, *L'homme et le miracle*; on miracles as 'une relation d'échange', chapter 2. For later medieval developments, see Vauchez, *La sainteté*, especially chapter 15.
4. *Vita Wulfstani*, ed. R. Darlington (*CS*, 40); translated by J. H. F. Peile as *William of Malmesbury's Life of Saint Wulstan Bishop of Worcester* (Oxford, 1934; reprint, Felinfach, 1996), from which the quotations here are taken.
5. *William of Malmesbury's Life*, p. 99.
6. *GP*, pp. 288–89.
7. *Vita Wulfstani*, ed. Darlington, pp. 115–80.
8. *GP*, pp. 317–18; *The Peterborough Chronicle of Hugh Candidus*, pp. 105–6.
9. *Sanctuarium Dunelmense et Sanctuarium Beverlacense (SS, 5)*, pp. 97–107.
10. *Liber Eliensis*, ed. E. O. Blake (*CS*, third series, 92, 1962).
11. *Liber Eliensis*, pp. 228–29.
12. *Liber Eliensis*, p. 265.
13. *Liber Eliensis*, p. 274.
14. *Liber Eliensis*, p. 379.
15. *Liber Eliensis*, p. 266.
16. *Liber Eliensis*, pp. 365–67.
17. *Sanctuarium Dunelmense et Sanctuarium Beverlacense*, p. 107.
18. *GP*, p. 428.
19. There is a certain irony in the gift of some 'tawdry laces' to Thomas Cromwell. Richard Lyst wrote to him from Cambridge on 12 October 1533: 'I send you for a poor token some hallowed Tawdry laces' (*LP*, 6, p. 516).
20. *The Register of St Osmund*, ed. W. H. Rich Jones (2 vols, *RS*, 78), i, pp. 202, 204, 227.
21. *Chronicon Abbatiae Rameseiensis*, pp. lxxv-lxxvi.
22. C. Taylor, *Roads and Tracks of Britain* (2nd edn, London, 1994), p. 134, with a map; *VCH, Huntingdon*, ii, pp. 211, 214–18.
23. *The Chronicle of Jocelin of Brakelond*, ed. H. E. Butler (London, 1949), pp. 75–79.

24. *Memorials of St Edmund's Abbey*, i, pp. 173–75.
25. *Jocelin of Brakelond*, p. 40.
26. *Jocelin of Brakelond*, pp. 106–16
27. Reginald fitzUrse, Hugh de Morville (or Mauclerc), William de Tracy and Richard le Breton.
28. Of the enormous bibliography on Becket I cite here only the biography by F. Barlow, *Thomas Becket* (London, 1986; revised edn, 1997), and the posthumously published work of W. Urry, *Thomas Becket: His Last Days* (Stroud, 1999). Many of the contemporary sources are gathered together in *Materials*.
29. Few in later medieval England would have had any difficulty in distinguishing between *Thomas apostolus* (the doubter), *Thomas martyr* (Becket) and *Thomas confessor* (Thomas Cantilupe, bishop of Hereford).
30. Similar attempts were later made on behalf of 'political martyrs' such as Simon de Montfort and Thomas, earl of Lancaster, either because there was an underlying unease about the sufficiency of their qualifications as true martyrs or because it was assumed that a martyr in death must have been a true saint in life.
31. *Materials*, ii, p. 9.
32. *Materials*, ii, pp. 434–35.
33. *Materials*, ii, p. 320.
34. The attachment of similar emotions to anointed kings may help to account for the otherwise implausible cult which arose around the deposed Edward II, and also perhaps for the reputation of Henry VI, although he presented a more obviously saintly *persona*.
35. *Materials*, ii, pp. 15–16.
36. These were the first known 'souvenirs' to be produced at an English shrine: Santiago de Compostela seems to have been first in the field in western Europe, earlier in the twelfth century. For a general view of this subject see B. Spencer, 'Medieval Pilgrim Badges: Some General Observations Illustrated Mainly from English Sources', *Rotterdam Papers: A Contribution to Medieval Archaeology*, 1 (1968), pp. 137–53.
37. *Opera*, ed. J. S. Brewer (8 vols, *RS*, 21), i, pp. 52–53.
38. *Memorials of Saint Dunstan*, pp. 248–49: 'For almost every day, people come running for it and a sure medicine for the sick is taken away.' Dunstan had enclosed a tooth of St Andrew in the stick.
39. *Historical Works*, ed. W. Stubbs (2 vols, *RS* 73), i, p. 18.
40. *Materials*, i, pp. 416–17; ii, pp. 242–43.
41. These collections, with William's *Life* of the saint and other lives, are contained in the first two volumes of *Materials*. William's dedication to Henry is in *Materials*, i, pp. 137–39.
42. *Materials*, i, pp. 487–89.
43. *Chronica Magistri Rogeri de Hovedene*, ed. W. Stubbs (4 vols, *RS*, 51), ii, pp. 61–62.
44. *Historical Works*, i, pp. 248–49.

45. *Chronicles of the Reigns of Stephen, Henry II and Richard I*, ed. R. Howlett (4 vols, *RS*, 82), i, pp. 188–89.
46. *Opera Historica*, ed. W. Stubbs (2 vols, *RS*, 68), i, p. 399.
47. *Gesta Regis Henrici Secundi Benedicti Abbatis*, ed. W. Stubbs (2 vols, *RS*, 49), i, p. 158.
48. *Gesta Henrici*, i, p. 207.
49. *Gesta Henrici*, i, pp. 240–41.
50. *Gesta Henrici*, i, p. 281
51. *Gesta Henrici*, i, pp. 313, 318–19.
52. *VCH, London*, i, pp. 491–95.
53. *Materials*, ii, pp. 164–71.
54. *Materials*, i, p. 309. This miracle probably took place at Ledbury.
55. *English Episcopal Acta*, vii, *Hereford, 1079–1234*, ed. J. Barrow (1993), pp. 176–77.
56. *Materials*, i, p. 531.
57. *Materials*, i, p. 244; ii, pp. 146–47.
58. H. Summerson, *Medieval Carlisle* (2 vols, Kendal, 1993), i, p. 158; *VCH, Cumberland*, ii, pp. 139–40.
59. *Materials*, ii, pp. 96–97.
60. *Miracula S. Frideswide* in *AS*, October, viii, pp. 568–89; H. Mayr-Harting, 'Functions of a Twelfth-Century Shrine: The Miracles of St Frideswide', in *Studies in Medieval History Presented to R. H. C. Davis*, ed. H. Mayr-Harting and R. I. Moore (London, 1985), pp. 193–206.
61. *Miracula S. Frideswide*, pp. 570, 583 , 585, 586.
62. The following references are to *Reginaldi Monachi Dunelmensis Libellus de Admirandis Beati Cuthberti Virtutibus* (*SS*, 1). Cf. the observations of V. Tudor, 'The Cult of St Cuthbert in the Twelfth Century'.
63. *Reginaldi Monachi Libellus*, p. 38.
64. Ibid., p. 164.
65. Ibid., pp. 208–10.
66. Ibid., pp. 248–54.
67. Ibid., pp. 254–55.
68. Ibid., pp. 255–59.
69. Ibid., pp. 260–61.
70. Ibid., pp. 261–62.
71. Ibid., p. 270.
72. Ibid., pp. 270–71.
73. Ibid., pp. 271–72.
74. *Libellus de Vita et Miraculis S. Godrici, Heremitae de Finchale, auctore Reginaldo Monacho Dunelmensis* (*SS*, 20), pp. 366–67.
75. Ibid., p. 374.
76. Ibid., p. 376.
77. Ibid., p. 379.
78. Ibid., p. 381.
79. Ibid., pp. 389–90.

80. Ibid., pp. 397–98.
81. Ibid., p. 398.
82. Ibid., p. 409.
83. Ibid., p. 412.
84. Ibid., p. 423.
85. Ibid., pp. 427–29.
86. Ibid., pp. 441–42.
87. Ibid., p. 441.
88. Ibid., pp. 442–43.
89. Ibid., pp. 445–46.
90. Ibid., pp. 451–52.
91. Ibid., pp. 459–60.
92. *Materials*, i, p. 386: 'Neque enim Eadmundo regi martyri et emerito post insignia miraculorum novum pondus laboris hujus imponendum erat . . .'
93. *Memorials of St Edmund's Abbey*, i, pp. 364–65, 366, 368.
94. *The Life and Miracles of St William of Norwich by Thomas of Monmouth*, ed. A. Jessopp and M. R. James (Cambridge, 1896), pp. 289–94.
95. *Nova Legenda Anglie*, ed. C Horstmann (2 vols, Oxford, 1901), i, pp. 88–89.
96. *Materials*, ii, p. 148.
97. B. Kemp, 'The Miracles of the Hand of St James', *Berkshire Archaeological Journal*, 65 (1970), pp. 1–19. For the relic, see K. J. Leyser, 'Frederick Barbarossa, Henry II and the Hand of St James' , in *Medieval Germany and its Neighbours* (London, 1982), pp. 215–40.
98. Kemp, 'The Miracles', p. 15. Kemp (p. 5) comments on the strong theme of rivalry in this collection.
99. *Materials*, i, pp. 210–11, 416–19; ii, pp. 242–43, 251–52; Leyser, 'Frederick Barbarossa, Henry II and the Hand of St James', p. 232.
100. *Historians of the Church of York* (*RS*, 71), ii, p. 537.
101. *The Flowers of History*, ed H. S. Hewlett (3 vols, *RS*, 84), i, pp. 109–16; *CM*, ii, pp. 301–8.
102. *GA*, i, pp. 192–93.
103. *Materials*, i, p. 166.
104. Sigal, *L'homme et le miracle*, pp. 207, 217–18, cites examples from St-Bertin and St-Bertrand de Comminges.
105. *AM*, ii, p. 62.
106. *Chronicon Abbatiae de Evesham*, pp. 101–2; *AM*, i, p. 53.
107. B. Spencer, 'An Ampulla of St Egwin and St Edwin', *Antiquaries Journal*, 51 (1971), pp. 316–18. In 1044 Abbot Elfward of Evesham retired to Ramsey, where he had originally been a monk, with relics which included the jawbone of St Ecgwin.
108. B. Spencer, 'Two Leaden Ampullae from Leicestershire', *Leicestershire Architectural and Archaeological Society Transactions*, 55 (1979), pp. 88–89; *AM*, 1, p. 209.
109. The miracles are printed in *Vita Wulfstani*, ed. R. Darlington.
110. *Vita Wulfstani*, pp. 119–20.

111. *Vita Wulfstani*, pp. 135–36.
112. *Vita Wulfstani*, pp. 154–57. For the earlier story see *William of Malmesbury's Life*, pp. 64–65.
113. B. Spencer, 'A Thirteenth-Century Pilgrim's Ampulla from Worcester', *Transactions of Worcestershire Archaeological Society*, third series, 9 (1984), pp. 7–11. Spencer judged it to resemble 'the transitional Canterbury types that were probably being distributed throughout the land during the second quarter of the thirteenth century'.
114. For this episode, see especially A. Gransden, 'The Growth of the Glastonbury Traditions and Legends in the Twelfth Century', *Journal of Ecclesiastical History* 27 (1976), pp. 337–58. For Glastonbury in general, see P. Rahtz, *Glastonbury* (London, 1993); J. P. Carley, *Glastonbury Abbey: The Holy House at the Head of the Moors Adventurous* (2nd edn, Glastonbury, 1996); J. P. Carley, *The Chronicle of Glastonbury Abbey: An Edition, Translation and Study of John of Glastonbury's Cronica sive Antiquitates Glastoniensis Ecclesie* (Woodbridge, 1985).
115. On 'the geography of pilgrimage' see Finucane, *Miracles and Pilgrims: Popular Beliefs in Medieval England* (London, 1977), especially ch. 9.

Notes to Chapter 4: Saints, Bishops and Shrine Promotion

1. For the background to papal canonisation, with much detail about individual cases, see E. Kemp, *Canonisation and Authority in the Western Church* (Oxford, 1948), and A. Vauchez, *La sainteté en Occident aux derniers siècles du moyen âge* (Rome, 1988). R. Foreville and G. Keir, ed., *The Book of St Gilbert* (Oxford, 1987), conveniently makes available the dossier of Gilbert of Sempringham's canonisation, including his miracles.
2. P. Grosjean, 'Thomas de la Hale, moine et martyr à Douvres en 1295', *AB*, 72 (1954), pp. 157–91.
3. On Becket's Jubilees and the indulgences granted for them, see R. Foreville, *Le Jubelé de S. Thomas Becket du XIII au XV siècle (1220–1470)* (Paris, 1958).
4. *GA*, i, p. 71.
5. *The Register, or Rolls, of Walter Gray, Lord Archbishop of York* (*SS*, 56), pp. 148–49. The archbishop's examination of the relics derives particular point from the Canterbury claim that they had been taken there in the tenth century: *Historians of the Church of York* (*RS*, 71), i, pp. xlvi–xlvii.
6. J. Alberigo, G. Dossetti, P.-P. Joannou, C. Leonardi and P. Prodi, *Conciliorum Oecumenicorum Decreta* (3rd edn, Bologna, 1973), pp. 263–64.
7. *The Flowers of History* (*RS*, 84), i, pp. 4–9, 65–78, 203, 302–10; ii, pp. 253–54, 274–76.
8. *CM*, iii, pp. 42, 47.
9. *Historia Anglorum, sive Historia Minor*, ed. F. Madden (3 vols, *RS*, 44), ii, pp. 93–94.

10. Matthew Paris noted that this permission was not granted to other women: *CM*, v, p. 113.
11. *The Register of William Wickwane, Lord Archbishop of York, 1279–1285* (*SS*, 114), p. 333.
12. *CM*, v, p. 324.
13. *AM* , ii, pp. 351–52; iv, p. 499.
14. D. J. Jones, 'The Cult of St Richard of Chichester in the Middle Ages', *Sussex Archaeological Collections*, 121 (1983), pp. 79–86; Leland, ii, p. 93. See also D. Jones, ed., *Saint Richard of Chichester: The Sources for his Life* (*Sussex Record Society*, 79, 1995).
15. *CM* , v, pp. 369–70, 380, 384, 419–20, 621, 691. For Matthew's life of Edmund, see *The Life of St Edmund by Matthew Paris*, translated, edited and with a biography by C. H. Lawrence (Stroud, 1996).
16. *English Episcopal Acta*, xii, *Exeter, 1186–1257*, ed. F. Barlow, p. 287.
17. *CM*, v, pp. 490–91, Matthew had already referred to miracles at Lincoln under the year 1253 (p. 419).
18. *AM*, i, p. 159
19. E. Kemp, 'The Attempted Canonization of Robert Grosseteste', in *Robert Grosseteste: Scholar and Bishop*, ed. D. A. Callus (Oxford, 1955), p. 246; cf. Vauchez, *La sainteté*, p. 107 n. 25.
20. *AM*, iv, pp. 389, 392.
21. *Registrum Robert Winchelsey Cantuariensis Archiepiscopi, AD 1294–1313*, ed. R. Graham (2 vols, *CYS*, 51–52), i, pp. 761–62.
22. *CM*, v, p. 638.
23. J. R. Shinners, 'The Veneration of Saints at Norwich Cathedral in the Fourteenth Century', *Norfolk Archaeology*, 40 (1987), pp. 133–44.
24. C. Rawcliffe, *Medicine for the Soul: The Life, Death and Resurrection of an English Medieval Hospital* (Stroud, 1999), pp. 18–29.
25. N. Orme, 'Two Saint-Bishops of Exeter: James Berkeley and Edmund Lacy' , *AB*, 104 (1986), pp. 403–18; U. M. Radford, 'The Wax Images Found in Exeter Cathedral', *Antiquaries Journal*, 29 (1949), pp. 164–68. John Wadham in 1501 wanted several pilgrimages done on his behalf, including one to 'Bysshope Lacy', and in 1534 Sir Richard Place, vicar of Kingston, wanted twenty pence offered at Lacy's tomb: *Somerset Medieval Wills, 1383–1500*, ed. F. W. Weaver (*Somerset Record Society*, 16, 1901), p. 30; *Wells Wills*, ed. F. W. Weaver (London, 1890), p. 98.
26. William Worcestre, *Itineraries*, ed. J. H. Harvey (Oxford, 1969), pp. 115–16; Leland, i, p. 227.
27. The king's letters are printed in *Foedera*, ii, pt 2, pp. 181–82, 183, 184; ii, pt 3, pp. 6, 21, 39–40, 61–62, 132.
28. Printed by David Wilkins, *Concilia Magna Britanniae et Hiberniae ab anno MCCCL ad annum MDXLV* (4 vols, London, 1837), ii, pp. 486–90. For Thomas of Lancaster's support of Winchelsey's cause, see *LC*, 3, pp. 398–401.
29. L. S. Colchester, ed., *Wells Cathedral: A History* (Wells, 1982), pp. 36, 49n., 72,

79, 86, 124–25; *Calendar of the Register of John de Drokensford* (*Somerset Record Society*, 1, 1887), pp. 215, 273–74, 297.

30. Rymer, *Foedera*, ii, pt 2, p. 183. On 2 February 1323 Edward II complained to the pope about the subversive activities of the bishops of Lincoln and Bath and Wells (*Foedera*, ii, pt 2, pp. 60–61).

31. Orme, 'Two Saint-Bishops', p. 404 n. 7; Radford, 'The Wax Images', pp. 167–68.

32. *The Register of Ralph of Shrewsbury*, ed. T. S. Holmes (2 vols, *Somerset Record Society*, 9, 10, 1896) i, p. xxx.

33. *St Thomas Cantilupe Bishop of Hereford: Essays in his Honour*, ed. M. Jancey (Hereford, 1982). On the subsequent history of the cult and its financial aspects, see P. E. Morgan, 'The Effect of the Pilgrim Cult of St Thomas Cantilupe in Hereford Cathedral', in *St Thomas Cantilupe*, pp. 145–52, and R. N. Swanson, 'Devotional Offerings at Hereford Cathedral in the Later Middle Ages', *AB*, 111 (1993), pp. 93–99.

34. R. Finucane, 'Cantilupe as Thaumaturge: Pilgrims and their "Miracles"', in *St Thomas Cantilupe*, pp. 137–44, and *Miracles and Pilgrims*, esp. ch. 10. A printed version of the miracles, which has been used here, is to be found in *AS*, October 1 (2nd edn, Brussels, 1859), pp. 549–629, but Finucane (who uses the first edition, Antwerp, 1765) also cites manuscript sources.

35. *AS*, October 1, pp. 568–69.

36. *AS*, p. 622.

37. *AS*, p. 562.

38. *AS*, p. 573.

39. *AS*, p. 579.

40. *AS*, p. 612.

41. *AS*, p. 615.

42. *AS*, pp. 549–52.

43. *AS*, p. 576.

44. *AS*, p. 604. Becket too performed several cures of hawks.

45. *AS*, p. 576.

46. *AS*, p. 528. The king's presence at Hereford is recorded only in November-December 1283, October-November 1291 and April 1301. He was married to Margaret in September 1299.

47. *AS*, pp. 628–29, 593.

48. *AS*, p. 494. The miracles did not meet with the approval of the bishop of Lincoln. See Chapter 7 below.

49. *Registrum Ricardi de Swinfield, 1283–1317*, ed. W. W. Capes (*CYS*, 6), pp. 281–82.

50. *Registrum Swinfield*, pp. 230–31, 297–99, 315–16. The treasurer received two-thirds, after the expenses of lighting had been deducted from the total; a man appointed by him, and another appointed by the other canons, took turns to collect the offerings and lay out on the expenses of the lighting.

51. *Registrum Ade de Orleton, 1317–1327*, ed. A. T. Bannister (*CYS*, 5), p. 143.

52. *Calendar of the Register of Simon de Montacute, Bishop of Worcester, 1334–1337*, ed. R. M. Haines (*Worcester Historical Society*, new series, 15, 1996), p. 198.

53. *Registrum Johannis de Trillek, 1344–1361*, ed. J. H. Parry (*CYS*, 8), p. 147.

54. *English Episcopal Acta*, iii, *Canterbury, 1193–1205*, ed. E. Johns (2 vols, 1986), pp. 81–83.

55. *AM*, i, pp. 84–86, 96, 141, 148.

56. *The Register of St Osmund*, i, p. 227; *The Register of Roger Martival, Bishop of Salisbury, 1315–1330*, ed. C. Elrington and S. Reynolds (3 vols in 4, *CYS*, 55–58, 59), ii, p. 293.

57. *GA*, i, pp. 105–6.

58. *CM*, v, pp 608–9, 617.

59. C. E. Woodruff, 'The Financial Aspect of the Cult of St Thomas of Canterbury', *Archaeologia Cantiana*, 44 (1932), pp. 525–27. B. Nilson, *Cathedral Shrines of Medieval England* (Woodbridge, 1998), pp. 211–15, tabulates the offerings to the four 'stations' connected with St Thomas. For 'souvenirs' of Our Lady Undercroft and royal patronage, especially that of the Black Prince, see B. Spencer, *Pilgrim Souvenirs and Secular Badges: Medieval Finds from Excavations in London* (London, 1998), pp. 131–33.

60. For pilgrim itineraries around major churches and the way they were organised and controlled, see Nilson, *Cathedral Shrines*, especially chapter 4.

61. Orme, 'Two Saint-Bishops', pp. 403–4.

62. *Memorials of the Church of SS. Peter and Wilfrid, Ripon*, iii (*SS*, 81), pp. 88–196, 224–88.

63. E. Craster, 'The Miracles of St Cuthbert at Farne', *AB*, 70 (1952), pp. 5–19; *CEPR*, 4, p. 176.

64. *LP*, 10, p. 138.

65. *Somerset Medieval Wills*, second series, *1501–30* (*Somerset Record Society*, 19, 1903), p. 174; Carley, *Glastonbury Abbey*, pp. 8–9, 20.

66. *Memorials of St Edmund's Abbey* (*RS*, 96), iii, pp. 327–39.

67. B. Kemp, 'The Miracles of the Hand of St James', p. 18.

68. B. Spencer, *Salisbury and South Wiltshire Museum, Medieval Catalogue*, pt 2, *Pilgrim Souvenirs and Secular Badges* (Salisbury, 1990), pp. 54–55.

69. N. Pevsner and D. Lloyd, *The Buildings of England: Hampshire and the Isle of Wight* (Harmondsworth, 1967), p. 307.

70. *CM*, iv, p. 227. Matthew's phrasing does not make it entirely clear whether this was planning or a fortuitous outcome which he had noticed. In fact he had already reported the dedication of St Paul's on 1 October in 1240, not 29 September as he implies here, but his essential point is unaffected.

71. *AS*, October 1, p. 528. The point of the last part of Wich's testimony was presumably to emphasise that pilgrims were coming in numbers; these were not the costly oblations of a few wealthy individuals.

72. Spencer, *Pilgrim Souvenirs and Secular Badges*, p. 195.

73. On the pilgrim's experience at the shrine, and on the management and physical lay-out of shrines, see especially Nilson, *Cathedral Shrines*, and Crook, *Architectural Setting of the Cult of Saints*.

74. *AM*, ii, p. 336.

75. *Materials,* ii, pp. 81–83.

76. J. Crook, 'St Swithun of Winchester', in J. Crook, ed., *Winchester Cathedral: Nine Hundred Years* (Chichester, 1993), pp. 57–68.

77. *The Register of William Greenfield, Lord Archbishop of York,* i (*SS,* 145), pp. 234–35.

78. Their works are conveniently summarised, from the *Gesta Abbatum* and other sources, in *VCH, Hertfordshire,* ii, pp. 483–88.

79. *GA,* i, p. 287.

80. *GA,* ii, p. 379. The recently completed Lady chapel was probably the new location for the shrine: R. N. Hadcock, *Tynemouth Priory and Castle* (London, 1952), p. 12.

81. *Rites of Durham: Being a Description or Brief Declaration of All the Ancient Monuments, Rites and Customs Belonging or Being within the Monastical Church of Durham before the Suppression. Written 1593* (*SS,* 107), p. 94.

82. *Materials,* ii, p. 131.

83. *Materials,* i, pp. 308–9.

84. Erasmus, *Pilgrimages to Saint Mary of Walsingham and Saint Thomas of Canterbury,* translated by J. G. Nichols (London, 1875).

85. On 9 May 1512 Erasmus informed a friend that he had made a vow for the success of the church and would make a pilgrimage to Walsingham to hang a Greek ode there (*LP,* 1, p. 556).

86. Edited by J. Krochalis, '*Magna Tabula*: The Glastonbury Tablets', *Arthurian Literature,* ed. J. P. Carley and F. Riddy, 15 (1997), pp. 93–183; 16 (1998), pp. 41–82; illustrated by J. Carley, *Glastonbury Abbey,* p. 140.

87. P. Rahtz, *Glastonbury,* p. 37.

88. *Memorials of St Edmund's Abbey* i, p. 84.

89. Printed by J. C. Dickinson, *The Shrine of Our Lady of Walsingham* (Cambridge, 1956), pp. 124–29. Only one copy of the ballad survives.

90. *Itineraries,* pp. 100–1.

91. P. Needham, *The Printer and the Pardoner: An Unrecorded Indulgence Printed by William Caxton for the Hospital of St Mary Rounceval, Charing Cross* (Washington, 1986) includes a brief discussion of indulgence printing.

92. J. Adair, *The Pilgrims' Way* (London, 1978), p. 117.

93. *The Tale of Beryn,* pp. 6–7.

94. *CEPR,* 11, pp. 53–54.

95. *AM,* ii, p. 293.

96. *AM,* iii, p. 58.

97. *Historia Anglicana,* ed. H. R. Luard (*RS,* 16), p. 110.

98. *CM,* iv, pp. 640–44; M. E. Roberts, 'The Relic of the Holy Blood and the Iconography of the Thirteenth-Century North Transept Portal of Westminster Abbey', in *England in the Thirteenth Century: Proceedings of the 1984 Harlaxton Symposium,* ed. W. M. Ormrod (Woodbridge, 1986), pp. 129–48.

99. *CM,* v, pp. 29, 333–34. The evidence suggests that the shrine was at its most popular in the third quarter of the fourteenth century, and Spencer attributes

many of the surviving pilgrim badges to this period: *Pilgrim Souvenirs and Secular Badges*, pp. 182–85.

100. *CEPR*, 8, pp. 239–40; Spencer, *Salisbury Museum Medieval Catalogue*, pt 2, pp. 29–30. See also Spencer, *Pilgrim Souvenirs and Secular Badges*, pp. 148–49.

101. *CEPR*, 10, p. 8.

102. *A Dialogue Concerning Heresies*, in *Complete Works*, ed. T. Lawler, G. Marc'-hadour and M. Marius, vi, pt 1 (New Haven, 1981), p. 52.

103. Nilson, *Cathedral Shrines*, pp. 134–35.

Notes to Chapter 5: Images and Indulgences

1. *Registrum Roberti Mascall, 1404–1416*, ed. J. H. Parry (*CYS*, 21), pp. 15–16.

2. *English Wills, 1498–1526*, ed. A. F. Cirket, *Bedfordshire Historical Record Society Publications*, 37 (1957), p. 29.

3. Walsingham, ii, p. 253.

4. See the observations of N. Orme, 'Indulgences in the Diocese of Exeter, 1100–1536', *Report and Transactions of the Devon Association for the Advancement of Science*, 120 (1988), pp. 15–32.

5. *The Register of John le Romeyn, Lord Archbishop of York, 1286–1296* (2 vols, SS 123, 128), i, p. 4.

6. *Registrum Ade de Orleton*, p. 347.

7. *Registrum Johannis de Trillek*, pp. 143–44. Here, the appearance of representative saints of the diocese of Hereford (Ethelbert, Thomas Cantilupe and Milburga), as well as the special attention paid to soliciting contributions for the provision of images, should be noted.

8. *CM*, v, pp. 490–91.

9. W. St. Clair Baddeley, *A Cotteswold Shrine: Being a Contribution to the History of Hailes, County Gloucester, Manor, Parish and Abbey* (Gloucester, 1908), pp. 57–58.

10. *CEPR*, 6, p. 376. Eugenius IV reissued the Corpus Christi indulgence in 1438, and a renewal was sought in 1457 because the church still claimed to need repairs: 9, p. 36; 11, p. 190. A 'quarantine' was a period of forty days, a unit in which indulgences were frequently granted.

11. *CEPR*, 15, p. 37.

12. *The Book of Margery Kempe*, pp. 232–35; Webb, *Pilgrims and Pilgrimage*, pp. 147, 221, 222. For English finds of badges from Wilsnack, see B. Spencer, *Medieval Pilgrim Badges from Norfolk* (Norwich, 1980), p. 24; *Pilgrim Souvenirs and Secular Badges*, pp. 266–67.

13. F. Wormald, 'The Rood of Bromholm', *Journal of the Warburg Institute*, 1 (1937–39), pp. 31–45; *CEPR*, 5, p. 384; L. J. Redstone, 'The Cellarer's Account for Bromholm Priory, Norfolk, 1415–16', *Norfolk Record Society*, 17 (1944), pp. 47–91.

14. Walsingham, ii, pp. 188–89.

15. Rose Graham, 'The Priory of La Charité sur Loire and the Monastery of

Bermondsey', in *English Ecclesiastical Studies* (London, 1929), pp. 91–124. It is possible that the Rood was a copy of the famous Volto Santo of Lucca, which was widely known in England.

16. *GA* , ii, p. 355.

17. *Chronica Monasterii de Melsa, Auctore Thoma Burton*, ed. E. A. Bond (3 vols, *RS*, 43), iii, pp. 35–36.

18. *CEPR*, 5, pp. 257–58.

19. *CEPR*, 5, p. 253; 7, p. 327.

20. *CEPR*, 8, p. 117.

21. *CEPR*, 9, p. 280.

22. *CEPR*, 13, p. 446.

23. Spencer, *Pilgrim Souvenirs and Secular Badges*, pp. 167–70.

24. Dickinson, *The Shrine of Our Lady of Walsingham*, summarises the history and topography of the shrine.

25. *English Episcopal Acta*, vi, *Norwich, 1070–1214*, ed. C. Harper-Bill, pp. 268–69.

26. *Heresy Trials in the Diocese of Norwich, 1428–31*, ed. N. Tanner (*CS*, fourth series, 20, 1977), p. 148.

27. B. Wolffe, *Henry VI* (London, 1981), pp. 367, 368; N. H. Nicolas, *Testamenta Vetusta* (2 vols, London, 1826), i, p. 329.

28. R. W. Dunning, 'The Last Days of Cleeve Abbey', in *The Church in Pre-Reformation Society: Essays in Honour of F. R. H. Du Boulay*, ed. C. M. Barron and C. Harper-Bill (Woodbridge, 1985), pp. 158–67.

29. *CEPR*, 2, p. 256.

30. W. M. Ormrod, 'The Personal Religion of Edward III', *Speculum*, 64 (1989), p. 857 and n. 46; *AS*, October, 1, pp. 573–74.

31. *The Register of Thomas de Cobham, Bishop of Worcester, 1317–1327*, ed. E. H. Pearce, *Worcestershire Historical Society* (1930), p. 15; *CEPR*, 4, p. 38.

32. *CEPR, Calendar of Petitions*, 1, p. 483. In 1375 Kingswood was still in need of costly repairs and obtained what was in effect a renewal of the earlier grant, while in 1398 the notoriously generous Boniface IX granted it a plenary indulgence: *CEPR* 4, p. 205; 5, p. 263.

33. *CEPR* 6, p. 452.

34. *CEPR* 5, p. 24.

35. *CEPR* 5, p. 256; 13, p. 260.

36. *CEPR* 13, p. 498. Woodville went to Rome in 1475 for the Jubilee indulgence; on 1 March 1476 the pope was offering pardon and reward to anyone who should supply information relating to the robbery Woodville had suffered at Sutri (p. 221).

37. C. L. Kingsford, 'Our Lady of the Pew: The King's Oratory or Closet in the Palace of Westminster', *Archaeologia*, 68 (1917), pp. 1–20; *Testamenta Eboracensia*, iv (*SS* 53), p. 153.

38. *CEPR*, 13, p. 225, 244–45.

39. Spencer, *Pilgrim Souvenirs*, pp. 151–52.

40. H. E. Craster, *A History of Northumberland*, x, *The Parish of Corbridge*

(Newcastle, 1914), pp. 34–35, 64–65, 110–11. The 1401 indulgence is in *CEPR*, 5, p. 408. The later indulgence was available 'at the principal feasts of the year' and also at the feast of the dedication of the chapel. Bishop Langley of Durham granted his own indulgences in January 1428 and again in February 1435.

41. E. Mackenzie, *A Descriptive and Historical Account of the Town and County of Newcastle-upon-Tyne* (Newcastle, 1827), pp. 149, 193; F. W. Dendy, 'An Account of Jesmond', *Archaeologia Aeliana*, third series, 1 (1904), pp. 139–47; P. Brewis, 'St Mary's Chapel and the Site of St Mary's Well, Jesmond', *Archaeologia Aeliana*, fourth series, 5 (1928), pp. 102–11. It is stated by H. M. Gillett, *Walsingham: The History of a Famous Shrine* (London, 1946), pp. 10, 33, that Jesmond was frequented by pilgrims on their way south to Walsingham, but he cites no evidence for this.

42. *CEPR* 8, pp. 22, 27; *Testamenta Eboracensia*, iii (*SS*, 45), p. 200.

43. *CEPR* 4, p. 455; 9, p. 253.

44. *CEPR*, 4, p. 454; T. Burton, *The History and Antiquities of the Parish of Hemingbrough* (York, 1888), p. 24; *VCH, East Riding*, iii, p. 43.

45. *The Book of Margery Kempe*, p. 148.

46. *CEPR*, 5, p. 207; 12, pp. 419–20.

47. *CEPR*, 13, p. 219.

48. *The Priory of Hexham: Its Chroniclers, Endowments and Annals*, i (*SS*, 44), pp. xcvii–xcviii.

49. *CEPR*, 4, pp. 163, 165.

50. *CEPR*, 10, p. 63.

51. *CEPR*, 9, pp. 376–77. For the disputes at Ilfracombe see below, Chapter 7.

52. *CEPR*, 11, p. 108.

53. *CEPR*, 3, p. 538.

54. *CEPR*, 10, p. 612.

55. *CEPR*, 11, pp. 657–58; Nicholls and Taylor, *Bristol Past and Present*, ii, pp. 123–24.

56. In August 1538 William Bassett suppressed the shrine at Buxton and 'locked up the baths and wells that none may wash therein': *LP*, 13, pt 2, p. 95.

57. *CEPR* 15, p. 391.

58. *CEPR*, 13, p. 117; J. C. Cox, 'Benefactions of Thomas Heywood, Dean (1457–1492) to the Cathedral Church of Lichfield', *Archaeologia*, 52 (1890), p. 627. On St Anne's cult in general, see K. Ashley and P. Sheingorn, ed., *Interpreting Cultural Symbols: Saint Anne in Late Medieval Society* (Athens, Georgia, 1990).

59. *CEPR*, 9, pp. 334–34.

60. *CEPR*, 11, p. 146.

61. *CEPR*, 12, p. 411.

62. *CEPR*, 5, p. 589.

63. *CEPR*, 8, p. 482.

64. *CEPR*, 6, p. 290; N. Orme, *English Church Dedications: With a Survey of Cornwall and Devon* (Exeter, 1996), p. 111.

65. *CEPR*, 11, pp. 603–4; Leland, i, p. 190.

66. *CEPR*, 5, p. 280; 6, p. 283.

67. *CEPR*, 11, p. 506.
68. *The Fabric Rolls of York Minster*, ed. J. Raine (*SS*, 35), p. 240.
69. *CEPR*, 6, p. 22.
70. *CEPR*, 11, p. 536.
71. *The Register of Edmund Lacy, Bishop of Exeter, 1420–1455*, ed. G. R. Dunstan (4 vols, *CYS*, 60–64, 66), i, pp. 51, 279.
72. *CEPR*, 10, pp. 102–3.

Notes to Chapter 6: Royal Pilgrimage

1. *AM*, i, pp. 137, 140–41.
2. *CM*, iv, p. 46; v, p. 111; *AM*, i, p. 345.
3. Edward's movements can be followed in H. Gough, *Itinerary of King Edward the First* (2 vols, Paisley, 1900).
4. *Chronicles of the Reigns of Edward I and Edward II*, ed. W. Stubbs (2 vols, *RS* 76), ii, p. 19.
5. *Chronicon Johannis de Reading et Anonymi Cantuariensis, 1346–1367*, ed. J. Tout (Manchester, 1914), pp. 120, 132–33. Reading misdates the gift of St Benedict's head to 1355, ibid., p. 260.
6. *AM*, ii, pp. 401–2; 4, p. 489; M. Ormrod, 'The Personal Religion of Edward III', pp. 855–56.
7. R. Fletcher, *St James's Catapult: The Life and Times of Diego Gelmírez of Santiago de Compostela* (Oxford, 1984), pp. 73–74.
8. *Symeonis Monachi Opera*, i, pp. 75, 211–12. Athelstan's gifts to St Cuthbert are believed to have included an embroidered stole of English workmanship which was found in the saint's tomb in 1827, but the Byzantine silk of which remains were also discovered is thought more likely to have been given by Edmund. See C. Higgins, 'Some New Thoughts on the Nature Goddess Silk', in *St Cuthbert: His Cult and his Community*, ed. Bonner, Rollason and Stancliffe, pp. 329–87; H. Granger-Taylor, 'The Earth and Ocean Silk from the Tomb of St Cuthbert at Durham: Further Details', *Textile History*, 20 (1989), pp. 151–66.
9. *Sanctuarium Dunelmense et Sanctuarium Beverlacense*, p. 98; *Historians of the Church of York*, i, pp. 263–64, 294–98.
10. *Opera Symeonis*, i, p. 90.
11. *Memorials of St Edmund's Abbey*, i, pp. 46–47.
12. *Liber Eliensis*, pp. 153–54.
13. *Opera Symeonis*, i, pp. 101, 106.
14. *AM*, ii, pp. 44–45
15. Ormrod, 'The Personal Religion of Edward III', p. 859.
16. E. Rupin, *Roc Amadour: étude historique et archéologique* (Paris, 1904), p. 195; *Gesta Henrici Secundi* (*RS*, 49), i, p. 7.
17. *Gesta Henrici Secundi*, i, pp. 157, 159, 179–80.
18. *Chronicles and Memorials of the Reign of Richard I*, ed. W. Stubbs (2 vols, *RS*, 38) i, pp. 145, 446.

19. Roger of Wendover, *The Flowers of History* (*RS*, 84), i, p. 288; *Chronicle of Jocelin of Brakelond*, pp. 116–17.

20. P. Draper, 'King John and St Wulfstan', *Journal of Medieval History*, 10 (1984), pp. 41–50.

21. F. Wormald, 'The Rood of Bromholm'; J. Dickinson, *The Shrine of Our Lady of Walsingham*, pp. 17–19.

22. Henry's itineraries have been derived here principally from the entries in the published *Calendars of Patent Rolls* (*CPR*) and *Close Rolls* (*CCR*). The latter include many instructions to officials, while details of his household expenditures and outlay on gifts and offerings come mostly from the *Calendars of Liberate Rolls* (*CLR*). Only selected references are given here.

23. *CCR, 1242–1247*, p. 208.

24. *CCR, 1242–1247*, p. 295

25. D. Gordon, *Making and Meaning: The Wilton Diptych* (London, 1993), p. 53.

26. Matthew Paris, *Historia Anglorum sive Historia Minor*, i, p. 347; *Memorials of St Edmund's Abbey*, iii, p. 27; *AM*, i, p. 92.

27. *The Chronicle of Bury St Edmunds, 1212–1291*, ed. A. Gransden (London, 1964), p. 27; for later refugees see *Memorials of St Edmund's*, iii, pp. 30–31.

28. *Chronicle of Bury*, p. 13.

29. *CLR*, 2, p. 306.

30. *CPR, 1266–1272*, p. 139; *CCR, 1242–1247*, p. 19.

31. *CCR, 1251–1253*, pp. 152, 427.

32. *CCR, 1251–1253*, p. 465.

33. *CLR*, 1, pp. 18–19. Henry did not in fact undertake his Lenten tour this year.

34. *CLR*, 4, p. 200.

35. These details are to be found in *CCR, 1254–1256*, pp. 274, 282, 284; *CLR*, 4, p. 275.

36. *Receipt and Issue Rolls for the 26th Year of the Reign of King Henry III, 1241–2*, ed. R. C. Stacey (*Publications of the Pipe Roll Society*, 87, new series, 49, 1987–88), p. 87; *CCR, 1242–1247*, p. 36.

37. *CLR*, 4, p. 297.

38. *CCR, 1254–1255*, p. 275. The reference to 'the other saints' who rested at Canterbury recalls the fact that earlier in the reign Henry had accorded recognition to the cult of St Adrian (often Hadrian), the African monk who had accompanied Theodore of Tarsus when he came to England as archbishop of Canterbury in 669. The king sent offerings in wax and coin to his tomb at St Augustine's Abbey in 1240 and again in 1251, when he also remembered St Mildred (*CLR*, 2, p. 17; *CCR, 1247–1251*, p. 463). In 1244 he ordered an altar of St Adrian, with appropriate windows, to be set up in the new chapel of St Mary at Westminster (*CCR, 1247–1251*, p. 208); and in 1247 he instructed the sheriff of Kent to make three altars in the chapel of Dover Castle, in honour of the Confessor, St Edmund and St Adrian (*CLR*, 3, p. 112).

39. *CCR, 1254–1256*, p. 128; *CLR*, 4, p. 247.

40. *CCR, 1261–1264*, pp. 162–63.

41. *Chronicle of Bury*, p. 37. Some of the Disinherited stole horses from the lands of St Edmund, but were traced and offered their swords at the shrine in recompense (pp. 39–40).

42. *Chronicle of Bury*, p. 52. Edward I also several times went on to Norwich from Bury.

43. *CLR*, 6, pp. 231, 232.

44. *CM*, 4, p. 402.

45. *CM*, 5, pp. 319–20.

46. *CM*, 5, p. 489. Edward at the time was in Gascony.

47. *CM*, 5, p. 574.

48. *CM*, pp. 489, 562–63.

49. *CM* 5, pp. 617–18. Henry gave at least passing attention to the cult of Edward the Martyr at Shaftesbury Abbey, but a hitch occurred in his relations with the nuns when they elected Agnes Ferrers as their abbess. For a long time the king refused to accept her nomination, claiming that she was 'sprung from a race of traitors'. He relented only in January 1247. A few months later he ordered the sheriff of Wiltshire to make a 100 pound taper and place it before the high altar on the day of St Edward's translation, 13 June (*CLR*, 3, p. 128).

50. William Rishanger, *Chronica et Annales, AD 1259–1307*, ed. H. T. Riley (*RS*, 28, pt 2), p. 75.

51. *AM*, iv, pp. 142–43; *CLR*, 5, p. 144. Subsequent payments were made on the same account, e.g. *CLR*, 5, p. 246; 6, pp. 4, 73.

52. *AM*, iv, p. 264.

53. Dickinson, *The Shrine of Our Lady*, pp. 19–21, 39–40, summarises Edward's devotion and benefactions to Walsingham.

54. Rishanger, *Chronica*, pp. 76–77.

55. *Chronicle of Bury*, p. 57.

56. John of Oxenden, *Chronica*, ed. H. Ellis (*RS*, 13), pp. 273, 285. He visited Camnterbury and Bury *en route*.

57. Bartholomew Cotton, *Historia Anglicana*, p. 316. Edward's treaty with the count of Flanders had been sworn on his behalf at Walsingham on the day of the Purification in 1296: *AM*, iv, p. 529.

58. A. J. Taylor, 'Edward I and the Shrine of St Thomas at Canterbury', *Journal of the British Archaeological Association*, 132 (1979), pp. 22–28.

59. These were in August 1274, when he had just returned to the country as king; in May-June and again in October of 1279; in May 1286 and August 1289; and in March 1298 when he was returning from Flanders.

60. Rishanger, *Chronica*, p. 191; Taylor, 'Edward I and the Shrine of St Thomas', p. 26.

61. *AM*, ii , p. 120.

62. Draper, 'King John and St Wulfstan', p. 46; *AM*, iv, p. 96.

63. The Worcester annalist noted the king's visits and offerings as follows: 1278 (*AM*, iv, p. 476); 1281 (p. 480); 1283 (p. 488); 1291 (p. 506); 1293 (p. 514); 1294 (p. 514); 1295 (p. 521); 1297 (p. 536); 1299 (p. 544); 1300 (p. 549).

64. *AM*, iv, p. 474; cf. ii, p. 389, and Carley, *The Chronicle of Glastonbury Abbey*,

pp. 244–47. According to the Waverley annalist, the crown of King Arthur, long prized by the Welsh, was offered to Edward in 1283. His eldest son Alphonse (who died the same year) offered the crown of Llewellyn and other jewels at the shrine of the Confessor (*AM*, ii, p. 401).

65. A. J. Taylor, 'Royal Alms and Oblations in the Later Thirteenth Century: An Analysis of the Alms Roll of 12 Edward 1 (1283–4)', in F. Emmison and R. Stephens, ed., *Tribute to an Antiquary: Essays Presented to Marc Fitch* (London, 1976), p. 113.

66. *Registrum Ricardi de Swinfield*, pp. 421–22, 432–38.

67. *AM*, iii, pp. 392, 399. The annalist recorded visits made by Edward to Dunstable Priory itself, with his father in 1247 and as king in 1275 (pp. 173, 266).

68. John of Oxenden, *Chronica*, p. 264.

69. A. J. Taylor, 'Edward I and the Shrine of St Thomas', pp. 25–26; 'Royal Alms and Oblations', p. 118.

70. *Chronicle of Bury*, p. 113; *Memorials of St Edmund's Abbey*, iii, pp. 35–36; John of Oxenden, p. 285.

71. *Chronicle of Bury*, p. 118.

72. *Chronicle of Bury*, pp. 133–36. He had already visited Bury, and feasted the convent, in January (p. 130).

73. Rishanger, *Chronica*, p. 192; see also the somewhat fuller account in the *Annales Anglie et Scotie*, published with Rishanger, pp. 397–99.

74. Rishanger, p. 194; *Annales Anglie et Scotie*, pp. 401–2.

75. *Annales Anglie et Scotie*, p. 406.

76. *Chronicle of Bury*, pp. 156–57.

77. Taylor, 'Royal Alms and Oblations', p. 100.

78. *VCH, Cumberland*, ii, p. 140; *CPR, 1301–1307*, p. 516.

79. *CPR, 1292–1301*, pp. 204, 208, 255. On 13 October he awarded a Scottish benefice to the royal clerk who had brought the banner of St John to him in Scotland and bore it throughout the campaign.

80. Walsingham, i, p. 75.

81. Edward sent them back on 27 November: *CCR, 1296–1302*, p. 414.

82. *Chronicles of the Reigns of Edward I and Edward II*, i, p. 114; *The Chronicle of Walter of Guisborough*, ed. H. Rothwell (*CS*, third series, 89, 1957), p. 339. Many years previously Edward had demonstrated reverence for Athelstan himself, when on his way south in March 1284 he visited the priory church of Stone in Staffordshire and made an offering to the 'shrine of St Athelstan, king' (Taylor, 'Royal Alms and Oblations', pp. 115, 125). This offering was not to the king's remains but, apparently, to a shrine given by him. Athelstan is not otherwise known as a saint.

83. *Foedera*, i, pt 1, p. 146; *CLR*, 2, p. 212.

84. *AM*, 1, p. 101; *CM*, v, pp. 653–54.

85. In November 1244 the sheriff of Kent was ordered to provide one thousand half-pound tapers for the Feast of St Thomas, and the like for St Augustine's, for the safe delivery of the queen: *CLR*, 2, p. 275.

86. Rishanger, *Chronica*, p. 438.

87. *GA*, ii, p. 366.

88. Walsingham, i, p. 327; ii, p. 344.

89. Johannes de Trokelowe, *Annales*, ed. H. T. Riley (*RS*, 28, pt 3), pp. 83, 92.

90. Dickinson, *The Shrine of Our Lady*, p. 24.

91. *Chronicles of the Reigns of Edward I and Edward II*, i, pp. 298–99; Trokelowe, pp. 110–11.

92. *CPR, 1321–1324*, p. 227

93. *Chronicles of the Reigns of Edward I and Edward II*, i, p. 314.

94. *CEPR*, 3, p. 605.

95. In the earlier years of his reign, Edward's movements, like those of his predecessors, can broadly be traced in the chancery enrolments of letters patent, close, etc. Ormrod, 'The Personal Religion of Edward III', especially pp. 857–60, supplies much detail of his pilgrimages and offerings.

96. *LC*, i, p. 496.

97. *Adae Murimuth Continuatio Chronicorum*, ed. E. M. Thompson (*RS*, 93), p. 69.

98. *Adae Murimuth Continuatio Chronicorum*, p. 135.

99. Ormrod, 'Personal Religion', p. 859.

100. J. P. Carley, *The Chronicle of Glastonbury Abbey*, pp. xxvii, xxxi.

101. Ormrod, 'Personal Religion', pp. 859–60. While it may be true that Edward had no time and no need to go to Compostela, as some of his greater subjects did, in 1353 he had to be absolved from a vow to do so, whether or not he ever seriously intended to fulfil it (*CEPR*, 3, p. 560).

102. For the Prince's pilgrimages in England and France, see R. Barber, *Edward, Prince of Wales and Aquitaine* (Woodbridge, 1978), pp. 46, 105, 109, 131, 159, 163; on his special devotion to the Holy Trinity, pp. 240–41.

103. *Chronicon Johannis de Reading et Anonymi Cantuariensis*, pp. 208–9, 220–21. On permissions to 'prisoners of war' and Scots to visit Walsingham, see Dickinson, *The Shrine of Our Lady*, p. 25; Webb, *Pilgrims and Pilgrimage*, pp. 229–30.

104. For Richard's piety, including his pilgrimages and his patronage of shrines, see N. Saul, *Richard II* (London, 1997), especially pp. 303–26. The king's itinerary is given, pp. 468–74.

105. *Polychronicon Ranulphi Higden Monachi Cestrensis*, ed. J. R. Lumby (9 vols, RS, 41), ix, pp. 20–21.

106. *Annales Ricardi Secundi Regis Angliae*, in Trokelowe, *Annales*, p. 167.

107. D. Wilkins, *Concilia Magnae Britanniae et Hiberniae ab Anno MCCCL ad Annum MDXLV* (4 vols, London, 1837), iii, pp. 234–36; *The Register of Henry Chichele, Archbishop of Canterbury, 1414–1443*, ed. E. F. Jacob (4 vols, CYS, 42), iii, pp. 8–9. Chichele's decree followed his celebration of a requiem mass at St Paul's for the souls of the dead at Harfleur and Agincourt (p. 7).

108. *Eulogium Historiarum sive Temporis Chronicon*, ed. F. S. Haydon (3 vols, RS, 9), iii, pp. 379–80.

109. *Expedition to Prussia and the Holy Land Made by Henry Earl of Derby*

(Afterwards King Henry IV) in the Years 1390–1 and 1392–3: Being the Accounts Kept by his Treasurer during Two Years, ed. L. Toulmin-Smith (*CS*, new series, 52, 1894).

110. J. H. Wylie, *History of England under Henry the Fourth* (4 vols, London, 1884–98), iii, p. 334. Henry of Derby had visited Bridlington, and also Beverley, in 1391 on his return from Prussia (p. 336; *Expenditures*, p. 117). Henry V named John of Bridlington as his special patron in the will he made in July 1415 before leaving England for the Agincourt campaign: Wylie, *The Reign of Henry V* (3 vols, London, 1914–29), i, p. 539. The battle of Agincourt was fought on 25 October, the feast day of Yorkshire's other St John, John of Beverley, and Henry believed that both were to be thanked for his victory, although Shakespeare (perhaps for metrical reasons) has him give the preference to 'Crispian', who shared the same date. On 17 December 1416 Archbishop Chichele, with specific reference to Agincourt, decreed that 25 October was to be celebrated 'throughout our province' (*Register*, iii, pp. 28–29). The Yorkshire saints were also available for use against the Scots: in 1417 Thomas Beaufort went on pilgrimage to Bridlington, where he was joined by the king's brother John, duke of Bedford, before campaigning in Scotland: Walsingham, ii, p. 325.

111. *The Chronicle of Adam of Usk, 1377–1421*, ed. C. Given-Wilson (Oxford, 1997), pp. 262–63. Adam implies that this event took place early in 1416, and seems to associate it with rumours about the burial place of Owen Glendower. Given-Wilson (p. 262 n. 4) suggests that Henry's visit is likely to have followed Archbishop Arundel's promotion of the feast in January 1416. Other evidence suggests the possibility that Henry went to Holywell before Agincourt: Wylie, *The Reign of Henry V*, i, pp. 483, 495.

112. *A Collection of the Chronicles and Ancient Histories of Great Britain, Now Called England, by John de Waurin, Lord of Forestel*, translated Sir W. Hardy and E. L. C. P. Harding (3 vols, *RS*, 40, pt 5), i, p. 219; *Chronicle of Adam of Usk*, p. 262.

113. Walsingham, ii, pp. 335, 337; Wylie, *The Reign of Henry V*, iii, pp. 270–72.

114. A. Goodman, *John of Gaunt* (London, 1992), p. 132: Constance, duchess of Lancaster, was received into the St Albans fraternity in 1386.

115. So-called by the chronicler, although the see of Chester was not established until the sixteenth century; he should more properly have been denoted 'of Lichfield'.

116. *Annales Monasterii S. Albani a Johanni Amundesham monaco, ut videtur, conscripto, AD 1421–1440*, ed. H. T. Riley (2 vols, *RS*, 28, pt 5), i, pp. 4–28.

117. *Dialogue Concerning Heresies*, pp. 86–87.

118. R. A. Griffiths, *The Reign of King Henry VI* (Berkeley, 1981), p. 53; B. Wolffe, *Henry VI*, pp. 74–75.

119. Wolffe supplies the royal itinerary down to 1461: *Henry VI*, pp. 361–71.

120. *Rites of Durham* (*SS*, 107), pp. 122–23.

121. *Registra quorundam Abbatum Monasterii S. Albani qui saeculo XVmo floruere*, ed. H. T. Riley (2 vols *RS*, 28, pt 6), i, pp. 171–73.

122. *Registra quorundam Abbatum*, i, p. 323.

123. C. Ross, *Edward IV* (London, 1974), p. 273.

124. C. L. Scofield, *The Life and Reign of Edward the Fourth* (2 vols, London, 1923), i, p. 574.

125. *The Paston Letters*, ed. J. Gairdner (6 vols, London, 1904; reprinted, Gloucester, 1984), iii, pp. 112, 314; v, pp. 28, 31,109, 112, 329.

126. Gillett, *Walsingham*, p. 36; T. Astle, *The Will of King Henry VII* (London, 1775), p. 37.

127. Nicholls and Taylor, *Bristol Past and Present*, ii, p. 124.

128. J. Cave-Browne, *The History of Boxley Parish* (Maidstone, 1892), p. 52.

129. Dickinson, *The Shrine of Our Lady*, pp. 42–47; Gillett, *Walsingham*, p. 37.

130. *LP*, 1, pp. 813, 1016.

131. *LP* 2, pt 1, pp. 131; 2, pt 2, pp. 1154, 1160, 1166, 1412. Wingfield was still in post, and still hoping to make his pilgrimage, in 1517 (p. 1029).

132. *LP* 2, pt 2, pp. 1447–48.

133. *LP* 4, pt 1, p. 285.

134. In March 43s. 4d. was paid for the king's candles before Our Lady of Walsingham and 100s. to the prior 'for the king's salary before Our Lady' (*LP*, 13, pt 1, p. 529). There is no such payment subsequently. Payments in arrears were also made for the king's candles burning before King Henry of Windsor and Our Lady of Doncaster (p. 526). In September, the king was paying for the demolition of the shrine at Canterbury (p. 534).

135. J. R. L. Highfield, 'Catherine of Aragon's Visit to the Shrine of St Frideswide', in J. Blair, ed., *Saint Frideswide's Monastery at Oxford: Archaeological and Architectural Studies* (Gloucester, 1990), pp. 274–75.

Notes to Chapter 7: Unofficial Pilgrimage

1. *Councils and Synods with Other Documents Relating to the English Church, AD 1205–1313*, ed. F. M. Powicke and C. R. Cheney (2 vols, Oxford, 1964), i, pp. 303, 622, 722; ii, p. 1044.

2. *Chronica* (*RS*, 51), iv, pp. 123–24.

3. *LP*, 18, pt 2, p. 296. The name of the spring commemorates Richard Plantagenet, illegitimate son of Richard III, who survived until 1550, working as a bricklayer at Eastwell: S. Jennett, *The Pilgrims' Way from Winchester to Canterbury* (London, 1971), p. 257.

4. A. Everitt, *Continuity and Colonization*, p. 296. Everett has considered the possible significance of such springs for early settlement patterns and the location of churches in Kent, concluding judiciously, if reluctantly, that the existence of water cults before the Conquest can so rarely be established with certainty that the question must be left open.

5. *The Rolls and Register of Oliver Sutton, 1280–1299*, ed. R. Hill, iii (*Lincoln Record Society*, 48), p. 37.

6. *Oxford Formularies*, i, ed. H. Salter (*Oxford Historical Society*, new series, 4), pp. 7–9.
7. *Register of Oliver Sutton*, vi (*Lincoln Record Society*, 64), pp. 186–87; *VCH, Buckinghamshire*, iii, pp. 387, 389.
8. *AS, October*, 1 (2nd edn, Brussels, 1859), p. 626.
9. *Itineraries*, pp. 64–65, 160–61.
10. Leland, ii, pp. 37, 99.
11. *The Register of Thomas Bekynton, Bishop of Bath and Wells, 1443–1465*, ed. H. C. Maxwell-Lyte and M. C. B. Dawes (2 vols, *Somerset Record Society*, 49–50), i, p. 414.
12. *Bekynton's Register*, i, pp. 116–17.
13. *GP*, p. 194.
14. Leland, i, pp. 141–43. For Elias of Reading see above, Chapter 3. It is interesting to note that the modern excavators of the Roman bath complex have found very little medieval material and apparently no coins. Was a very careful watch kept on bathers, or were their offerings successfully diverted to churches in the town?
15. *Register of Oliver Sutton*, vi, p. 104.
16. *Register of Oliver Sutton*, v (*Lincoln Record Society*, 60), pp. 143–44, 176, 212.
17. *AS*, October 1 (2nd edn, Brussels 1859) p. 494.
18. *Register of Oliver Sutton*, v, p. 32.
19. *The Register of William Greenfield, Lord Archbishop of York, 1300–1315*, ed. W. Brown and A. Hamilton Thompson, iii (*SS*, 151), pp. 209–10. The story of the Fraisthorpe Madonna is outlined in *VCH, Yorkshire, East Riding*, ii, pp. 187–88, but this account is in need of correction on several points.
20. *Abstracts of the Charters and Other Documents Contained in the Chartulary of the Priory of Bridlington*, ed. W. T. Lancaster (Leeds, 1912), pp. 448–49.
21. *Greenfield's Register*, iii, pp. 215–17.
22. *CPR, 1313–1317*, p. 60. Commissions of oyer and terminer on the rector's complaint were issued again on 28 April and 20 November 1314 (pp. 148, 245).
23. *Calendar of Inquisitions Miscellaneous*, 1, pp. 358–59. The inquest was misdated to 28 October in 8 Edward I (i.e. 1280), but must have taken place in 1314 (8 Edward II) or possibly 1315.
24. *Greenfield's Register*, v (*SS*, 153), p. 266. In 1331 Robert of Scarborough, prior of Bridlington, complained to the king that in the time of Prior Gerald, that is before early 1315, certain members of the Grimston family had come to Fraisthorpe church, broken down the doors and carried the image off (*CPR, 1330–1334*, p. 203). The prior valued it at £60, a healthy sum. As all the indications are that the image was safely at Bridlington in January 1316, it is not clear what he was hoping to achieve, unless it was retrospective compensation. The subsequent history of the image is obscure, but in 1463 the vicar of Topcliffe bequeathed 8*d.* to be offered 'to the image of the Blessed Mary called Melrose' at Bridlington: *VCH, Yorkshire*, iii, p. 201 n. 19. The nickname

is arresting and may recall the Scottish origins of the image Thomas Poynton had brought to Fraisthorpe a century and a half earlier.

25. *Registrum Radulphi Baldock, Gilberti Segrave, Ricardi Newport et Stephani Gravesend Episcoporum Londoniensium AD MCCCIV-MCCCXXXVIII*, ed. R. C. Fowler (*CYS*, 7), pp. 25–26.

26. *Les registres d'Innocent IV*, ed. E. Berger (3 vols and index, Paris, 1884), iii, p. 131.

27. *Greenfield's Register*, iv (*SS*, 152), pp. 88–89.

28. *Registrum Ade de Orleton* (*CYS*, 5), p. 61; *Charters and Records of Hereford Cathedral*, ed. W. W. Capes (Hereford, 1908), pp. 183–84.

29. *The Register of Walter de Stapeldon, Bishop of Exeter, AD 1307–1326*, ed. F . C. Hingeston-Randolph (London and Exeter, 1892), p. 182.

30. *CEPR*, 9, pp. 376–77.

31. *The Register of Thomas de Brantyngham, AD 1370–1394*, ed. F. C. Hingeston-Randolph (2 vols, London and Exeter 1901–6), i, p. 507.

32. *Brantyngham's Register*, i, pp. 164–65; 2, p. 609.

33. *Brantyngham's Register*, ii, p. 695.

34. *Greenfield's Register*, ii (*SS* 149), p. 135.

35. In the mid fourteenth century 'a picture painted in Lombardy' was bought in London for the high altar of St Albans: *GA*, iii, p. 381.

36. S. Sutcliffe, 'The Cult of St Sitha in England: An Introduction', *Nottingham Medieval Studies*, 37 (1993), pp. 83–89; P. J. Goldberg, *Women in England, c. 1275–1525* (Manchester, 1995), p. 284; E. Duffy, 'Holy Maydens, Holy Wyfes: The Cult of Women Saints in Fifteenth- and Sixteenth-Century England' , in *Women in the Church*, ed. W. J. Sheils and D. Wood (*Studies in Church History*, 27, 1990), pp. 175–96. On badges of Zita, see Spencer, *Pilgrim Souvenirs and Secular Badges*, pp. 198–99.

37. *Dialogue concerning Heresies*, p. 77; *Selections from English Wycliffite Writings*, ed. Hudson, pp. 87–88.

38. *The Register of John de Grandisson, Bishop of Exeter, AD 1327–1369*, ed. F. C. Hingeston-Randolph (2 vols, London, 1894), ii, pp. 941–43.

39. Orme, 'Two Saint-Bishops of Exeter', pp. 409–11.

40. B. Spencer, 'King Henry of Windsor and the London Pilgrim', in *Collectanea Londiniensia: Studies Presented to Ralph Merrifield*, ed. J. Bird, J. Chapman and J. Clark (*London and Middlesex Archaeological Society Special Papers*, 2, 1978), pp. 235–64. In *Pilgrim Souvenirs and Secular Badges*, pp. 192–95, Spencer contrasts Schorne's longlasting fame with the swift rise and fall of John Warton at Durham.

41. *Chronica Monasterii de Melsa* (*RS*, 43), iii, p. 195; *VCH, Yorkshire, East Riding*, v, pp. 57, 63.

42. Spencer, *Pilgrim Badges*, pp. 196–98.

43. J. W. McKenna, 'Popular Canonization as Political Propaganda: The Cult of Archbishop Scrope', *Speculum*, 45 (1970), pp. 609–10.

44. *Grandisson's Register*, ii, pp. 1231–34.

45. *Registrum Palatinum Dunelmense: The Register of Richard de Kellawe, Lord Palatine and Bishop of Durham, 1311–1316*, ed. T. Duffus-Hardy (4 vols, London, 1873–78), i, p. 264.

46. *Extracts from the Account Rolls of the Abbey of Durham*, ii (*SS*, 100), pp. 476–83.

47. N. Vincent, 'Simon of Atherfield (d. 1211), a Martyr to his Wife', *AB*, 113 (1995), pp. 349–61.

48. *CPR, 1350–1354*, p. 7; D. M. Webb, 'The Saint of Newington: Who Was Robert le Bouser?' *Archaeologia Cantiana*, 119 (2000), pp. 173–88.

49. William Dene, *Historia Roffensis*, in H. Wharton, *Anglia Sacra*, i, pp. 346, 350, 352; W. H. St John Hope, 'The Architectural History of the Cathedral Church and Monastery of St Andrew at Rochester', *Archaeologia Cantiana* (1898), pp. 232n, 320–21.

50. J. Shinner, 'The Veneration of Saints at Norwich Cathedral', pp. 133–37; *The Life and Miracles of St William of Norwich by Thomas of Monmouth*; Finucane, *Miracles and Pilgrims*, pp. 118–21, 161–62; Nilson, *Cathedral Shrines*, pp. 156–57, 170, 218–21.

51. *Chronicle of Jocelin of Brakelond*, p. 16.

52. *AM*, ii, p. 86; *CM*, iv, pp. 377–78. A later incident, at Northampton in 1279, was noted by John of Oxenden, *Chronica* (*RS*, 13), p. 254.

53. *AM*, i, pp. 340–48, 371. Chaucer's Prioress ends her tale by invoking Little St Hugh.

54. *Historia Rerum Anglicarum*, in *Chronicles of the Reigns of Stephen, Henry II and Richard I* (*RS* 82), i, pp. 311–12.

55. *Historia*, in *Chronicles*, ii, pp. 466–73; Ralph Diceto, *Opera Historica* (2 vols, RS, 68), ii, pp. 143–44; Gervase of Canterbury, *Historical Works* (*RS*, 73), i, pp. 532–34; *Chronica Magistri Rogeri de Hovenden* (*RS*, 51), iv, pp. 5–6; Roger of Wendover, *Flowers of History* (*RS*, 84) i, p. 244; *CM*, ii, pp. 418–19.

56. *Gesta Henrici Secundi et Ricardi Primi*, ii, p. 116. The story was either unknown to, or ignored by, Newburgh, Diceto and Gervase, but Roger of Hoveden got it from the *Gesta* and Wendover and Matthew Paris both included it.

57. *Episcopal Registers, Diocese of Worcester: Register of Bishop Godfrey Giffard, September 23rd 1268 to August 15th 1301*, ed. J. Willis Bund (2 vols, Worcestershire Historical Society, 1902), ii, pp. 110–13. Nicholls and Taylor report both this incident and the quarrels between the citizens and the constable, but do not connect the two (*Bristol Past and Present*, i, pp. 145–46).

58. On this subject in general see McKenna, 'Popular Canonization as Political Propaganda'; J. C. Russell, 'The Canonization of Opposition to the King in Angevin England', in *Anniversary Essays in Mediaeval History by Students of Charles Homer Haskins* (Boston, 1929), pp. 279–90; J. Theilmann, 'Political Canonization and Political Symbolism in Medieval England', *Journal of British Studies*, 29 (1990), pp. 241–66.

59. *Historia*, in *Chronicles*, i, p. 234. An adulatory account of the young Henry's death and miracles is printed in Ralph Coggeshall, *Chronicon Anglicarum*, ed. J. Stevenson (*RS*, 66), pp. 265–73.

60. *Historia Anglorum* (RS, 44), i, p. 136. Roger (*Flowers of History*, ii, pp. 62–63) says only that Peter died *pro assertione veritatis*.
61. *CM*, iv, pp. 93–94.
62. Rishanger, *Chronica et Annales* (RS, 28, pt 2), p. 53.
63. *LC*, iii, pp. 398, 400–1.
64. C. Valente, 'Simon de Montfort, Earl of Leicester, and the Utility of Sanctity in Thirteenth-Century England', *Journal of Medieval History*, 21 (1995), pp. 27–49. The miracles are printed with *The Chronicle of William de Rishanger of the Barons' Wars*, ed. J. Halliwell (CS, 15, 1840), pp. 67–110. For analysis of them see also Finucane, *Miracles and Pilgrims*, pp. 131–35.
65. *AM*, iv, pp. 170–71; *The Chronicle of Walter of Guisborough*, p. 201; *AM*, ii, p. 365.
66. *Chronicle of Melrose*, ed. A. and M. Anderson (London, 1936), pp. 135–40. The translation quoted is that of Joseph Stevenson, recently reprinted as *A Medieval Chronicle of Scotland* (Llanerch, 1991), pp. 107–16. Another eulogistic account is in the *Chronicon de Lancercost* (Bannatyne Club, 65, Edinburgh, 1839), pp. 75–78.
67. *Chronicon de Lanercost*, p. 78.
68. Valente, 'Simon de Montfort', p. 34: 'The entire village of Brill, Northants., which had wholeheartedly embraced the reform and was condemned as "contumacious" after the revolt, bore witness to the cure of one of its residents.' Brill is in fact in Buckinghamshire, but very near the present border with Northamptonshire; there was a royal manor there.
69. J. R. Maddicott, 'Follower, Leader, Pilgrim, Saint: Robert de Vere, Earl of Oxford, at the Shrine of Simon de Montfort, 1273', *English Historical Review*, 109 (1994), pp. 641–53.
70. *AS, October*, i, p. 600. Thomas's use of the phrase 'servants of God' as a description of himself and (implicitly) Simon was impeccably correct.
71. J. Edwards, 'The Cult of "St" Thomas of Lancaster and its Iconography', *Yorkshire Archaeological Journal*, 64 (1992), pp. 103- 91; H. Tait, 'Pilgrim-Signs and Thomas, Earl of Lancaster', *British Museum Quarterly*, 20 (1955), pp. 39–47.
72. *The Brut*, ed. F. W. D. Brie (2 vols, *Early English Text Society*, 131, 135), i, pp. 228–31.
73. *Calendars of Inquests Miscellaneous, 1307–1347*, pp. 528–29.
74. *Chroniques de Londres depuis l'an 44 Hen. III jusqu' à l'an 17 Edw. III*, ed. G. J. Aungier (CS, 28, 1840), p. 46; *Flores Historiarum*, ed. H. R. Luard (3 vols, RS, 95), iii, pp. 213–14.
75. *Foedera*, ii, pt 2, p. 77.
76. *Foedera*, ii, pt 2, p. 86. Edward wrote further letters on the same subject from Liverpool on 24 October, and from Westminster on 16 March of the following year.
77. *Historical Papers and Letters from Northern Registers*, ed. J. Raine (RS, 61) pp. 323–26, 339–42.
78. *Foedera* ii, pt 2, pp. 182–83; ii, pt 3, pp. 39–40, 61–62.
79. *CPR, 1330–1334*, p. 334.

80. *Polychronicon*, viii, pp. 312–14.
81. J. Nichols, *Collection of All Wills Extant of Kings and Queens of England* (London, 1780), p. 54; *Chronica Johannis de Reading*, ed. Tout, pp. 133–34.
82. Tait, 'Pilgrim-Signs'; Spencer, *Pilgrim Souvenirs*, pp. 198–203. Spencer is inclined to date these badges predominantly to the fourteenth century and comments that some of them 'were clearly politically propagandist as well as devotional in intent'; they 'were large and intricate and they have tended to survive as isolated fragments'.
83. As discovered by Henry VIII's commissioners in 1536: *LP*, 10, p. 141.
84. *Polychronicon*, viii, pp. 324–26.
85. *Historia et Cartularium Monasterii Sancti Petri Gloucestriae*, ed. W. H. Hart (3 vols, RS, 33), i, pp. 44–46.
86. *Registrum Hamonis de Hethe Diocesis Roffensis, AD 1319–1352*, ed. C. Johnson (2 vols, CYS, 48, 91), ii, p. 938.
87. See especially Theilmann, 'Political Canonization'. It has been suggested that the Confessor as depicted in the Wilton Diptych bears the features of Edward III and St Edmund those of Edward II (pp. 259–60).
88. Walsingham, i, p. 401.
89. Walsingham, ii, p. 114; *Polychronicon*, ix, p. 40
90. Walsingham, ii, p. 195.
91. McKenna, 'Popular Canonization', p. 622.
92. *Chronicle of Adam of Usk*, p. 30; Walsingham, ii, pp. 225–26; Theilmann, 'Political Canonization', pp. 261–63.
93. See especially McKenna, 'Popular Canonization'.
94. *Historians of the Church of York* (RS, 71), iii, pp. 292–94.
95. *Historians of the Church of York*, iii, pp. 388–90.
96. See especially Spencer, 'Henry VI and the London Pilgrim'. The miracles were published in full by P. Grosjean, *Henrici VI Angliae Regis Miracula Postuma ex Codice Musei Britannici Regio 13.C.VIII* (Brussels, 1935) and in part, with English summaries, by R. Knox and S. Leslie, *The Miracles of King Henry VI* (Cambridge, 1923). Grosjean also gives a full account of the cult and of the campaign for Henry's canonisation.
97. These measures will be more fully considered below, in Chapter 9.
98. *The Fabric Rolls of York Minster*, ed. J. Raine (SS, 35), pp. 208–10.
99. Spencer, 'King Henry of Windsor', p. 240; R. Swanson, 'Devotional Offerings at Hereford Cathedral', p. 96. Cf. the observations of Grosjean, *Henrici VI Angliae Regis Miracula*, pp. 94–97.
100. J. R. Maddicott, *Thomas of Lancaster, 1307–1322: A Study in the Reign of Edward II* (Oxford, 1970), pp. 329–30.
101. Grosjean, pp. 239–43; Knox and Leslie, p. 182.
102. Grosjean, pp. 122–23; Knox and Leslie, pp. 109–10.
103. Grosjean, pp. 164–65, 185–90, 231–34; Knox and Leslie, pp. 133–34, 149, 179.
104. Grosjean, pp. 181–84, 298–99; Knox and Leslie, pp. 142, 211.
105. *CEPR*, 17, pp. 150, 152.

Notes to Chapter 8: The Pilgrim's Voice

1. *Materials*, i, pp. 395–97.
2. D. Stroud, 'The Cult and Tombs of St Osmund at Salisbury', *Wiltshire Archaeological and Natural History Magazine*, 78 (1984), pp. 50–54.
3. *LC*, iii, pp. 26–29, 191–92.
4. Grosjean, p. 102; Knox and Leslie, p. 84
5. N. Pevsner, *The Buildings of England: Wiltshire* (Harmondsworth, 1963), p. 112. The church of Box is now dedicated to St Thomas Becket.
6. *CIPM*, 13, p. 258.
7. *CIPM*, 3, p. 328.
8. *CIPM*, 5, p. 36.
9. *CIPM*, 5, p. 84
10. *CIPM*, 10, pp. 176–77.
11. *CIPM*, 10, p. 241.
12. *CIPM*, 10, p. 180. The only female pilgrims mentioned in these records are one or two who had gone to the Holy Land and, having died there, were unable to take up their inheritances.
13. *CIPM*, 6, p. 263.
14. *CIPM*, 11, p. 468.
15. *CIPM*, 13, p. 214.
16. *CIPM, Henry IV*, 1, pp. 406–407.
17. *CIPM*, 10, p. 365.
18. *CIPM*, 10, p. 379.
19. *CIPM*, 10, p. 177.
20. *CIPM*, 15, p. 351.
21. *CIPM*, 7, p. 136.
22. *CIPM*, 10, p. 178.
23. *CIPM*, 11, p. 119; 13, p. 212; 14, p. 69.
24. *CIPM*, 17, pp. 180, 511.
25. *CIPM*, 8, p. 33. 1315 was the first of of a run of disastrous famine years which afflicted England and much of northern Europe and brought a great deal of pilgrimage to Canterbury. The priory received £501 10s. in oblations that year: M. Mate, 'Coping with Inflation: A Fourteenth-Century Example', *Journal of Medieval History*, 4 (1978), p. 100.
26. *CIPM*, 10, p. 113.
27. *CIPM*, 10, p. 434; 11, p. 127.
28. *CIPM, Henry IV*, 1, p. 221.
29. *CIPM, Henry VII*, 1, p. 253; 2, pp. 359, 357, 402, 403.
30. *Testamenta Eboracensia*, iv (*SS*, 53), p. 276.
31. *The Register of Henry Chichele* (*CYS*, 42), ii, p. 411.
32. *Sussex Wills*, i (*Sussex Record Society*, 41), pp. 210–11.
33. *Calendar of Wills Proved and Enrolled in the Court of Husting, London, AD 1258-AD 1688*, ed. R. R. Sharpe (2 vols, London 1889–90), ii, p. 234.

34. *Sussex Wills*, iv (*Sussex Record Society*, 45), p. 52. A 'trentall' was a set of thirty masses.
35. *Somerset Medieval Wills*, second series, *1501–30*, ed. F. W. Weaver (*Somerset Record Society*, 19), p. 276.
36. *Testamenta Eboracensia*, v (*SS*, 79), p. 125.
37. *Wills and Inventories from the Registers of the Commissary of Bury St Edmund's and the Archdeacon of Sudbury*, ed. S. Tymms (*CS*, 49), pp. 83, 109.
38. *Register of Henry Chichele*, ii, p. 74.
39. J. Nichols, *Collection of All Wills Extant of Kings and Queens of England*, p. 54; also in *Testamenta Vetusta*, ed. Nicolas, i, p. 68.
40. *Somerset Medieval Wills, 1383–1500*, ed. F. W. Weaver (*Somerset Record Society*, 16), p. 201.
41. *Sussex Wills*, iv, p. 244.
42. *Testamenta Cantiana, East Kent*, ed. A. Hussey (London, 1907), pp. 271, 348.
43. *Register of Henry Chichele*, ii, pp. 385, 539.
44. *Testamenta Eboracensia*, v (*SS*, 79), p. 95.
45. *Sussex Wills*, i, p. 308.
46. *Register of Henry Chichele*, ii, p. 485.
47. R. M. Serjeantson and H. I. Longden, 'The Parish Churches and Religious Houses of Northamptonshire', pp. 46–47.
48. *Lincoln Wills Registered in the District Probate Registry at Lincoln*, i, *AD 1271 to AD 1526*, ed. C. W. Fowler (*Lincoln Record Society*, 5, 1914), p. 71; ii, *1505–1530* (*Lincoln Record Society*, 10, 1918), p. 76.
49. *Calendar of Wills Proved in the Court of Husting*, ii, p. 107.
50. *Register of Philip Repingdon, Bishop of Lincoln, 1405–19*, i, ed. M. Archer (*Lincoln Record Society* 57), p. 122.
51. *Testamenta Eboracensia*, v (*SS*, 79), p. 74.
52. *Testamenta Eboracensia*, i (*SS*, 4), p. 187.
53. *Testamenta Eboracensia*, iv (*SS*, 53), p. 257.
54. *Testamenta Eboracensia* iv, p. 153; v (*SS*, 79), pp. 137–38, 186.
55. *Testamenta Eboracensia*, ii (*SS*, 30), p. 276. A *saluz* was a coin depicting the Angelic Salutation, or Annunciation.
56. *Testamenta Eboracensia*, iv, p. 182n.
57. *Testamenta Eboracensia*, i, p. 42.
58. *Testamenta Vetusta*, ed. Nicolas, i, pp. 232, 240.
59. *Testamenta Vetusta*, i, p. 345.
60. *Somerset Medieval Wills, 1383–1500*, pp. 269–69.
61. *Somerset Medieval Wills*, second series, *1501–1530*, p. 501; *Somerset Medieval Wills, 1383–1500*, p. 226.
62. *Somerset Medieval Wills*, third series, *1531–1538* (*Somerset Record Society*, 21), p. 14.
63. *Wells Wills*, ed. F. W. Weaver (London, 1890), p. 98.
64. *Testamenta Eboracensia*, ii, pp. 200–1. The editor, James Raine, commented: 'I am not aware of the existence of any other document from which we can

ascertain that some of these shrines were places of fame. This passage, therefore, is of singular interest.'

65. *Testamenta Eboracensia*, ii, p. 283.
66. Serjeantson and Longden, 'The Parish Churches of Northamptonshire', p. 47.
67. *Early Lincoln Wills*, ed. A. Gibbons (Lincoln, 1888), p. 66.
68. *Testamenta Eboracensia*, v, p. 114.
69. *Acts of Chapter of the Collegiate Church of SS. Peter and Wilfrid, Ripon, AD 1452 to AD 1506* (*SS*, 64), p. 265.
70. Serjeantson and Longden, 'The Parish Churches of Northamptonshire', p. 47.
71. *Testamenta Cantiana, East Kent*, pp. 127, 135.
72. *Testamenta Vetusta*, ed. Nicolas, p. 349.
73. *Calendar of the Register of John de Drokensford*, ed. Bishop Hobhouse (*Somerset Record Society*, 1), p. 144.
74. *CPR, 1364–1367*, p. 375.
75. *CPR, 1361–1364*, pp. 473–74.
76. *Calendar of the Register of Simon de Montacute, Bishop of Worcester, 1334–1337*, ed. R. M. Haines (*Worcester Historical Society*, new series, 15), pp. 7, 187, 209.
77. *Calendar of the Register of John de Drokensford*, p. 17; *Calendar of the Register of Wolstan de Bransford, Bishop of Worcester, 1339–1349*, ed. R. H. Haines (*Worcester Historical Society*, new series, 9), p. 19.
78. *Calendar of the Register of Adam de Orleton, Bishop of Worcester 1327–1333*, ed. R. M. Haines (*Worcester Historical Society*, new series, 10), pp. 141–42.
79. Quotations are from *The Book of Margery Kempe*, ed. S. B. Meech (*Early English Text Society*, 212). There is a recent version in modern English by R. Windeatt (Harmondsworth, 1985). Of an extensive secondary literature I cite only C. W. Atkinson, *Mystic and Pilgrim: The Book and the World of Margery Kempe* (Ithaca, New York, 1985), and G. Gibson, *The Theater of Devotion: East Anglian Drama and Society in the Late Middle Ages* (Chicago, 1989). especially chapter 3.
80. *The Book of Margery Kempe*, p. 22.
81. Ibid., p. 27.
82. Ibid., p. 122.
83. Ibid., p. 110.
84. Ibid., pp. 245–46.
85. Ibid., pp. 79, 95.
86. Ibid., pp. 136, 227.
87. Ibid., pp. 24–25.
88. Ibid., pp 128–29, 132.
89. Ibid., pp. 38–40, 102.
90. Ibid., pp. 147–48.
91. Ibid., p. 200.
92. Ibid., p. 224.
93. *The Cely Letters, 1472–1488*, ed. A. Hanham (*Early English Text Society*, 273), pp. 62–63, 66.
94. The suggested identification is Alison Hanham's (*Cely Letters*, p. 264). The

(Victorian) parish church of Brentwood is at the present day dedicated to St Thomas, and there are fourteenth-century remains of a chapel dedicated to him: N. Pevsner, *The Buildings of England: Essex* (2nd edn, Harmondsworth, 1965), p. 101.

95. *Cely Letters*, p. 55.

96. *The Paston Letters*, ed. J. Gairdner, ii, pp. 55–57.

97. *Paston Letters*, v, pp. 76–77.

98. *Paston Letters*, vi, p. 119.

99. *Paston Letters*, iv, p. 186.

100. *Paston Letters* v, p. 74.

101. *Paston Letters*, v, pp. 186, 190.

102. Foreville, *Le Jubilé de Saint Thomas Becket*, pp. 71–81; B. Schimmelpfennig, 'Die Anfange des Heiligen Jahres in Santiago de Compostela im Mittelalter', *Journal of Medieval History*, 4 (1978), pp. 285–303.

103. Ibid, pp. 133–34; *Annales Monasterii S. Albani, AD 1421–1440* (*RS*, 28, pt 5), i, p. 24.

104. *Stonor Letters and Papers*, ed. C. L. Kingsford (2 vols, *CS*, third series 29, 30), ii, p. 14.

105. *Stonor Letters*, ii, pp. 68–69.

106. C. Platt, *Medieval Southampton* (London, 1973), p. 104.

107. H. Lubin, *The Worcester Pilgrim* (*Worcester Cathedral Publications*, 1, 1990).

Notes to Chapter 9: Pilgrims in a Landscape

1. *CPR, 1345–1348*, pp. 464–65.

2. *The Register of John de Grandisson*, ed. Hingeston-Randolph, ii, p. 1021.

3. *The Register of Walter de Stapeldon*, ed. Hingeston-Randolph, p. 108.

4. That is, the ubiquitous Cut-Me-Own Throat Dibbler of Ankh Morpork and his clones in other parts of Terry Pratchett's Discworld.

5. *CPR, 1335–1338*, pp. 6, 188.

6. *Materials*, i, p. 327.

7. *Materials*, i, p. 154.

8. *Materials*, ii, pp. 210–11.

9. *Materials*, i, p. 278.

10. *Materials*, i, pp. 499–501,

11. *Materials*, i, pp. 286–87.

12. *Materials*, i, pp. 534–35.

13. *Materials*, i, p. 395.

14. *AS, October*, i, p. 602: 'una cum aliis, causa devotionis euntibus ad tumulum memoratum, dietam integram peregrinis huiusmodi consuetam perficere potuit, propriis pedibus ambulando per auxilium servi Dei'.

15. *AS, October*, i, pp. 560–61.

16. E. Cohen, 'Roads and Pilgrimage: A Study in Economic Interaction', *Studi Medievali*, 2 (1980), pp. 321–41.

17. A. Shaver-Crandell and P. Gerson, *The Pilgrim's Guide to Santiago de Compostela* (London, 1995), p. 89.

18. Webb, *Pilgrims and Pilgrimage*, pp. 93–94, 117–22.

19. C. Aldridge, 'The Priory of the Blessed Virgin and Saint James, Birkenhead', *Transactions of the Historic Society of Lancashire and Cheshire*, 42 (1892), pp. 141–58; R. Stewart-Brown, *Birkenhead Priory and the Mersey Ferry* (Liverpool, 1925); *VCH, Chester*, iii, pp. 128–32.

20. H. Belloc, *The Old Road* (new edn, 1910), pp. 29–71.

21. A. Everitt, *Continuity and Colonization*, p. 249.

22. S. Jennett, *The Pilgrims' Way*, pp. 260–261.

23. *The Paston Letters*, ed. Gairdner, v, pp. 74–75.

24. *CIPM*, 10, p. 113.

25. These references are in the *Canon Yeoman's Prologue*, fragment 8, lines 555–92, and the *Manciple's Prologue*, fragment 9, lines 1–8.

26. *Materials*, i, p. 530.

27. *VCH, Kent*, ii, pp. 214–24. See also 'Hospitals in Kent' , *Archaeologia Cantiana*, 29 (1911), pp. 259–67; S. E. Rigold, *Maison Dieu, Ospringe* (London, 1958); G. H. Smith, 'The Excavation of the Hospital of St Mary of Ospringe, Commonly Called Maison Dieu', *Archaeologia Cantiana*, 95 (1979), pp. 81–184; M. Frohnsdorff, *The Maison Dieu and Medieval Faversham* (Faversham, 1997).

28. *LC*, ii, pp. 251–57.

29. On Canterbury's inns, see A. P. Stanley, *Historical Memorials of Canterbury* (11th edn, London, 1912), pp. 212–14; M. Lyle, *Canterbury* (London, 1994), pp. 81–84.

30. *CEPR*, 4, p. 36, The word *Romipetae* was often used generically to mean 'pilgrims', although it might more specifically designate people on their way to Rome.

31. *Chronica Johannis de Reading*, pp. 208–9.

32. *CEPR* 17, p. 4.

33. C. Rawcliffe, *Medicine for the Soul*, p. 60. On the general subject of hospitals and their very varied character, see N. Orme and M. Webster, *The English Hospital, 1070–1570* (New Haven, 1995).

34. *Registrum Robert Winchelsey*, ii (*CYS*, 52), pp. 822–23.

35. *GA*, i, p. 314.

36. *Registra Abbatis Johannis Whethamstede*, ed. H. T. Riley (2 vols, *RS*, 28, pt 6) ii, p. 269.

37. *Annales Monasterii S. Albani* (*RS* 28, pt 5), i, p. 62. Many of the inns of Walsingham are named by H. Gillett, *Walsingham*, p. 32.

38. P. Rahtz, *Glastonbury*, p. 104.

39. D. Verey, *The Buildings of England: Gloucestershire. The Vale and the Forest of Dean* (Harmondsworth, 1970), pp. 245, 248; J. Adair, *The Pilgrims' Way* (London, 1978), p. 92.

40. *Itinerary*, i, p. 165.

41. *CPR, 1258–1266*, p. 182.

42. *Materials*, i, pp. 187–88.
43. J. Ravensdale, *In the Steps of Chaucer's Pilgrims*, pp. 90, 94. The reference to the alestake is in the Introduction to the *Pardoner's Tale*, fragment 6, line 321.
44. *Expedition to Prussia and the Holy Land*, pp. 16, 256.
45. *The Tale of Beryn*, p. 2.
46. *The Registers of Roger Martival*, ii, pp. 265–67.
47. *Itinerary*, v, p. 38; iv, p. 14.
48. J. Dunkin, *The History and Antiquities of Dartford* (London, 1844), pp. 187–89; S. K. Keyes, *Dartford: Further Historical Notes* (Dartford, 1933), p. 100; *CIPM*, 7, p. 223. P. Boreham and C. Baker, *Medieval Dartford* (Dartford, 1994), is an attractive illustrated summary.
49. J. Thorpe, *Registrum Roffense* (London, 1769), p. 374. A hospital at Milton by Gravesend is first recorded early in the reign of Henry II: *VCH, Kent*, ii, pp. 221–22.
50. C. Taylor, *Roads and Tracks of Britain*, pp. 112–15 (with map). Gough, *Itinerary*, ii, p. 60, has the king at Leeds Castle on 27 August and at Rayleigh on the 30th, but has no entries for the intervening days.
51. Gough, *Itinerary*, ii, p. 116. There are numerous other examples; *Itinerary*, i, pp. 79 (January 1278), 100 (October 1279), 122 (August 1281); ii, pp. 133 (September 1295), 163 (March 1298), 214 (June 1302), 252 (August 1305).
52. *Materials*, ii, p. 72.
53. A. K. Astbury, *Estuary: Land and Water in the Lower Thames Basin* (London, 1980), pp. 45–46, 90, 230–31; N. Pevsner, *The Buildings of England: Essex* (2nd edn, Harmondsworth, 1965), pp. 170, 420.
54. N. Yates and J. Gibson, *Traffic and Politics: the Construction and Management of Rochester Bridge, AD 43–1993* (Woodbridge, 1994). In the eyre roll of 1292–94 the deaths of *quidam peregrini ignoti* are recorded (p. 39 n. 98).
55. *CPR, 1364–1367*, p. 256.
56. *CPR, 1391–1396*, pp. 712–13.
57. *Chronica Monasterii de Melsa*, ii, pp. 92, 108. Routh is not included among the hospitals of Yorkshire in *VCH, Yorkshire*, iii, but Archbishop Romeyn mentioned it when in 1280 he granted an indulgence to those contributing 'ad emendacionem, reparacionem seu fabricam vie regie ab hospitali de Routh usque pontem de Hull' nostre diocesis ducentis': *Register*, i (*SS*, 123), p. 11n.
58. St Claire Baddeley, *A Cotteswolde Shrine*, p. 87.
59. Gillett, *Walsingham*, pp. 32–34; Adair, *The Pilgrims' Way*, pp. 115–17.
60. *Itinerary*, v, p. 126; N. Pevsner and I. Richmond, *The Buildings of England: Northumberland* (2nd revised edn, Harmondsworth, 1992), pp. 409, 412, 484–85; Mackenzie, *Descriptive Account of Newcastle upon Tyne*, pp. 113, 177; Dendy, 'Account of Jesmond', p. 130. Pilgrim Street was until recent times part of the A1.
61. Brewis, 'St Mary's Chapel, Jesmond', p. 105, and Dendy, 'Account of Jesmond', p. 140n., both citing William Gray's *Chorographia: or A Survey of Newcastle upon Tyne* (1649).

62. Webb, *Pilgrims and Pilgrimage*, p. 46.

63. C. Platt, *Medieval Southampton*, p. 28.

64. *Itinerary*, i, pp. 280, 284.

65. N. Pevsner, *The Buildings of England: North Somerset and Bristol* (Harmondsworth, 1958), pp. 395–404. Pevsner cites indulgences of 1232, 1246, 1278 and 1287 in aid of building. The present church was built, or rebuilt, later than the double porch.

66. Walsingham, i, pp. 454–55.

67. *Statutes of the Realm*, 12 Richard II, cc. 3, 7.

68. *Paston Letters*, ed. Gairdner, v, pp. 110, 112.

69. *CCR*, *1468–1476*, pp. 298–99; Spencer, 'King Henry of Windsor', pp. 240–41.

70. *CCR*, *1485–1500*, pp. 434–47.

Notes to Chapter 10: Penitents and Critics

1. *The Register of Thomas Langton, Bishop of Salisbury, 1485–93*, ed. D. P. Wright (*CYS*, 74), pp. 70–71, 72, 79, 82–83. I have been unable to find the word 'bitynel'; it might plausibly mean 'beggar' (by analogy with the German *Bettler*), or could perhaps be a variant of a dialect word meaning 'blind' or 'sight-impaired' and which appears in a variety of forms including 'bisne', 'bisen' etc.

2. There is a translation of this canon in Webb, *Pilgrims and Pilgrimage*, p. 32.

3. Webb, *Pilgrims and Pilgrimage*, pp. 51–63, gives a brief account.

4. Webb, *Pilgrims and Pilgrimage*, pp. 60–61, 225–26.

5. *The Register of John Pecham, Archbishop of Canterbury, 1272–1292*, ed. F. N. Davis and D. Douie (2 vols and index, *CYS*, 64, 65), ii, p. 64.

6. There is a table of these penances in Webb, *Pilgrims and Pilgrimage*, pp. 52–53.

7. *Registrum Hamonis de Hethe*, i, p. 217.

8. *Registrum Hamonis de Hethe*, i, pp. 467–68.

9. *Registrum Hamonis de Hethe*, i, pp. 233–34.

10. *Registrum Hamonis de Hethe*, i, pp. 200, 245. There are inaccuracies in the description of these penances in Webb, *Pilgrims and Pilgrimage*.

11. *Registrum Hamonis de Hethe*, i, p. 472.

12. *Registrum Hamonis de Hethe*, ii, p. 938.

13. *Register of Ralph of Shrewsbury* ii, p. 495.

14. *Register of Ralph of Shrewsbury*, ii, p. 599.

15. *The Episcopal Register of Robert Rede, OP, Lord Bishop of Chichester 1397–1415*, ed. C. Deedes (2 vols, *Sussex Record Society*, 8, 11), i, pp. 44–46, 56–57.

16. *The Register of John Waltham, Bishop of Salisbury, 1388–1395*, ed. T. C. Timmins (*CYS*, 80), pp. 124, 128, 145, 148, 168, 169–70.

17. *Registrum Henrici Woodlock, Diocesis Wintoniensis, 1305–16*, ed. A. W. Goodman (2 vols, *CYS*, 43–44), i, p. 286.

18. *Wykeham's Register*, ed. T. F. Kirby (2 vols, *Hampshire Record Society*, 11, 13), ii, p. 100.

19. *The Register of William Wickwane, Lord Archbishop of York, 1279–1285* (SS, 114), pp. 15–16, 40–41.

20. *The Register of William Greenfield,* iii (SS 151), pp. 182–83.

21. Walsingham, ii, pp. 183–86, 188–89.

22. See Webb, *Pilgrims and Pilgrimage,* pp. 235–54.

23. *Chronicle of Jocelin of Brakelond,* p. 54; *Registrum Roberti Winchelsey,* i (CYS, 51), p. 413.

24. *VCH, Yorkshire,* iii, pp. 171–72.

25. *Registrum Hamonis de Hethe,* ii, pp. 735–36.

26. *Register of Henry Chichele,* iv, p. 167.

27. *CEPR,* 5, p. 471.

28. *Pilgrimages to Walsingham and Canterbury,* pp. 58–59.

29. H. Wharton, *Anglia Sacra* (2 vols, London, 1691), i, p. 49

30. *The Vision of Piers Plowman: A Critical Edition of the B-Text Based on Trinity College Cambridge MS. B.15.17,* ed. A. V. Schmidt (2nd edn, London, 1978), pp. 3–4, 58–59, 73, 89.

31. *Selections from English Wycliffite Writings,* ed. Hudson, pp. 24–29.

32. Part of Thorpe's exchange with Arundel is printed in the introduction to Erasmus, *Pilgrimages to Walsingham and Canterbury,* pp. xxi–xxvi.

33. *The Register of Robert Hallum, Bishop of Salisbury, 1407–17,* ed. J. Horn (CYS, 72), p. 142.

34. *Register of Robert Hallum,* p. 219.

35. *Foedera,* iv, pt 2, p. 50.

36. *Register of Henry Chichele,* iv, p. 157.

37. *The Repressor of Over-Much Blaming of the Clergy,* ed. C. Babington (2 vols, RS, 19), i, pp. 131–274. Ironically, Pecock's participation in vernacular polemic led to accusations of heresy and he was deprived of office.

38. Pecock, *Repressor,* i, p. 252.

39. For an analysis of the whole issue of image-worship, including the defences undertaken by Pecock and More, see M. Aston, *England's Iconoclasts,* i, *Laws against Images* (Oxford, 1988).

40. More, *Dialogue Concerning Heresies,* p. 232.

41. Pecock, *Repressor,* i, p. 223.

42. Pecock, *Repressor,* i, p. 192.

43. *Register of Henry Chichele,* iv, pp. 137, 157.

44. *Selections from English Wycliffite Writings,* pp. 87–88.

45. Pecock, *Repressor,* i, p. 221.

46. *LP,* 8, p. 185.

47. More, *Dialogue Concerning Heresies,* pp. 50–51.

48. More, *Dialogue Concerning Heresies,* pp. 77–81.

49. *Heresy Trials in the Diocese of Norwich, 1428–31,* ed. N. P. Tanner (CS, 4th Series, 20), pp. 142, 160, 166. Hawisia Moon's testimony is also in *Selections from English Wycliffite Writings,* pp. 34–37.

50. *Register of Henry Chichele,* iii, p. 222.

51. *The Register of Thomas Bekynton*, i, pp. 120–27.
52. *Registrum Johannis Stanbury Episcopi Herefordensis*, ed. A. T. Bannister (*CYS*, 25), p. 120.
53. Pecock, *Repressor*, i, p. 254.
54. Tanner, *Heresy Trials in the Diocese of Norwich*, p. 148.
55. *The Register of Thomas Bekynton*, i, p. 337.
56. Swanson, 'Devotional Offerings at Hereford Cathedral'.
57. *Memorials of the Church of SS. Peter and Wilfrid, Ripon*, i (*SS*, 74).
58. Summaries of the commissioners' findings are in *LP*, 10, pp. 138–44.
59. Cf. Nilson's suggestion, *Cathedral Shrines*, p. 193: 'Much of the devotion formerly directed towards saints' shrines in cathedral was now given to those in smaller churches and in Marian shrines.'
60. See, notably, E. Duffy, *The Stripping of the Altars* (New Haven, 1992).
61. *Yorkshire Monasteries: Suppression Papers*, ed. J. EW. Clay (*Yorkshire Archaeological Society*, Record Series, 48, 1912), pp. 46–47, 53.
62. *Kent Heresy Proceedings, 1511–12*, ed. N. Tanner (Maidstone, 1997), pp. 45–46, 65.
63. Erasmus, *Pilgrimages*, pp. 6–10.
64. *LP*, 4, pt 1, pp. 1845, 1984.
65. *LP*, 4, pt 1, p. 1935.
66. *LP*, 4, pt 1, p. 127.
67. William Lambarde, *Perambulation of Kent* (new edn, Bath, 1970), pp. 205–11.
68. *LP* 13, pt 1, pp. 79, 117, 120, 152, 283–84. The destruction of the Rood was reported with great excitement to the Swiss reformer Bullinger.
69. *Repressor*, i, p. 187.
70. *The Book of Sainte Foy*, translated by P. Sheingorn (Philadelphia, 1995), pp. 77–79.
71. *LP*, 14, pt 1, pp. 480–81.
72. *Pilgrimages to Walsingham and Canterbury*, pp. 3, 22
73. *LP* 6, p. 196; *Sermons and Remains of High Latimer* (Cambridge, 1845), p. 366. The text in question was Matthew 19:29: 'And everyone who has left houses or brothers or sisters or father or mother or children or fields, for my name's sake, will receive hundredfold, and will inherit eternal life.'
74. *Selected Sermons of Hugh Latimer*, ed. A. G. Chester (Charlottesville, Virginia, 1968), p. 23.
75. *Selected Sermons*, p. 23–25.
76. More, *Dialogue Concerning Heresies*, p. 99; Spencer, *Pilgrim Souvenirs*, pp. 151–52.
77. *Sermons and Remains*, p. 364.
78. St Clair Baddeley, *A Cotteswolde Shrine*, pp. 116–120; *Sermons and Remains*, pp. 407–408; *LP*, 13, pt 1, pp. 119.
79. *Pilgrimages to Walsingham and Canterbury*, p. 20.
80. Nilson, *Cathedral Shrines*, p. 165.
81. *LP*, 13, pt 1, p. 437.
82. *LP*, 12, pt 2, p. 218; 13, pt 2, p. 211

83. *LP*, 14, pt 1, p. 155.

84. *LP*, 13, pt 1, p. 214.

85. *LP*, 13, pt 2, pp. 143, 147; *Three Chapters of Letters Relating to the Suppression of the Monasteries*, ed. T. Wright (*CS*, 26, 1843), pp. 221–26.

86. It is reviewed by J. Butler, *The Quest for Becket's Bones* (London, 1995). In September 1538 the king paid 'sundry servants travailing about the disgarnishings of a shrine and other things' at Canterbury £23 6s. (*LP*, 13, pt 2, p. 534).

87. *Rites of Durham*, pp. 102–3.

88. *LP*, 13, pt 2, pp. 259, 287, 427, 459.

89. *LP*, 13, pt 2, p. 23.

90. See the documentation headed 'Cranmer and the Heretics of Kent', in *LP* 18, pt 2, pp. 291–378.

91. Ben Nilson calls it 'the golden age' (*Cathedral Shrines*, p. 190). For his analysis of what he terms 'the underlying influences on the level of shrine offerings', see pp. 172–82.

Index

Saints, kings and popes are normally indexed separately under their names; bishops in order of succession under the name of their diocese unless themselves saints or reputed saints.